Contested Commemorations

This innovative study of remembrance in Weimar Germany analyses how experiences and memories of the Great War were transformed along political lines after 1918. Examining the symbolism, language and performative power of public commemoration, Benjamin Ziemann reveals how individual recollections fed into the public narrative of the experience of war. Challenging conventional wisdom that nationalist narratives dominated commemoration, this book demonstrates that Social Democrat war veterans participated in the commemoration of the war at all levels: supporting the 'no more war' movement, mourning the fallen at war memorials and demanding a politics of international solidarity. It describes how the moderate socialist left related the legitimacy of the Republic to their experiences in the Imperial Army, and acknowledged the military defeat of 1918 as a moment of liberation. This is the first comprehensive analysis of war remembrances in post-war Germany and a radical reassessment of the democratic potential of the Weimar Republic.

BENJAMIN ZIEMANN is Professor of Modern German History at the University of Sheffield. An expert on the social, political and cultural history of modern Germany, his many previous books include *War Experiences in Rural Germany, 1914–1923* (2007) and *German Soldiers of the Great War: Letters and Eyewitness Accounts* (co-edited with Bernd Ulrich, 2010).

Studies in the Social and Cultural History of Modern Warfare

In recent years the field of modern history has been enriched by the exploration of two parallel histories. These are the social and cultural history of armed conflict, and the impact of military events on social and cultural history.

Studies in the Social and Cultural History of Modern Warfare presents the fruits of this growing area of research, reflecting both the colonisation of military history by cultural historians and the reciprocal interest of military historians in social and cultural history, to the benefit of both. The series offers the latest scholarship in European and non-European events from the 1850s to the present day.

A full list of titles in the series can be found at:
www.cambridge.org/modernwarfare

Contested Commemorations

Republican War Veterans and Weimar Political Culture

Benjamin Ziemann

University of Sheffield

CAMBRIDGE UNIVERSITY PRESS
Cambridge, New York, Melbourne, Madrid, Cape Town,
Singapore, São Paulo, Delhi, Mexico City

Cambridge University Press
The Edinburgh Building, Cambridge CB2 8RU, UK

Published in the United States of America by Cambridge University Press, New York

www.cambridge.org
Information on this title: www.cambridge.org/9781107028890

First published 2013

Printed and bound in the United Kingdom by the MPG Books Group

A catalogue record for this publication is available from the British Library

Library of Congress Cataloguing in Publication data
Ziemann, Benjamin.
Contested commemorations : republican war veterans and Weimar political culture / by Benjamin Ziemann.
p. cm. – (Studies in the social and cultural history of modern warfare)
Includes bibliographical references and index.
ISBN 978-1-107-02889-0 (hardback)
1. World War, 1914–1918–Veterans–Germany. 2. World War, 1914–1918–Influence. 3. World War, 1914–1918–Personal narratives, German. 4. World War, 1914–1918–Social aspects–Germany. 5. Veterans–Germany–History–20th century. 6. Political culture–Germany–History–20th century. 7. War memorials–Germany–History–20th century. 8. Memory–Political aspects–Germany–History–20th century. 9. Germany–Politics and government–1918–1933. 10. Germany–Social conditions–1918–1933. I. Title.
DD238.Z54 2013
940.4'6094309042–dc23
2012024506

ISBN 978-1-107-02889-0 hardback

Contents

Table and illustrations

Table

Illustrations

Every effort has been made to contact the relevant copyright-holders for the images reproduced in this book. In the event of any error, the publisher will be pleased to make corrections in any reprints or future editions.

Acknowledgements

My engagement with the issues discussed in this book dates back to the late 1990s. In the wake of my monograph on rural Bavaria from 1914 to 1923, I first came across the Reichsbanner, and discussed its significance in a journal article. At this time, and on many later occasions, I received generous advice from Belinda Davis, Christa Hämmerle, Wolfgang Hardtwig, Bedrich Loewenstein, Josef Mooser and Bernd Ulrich, for which I am extremely grateful. Work on the current book could finally commence after I had joined the University of Sheffield. I have benefited immensely from conversations with friends and colleagues at Sheffield, especially Miriam Dobson, Mike Foley, Ian Kershaw, Miles Larmer and my mentor Bob Moore. I am also grateful to Richard Bessel, Michael Geyer, Thomas Kühne, Thomas Mergel, Helmut W. Smith and Jay Winter for their intellectualism and unwavering support, and for important conversations with Martin H. Geyer, Rüdiger Graf, Daniel Morat, Nadine Rossol and Meik Woyke. Mike Geheran, Patrick Houlihan and Thomas F. Schneider have offered constructive feedback on individual chapters – thanks a lot! Moritz Föllmer and Matthew Stibbe have commented on a draft of the whole book. Both have written trail-blazing books and articles on Weimar Germany, and their work has deeply influenced my own thinking on the subject. Both are also trusted friends, and I owe a lot to their support and generosity.

Also important was the practical and material support I have received along the way. I very much appreciate the valuable support of the staff of the many archives and libraries I have consulted. Special thanks go to my friend Anja Kruke, head of the Archiv der sozialen Demokratie in the Friedrich Ebert Foundation in Bonn; to my former student Alexander Schwitanski, now head of the Archiv der Arbeiterjugend in Oer-Erkenschwick; to Michael Hensle of the Stadtarchiv Schiltach; to Ute Simon of the Stadtarchiv Schmalkalden; and to the staff of the library of the Friedrich Ebert Foundation, of the Bibliothek des Ruhrgebiets in Bochum, and of the Bayerische Staatsbibliothek in Munich. Martin Brost has generously funded the digitisation of Social

Democrat journals and newspapers, which are hosted by the online portal of the Friedrich Ebert Foundation. I am extremely grateful for this invaluable resource. Archival research in Germany was supported by a British Academy Small Grant, and facilitated by invitations to work as a Visiting Scholar at Humboldt-Universität zu Berlin and as a Visiting Professor at the Eberhard Karls Universität Tübingen. Ewald Frie, Daniel Menning, Jörg Neuheiser, Sebastian Kraffzig, Lena Gautam, Claudia Prinz, Andreas Weiß and many others turned these trips into convivial occasions. Thanks also to Franz and Joan Brüggemeier for putting me up during a trip to Freiburg! I am grateful to Laura King and Robert Whitelock, who carefully copy-edited my manuscript, and to Conny Schneider, whose diligent work as a research assistant was indispensable. At various stages, James Pearson kindly offered crucial technical support. The Arts and Humanities Research Council has generously supported the completion of the manuscript through a grant in its Fellowship Scheme. Michael Watson, my editor at Cambridge University Press, offered crucial support, and commissioned very helpful feedback by two anonymous reviewers. Permission to reproduce copyright material by the following is gratefully acknowledged: Berliner Vorwärts Verlagsgesellschaft, Archiv der sozialen Demokratie der Friedrich-Ebert-Stiftung Bonn, Bundesarchiv Koblenz, Archiv der Münchener Arbeiterbewegung, Münchener Stadtmuseum and Museum Schloss Wilhelmsburg in Schmalkalden.

Finally, my most heartfelt thanks go to my family: to Christine, Jonathan and Sophie; to my brothers Alexander and Jakob; and to my mother, Susanne Lücke, née Plojetz, who taught me all about the importance of books.

Abbreviations

AdK, Kempowski-BIO	Akademie der Künste Berlin, Kempowski-Biographienarchiv
AdsD	Archiv der sozialen Demokratie
AfS	*Archiv für Sozialgeschichte*
BA/MA	Bundesarchiv/Miltärarchiv Freiburg im Breisgau
BArch	Bundesarchiv Berlin-Lichterfelde
BHStA	Bayerisches Hauptstaatsarchiv München
BVP	Bayerische Volkspartei (People's Party of Bavaria)
BVZ	*Berliner Volks-Zeitung*
CEH	*Central European History*
DAZ	*Deutsche Allgemeine Zeitung*
DDP	Deutsche Demokratische Partei (German Democratic Party)
DFG	Deutsche Friedensgesellschaft (German Peace Society)
DHV	Deutschnationaler Handlungsgehilfen-Verband
DNVP	Deutschnationale Volkspartei (German National People's Party)
DVP	Deutsche Volkspartei (German People's Party)
FdK	Friedensbund der Kriegsteilnehmer (Associations of War Veterans for Peace)
GG	*Geschichte und Gesellschaft*
GStA	Geheimes Staatsarchiv Preußischer Kulturbesitz Berlin
HStASt	Hauptstaatsarchiv Stuttgart
HZ	*Historische Zeitschrift*
IfZ	Institut für Zeitgeschichte München, Archiv

JCH	*Journal of Contemporary History*
KPD	Kommunistische Partei Deutschlands (German Communist Party)
LAB	Landesarchiv Berlin
MGZ	*Militärgeschichtliche Zeitschrift*
MSPD	Mehrheitssozialdemokratische Partei Deutschlands (Majority Social Democratic Party of Germany)
NCO	Non-commissioned officer
NHStAH	Niedersächsisches Hauptstaatsarchiv Hannover
PND	Politischer Nachrichtendienst der Polizeidirektion München (Political News Service of the Munich Police Headquarters)
POW	prisoner of war
RB	*Das Reichsbanner: Zeitung des Reichsbanner Schwarz–Rot–Gold*
ReK	Reichsvereinigung ehemaliger Kriegsgefangener (Reich Association of Former Prisoners of War)
RjF	Reichsbund jüdischer Frontsoldaten (Reich Federation of Jewish Front Soldiers)
SAJ	Sozialistische Arbeiterjugend (Socialist Labour Youth)
SBPK	Staatsbibliothek Preußischer Kulturbesitz zu Berlin, Handschriftenabteilung
SPD	Sozialdemokratische Partei Deutschlands (German Social Democratic Party)
StA Bremen	Staatsarchiv Bremen
StAM	Staatsarchiv München
StA Schiltach	Stadtarchiv Schiltach
USPD	Unabhängige Sozialdemokratische Partei Deutschlands (Independent Social Democratic Party of Germany)
VeK	Vereinigung ehemaliger Kriegsgefangener (Union of Former Prisoners of War)
WUA	*Das Werk des Untersuchungsausschusses der Verfassunggebenden Deutschen Nationalversammlung und des Deutschen Reichstages 1919–1930*, 4. Reihe, II. Abteilung

Introduction

When the bloodshed and fighting of the First World War ended on 11 November 1918, Germans, along with the people of other belligerent nations, began to transform their war experiences into a set of personal recollections and memories. This was a highly selective process: while some aspects of the war receded quickly into the background, others acquired a heightened symbolic meaning with growing temporal distance from the actual events. These personal recollections, to be sure, not only had relevance for the individual and his close family and friends; they also fed into a pattern of public commemorations of war that ultimately served political purposes. German veterans' associations in particular were highly politicised, and dwelled upon those commemorative themes that they knew would resonate among their members. Compared with France and Great Britain, however, the commemoration of war in Germany took place in a radically altered political context. Only two days before the armistice, on 9 November 1918, Majority Social Democrat Philipp Scheidemann had pronounced the German Republic from the Reichstag in Berlin. Yet there was more than only a temporal coincidence between the abolition of the Hohenzollern monarchy and German military defeat. In the recollection of many German war veterans, the proclamation of the Republic was the positive corollary of a defeat that had been, in the first instance, the result of the extreme imperialist ambitions of the monarchy and its ruling elites.

These pro-republican recollections of the First World War are the subject of this study. This book will investigate the shaping of those war memories that were, in one way or another, supportive of the Weimar Republic as a political project. It will scrutinise the symbolism, language and performative power of public commemorations of war that were based on these more private reminiscences. With such a focus, this book goes against the grain of a long-established interpretation that found its seminal formulation in the late George L. Mosse's comparative study of war remembrances. Here, Mosse analysed a pattern of public representations and symbols that he called the 'myth of the war experience, which looked back upon the war as a meaningful and even sacred event'. This myth 'was designed to mask war and to legitimize the war experience'.[1] While such mythological representations of the front-line experiences emerged in all belligerent nations, they were most 'urgently needed' and most widely appreciated 'in the defeated nations'. But it was only in Germany, Mosse insisted, that nationalist war remembrances 'informed most postwar politics', and it was this country that 'proved most hospitable to the myth'.[2] This argument chimes in with the more general and widely accepted point that post-war Germany was in denial about the inevitability of military defeat in 1918, and that the majority of German war veterans had tremendous difficulties adapting to peace and contributing to a 'cultural demobilization'.[3]

Experts in the field have argued for some time that it would be wrong to assume that the war experience forced a whole generation of former German soldiers to seek refuge 'in a life of violence in paramilitary uniform' or at least to 'glorify violence and things military'.[4] Such an interpretation of war remembrances in Weimar Germany is, as Richard Bessel has pointed out, 'inconsistent with the fact that the largest interest-group formed by veterans' was actually organised by Social Democrats.[5] The 'Reichsbund of War Disabled, War Veterans and War Dependants' (Reichsbund der Kriegsbeschädigten, Kriegsteilnehmer und Kriegerhinterbliebenen), founded in the spring of 1917, and with a

[1] George L. Mosse, *Fallen Soldiers: Reshaping the Memory of the World Wars* (New York; Oxford: Oxford University Press, 1990), p. 7.

[2] *Ibid.*, pp. 7, 10. It is a testament to the innovative nature of Mosse's research that he actually discussed the war experience as a challenge for the post-1918 political left, particularly in Germany, also touching upon the Reichsbanner. As often, however, he presented sweeping generalisations, here on the militarism of the Reichsbanner and its 'imitation of the right', with hardly any empirical evidence. See George L. Mosse, 'La sinistra Europea e l'esperienza della guerra (Germania e Francia)', in *Rivoluzione e reazione in Europa, 1917–1924: Convegno storico internazionale, Perugia, 1978* (Rome: Avanti, 1978), pp. 151–67 (quotes on p. 159).

[3] See, for instance, Wolfgang Schivelbusch, *The Culture of Defeat: On National Trauma, Mourning, and Recovery* (London: Granta, 2004), pp. 189–230; Boris Barth, *Dolchstoßlegenden und politische Desintegration: Das Trauma der deutschen Niederlage im Ersten Weltkrieg 1914–1933* (Düsseldorf: Droste, 2003); Laurence Van Ypersele, 'Mourning and Memory, 1919–45', in John Horne (ed.), *A Companion to World War I* (Chichester: Wiley, 2010), pp. 576–90 (p. 583). On the notion of 'cultural demobilization' see John Horne, 'Kulturelle Demobilmachung 1919–1939: Ein sinnvoller Begriff?', in Wolfgang Hardtwig (ed.), *Politische Kulturgeschichte der Zwischenkriegszeit 1918–1939* (Göttingen: Vandenhoeck & Ruprecht, 2005), pp. 129–50.

[4] Richard Bessel, *Germany after the First World War* (Oxford: Clarendon Press, 1993), p. 258. See also the pathbreaking study by Bernd Ulrich, *Die Augenzeugen: Deutsche Feldpostbriefe in Kriegs- und Nachkriegszeit 1914–1933* (Essen: Klartext, 1997).

[5] Bessel, *Germany*, p. 258.

peak membership of 830,000 in 1922, was by far the largest of all associations that represented disabled war veterans in Weimar Germany.[6] In the latter half of the 1920s, the Reichsbund often collaborated with the 'Reichsbanner Black–Red–Gold' (Reichsbanner Schwarz–Rot–Gold), established in the spring of 1924 as a 'League of Republican Ex-Servicemen'. The designated purpose of the Reichsbanner was to defend the Republic, and support the campaigning of the parties that had formed the Weimar coalition in 1919, i.e. the Social Democrats, the Catholic Centre Party and the left-liberal German Democratic Party (DDP). In practice, however, the Reichsbanner was dominated by members and supporters of the Social Democratic Party (SPD), who accounted for 90 per cent of its membership. With its very substantial presence in a wide array of associations in the socialist working-class milieu, the Reichsbanner and its approximately one million members played a pivotal role in the representation of republican war memories both for individuals and the wider public. As the following chapters will demonstrate, Reichsbund and Reichsbanner were at the forefront of attempts to develop a pro-republican language of war remembrance, and to elaborate an appropriate set of commemorative symbols and rituals in the public sphere. Yet these champions of a democratic commemoration of war did not act in a political vacuum. Rather, their interventions have to be understood against the backdrop of narratives established in nationalist circles, by, for example, former members of the *Freikorps*, writers and novelists who wrote using the tropes of soldierly nationalism, and, last but not least, the Stormtroopers and other members of the National Socialist Party.[7]

Contested commemorations

Throughout the Weimar Republic, right-wing authors and associations on the one hand, and Social Democrats on the other, were locked into an intense and often bitter dispute over public representations of the war experience. For this reason, and owing to the substantial range and

6 Robert W. Whalen, *Bitter Wounds: German Victims of the Great War, 1914–1939* (Ithaca, NY; London: Cornell University Press, 1984), p. 150.

7 On these nationalist narratives and mythologies, see, among others, Matthias Sprenger, *Landsknechte auf dem Weg ins Dritte Reich? Zu Genese und Wandel des Freikorpsmythos* (Paderborn: Schöningh, 2008); Roger Woods, 'Die neuen Nationalisten und ihre Einstellung zum 1. Weltkrieg', *Krieg und Literatur/War and Literature* 1 (1989), 59–79; and Gerd Krumeich (ed.), *Nationalsozialismus und Erster Weltkrieg* (Essen: Klartext, 2010); as well as the older but still valuable study by Kurt Sontheimer, *Antidemokratisches Denken in der Weimarer Republik* (Munich: Deutscher Taschenbuch-Verlag, 1978 [1962]), pp. 93–111.

presence of pro-republican recollections of the Great War, there was 'no dominant memory of the war' in Germany until 1933, as Alan Kramer has observed.[8] When members of Reichsbund and Reichsbanner contemplated the meaning of their front-line service and constructed its memory in various ways, their contributions were part and parcel of the contested commemorations of the Great War in Weimar Germany. In the highly polarised public sphere of post-war Germany, the mechanisms of contestation worked both ways. Social Democrats were indeed able to deny the legitimacy of many powerful right-wing war myths. But when they offered their own symbols and narratives of the war experience and claimed that these would express popular sentiment more properly, their interventions also reflected the discursive limits imposed by the already existing nationalist framework of interpretation.[9]

In the following, I will focus on the two associations, Reichsbund and Reichsbanner, in order to investigate the politics of republican commemorations of war, to analyse the selective nature of these memories and to unravel the key narratives that Social Democrats used to engage with their past participation in a brutal conflict. Such an endeavour requires more than a simple, conventional institutional history of these two associations and their relative position in the field of German veterans' politics.[10] As far as the primary source material allows, the construction of war memories will be contextualised in the

[8] Alan Kramer, 'The First World War and German Memory', in Heather Jones, Jennifer O'Brien and Christoph Schmidt-Supprian (eds.), *Untold War: New Perspectives in First World War Studies* (Leiden; Boston, MA: Brill, 2008), pp. 385–415 (p. 390); Bernd Ulrich, 'Die umkämpfte Erinnerung: Überlegungen zur Wahrnehmung des Ersten Weltkrieges in der Weimarer Republik', in Jörg Duppler and Gerhard P. Groß (eds.), *Kriegsende 1918: Ereignis–Wirkung–Nachwirkung* (Munich: Oldenbourg, 1999), pp. 367–75 (p. 368).

[9] As a first provisional outline of this argument see my 'Republikanische Kriegserinnerung in einer polarisierten Öffentlichkeit: Das Reichsbanner Schwarz–Rot–Gold als Veteranenverband der sozialistischen Arbeiterschaft', *HZ* 267 (1998), 357–98. For Austria, see now the innovative study by Oswald Überegger, *Erinnerungskriege: Der Erste Weltkrieg, Österreich und die Tiroler Kriegserinnerung in der Zwischenkriegszeit (1918–1939)* (Innsbruck: Wagner, 2011).

[10] The standard account on the Reichsbanner is Karl Rohe, *Das Reichsbanner Schwarz Rot Gold: Ein Beitrag zur Geschichte und Struktur der politischen Kampfverbände zur Zeit der Weimarer Republik* (Düsseldorf: Droste, 1966); two valuable regional studies, on Munich and Saxony respectively, are Günther Gerstenberg, *Freiheit! Sozialdemokratischer Selbstschutz im München der zwanziger und frühen dreißiger Jahre*, 2 vols. (Andechs: Edition Ulenspiegel, 1997); and Carsten Voigt, *Kampfbünde der Arbeiterbewegung: Das Reichsbanner Schwarz–Rot–Gold und der Rote Frontkämpferbund in Sachsen 1924–1933* (Cologne: Böhlau, 2009). All three studies touch upon the commemorative politics of the Reichsbanner only briefly, and are mostly concerned with its role as a republican defence league. Cf. James M. Diehl, 'Germany: Veterans' Politics under Three Flags', in Stephen R. Ward (ed.), *The War Generation: Veterans of the First World War* (Port Washington: Kennikat Press, 1975), pp. 135–86.

associational culture of the local Reichsbanner branches in particular. Both Reichsbund and Reichsbanner were democratic and hence by definition pluralistic organisations, in which ordinary members were able to voice the symbols, ideas, and narratives that they thought best represented their personal memories of the Great War, in meetings, in articles for the membership journals and in public speeches. Little is still known 'about the historical circumstances that encourage practices of personal remembering and vernacular commemoration'.[11] It is thus necessary to question whether Reichsbanner members tended to gloss over memories of hardship and disillusionment at the front and started to frame their recollections in more positive terms, emphasising their ability to cope with and endure the circumstances of war. Which notions of German national identity did pro-republican war veterans prioritise, and how were they embedded in their own personal experiences, both during the war and in post-war society? Situating republican war memories in their proper social and cultural context also requires an understanding of the problems and constraints Reichsbanner members faced when they tried to reconcile their personal recollections with the public discourse on the mythologised 'war experience'.

Performative aspects of Weimar democracy

As an investigation of republican war memories in Weimar Germany, this study contributes to the growing literature on the remembrance of the First World War, both with regard to Germany, and in a wider, European perspective.[12] Yet it is necessary to admit that memory as a field of research, as Alon Confino noted fifteen years ago, does 'not offer any true additional explanatory power. Only when linked to historical questions and problems' can it be 'illuminating'.[13] Heeding this

11 Peter Fritzsche, 'The Case of Modern Memory', *Journal of Modern History* 73 (2001), 87–117 (p. 108).

12 On Germany, see in particular Stefan Goebel, *The Great War and Medieval Memory: War, Remembrance and Medievalism in Britain and Germany, 1914–1940* (Cambridge University Press, 2007); Greg Caplan, *Wicked Sons, German Heroes: Jewish Soldiers, Veterans and Memories of World War I in Germany* (Saarbrücken: VDM Verlag, 2008); Philipp Stiasny, *Das Kino und der Krieg: Deutschland 1914–1929* (Munich: edition text + kritik, 2009); and Anton Kaes, *Shell Shock Cinema: Weimar Culture and the Wounds of War* (Princeton University Press, 2009). More generally, see the seminal studies by Jay Winter, *Sites of Memory, Sites of Mourning: The Great War in European Cultural History* (Cambridge University Press, 1996); and *Remembering War: The Great War between Memory and History in the Twentieth Century* (New Haven; London: Yale University Press, 2006).

13 Alon Confino, 'Collective Memory and Cultural History: Problems of Method', *American Historical Review* 102 (1997), 1386–1403 (p. 1388). An excellent overview on the growing literature on memory studies is Karin Tilmans, Frank van Vree and

important suggestion, this study of republican war memories above all aims to contribute to our understanding of the participatory potential and performative power of Weimar democracy. Earlier historiography on Germany after 1918 faced no difficulties at all when explaining the failure and ultimate destruction of the republican system by the Nazis in 1933 in terms of a multiplicity of problems. Inherent weaknesses of the republican settlement were crucial in this historiographical framework, as was the assumed 'lack of legitimacy' of the democratic system, which seemed to be based on a more general 'lack of active commitment to the new order'.[14] The determination and brutality of those who resented the Republic from its inception added to these difficulties. By drawing lines of continuity from the war experience, and especially from the experience of the trenches, it seemed appropriate to explain the rise of Nazism and the concomitant surge of political violence in the post-war period in terms of a brutalisation thesis. Participation in the killing and shelling from 1914 to 1918 had prepared the ground for authoritarian attitudes and hatred against Jews, and indeed anyone else who seemed to symbolise the democratic system.[15] All in all, then, the primary aim for historians was to account for the failure of the Weimar Republic.

However, the historiographical agenda has fundamentally changed, instigated by a landmark article by Peter Fritzsche, in which he asked the provocative question, 'Did Weimar fail?'[16] His intention was not to suggest 'no' as a possible answer. Rather, his essay was an invitation to think outside the box and to develop more imaginative lines of argument for the study of the first German Republic. In this view, it seems appropriate to consider Weimar as a laboratory of modernity, in which a broad range of social, political and cultural experiments were conducted, and people tried to grapple with the modern condition in a variety of ways. Some of these experiments led to no conclusive results, some were disappointing, others ended soon in outright failure even before the Nazi seizure of power moved the goalposts in the political field. But seen together, all these experiments make it abundantly clear

Jay Winter (eds.), *Performing the Past: Memory, History and Identity in Modern Europe* (Manchester University Press, 2010).

14 Detlev Peukert, *The Weimar Republic: The Crisis of Classical Modernity* (New York: Hill & Wang, 1993), p. 6.

15 Again, Mosse, *Fallen Soldiers*, pp. 159–81, was a crucial reference point. As a critique, see Benjamin Ziemann, 'Germany after the First World War: A Violent Society? Results and Implications of Recent Research on Weimar Germany', *Journal of Modern European History* 1 (2003), 80–95.

16 Peter Fritzsche, 'Did Weimar Fail?', *Journal of Modern History* 68 (1996), 629–56.

that the history of the Weimar Republic cannot simply be written as a narrative of tragic demise.[17]

Amidst this wider shift in the overall framework of historical work on Weimar, two aspects are of particular importance with regard to the contested republican commemorations of the Great War. First, this shift has led to a renewed emphasis on the semantic structures that framed temporality and informed the horizon of expectations among contemporary actors. From this perspective, it makes sense to investigate the present futures, i.e. the possible states of politics and society in ten or fifteen years as they were anticipated and expressed at any given point after 1918. Such an inquiry reveals the large number of rather optimistic visions of the future throughout the 1920s. Even after the carnage of war, Weimar contemporaries did not simply abandon their belief in the possibility of progress, not least because the constitutional framework of the Republic itself opened up a whole raft of promising opportunities and allowed people to work towards positive change.[18] This reassessment of the semantics of the future has crucial implications for the attempts of Social Democratic war veterans to boost support for the republican project. Leaders of the Reichsbanner in particular used every opportunity to stress that they were working towards a better future for Germany, and that only a fair and democratic society could ensure a recovery of the nation. Yet such a rhetorical orientation towards the future stood in a stark contrast to the ceaseless exploitation of the legacy of the fallen soldiers. With their immersion in the remembrance of the First World War, the Reichsbanner members defended the Republic against right-wing mythologies. But at the same time, they tended to neglect or perhaps even to obfuscate Weimar's present future, a temporal marker that was of paramount importance as a motivation for republican activism. In that sense, the obvious obsession of a veterans' association with the past hindered the equally necessary engagement with the future.

A second relevant aspect of this historiographical shift is the attention devoted to the performative aspects of politics. In this perspective, the theatrical dimensions of the political process are seen not only as a mere façade or an empty shell that adds nothing to the political content. On the contrary, this approach focuses on the ways in which rituals and public speech acts regulate change in the status of individuals

[17] For further references and reflections see Benjamin Ziemann, 'Weimar was Weimar: Politics, Culture and the Emplotment of the German Republic', *German History* 28 (2010), 542–71.

[18] See Rüdiger Graf, *Die Zukunft der Weimarer Republik: Krisen und Zukunftsaneignungen in Deutschland 1918–1933* (Munich: Oldenbourg, 2008).

or institutions and facilitate or reintegrate challenges to an established social order.[19] Such a perspective is vital for an understanding of the promises and pitfalls of republican politics in the 1920s. The new regime itself was based on the transition from monarchy to a republic, and hence lively and attractive performative rituals were required in order to make the structures of a participatory democracy tangible.[20] Earlier historiography has often stated that the proponents of Weimar, and the Social Democratic left in particular, tended to underestimate the significance of symbolic politics. Based on a sober, rationalistic notion of politics as a debate among the reasonable, they neglected the persuasive potential of colourful and emotional rituals, speech acts and other symbolic performances.[21] Recent research, notably the important study by Nadine Rossol of the 'staging of the republic', has substantially revised this interpretation. These studies have highlighted how the office of the Reichskunstwart and its ambitious head, Edwin Redslob, who was responsible for the official state pageantry and the shape of state symbols, aimed to develop an appropriate symbolism for the Republic. One important part of these endeavours was the festivities on 11 August. From 1921 onwards, the day on which Reich President Friedrich Ebert had signed off and thus promulgated the constitution in 1919 was celebrated as Constitution Day. Beginning on 11 August 1924, the Reichsbanner was a key driving force for attempts to stage marches, speeches and other Constitution Day festivities in even the remotest corners of the Reich, and thus to shape a distinctively democratic and inclusive political ritual around the founding document of the new polity.[22]

Against this backdrop of recent work on the performative aspects of Weimar democracy, pro-republican commemorations of war have a wider significance that goes far beyond the field of memory studies.

[19] In memory studies, performative aspects were analysed in the pathbreaking study by Adrian Gregory, *The Silence of Memory: Armistice Day, 1919–1946* (Oxford: Berg, 1994).

[20] See Ziemann, 'Weimar was Weimar', pp. 560–4.

[21] See the references in Manuela Achilles, 'With a Passion for Reason: Celebrating the Constitution in Weimar Germany', *CEH* 43 (2010), 666–89 (pp. 666f.).

[22] Nadine Rossol, *Performing the Nation in Interwar Germany: Sport, Spectacle and Political Symbolism 1926–1936* (Basingstoke: Palgrave, 2010), esp. 58–79. See also Achilles, 'Celebrating'; and Manuela Achilles, 'Performing the Reich: Democratic Symbols and Rituals in the Weimar Republic', in Kathleen Canning, Kerstin Barndt and Kristin McGuire (eds.), *Weimar Publics/Weimar Subjects: Rethinking the Political Culture of Germany in the 1920s* (New York: Berghahn, 2010), pp. 175–91; Bernd Buchner, *Um nationale und republikanische Identität: Die deutsche Sozialdemokratie und der Kampf um die politischen Symbole in der Weimarer Republik* (Bonn: J. H. W. Dietz, 2001).

The legacy of the First World War was one of the pivotal political battlegrounds in Weimar. When Reichsbund and Reichsbanner members intervened in this field, they not only offered an alternative reading of past events that were of primary interest for the community of war veterans, widows and orphans. Unveiling a war memorial, paying tribute to the fallen soldiers on Constitution Day or on other national holidays, or displaying military decorations during a republican rally were only some examples of a whole raft of symbolic performances that ultimately contributed to the political fabric of Weimar democracy. From this perspective, it should also be clear that the history of republican war remembrances is more than a mere complement to the existing historiography on the nationalist war mythologies of the anti-democratic right. To be sure, a proper assessment of the memory politics of Social Democratic war veterans can add both nuance and substance to the already established arguments about the contingent nature of Weimar's collapse, and for the openness of political possibilities in the 1920s.[23]

Nonetheless, the story of the Reichsbund and Reichsbanner war veterans is not simply a straightforward alternative narrative that can offer consolation and historical optimism, based on the insight that not all German war veterans were brutalised, ready to glorify violence and use war remembrances for an assault on the Republic. The history of republican war memories has to be cast in a wider and more complicated fashion. It should not merely underpin a superficial success story, and should instead highlight the ambivalence of Social Democratic engagement with the past. These ambivalences stemmed from the fact that Social Democrats had their own difficulties in coming to terms with the initial support of the party for the war in 1914, and the subsequent division into pro- and anti-war factions as the fighting continued.[24] However, these legacies of the decision to support national unity in 1914 were not the only ambivalence of republican commemorations of war. As the following chapters will explore in more detail, Reichsbanner activism was characterised by substantial inherent contradictions, especially with regard to the articulation of gender roles and the formulation of a coherent anti-war stance. While the association affirmed progressive Social Democratic ideals of female emancipation in principle, it did not

[23] As a summary, see Ziemann, 'Weimar was Weimar'; an important case study is the book on the political culture of parliamentary debates by Thomas Mergel, *Parlamentarische Kultur in der Weimarer Republik: Politische Kommunikation, symbolische Politik und Öffentlichkeit im Reichstag* (Düsseldorf: Droste, 2002).

[24] The most thorough account of this decision and its consequences is Wolfgang Kruse, *Krieg und nationale Integration: Eine Neuinterpretation des sozialdemokratischen Burgfriedensschlusses 1914/15* (Essen: Klartext, 1993).

admit women as members and thus excluded them from pro-republican work. Additionally, although Reichsbanner members supported moderate pacifist and anti-militarist ideals, they presented themselves – at least to some degree – as a paramilitary formation. These are only the two most important contradictions in Social Democratic attempts to turn the trauma of war from a liability into an asset of the new democratic system.

However, it would be unbalanced and counterintuitive to stress only ambivalence in the attempts by moderate socialists to come to terms with their own participation in total war, and to foster political allegiances on these shared memories. Republican commemorations of war were an important element of the political culture in 1920s Germany. They mattered because they injected a convincing point of reference and a strong sense of commitment and emotional justification into the social democratic discourse on the Republic, harking back to the injustice workers had experienced in the Imperial Army. Contrary to conventional wisdom, the term 'republic' had not lost semantic currency, but encapsulated the hopes and achievements of the many front-line soldiers among Weimar's Social Democrats.[25] It is all the more surprising that historians who have studied the rich organisational culture of Social Democracy during the Weimar period, and the attempts of party members to defend the Republic against the onslaught from the right, have failed to identify war remembrances as an important cultural element in the tightly knit associational fabric of the Social Democratic milieu.[26]

Comparative aspects

Thus, a historical investigation of republican war remembrances has relevance beyond the field of memory studies. It casts light on the wider problem of how the moderate German left tried to turn the social and cultural legacy of total war into symbolic capital that could strengthen their overall political stance. Ultimately, such a re-description of collective war remembrances in Weimar Germany also has implications

[25] For the claim that the term 'Republik' had lost semantic currency, see Dieter Langewiesche, *Republik und Republikaner: Von der historischen Entwertung eines Begriffs* (Essen: Klartext, 1993), p. 46.

[26] See for instance Peter Lösche and Franz Walter, 'Zur Organisationskultur der sozialdemokratischen Arbeiterbewegung in der Weimarer Republik: Niedergang der Klassenkultur oder solidargemeinschaftlicher Höherpunkt?', *GG* 15 (1989), 511–36; Donna Harsch, *German Social Democracy and the Rise of Nazism* (Chapel Hill: University of North California Press, 1993).

for a comparative history of the post-war period in the main belligerent nations. In George L. Mosse's seminal account, the cult of the fallen soldiers was a more general phenomenon, as heroic mythologies were also voiced in France and Britain. Yet a pervasive and much more aggressive hero-worshipping and poisoned political culture only emerged in Germany, paving the way for the violent Nazi onslaught on democratic institutions.[27] The slightly paradoxical nature of this highly influential argument is rather obvious. Commemorative practices faced similar challenges in all countries where young men had died for their nation since 1914: they had to transcend the contingency of violent mass death and endow it with higher meaning, to offer consolation to the grieving and bereaved, and to demonstrate how the loss of the fallen soldiers could be turned into a positive example for the living. These tasks transcended national borders, and their form and urgency rested on the similar patterns of war experience that the battles of materiel had created on both sides of no man's land. Only by a sleight of hand could the more universal aspects of war remembrance be turned into an argument that made the case for a German *Sonderweg* or 'special path' of remembrance that directly led to 1933.

Critics spotted this paradox early on and have suggested framing the comparative history of war remembrances more broadly. Rather than being a direct result of the war experience, Antoine Prost argued, the greater acceptance of mass death in inter-war Germany was actually 'a continuation of prewar attitudes into postwar conditions'.[28] From this perspective, the strong chauvinistic currents in the German 'cult of the fallen soldier' were not the consequence of a mysterious wartime brutalisation, but have to be contextualised in the long-term affirmation of force in German power politics and in the stronger exclusionary tendencies of its nationalism. When we compare Germany with France in a more subtle fashion, Prost insisted, it becomes obvious that the veterans' pacifism of the French *anciens combattants* was firmly rooted in the more inclusionary rhetoric of nationalism in the Third Republic, in which individuals could easily reconcile their decision to join and cherish the nation with an emphatic commitment to humanism.[29] Comparative study of commemorations has also dismissed the rather simplistic notion that the German special path in terms of war remembrance was due to its status as a vanquished nation. Investigating the symbolism of war memorials in Germany and the UK, Stefan Goebel

[27] Mosse, *Fallen Soldiers*, p. 159.

[28] Antoine Prost, 'The Impact of War on French and German Political Cultures', *Historical Journal* 37 (1994), 209–17 (p. 211).

[29] *Ibid.*, p. 212–14.

has detailed how medievalism was a common theme, and how commemorative practices in both countries harked back to an 'idealised past' in order to link the hope for 'personal salvation and national regeneration'. In their quest to find cultural pillars of stabilisation in the face of an unprecedented catastrophe, victors and losers shared a yearning for an 'affirmation of continuity'.[30]

Building on these insights, the results of this study suggest a more complicated picture of the comparative position of German war remembrances. Taking the scope and scale of republican activism in the Reichsbund and Reichsbanner into account, the story of German war veterans moves even closer to their French counterparts than previously thought. To be sure, not many French veterans were organised in associations with a close affiliation to one political party. Founded by Henri Barbusse and close to the Communist Party, the 'Association républicaine des anciens combattants' (ARAC) was an exception, and could muster no more than 20,000 members. Most former front-line soldiers were represented by the 'Union fédérale', a left-leaning league of disabled veterans, and by the 'Union nationale des combattants', founded in 1918 and representing Christian-conservative political opinions. The most striking and overarching feature of the French anciens combattants was their republican anti-militarism and their commitment to peace, disarmament and international reconciliation. These core values accompanied a sometimes righteous patriotic attitude, which denounced the hypocrisy of jingoistic and chauvinistic nationalism and proudly demanded that France should be a beacon of humanity. Only as a democracy and republic, these veterans insisted, could France claim to be a superior nation and to represent universal rights.[31] Thus, they all shared a 'patriotic pacifism', even though tremendous differences in the relative significance and actual meaning of these two terms existed.[32]

In many respects, these republican and anti-militaristic values resembled those held by the veterans gathered in the Reichsbund and

[30] Goebel, *Great War*, pp. 287, 290.

[31] Antoine Prost, *Les Anciens Combattants et la société francaise, 1914–1939*, 3 vols. (Paris: Presse de la Fondation Nationale des Sciences Politiques, 1977); see the abridged translation as Antoine Prost, *In the Wake of War: 'Les Anciens Combattants' and French Society 1914–1939* (Providence, RI; Oxford: Berg, 1992), pp. 40, 51–93. For a revisionist interpretation see Chris Millington, *From Victory to Vichy: Veterans in Inter-War France* (Manchester University Press, 2012).

[32] Prost, *In the Wake of War*, quote on p. 79; for context, see John Horne, 'Der Schatten des Krieges: Französische Politik in den zwanziger Jahren', in Hans Mommsen (ed.), *Der Erste Weltkrieg und die europäische Nachkriegsordnung: Sozialer Wandel und Formveränderung der Politik* (Cologne: Böhlau, 2000), pp. 145–64 (pp. 146–57).

Reichsbanner. 'Patriotic pacifism' is indeed an appropriate term for the political core values of the Reichsbanner members in particular, as they abhorred war, criticised armaments and were convinced that the Republic represented a better Germany which had left the legacy of Prussian militarism behind. Since the members of these two organisations represented a substantial proportion of all German war veterans, it would be misleading to construe a German *Sonderweg* in the commemoration of the Great War by former front-line soldiers. Major differences between the remembrances in France and Germany existed. Yet the crucial point was not the insignificance or even total lack of any republican currents in the German 'cult of the fallen soldier'.[33] Where Germany indeed diverged from France was in the lack of a shared framework of core political assumptions that allowed veterans to speak with one unified voice whenever they thought it was necessary. The various French associations were able to establish a national confederation in 1927 'which left each association independent but which coordinated collaboration'.[34] Such a limited cooperation stood in stark contrast to Weimar, where polarisation and confrontation between competing political camps were the hallmarks of a highly fragmented political culture. Lack of even basic agreement on how a good polity was meant to work, and on a set of shared symbols for the unity of the German nation, characterised political communication across the Rhine. The three major political camps – Social Democrats and Left Liberals as the main proponents of the Republic; the nationalist and conservative right as its main opponents; and the Catholics, represented by the Centre Party, in the middle – were worlds apart in their core assumptions on the rules of political engagement.[35] Veterans' politics, and hence also the commemoration of war, reflected these fissures and even aggravated them further. Disagreement about the aims and content of remembrance abounded. As will be explained in more detail below, there were only very few instances when the pro-republican veterans and their counterparts on the right could agree on the symbolism and significance of the Great War. Post-war Germany saw a proliferation of veterans' leagues of different political leaning and different purposes, such as specialist

[33] A point that is reiterated by Oliver Janz, 'Trauer und Gefallenenkult nach 1918: Italien und Deutschland im Vergleich', in Ute Daniel, Inge Marszolek, Wolfram Pyta and Thomas Welskopp (eds.), *Politische Kultur und Medienwirklichkeiten in den 1920er Jahren* (Munich: Oldenbourg, 2010), pp. 257–78 (p. 277).

[34] Prost, *In the Wake of War*, p. 37.

[35] See the chapters in Detlef Lehnert and Klaus Megerle (eds.), *Politische Teilkulturen zwischen Integration und Polarisierung: Zur politischen Kultur in der Weimarer Republik* (Opladen: Westdeutscher Verlag, 1990).

leagues solely representing disabled veterans or former POWs. In order to facilitate an understanding of this crucial field for the commemoration of war, the most important veterans' leagues are mentioned in Table 1, with a first brief indication of their relative strength, purpose, and political orientation.

A systematic investigation of republican war remembrances will also allow a reassessment of the distinctiveness of the French *monuments aux morts*, or war memorials, relative to their German equivalents, the *Kriegerdenkmäler*. The different terminology is in itself indicative of the different meaning of these memorials. In France, local memorials were primarily a reaffirmation of the 'communities of mourning' that gathered around them, consisting of the relatives and former comrades of those who had lost their lives in service for the Third Republic.[36] Based on a widely shared and inclusive notion of republican citizenship, the dominant symbolism of French war memorials represented the soldier as a citizen in uniform, as someone who had served at the front in order to protect a community of civilians that he himself belonged to and was part of. Women and children were thus integral to this style of commemoration, and many memorials depicted the pivotal scene of mutual recognition and appreciation, when the soldier returned home to his loved ones.[37] The established German term *Kriegerdenkmäler*, however, invoked the soldier as a warrior and thus set him apart from the civilians who had stayed at the home front. Implicit in this terminology, and explicit in the iconography of many memorials that depicted combat-ready soldiers in uniform, bent on renewing the conflict against the Western Allies, was the idea that the example of the fallen should motivate the living to revise the Versailles settlement with violent means.[38] Such a comparison of local memorials in France and Germany is certainly correct with regard to the iconography and epigraphy of the *Kriegerdenkmäler*. A third and at least equally important dimension of the commemorative culture around war memorials was, however, their 'ceremonial role', or the interpretations and dedications

[36] See Stéphane Audoin-Rouzeau and Annette Becker, *14–18, Understanding the Great War* (New York: Hill and Wang, 2003), pp. 203–25 (quote on p. 204).

[37] Michael Jeismann and Rolf Westheider, 'Wofür stirbt der Bürger? Nationaler Totenkult und Staatsbürgertum in Deutschland und Frankreich seit der Französischen Revolution', in Reinhart Koselleck and Michael Jeismann (eds.), *Der politische Totenkult: Kriegerdenkmäler in der Moderne* (Munich: Fink, 1994), pp. 23–50; see also Daniel J. Sherman, 'Bodies and Names: The Emergence of Commemoration in Interwar France', *American Historical Review* 103 (1998), 443–66.

[38] See Jeismann and Westheider, 'Totenkult', pp. 29, 36–42; and the examples in Kai Kruse and Wolfgang Kruse, 'Kriegerdenkmäler in Bielefeld: Ein lokalhistorischer Beitrag zur Entwicklungsanalyse des deutschen Gefallenenkultes im 19. und 20. Jahrhundert', in Koselleck and Jeismann, *Der politische Totenkult*, pp. 91–128 (pp. 111–14).

Table 1 *Veterans' associations in the Weimar Republic*

Stahlhelm (Steel Helmet): founded in 1918, peak membership in 1932 = *c.* 350,000; radical nationalist, moving to the extreme right from the late 1920s.

Jungdeutscher Orden, or Jungdo (Young German Order): founded in 1920, peak membership in 1921 = 200,000, dropping to 100,000 from 1924; nationalist and 'bündisch', its leadership circle merged the Jungdo with the liberal DDP to form the Deutsche Staatspartei (German State Party) in July 1930.

Kyffhäuserbund: founded in 1900, peak membership during the Weimar years in 1929 = 2.6 million, up from 2.2 million in 1921; umbrella organisation of conservative but largely unpolitical local veterans' associations that were mostly founded in the wake of the war against France in 1870/1.

Reichsvereinigung ehemaliger Kriegsgefangener (Reich Association of former Prisoners of War): founded in 1919, peak membership was allegedly 400,000 in 1921, but this seems vastly exaggerated, given that in 1924 it was stated that there were as few as 10,000 members; on paper politically neutral, but increasingly promoting *völkisch*-nationalist ideals, triggering the foundation of the breakaway group Vereinigung ehemaliger Kriegsgefangener in 1925, which comprised Social Democrat and pacifist former POWs.

Reichsbund jüdischer Frontsoldaten (Reich League of Jewish Front-Line Soldiers): founded in 1919, peak membership in 1924 = 36,000; defence organisation of Jewish war veterans.

Reichsbanner Schwarz–Rot–Gold (Reichsbanner Black–Red–Gold): founded in 1924, peak membership perhaps in 1925/6 = *c.* 900,000; league of republican ex-servicemen, on paper non-partisan, de facto almost exclusively Social Democrat.

Reichsbund der Kriegsbeschädigten, Kriegsteilnehmer und Kriegerhinterbliebenen (Reich League of Disabled War Veterans, Ex-Servicemen and War Dependants): founded in 1917, peak membership in 1922 = 830,000; Social Democrat association of disabled war veterans and war widows, closely associated with the Reichsbanner.

Friedensbund der Kriegsteilnehmer (Peace League of Ex-Servicemen): founded in 1919, peak membership in 1919 = 30,000; disbanded itself in 1922, radical pacifist association.

Rote Frontkämpferbund (Red Front Fighters' League): founded in 1924, peak membership in 1927 = 127,000; combat league of the Communist Party.

This list is not comprehensive, and excludes officers' and regimental associations, as well as various smaller right-wing combat leagues. All membership figures are referenced in the following chapters, apart from the figures for Kyffhäuserbund: Dieter Fricke (ed.), *Lexikon zur Parteiengeschichte: Die bürgerlichen und kleinbürgerlichen Parteien und Verbände in Deutschland (1789–1945)*, 4 vols., Vol. III (Cologne: Pahl-Rugenstein, 1985), p. 326; Jungdo: *ibid.*, p. 138; Reichsvereinigung ehemaliger Kriegsgefangener: Rainer Pöppinghege, '"Kriegsteilnehmer zweiter Klasse?": Die Reichsvereinigung ehemaliger Kriegsgefangener 1919–1933', *MGZ* 64 (2005), 391–423 (pp. 401, 405); Reichsbund jüdischer Frontsoldaten: Greg Caplan, *Wicked Sons*, p. 128; Rote Frontkämpferbund: Heinrich-August Winkler, *Der Schein der Normalität: Arbeiter und Arbeiterbewegung in der Weimarer Republik 1924 bis 1930*, 2nd edn (Berlin; Bonn: J. H. W. Dietz, 1988), p. 455.

delivered during the unveiling of a monument and on subsequent festive occasions.[39] Only when these performative aspects of remembrance are properly investigated, and the presence of pro-republican interpretations of violent death during many of these celebrations has been established, is it possible to put Weimar's memorial culture properly into a comparative perspective. It is certainly wrong to state, as Reinhart Koselleck has done, that the Weimar Republic 'left the cult of the dead to the Conservatives alone', and that this is a 'key' to understanding the demise of the Republic.[40]

The populist framing of remembrance

In 1926 Hermann Cron, an archivist at the Reichsarchiv in Postdam, which kept – among many other records – the files of the Prussian army and the general staff for the years 1914–18, published the first of a series of short booklets for internal use in the archive. They were inventories of some of the many large collections of *Feldpostbriefe*, or war letters, that the Reichsarchiv had acquired from a variety of corporate donors, for instance those of various branches of the Social Democratic 'Free Trade Unions', including the miners' and transport workers' association, and some confessional student associations. In addition to a short description of the provenance and content of the collection, Cron included a number of significant excerpts from the letters themselves.[41] Introducing the series in a brief foreword, Ernst Müsebeck, head of the archive department in the Reichsarchiv, claimed that a 'German cultural history of the World War' could 'absolutely' not be written without collections of war letters like these. While the 'repercussions and consequences' of the war on 'all areas of national life' could still not be fully ascertained, it was already apparent to Müsebeck that the 'greatest event in universal history for the past few centuries' required a new approach to collective remembrance. It was a duty of the Reichsarchiv, Müsebeck was sure, to view the memory of the Great War 'not only from above, from the state', but also 'from the depth of the German people and from all its social strata'.[42] Collecting *Feldpostbriefe* served this aim, as they offered seemingly authentic insights into the

[39] See Goebel, *Great War*, pp. 23f.

[40] Reinhart Koselleck, *Zur politischen Ikonologie des gewaltsamen Todes: Ein deutsch–französischer Vergleich* (Basel: Schwabe, 1998), p. 39.

[41] See Ulrich, *Augenzeugen*, pp. 266f.

[42] Ernst Müsebeck, 'Vorwort', in Hermann Cron (ed.), *Das Archiv des Deutschen Studentendienstes von 1914*, Inventare des Reichsarchivs, Series 1: Kriegsbrief-Sammlungen 1 (Potsdam: Reichsarchiv, 1926), pp. 2f.

perceptions of those ordinary soldiers who had encountered the face of battle at close range.

Müsebeck's remark encapsulates two significant elements that shaped the wider framework of war remembrance in Germany. The first was its populist structure, which replaced the established notion that the elites, and the military elites in particular, had made a particularly important and privileged contribution to the overall war effort. Instead, a premium was placed on the sacrifice, endurance and perceptions of the wider populace. In the context of the army this implied that it was not the memoirs of officers or even generals that offered the best vanishing point for the broader canvas of war remembrances, but rather the worm's-eye perspective of the front-line soldier. Only here, in the mud of the trenches, had truly significant *Erlebnisse*, or experiences, been generated, that were worthy of remembrance as an example for future generations or as proper reflections of the consciousness of the German people during the war. As various social and political groups in Weimar embarked on a race to re-enact the proper meaning of the *Fronterlebnis* in rituals of collective remembrance, they all agreed that the testimony of ordinary soldiers was the crucial benchmark from which to establish the relative authenticity of certain recollections. Thus, whilst eyewitness accounts, such as the various edited collections of *Feldpostbriefe* by fallen soldiers, could be the subject of conflicting interpretations, all participants in these debates shared the understanding that these voices from the past had a specific dignity.[43]

To frame the memory of the war in a populist fashion, from the 'depth' of the people, also implied a second characteristic element of German war remembrance. More than in any other country with the one exception of France, former soldiers were the primary stakeholders in the raft of cultural activities that were intended to transform past events into a meaningful present. To some extent, this was simply a belated result of the vast scale of German mobilisation during the war. Throughout the 1920s, men who had served in the army during the war still accounted for 'more than one-quarter of the German electorate', and, if the lower turnout among women is factored in, for an even larger part of the actual voters.[44] But the hegemony of veterans in the embattled field of war remembrance had not only a quantitative dimension. It was first of all the result of a process by which other potential contributors to the commemoration of war, such as war widows as one severely affected constituency, were crowded out through the overwhelming presence of

[43] Ulrich, *Augenzeugen*, pp. 228–44.
[44] Bessel, *Germany*, p. 271.

veterans.[45] Any study of war memories in the Weimar period is thus also a contribution to the cultural and political contexts for the formation of the 'front generation'. This generation should not be understood literally. It was not bound together by a shared set of memories. Rather, it was the result of a complicated process by which a highly diverse range of experiences were transformed into the mythological notion of a generation.[46] As Jay Winter has observed, the 'soldiers' memory of the war is not at all the same as the cultural memory of the war'.[47] This cultural memory was the result of a permanent reinterpretation of the meaning of violent mass death that was centred around the 'soldier's tale', i.e. the notion that veterans were in a privileged position to talk authoritatively about these matters.[48]

There is no need here to consider in detail the vast theoretical literature on cultural memory and on the application of this concept to the study of the Great War.[49] Two brief remarks should suffice. The first concerns the transformation of individual memories into collective remembrances. War memories were not simply the preserve of the individual, even though each war veteran could refer back to an individual set of recollections that reflected the trajectory of his own biography. But 'every individual memory constitutes itself in communication with others', as Jan Assmann has contended, following Maurice Halbwachs in this point.[50] Only on rare occasions is it possible to identify the conversations that shaped individual memories. But there can be no doubt that the members of the Reichsbund and Reichsbanner attached significance primarily to those aspects of the past that they shared in many encounters with fellow socialist workers in their town or neighbourhood. These individual memories were

[45] For one of the few attempts to remember the fate of war widows see Helene Hurwitz-Stranz (ed.), *Kriegerwitwen gestalten ihr Schicksal: Lebenskämpfe deutscher Kriegerwitwen nach eigenen Darstellungen* (Berlin: Heymann, 1931); see also Bernd Ulrich and Benjamin Ziemann (eds.), *Krieg im Frieden: Die umkämpfte Erinnerung an den Ersten Weltkrieg* (Frankfurt am Main: Fischer, 1997), pp. 118f. See also Karin Hausen, 'The German Nation's Obligations to the Heroes' Widows of World War I', in Margaret Higonnet, Jane Jenson, Sonya Michel and Margaret Collins Weitz (eds.), *Behind the Lines: Gender and the Two World Wars* (New Haven; London: Yale University Press, 1987), pp. 126–40.

[46] Richard Bessel, 'The "Front Generation" and the Politics of Weimar Germany', in Mark Roseman (ed.), *Generations in Conflict: Youth Revolt and Generation Formation in Germany 1770–1968* (Cambridge University Press, 1995), pp. 121–36.

[47] Winter, *Remembering War*, p. 104.

[48] *Ibid.*, p. 116.

[49] For perceptive remarks, see Goebel, *Great War*, pp. 14–18; Winter, *Remembering War*, pp. 1–51.

[50] Jan Assmann, 'Collective Memory and Cultural Identity', *New German Critique* 65 (1995), 125–33 (p. 127).

transformed into collective remembrances when certain groups of people acted together to specify their understanding of the past and make it public.[51] The second remark is a reminder that the connotations of some key terms in English and German differ. Memory can be translated in straightforward fashion as *Erinnerung*, but the English term remembrance covers a wider range of connotations. Its German equivalents can be both *Erinnerung*, denoting the shifting, dynamic process through which individuals rework their past experiences, and *Gedächtnis* and *Gedenken*, terms that refer to the performative rituals that identify certain elements of the past as particularly noteworthy and exemplary for the living.

Available sources

Analysing republican war memories is not the easiest task, particularly when personal remembrances and their possible articulation in the framework of public commemorations constitute one element of the historical argument. As published sources, the membership journals of the Reichsbund and Reichsbanner respectively offer crucial insights into all aspects of this investigation. In addition, press coverage by a variety of local newspapers can illuminate the performative aspects of memory politics, during the inauguration of war memorials and on many other occasions.[52] As a result of the Nazi seizure of power in 1933, the paper trail of the head offices of the Reichsbund and Reichsbanner have not survived. An exceptionally rich documentation at the regional level are the files of the Reichsbanner Hanover *Gau*, which include correspondence with local branches.[53] The personal papers of some leading Reichsbanner members were also confiscated by the Gestapo and most probably later destroyed.[54] Others, such as Karl Höltermann, who served from 1924 as the deputy head of the Reichsbanner and finally headed the association from July 1932, had to leave their papers behind when they fled the Nazis and went into exile. Nonetheless, the still available personal papers of some leading Reichsbanner members and SPD politicians contain valuable material.[55]

[51] Winter, *Remembering War*, pp. 4f.

[52] For these and other aspects, the newspaper clippings produced by the head office of the former Reichslandbund provide an unparalleled range of coverage. See BArch, R 8034 II, 7690–2.

[53] See the files in NHStAH, Hann. 310 II A, nos. 2–25.

[54] See for instance, with regard to Karl Mayr, Wolfgang A. Mommsen (ed.), *Die Nachlässe in den deutschen Archiven*, 2 vols., Vol. I (Boppard: Boldt, 1971), p. 327.

[55] Most of these are held by the AdsD in Bonn.

It is ironic that the most comprehensive and systematic insights into the inner workings of local Reichsbanner branches are provided by sources that were gathered through police surveillance. Even though the Reichsbanner aimed to defend the democratic state, the political police in Bavaria, working on the premise that political disorder mainly emanated from the left, decided to put the Reichsbanner under constant surveillance. Desk-workers filed pertinent newspaper clippings, while police informers attended meetings of Reichsbanner *Kameradschaften* (comradeships) in various neighbourhoods across Munich.[56] These reports offer detailed insights into the inner workings of local Reichsbanner groups, and give a lively and vivid picture of the discussions held among rank-and-file members. Additional information was provided by a number of regional studies of the Reichsbanner that have been published in recent years, mostly relying on a thorough analysis of the local press and snippets of archival evidence.[57] The commemorative practices at war memorials are mainly documented in newspaper clippings. For the purposes of this book, it was also possible to extract relevant information from a number of regional studies.[58]

Structure of the argument

In the following chapters, the structure and the significance of republican war remembrances will be situated in their social, political and cultural context. While the bulk of the argument is based on the commemorative activities of the Reichsbund and Reichsbanner, other agents and media of memory occasionally come into play. In the first chapter in particular, a string of popular booklets and brochures on the inner workings of the German army during the war will be examined. Mostly published in the period from 1919 to 1922 by leftist and radical-democratic authors, they sketched out a republican narrative for the causes of the German collapse in 1918, laying the blame at the

[56] For context on the political police in Bavaria, see Martin Faatz, *Vom Staatsschutz zum Gestapo-Terror: Politische Polizei in Bayern in der Endphase der Weimarer Republik und der Anfangsphase der nationalsozialistischen Diktatur* (Würzburg: Echter, 1995), pp. 63–77.

[57] In addition to Voigt, *Kampfbünde*, see David Magnus Mintert, *'Sturmtrupp der deutschen Republik': Das Reichsbanner Schwarz–Rot–Gold in Wuppertal* (Wuppertal: Edition Wahler, 2002); and Axel Ulrich, *Freiheit! Das Reichsbanner Schwarz–Rot–Gold und der Kampf von Sozialdemokraten in Hessen gegen den Nationalsozialismus 1924–1938* (Frankfurt am Main: SPD–Bezirk Hessen Süd, 1988).

[58] See, for instance, Christian Saehrendt, *Der Stellungskrieg der Denkmäler: Kriegerdenkmäler im Berlin der Zwischenkriegszeit (1919–1939)* (Bonn: J. H. W. Dietz, 2004).

door of the Wilhelmine elites and quite effectively rejecting the stab-in-the-back myth. The chapter will situate these published recollections in the early debates about the legacy of the war.

When it was established in 1924 as a republican defence formation, the Reichsbanner Schwarz–Rot–Gold quickly attracted a mass membership of roughly one million men, mostly Social Democrats. But the Reichsbanner acted not only as the security guard of the Republic. Its members, two-thirds of whom were veterans of the First World War, also engaged in an intense and differentiated cultural practice of war remembrances. Chapter 2 will analyse the key features of these commemorations and their connections with the republican activism of these veterans. It will thus highlight the significance of the Reichsbanner as the veterans' association of the socialist working-class milieu. Chapter 3 will trace individual recollections of the war as personal motives that fed into the republican activism of ordinary Reichsbanner members. Drawing on an example from a small provincial town, these motives will be contextualised in the local setting of veterans' politics and working-class everyday life, thus avoiding the pitfall of detaching discourses about the war from the social contexts in which they were embedded. The chapter will also shed light on the problems Reichsbanner members faced when they tried to reconcile their personal memories with the public discourse on the 'war experience'.

Chapter 4 will outline the public rhetoric of war remembrances employed by the Reichsbanner and Reichsbund. Both associations tried to use the commemoration of the war dead as a means of strengthening the legitimacy of the Republic, thus criticising the exploitation of the legacy of the fallen for anti-republican purposes. A particular focus will be on the attempts to symbolise and to assign meaning to mass death, and on the ambivalent results of a discourse that focused on the victimisation of front-line soldiers. Chapter 5 will provide a detailed account of the unsuccessful attempts to build a *Reichsehrenmal*, a central national memorial for the commemoration of the fallen soldiers of 1914–18 in Germany. It will chart the various proposals, their political motives and symbolic implications. Outlining the reasons for the reluctance to adopt the idea of the 'Unknown Soldier', the chapter will explain the failure of the *Reichsehrenmal* in terms not of a lack but of an abundance of (contradicting) symbols for German national unity.

Military history was another crucial battleground for the contested commemorations of the First World War. Chapter 6 will outline how the republican camp aimed to attribute responsibility for German defeat to the imperial general staff and to criticise the smokescreens offered by the official historiography produced by Reichswehr officials. For these purposes, the Reichsbanner could rely on a number of former officers in the Imperial Army who had turned into outspoken and devoted supporters of the Weimar Republic, advocates of reconciliation with France and critics of the rearmament politics of the Reichswehr. The chapter will examine the biographies of these former officers and the reasons for this dramatic shift in their political allegiances. It will then analyse their contributions to the politics of military history up until 1933. Chapter 7 will focus on the years from 1928 to 1933, when the memories of the Great War became the subject of a massive wave of literary and other artistic representations.[59] It will explore how the increasing polarisation of war remembrances in this period affected the position and the interpretations of the republican camp.

Finally, some remarks on terminology. Throughout this book, men who had been conscripts in the German army during the First World War will be called 'veterans'. This English word has an equivalent in German parlance, *Veteranen*, but it was rarely ever used in the interwar period.[60] The political left and centre preferred to call veterans *Kriegsteilnehmer*, as the name of the Reichsbanner ('Bund republikanischer Kriegsteilnehmer') indicates, thus using a rather sober and descriptive term that simply indicated that someone had participated in the war. In the nationalist camp, *Frontsoldaten*, or front-line soldiers, was the preferred semantic label, as it situated the veterans at precisely those spots where the actual fighting had been taking place, and facilitated denunciations of the left as cowards who had never seen the enemy in the first place. Accusations like these forced the moderate left to adopt the term *Frontsoldaten* for themselves, and occasionally even to include the notion of *Kampf* or fighting into the set of connotations associated with a republican *Frontsoldat*.[61] Tapping into the competitive logic of ascribing proper wartime service only to the in-group, and injecting further militancy, veterans could also describe themselves as *Frontkämpfer*, or front-line fighters. This terminology largely remained the domain of the extreme left and right. Its systematic use

[59] The most comprehensive study of war literature in the Weimar Republic is Jörg Vollmer, 'Imaginäre Schlachtfelder: Kriegsliteratur in der Weimarer Republik. Eine literatursoziologische Untersuchung', Ph.D. dissertation (Freie Universität Berlin, 2003); on individual authors see Thomas F. Schneider and Hans Wagener (eds.), *Von Richthofen bis Remarque: Deutschsprachige Prosa zum I. Weltkrieg* (Amsterdam; New York: Rodopi, 2003).

[60] See Jakob Vogel, 'Der Undank der Nation: Die Veteranen der Einigungskriege und die Debatte um ihren "Ehrensold" im Kaiserreich', *MGZ* 60 (2001), 343–66 (pp. 356f.).

[61] As flagged up in the title of Hermann Schützinger, *Der Kampf um die Republik: Ein Kampfbrevier für republikanische Frontsoldaten* (Leipzig: Ernst Oldenburg, 1924).

was spearheaded by the Communist Party, which called its own veterans' league, founded in 1924, the *Rote Frontkämpferbund*, or Red Front Fighters' League.[62] But as we will see below, moderate Social Democrats were also sometimes tempted to adopt this aggressive term and thus to outbid the nationalist camp. In a nutshell, the semantics of these self-descriptions already indicate that contestation and disunity were key elements of war remembrances in Weimar Germany.

62 See Voigt, *Kampfbünde*, pp. 115–26, esp. p. 119.

1 'A short period of insight': symbolising defeat as liberation, 1918–1923

On 1 January 1919, a poem published in *Vorwärts*, the daily newspaper edited by the Majority Social Democratic Party (MSPD) in Berlin, addressed the final year of the war in a 'farewell to 1918' with these lines:

> ... There were hardly enough coffins to take all the dead,
> earth had become one mass grave,
> love had died away, reconciliation suffered from a lingering disease,
> hatred was the only master, and this eerie dance of death was insanely directed by a sceptre.
> ...
> Then suddenly, year (we started to believe you were a faint man, close to death),
> You turned into a young man, strong and marvellous,
> And you shouted with joy: the dawn of the new era has arrived!! ...
> Thrones were deposed. And the people, liberated and without shackles,
> were quick to raise love and peace to the throne ...
> You finished the battle, the need, serfdom and misery ...
> We will always pronounce you as the year of freedom,
> Of your horrors, we will no longer speak ...[1]

While the poetic substance of these stanzas is debatable, they indicate some of the persistent ambivalences in the Social Democratic remembrance of the Great War only shortly after its end. The destructive nature of war is spelled out in no uncertain terms, and the blame for this reign of death is clearly laid on the rulers of the monarchical system. Yet the revolutionary transformation to a regime of peace, freedom and love is presented in rather ambiguous fashion. Instead of celebrating the power and agency of soldiers and workers and their active contribution to the toppling of the Hohenzollern monarchy, the cause of political change is rather reified as a personification of time. Judging from this

[1] 'Abschied von 1918', *Vorwärts* no. 1, 1 January 1919. Throughout the book, all translations are mine unless stated otherwise.

poem, it was not at all clear that the people had liberated themselves, and that it had been the soldiers in the field army who brought an end to 'battle' and 'serfdom' by deserting in masses from August 1918 onwards and thus fatally undermining the cohesion of the Imperial Army.[2] The poem is equally ambivalent in its treatment of remembrance. It was certainly believed that the end of the war should be associated with the liberation of the German people, and not with the fact that Germany had been defeated, or with the terms of the armistice imposed by the Allies. Given the prospect of a future spent in freedom it seemed reasonable, though, to forget about the horrors of war, or at least to refrain from mentioning them any longer. Yet as we will see, the competitive structure of war remembrance in post-war Germany meant that it was essential for Social Democrats and progressive republicans to bring to mind the misery and bloodshed of life at the front time and time again.

This improvised poem was only one of the many forms through which supporters of the republican system voiced their recollections of the First World War during the first couple of years after the armistice. Indeed, one of the characteristic elements of republican war remembrance in the period up till 1923 was the lack of any stable and coherent framework or core institutional platform on which moderate socialists and radical democrats could rely for these purposes. A variety of media outlets was at their disposal for the representation of war memories, and they were eager to develop institutional structures that could support and sustain concerted efforts to communicate republican narratives of the war in a broader public. Yet while these efforts could at least temporarily be connected in a rather loose network, some of them were only short-lived, and others faced an increasing backlash from the Reichswehr, which had a vested interest in restoring the German public's *Wehrhaftigkeit*, or fitness to fight. The diverse and unstable nature of these endeavours goes a long way towards explaining both the remarkable strength and the ultimate weakness of republican war narratives in the turbulent years from 1919 to the stabilisation of both currency and political system in late 1923. Political and cultural struggles about the legacy of the war were deeply entwined; any success in this field rested both on the ability to foster support and draw a constituency of interested people together, and on the power of textual and pictorial symbols that resonated among those who had experienced the war first-hand. For these reasons, I will first outline some of the key media outlets and institutional players in the domain of pro-republican war remembrance

[2] See Wilhelm Deist, 'The Military Collapse of the German Empire', *War in History* 3 (1996), 186–207.

before the texture and symbolism of these recollections are explored in more detail.

Media outlets for the republican cause

The first crucial platform for republican war memories was provided by the main political newspapers of the moderate left. *Vorwärts* published a broad variety of articles on the war experiences in the immediate post-war years. In terms of form, these pieces ranged from poems and personal reflections on the problems of returning home from war to fictionalised short stories and opinion statements.[3] Apart from these more reflexive genres, *Vorwärts* also offered critical coverage and commentary on the 'stab-in-the-back' or *Dolchstoß* myth, the most important right-wing attempt to shape public opinion with regard to the causes of the German defeat.[4] One driving force for the publication of these recollections was Artur Zickler, a member of the Social Democratic Party (SPD) youth organisation *Jungsozialisten*, and a member of the *Vorwärts* editorial staff. Through the publishing house of *Vorwärts*, Zickler also published an account of his wartime service unter the title *In the Madhouse*. In this booklet, he detailed how the NCOs in his company had singled him out as a Social Democrat, and described his complete loss of faith in the notion of comradeship after suffering abuse from his roommates. After refusing to return to the front after a stay in hospital, he was transferred to a mental asylum for psychiatric treatment: an indication, for Zickler, of how the war had fundamentally altered the notions of reason and insanity.[5]

Another important outlet for democratic narratives of the war experience was the *Berliner Volks-Zeitung* (*BVZ*). Published by the liberal Jewish newspaper proprietor Georg Lachmann-Mosse, the *BVZ* was an influential political paper with a long-established tradition and a largely working-class readership. While its chief editor, Otto Nuschke, was a member of the Prussian parliament for the German Democratic Party (DDP), the newspaper itself did not follow any particular party directive, and was an open and diverse forum for left-liberal and radical-democratic ideas. In the aftermath of the war, a group of outspoken pacifists

[3] See for instance Kurt Juliusberger, 'Front-Frieden', *Vorwärts* no. 101, 24 February 1919; Walter Dornbusch, 'Die Heimkehr', *Vorwärts* no. 138, 27 March 1919.

[4] Kurt Heilbut, 'Von hinten erdolcht', *Vorwärts* no. 59, 9 February 1920.

[5] Artur Zickler, *Im Tollhause* (Berlin: Verlag Vorwärts, n.d. [1919]), pp. 14–19, 31–7. See the review by Ignaz Wrobel (i.e. Kurt Tucholsky), *Weltbühne* 16.I (1920), 282f. See also, without much detail on his anti-militarist writings, the autobiographical note by Zickler, 3 August 1945: BArch, SAPMO, SgY 30, 1052.

contributed to the *BVZ* either as writers, such as Carl von Ossietzky and Berthold Jacob, or as members of the editorial staff, such as Karl Vetter. Vetter was the driving force behind this energetic group of political journalists. Coming from a humble working-class background – his father was a bricklayer in Berlin-Neukölln – and invariably described as a swaggering type of 'Ur-Berliner', he had been involved in the youth movement before the war. Devastated by his impressions from his front-line service during the war, he returned home as a radical pacifist.[6] Like Artur Zickler and *Vorwärts*, Vetter was particularly eager to use the *BVZ* as a platform for reflection on and remembrance of the disastrous consequences of the war. Starting in March 1919, he published a series of articles based on his own reminiscences of the decisive final months of the war at the western front. Inundated with positive responses from the ranks of former *Kriegsteilnehmer*, and responding to their suggestion to make his reflections available in a more coherent fashion, Vetter published a booklet on *The Collapse of the Western Front* in 1919. Explicitly blaming Ludendorff, and speaking on behalf of the 'Feldgrauen', soldiers in field-grey uniform, he formulated an indictment against the 'deliberate collusion' and 'knowing untruth' spread by former members of the Third Army Supreme Command about the reasons for German military defeat.[7]

A number of pacifist and radical-left journals such as *Die Weltbühne* or *Das Tage-Buch* also continued to publish articles on the war experience throughout the early 1920s.[8] But in terms of readership and political significance, *Vorwärts* and the *BVZ* were by far the most important periodicals that promoted a progressive reading of wartime suffering to a broader audience. To be sure, compared with some of the tabloids and other mass papers published in the capital, such as the *Berliner Morgenpost*, the circulation figures for *Vorwärts* and *BVZ* were rather modest. In 1925, the first year for which comparative figures are available, their average print-runs were 95,000 and 90,000 copies respectively. Nonetheless, they were both vital tools for the representation of

[6] See the recollections by Margret Boveri, *Wir lügen alle: Eine Hauptstadtzeitung unter Hitler* (Olten; Freiburg: Walter, 1965), pp. 37f. (quote); Modris Eksteins, *The Limits of Reason: The German Democratic Press and the Collapse of Weimar Democracy* (Oxford University Press, 1975), pp. 110f., 136, 227–30.

[7] Karl Vetter, 'Wie es kam: Ein Beitrag zur Geschichte des Zusammenbruchs', *BVZ* no. 129, 25 March 1919; and *Der Zusammenbruch der Westfront: Ludendorff ist schuld! Die Anklage der Feldgrauen* (Berlin: Koch & Jürgens, n.d. [1919]), pp. 3f. (quotes).

[8] See Vanessa Ther, '"Humans are cheap and the bread is dear": Republican Portrayals of the War Experience in Weimar Germany', in Heather Jones, Jennifer O'Brien and Christoph Schmidt-Supprian (eds.), *Untold War: New Perspectives in First World War Studies* (Leiden; Boston, MA: Brill, 2008), pp. 357–84.

public opinion in the pro-republican camp, and had a significantly larger circulation than comparable conservative newspapers such as the *Deutsche Zeitung*.[9]

Newspapers offered an important outlet for reflections on the meaning of the war precisely because of the instantaneous nature of this medium, making it ideal for ad hoc interventions and as a forum for open debate. A different but closely related medium was that of short pamphlets and booklets on the nature of the war experience and on the systematic abuse of power in the German field army. Many of these brochures served a direct political purpose. From the early months of 1919, a campaign by nationalist circles of the extreme right and by high-ranking officers in the Imperial Army had gathered pace. Keen to deflect from their own failure as military commanders, and to blame the revolution, and by implication the Republic, for the defeat and the harsh terms of the Treaty of Versailles, these circles developed the core elements of the stab-in-the-back myth. In their view, the German army had been 'undefeated in the field' ('Im Felde unbesiegt'), a slogan first used in 1921. As officers such as Colonel Max Bauer relentlessly stressed in their newspaper articles and hastily published memoirs, it had been the socialists and Jews on the home front who had conspired to undermine the fighting power of the army, thus halting the German offensive in 1918, which would have otherwise led to victory. The first peak of this campaign was reached on 18 November 1919, when Paul von Hindenburg and Erich Ludendorff issued a joint statement in front of a parliamentary subcommittee investigating the causes of Germany's defeat. Here they reiterated and confirmed, with their authority as former leaders of the German military campaign, the *Dolchstoß* allegation.[10]

It would be wrong, though, to assume that the republican counter-attack was hindered by widespread 'veneration' for Hindenburg among 'republican circles'.[11] Under the headline 'Broken pillars', a Social Democrat newspaper in Magdeburg highlighted the appearance

[9] See Bernhard Fulda, *Press and Politics in the Weimar Republic* (Oxford University Press, 2009), p. 24.

[10] Barth, *Dolchstoßlegenden*, pp. 302–39 (quote on p. 326); on the appearance in front of the subcommittee see also the cynical commentary by Ignaz Wrobel, 'Zwei Mann in Zivil', *Weltbühne* 15.II (1919), 659–64.

[11] See Anna von der Goltz, *Hindenburg: Power, Myth, and the Rise of the Nazis* (Oxford University Press, 2009), pp. 66–9 (quote on p. 66). Throughout her book, Goltz grossly exaggerates the acceptance of the Hindenburg myth among Social Democrats, largely based on a few articles in *Vorwärts*; *ibid.*, pp. 50f. She also fails to recognise the almost total collapse of the Hindenburg myth among front-line soldiers in the autumn of 1918. For references, see Benjamin Ziemann, *War Experiences in Rural Germany, 1914–1923* (Oxford: Berg, 2007), p. 138; and Bernd Ulrich and Benjamin Ziemann

in front of the subcommittee as an act of denial by two disoriented elderly men. Their testimony had ultimately destroyed the 'legend' that Germany had had a brilliant army leadership during the war.[12] Other authors seconded, directing their ire against both Ludendorff and Hindenburg.[13] Unmasking the *Dolchstoß* myth as a deliberate smokescreen that served vested interests was the core aim of many booklets and pamphlets by Social Democrats and other republicans in the immediate post-war period. According to one survey of this literature, no fewer than twenty-three brochures, most of them published between 1919 and 1923, were devoted to this purpose.[14] This figure cannot be more than a rough indication, as a number of brochures that explicitly aimed to dispel nationalist myths about the collapse in 1918 are not included.[15] Nonetheless, it is important to note that the republicans did not simply surrender when they were blamed for Germany's defeat. On the contrary, they offered a detemined rebuttal of such allegations. One of their strategies was simple ridicule. In a booklet published in 1921, Erich Kuttner, the founder and first head of the Reichsbund of disabled soldiers, cited Ludendorff's war memoirs. Complaints that officers were living in luxury at the expense of private soldiers, the former general insisted, had been 'shameful slander by foreign and domestic propaganda'. Without any comment, Kuttner printed the menu from the officers' mess of an army headquarters on the next page.[16]

Many other publications effectively used the worm's-eye view of the front-line soldier as a narrative strategy.[17] Presenting the workings of the Imperial Army from the viewpoint of an ordinary private soldier offered a number of advantages for those authors who did not simply

(eds.), *German Soldiers in the Great War: Letters and Eyewitness Accounts* (Barnsley: Pen & Sword, 2010), pp. 150, 179.

12 'Geborstene Säulen', *Volksstimme* no. 272, 21 November 1919.

13 Vetter, *Zusammenbruch*, p. 6; *Der 'Dolchstoß': Warum das deutsche Heer zusammenbrach* (Berlin: Zentralverlag, 1920), pp. 4–6.

14 Rainer Sammet, *'Dolchstoss': Deutschland und die Auseinandersetzung mit der Niederlage im Ersten Weltkrieg (1918–1933)* (Berlin: Trafo, 2003), pp. 178f.

15 See for instance *Der Zusammenbruch der Kriegspolitik und die Novemberrevolution: Beobachtungen und Betrachtungen eines ehemaligen Frontsoldaten* (Berlin: Verlagsgenossenschaft Freiheit, 1919); *Der Etappensumpf: Dokumente des Zusammenbruchs des deutschen Heeres aus den Jahren 1916/1918. Aus dem Kriegstagebuch eines Gemeinen* (Jena: Volksbuchhandlung, 1920); Hermann Schützinger, *Zusammenbruch: Die Tragödie des deutschen Feldheeres* (Leipzig: Ernst Oldenburg, 1924).

16 Erich Kuttner, *Der Sieg war zum Greifen nahe! Authentische Zeugnisse vom Frontzusammenbruch* (Berlin: Verlag für Sozialwissenschaft, 1921), pp. 23f.

17 See Bernd Ulrich, 'Die Perspektive "von unten" und ihre Instrumentalisierung am Beispiel des Ersten Weltkrieges', *Krieg und Literatur/War and Literature* 1 (1989), 47–64.

want to indulge in rose-tinted recollections of a time of heroic adventures, but whose main aim was to unmask the deceptive lies of the former elites. Such a perspective allowed them to pitch the worm's-eye view against the detached position of those staff officers who had only ever observed the battlefield from a remote rear position and were thus never confronted with the brutal reality of the front. Many of the brochures foregrounded the suffering of the 'poor and betrayed' front-line soldiers and their 'still weeping wounds'. Thus, they effectively juxtaposed the authenticity of the real war experience with the bogus claims for superior leadership from nationalist officers.[18]

Another crucial advantage of those accounts that presented authentic experiences of ordinary soldiers was the claim to veracity. Republican authors tried to illuminate the corruption and dysfunctional organisation in the Imperial Army through the publication of war letters or personal testimony in the form of war diaries. Excerpts from the diary of a sergeant in the medical corps were published in 1919 under the main title *Indictment of the Tormented.* According to the subtitle, these recollections would provide the reader with the 'history of a field hospital'. In his introduction, Artur Zickler summed up the gist of these notes, describing them as a 'classical chronicle of the vileness, crying shame, exploitation, corruption and crimes against the poorest of the poor, the victims of war'. These pages, Zickler claimed, were 'nothing but an unvarnished description of the facts'. He was eager to pre-empt the standard rebuttal of right-wing authors against such accusations: the argument that the experiences of this particular observer were a deplorable exception, while the German army had generally functioned effectively despite adverse circumstances. On the contrary, Zickler insisted, the situation in this field hospital would have been 'impossible' if the 'whole system' and command structure of the army had not provided 'fertile soil for such decay'.[19] A brief foreword by the publisher underscored the main point. While he had advised the author to remain anonymous, the veracity of all claims had been subjected to scrutiny, and both the author himself and further eyewitnesses were ready to testify to their accuracy.[20]

From 1919 to 1923, the republican left used the worm's-eye view in many brochures as an effective instrument against right-wing denial with

[18] Vetter, *Zusammenbruch*, p. 4.

[19] *Anklage der Gepeinigten! Geschichte eines Feldlazarettes: Aus den Tagebüchern eines Sanitäts-Feldwebels* (Berlin: Firn-Verlag, 1919), pp. 6f. (on this book, see Ignaz Wrobel, 'Militaria', *Weltbühne* 15.II (1919), pp. 195f.; and Karl Vetter, 'Die Anklage der Gepeinigten', *BVZ* no. 193, 30 April 1919); a similar indictment of the 'system' can be found in *Der Etappensumpf*, p. 4.

[20] *Anklage der Gepeinigten*, p. 3.

regard to the causes of German defeat. But popular representations of the suffering at the front had an impact far beyond the core constituency of those who eagerly supported the new democratic system. One of the characteristic elements of the discourse on war remembrance during the immediate post-war period was that nationalist publications were forced to tap into similar sentiments, and to give voice to those bitter feelings of disillusionment that the left so effectively used for an indictment against the Wilhelmine system. One prominent example of nationalist attempts to accept responsibility and provide an honest account of the 'causes of the collapse' was a booklet of the same title, published by Walther Lambach in 1919. A leading official in the German National Union of Commercial Employees (Deutschnationaler Handlungsgehilfen-Verband; DHV), Lambach presented a cross-section of the many war letters by DHV members serving in the field army. The prevalent tone was highly critical: of the Jews – following the anti-Semitic ideology of the DHV – but also of the junior officers, who were keen to exploit the system for their personal advantage but completely uninterested in the welfare of their subordinates. Other letter writers complained about the lack of comradeship and the large discrepancy in pay between private soldiers and junior officers.[21] The ideas behind this critique of the national war effort from a nationalist perspective were summed up in the following letter from the western front in May 1917:

> I went to the front on the third day of mobilisation as a member of the *Landsturm*, full of ideals, true to my affiliation with the German National Association. But what I have experienced in the course of time from our officers has already destroyed my idealism. I could tell you incidents that would amaze you. The war is only considered as a profitable business, from which everyone is trying to earn as much as possible.[22]

When Lambach published these eyewitness accounts from the members of his association, he wanted to demonstrate that the DHV had tried to address the soldiers' grievances by including these materials in a petition it had filed in February 1916 with the Prussian War Ministry. Another reason, however, was the wave of post-revolutionary indictments of the injustice in the Imperial Army that used the worm's-eye perspective. Lambach clearly hoped for a restoration of 'order and for a new German advance'. But in 1919, far from being able to propagate any mythologies of the war experience, he faced a situation where

[21] Walther Lambach, *Ursachen des Zusammenbruchs* (Hamburg: Deutschnationale Verlagsanstalt, n.d. [1919]), pp. 23, 25f., 32f., 56f.

[22] Cited in *ibid.*, p. 59. For a related argument on the internal reasons for the military collapse in 1918 from a nationalist perspective see Otto Dietz, *Der Todesgang der deutschen Armee: Militärische Ursachen* (Berlin: Karl Curtius, 1919), pp. 5ff.

leftist currents effectively used these grievances 'to attract customers, in order to talk them into also accepting their other dubious products (anti-militarism, cosmopolitanism)'.[23] In addition, the presence and substance of these pacifist sentiments were reflected in his material, with letters pointing out how the war had turned nationalists into Social Democrats, and noting the increasing number of desertions towards the end of the war.[24] But when the left-liberal *Berliner Tageblatt*, published by the Mosse publishing house, and *Vorwärts* seized upon Lambach's publication, the author immediately backtracked and accused the left of cherry-picking only those quotations that served their agenda. Describing the army with the organicist metaphor of the 'body politic' (*Volkskörper*), Lambach insisted that DHV members had only meant to make it more resilient against the inevitable 'germs of corrosion'.[25]

Friedensbund der Kriegsteilnehmer

In addition to and in connection with newspapers and brochures, pro-republican war remembrances until 1923 were also fostered through a network of institutions that aimed, directly or indirectly, to utilise the raw memories of the carnage of war for pacifist and progressive political activism. One of them was the 'Peace League of Ex-Servicemen' (Friedensbund der Kriegsteilnehmer; FdK). On 2 October 1919, Karl Vetter invited a number of like-minded pacifists to the editorial offices of the *Berliner Volks-Zeitung*. Among them were pacifist luminaries such as the journalists and writers Carl von Ossietzky and Kurt Tucholsky, and Georg Friedrich Nicolai, a physician and professor at the University of Berlin who had famously fled to Denmark by plane in 1917 to avoid persecution and imprisonment for his book *Biology of War*. Other members of this gathering were less well known, including the former captain of the Saxon army, Willy Meyer, who had served as a test-pilot for the nascent German air force during the war and encountered flight aces such as the 'Red Baron', Manfred von Richthofen.[26] When the members of this gathering founded the

[23] Quotes from Lambach, *Ursachen*, pp. 111, 21f.

[24] *Ibid.*, pp. 59, 85.

[25] Walther Lambach, 'Die Zermürber der Front', *Deutsche Tageszeitung* no. 208, 5 May 1920; see Ulrich, 'Perspektive', p. 54.

[26] See the recollections by Carl von Ossietzky, 'Nie wieder Krieg: Der Rundlauf einer Parole' (1923), in *Sämtliche Schriften*, 8 vols., Vol. II: *1922–1924* (Reinbek: Rowohlt, 1994), pp. 267–70; on Nicolai, see Bernhard vom Brocke, '"An die Europäer": Der Fall Nicolai und die Biologie des Krieges. Zur Entstehung und Wirkungsgeschichte eines unzeitgemäßen Buches', *HZ* 240 (1985), 363–75; on Meyer, see Jürgen Schmidt and Bernd Ulrich, 'Pragmatischer Pazifist und Demokrat: Hauptmann a.D. Willy

FdK, they aimed to mobilise all ex-servicemen irrespective of their political allegiances, provided they were in favour of peace and reconciliation and would support the Republic. War veterans from all social strata were the core constituency because the founders agreed that only they had experienced the 'full horror of war' first-hand and were thus able to relay the 'misery' of war to the masses, and willing to work towards avoiding another war.[27]

Based on a general anti-militarist agenda that – among other points – included the rejection of general conscription, the League aimed to 'nip revanchist ideas in the bud'. Yet it also wanted to work with veterans in the 'former enemy countries' on a gradual improvement of those terms of the Treaty of Versailles that were deemed to be a 'violation of the spirit of reconciliation between peoples'.[28] Apart from pursuing a radical pacifist agenda, the FdK thus tried both to exploit and to harness the defiant mood that was prevalent in Germany vis-à-vis the peace treaty in 1919, precisely because its overall aim was to contribute to cultural demobilisation. Public rallies and speeches against the *Dolchstoß* myth were an intrinsic part of the league's activities.[29] The 'Peace League of Ex-Servicemen' was quickly able to establish itself in Berlin and in a number of other larger cities across Germany, including Bavaria. The police reckoned that between about 25,000 and 30,000 members had joined by late 1919. That was not a huge figure, but nonetheless quite remarkable against the backdrop of the chronic inability of the pacifist camp to attract larger crowds, with the German Peace Society (DFG) – the main established moderate pacifist organisation – never able to muster a higher membership throughout the Weimar Republic. Alongside Karl Vetter and Willy Meyer as founding members, the *Vorwärts* editor Artur Zickler appeared in public as the third member of the executive board. Among the members of the larger *Bundesausschuß*, or advisory board, was Emil Rabold, an editor of the Berlin-based newspaper *Freiheit*, which was published on behalf of the Independent Social Democratic Party (USPD).[30] Henning

Meyer (1885–1945)', in Wolfram Wette and Helmut Donat (eds.), *Pazifistische Offiziere in Deutschland 1871–1933* (Bremen: Donat, 1999), pp. 303–17.

27 Report by Staatskommissar für die Überwachung der öffentlichen Ordnung, 3 December 1919: StA Bremen, 4, 65, 1157.

28 'Der Friedensbund der Kriegsteilnehmer', excerpt from a report by the RKO, 25 January 1921: StA Bremen, 4, 65, 1157; see also 'Ein Aufruf des Friedensbundes der Kriegsteilnehmer', *Berliner Tageblatt*, 19 October 1919.

29 See for instance 'Gegen die Dolchstoß-Legende', *Freiheit* no. 193, 26 May 1920.

30 Berlin Police President to Prussian Ministry of the Interior, 8 December 1919: GStA, Rep. 77, Tit. 1137, Nr. 50; Report by Staatskommissar für die Überwachung der öffentlichen Ordnung, 3 December 1919.

Duderstadt, who worked as a journalist for the *Berliner Volks-Zeitung*, was also a member of the Friedensbund and a contributor to its journal.[31] It thus seems appropriate to describe the FdK as based on a cooperation of leftist newspaper editors and journalists representing the DDP, the SPD and the USPD respectively. While these political journalists agreed on the need to use the political leverage provided by the fresh recollections of war among former front-line soldiers, they were also involved in the infighting between different factions of the socialist camp. Looking back in 1923, Carl von Ossietzy identified these bitter internal struggles within the left as the main reason for the short-lived success of the FdK, which was formally disbanded in 1922.[32]

Associations for POWs and disabled soldiers

A survey of those organisations that contributed to the densely knit web of pro-republican war remembrances would not be complete without at least a brief mention of the Reichsvereinigung ehemaliger Kriegsgefangener (Reich Association of Former POWs; ReK). It was founded in early 1919, and by 1921 about 400,000 from a total of 1.2 million former POWs had joined the association; a remarkable degree of mobilisation among this particular group of war veterans. The ReK basically served as a pressure group for the social interests of its members, particularly with regard to an appropriate pension provision. In principle, the association claimed to pursue a non-partisan agenda and supported the Republic, although leading representatives did in fact represent a moderate conservatism and tried to translate the experiences of the camp-community into the wider ideal of a *Volksgemeinschaft*.[33] Yet political attitudes among the rank-and-file members, particularly those in Berlin and other larger cities, tilted further towards the left. At the grassroots level, cooperation with the Social Democratic Reichsbund was considered to be a matter of course, and many ReK members voiced strictly anti-militarist attitudes, favoured international reconciliation and warned against the dangers of another war. Aiming to

[31] See Henning Duderstadt, 'Die Internationale der Soldaten', *Nie wieder Krieg: Organ des Friedensbundes der Kriegsteilnehmer* no. 16/17 (November 1921): LAB, A Pr. Br. Rep. 030, 21643, fos. 147f.

[32] Ossietzky, 'Nie wieder Krieg', p. 268; see also the recollection by Kurt R. Grossmann, *Ossietzky: Ein deutscher Patriot* (Munich: Kindler, 1963), p. 80.

[33] Rainer Pöppinghege, '"Kriegsteilnehmer zweiter Klasse"? Die Reichsvereinigung ehemaliger Kriegsgefangener 1919–1933', *MGZ* 64 (2005), 391–423 (pp. 401, 412ff.).

turn such ideas into official policy, a number of local branches left the ReK in 1925 and founded the explicitly pacifist Vereinigung ehemaliger Kriegsgefangener (Association of Former Prisoners of War; VeK).[34] Prior to 1925, it was self-evident for the many Social Democrats among the ReK membership that this organisation should uphold in public the peaceful values they supported owing to their specific wartime experiences. Reconciliation with the former enemies was thus high on the agenda of official acts of remembrance. Kurt Grossmann (1897–1972), Social Democrat and one of the leading pacifists and active republicans of the Weimar period, recalled how he had joined the ReK immediately upon his return from British captivity in autumn 1919. Quickly progressing to head of the local branch in Berlin-Charlottenburg, he and his comrades used the *Totensonntag* in 1920, the last Sunday before Advent traditionally used by Protestants for the commemoration of the dead, to pay their respect to the former enemies. During a remembrance ceremony they laid down a wreath at the grave of an unknown French soldier who was buried at a cemetary in the Hasenheide, a public park in which many working-class Berliners spent their leisure time.[35]

In some respects, the third institutional platform for republican war remembrances was also connected to the *Vorwärts* newspaper, which certainly acted as the major hub for initiatives in this field. In April 1916, the Jewish Social Democrat and journalist Erich Kuttner had been severely wounded at the battle of Verdun. Nerves in his left arm had been severed, and Kuttner was hospitalised for a total period of eight months. With his treatment not yet finished and his arm still in a sling, Kuttner joined the editorial staff of *Vorwärts*, and quickly established himself as an expert on the plight of disabled war veterans and social policy initiatives that could improve their situation. Using *Vorwärts* as a 'forum' for a debate on the prospect of an organisation of disabled war veterans, Kuttner faced scepticism from the Social Democratic trade unions who insisted that no separate organisation was needed.[36] In May 1917, Kuttner and his supporters went ahead anyway, and founded the Bund der Kriegsbeschädigten und Kriegsteilnehmer (League of Disabled War Veterans and Ex-Servicemen), which was later renamed as Reichsbund der Kriegsbeschädigten, Kriegsteilnehmer und Kriegerhinterbliebenen (Reich League of Disabled War Veterans,

[34] *Ibid.*, pp. 395f., 398, 404.

[35] Grossmann, *Ossietzky*, p. 80. See the example from Bielefeld in Pöppinghege, 'Kriegsteilnehmer', p. 408.

[36] See Maximilian Ingenthron, *"Falls nur die Sache siegt". Erich Kuttner (1887–1942): Publizist und Politiker* (Mannheim: Palatium, 2000), pp. 132–45; Whalen, *Bitter Wounds*, quote on p. 122.

Ex-Servicement and War Dependants). The Reichsbund was by far the strongest of the various associations for disabled veterans, even though competitors both on the right and the left emerged in 1919, with radical leftists breaking away and forming the Communist Internationaler Bund. Formally non-partisan, but clearly embedded in the Social Democratic working-class milieu in terms of its ideology, rank-and-file members and its functionaries, the Reichsbund remained by far the largest organisation for disabled war veterans throughout the Republic. In 1921, the Reichsbund represented more veterans than the next three largest groups, all with a moderate conservative tendency, combined.[37]

In March 1922, the league claimed to have about 830,000 members in no fewer than 7,000 local branches. During the period of hyper-inflation from 1922 to 1923, the number of fee-paying members dropped significantly to less than a third of that figure, as the budgets of working-class families were squeezed. But membership figures had bounced back by the mid 1920s, and in 1930 the Reichsbund represented about 450,000 people in 5,800 local chapters.[38] It has been argued that the Reichsbund and other organisations for disabled veterans established themselves only as 'interest groups' and were 'inhospitable associations' that could not formulate a social and political identity for those who were still carrying the scars and mutilations of their wartime service.[39] This argument seems to neglect the relevance of moral claims and a sense of righteousness that disabled veterans developed as a result of their mutilation. These were driving forces both for their personal commitment to the Reichsbund and for the symbolic displays of their collective identity that the association staged. Heinrich Hoffmann, who later served in the regional excutive boards of the Reichsbund in Hamburg and Thuringia, recalled how he founded a local chapter of the League in a military hospital in the town of Schleswig after returning from British imprisonment in April 1919. He and his comrades responded enthusiastically to the demand for 'Same pay, same food and same clothing as the Noske-guards', voiced in leaflets they received from Berlin. Disabled veterans had to wear old, deloused and repeatedly mended field-grey uniforms when they were allowed into town. These former POWs

[37] James M. Diehl, 'The Organization of German Veterans, 1917–1919', *AfS* 11 (1971), 141–84; Whalen, *Bitter Wounds*, pp. 123–9.

[38] Erich Rossmann, 'Die Wirksamkeit des Reichsbundes in Staat und Gesellschaft', *Reichsbund* 15 (1932), no. 9/10, 99.

[39] Michael Geyer, 'Ein Vorbote des Wohlfahrtsstaates: Die Kriegsopferversorgung in Frankreich, Deutschland und Großbritannien nach dem Ersten Weltkrieg', *GG* 9 (1983), 256.

believed the better treatment of young soldiers who were recruited by defence minister Gustav Noske in order to crack down on the revolutionary movement, even though they had never 'smelled fire' at the front, compared to those who had 'lain in the mud', was an 'injustice that cries to heaven'.[40]

The Social Democrats in the Reichsbund also used street demonstrations and other gatherings to display the specific reasons for their intervention in the symbolic field of war remembrances in public. The first of these mass rallies took place immediately after a welcome reception for the returning troops, organised by the Reichsbund in the Circus Busch in Berlin on 22 December 1918. Here, and on many other occasions, the mutilated bodies of ex-soldiers were deliberately used to occupy public space and to underpin the moral claims of these disabled veterans in a highly visible manner. In a carefully choreographed arrangement, veterans with the most obvious mutilations – those with severe facial injuries, amputees in wheelchairs and blinded soldiers led by their dogs – were placed at the top of the marching column. As many disabled Reichsbund members in 1918/19 marched in their worn-out army uniforms, these street demonstrations could also be read as a 'parody' on the patriotic scenes in August 1914, when young war volunteers had paraded the streets of Berlin. Other organisations of disabled veterans criticised this public use of blind soldiers as a form of propaganda.[41] Nonetheless, Erich Kuttner worked tirelessly to remind the public of the very existence of the 'Kriegszermalmten' whose faces had been crushed by the war, even after he had stepped down as chairman of the Reichsbund in February 1919. Writing in 1920 about a visit to a number of hospitals in Berlin in which more than 2,000 veterans with extreme facial injuries were hidden from public view, he offered a vivid description of these living 'memorials of horror'.[42] The very ability of the Reichsbund to express – both politically and symbolically – the specific experiences of disabled war veterans and the next-of-kin of the deceased was also the main reason why it failed to attract non-disabled veterans. Even in the immediate post-war period, when Social Democratic war

[40] 'Erinnerungen Heinrich Hoffmann', n.d. [*c.* 1965]: BArch, SAPMO, SgY 30, 1365/2, fos. 501f.

[41] Sabine Kienitz, *Beschädigte Helden: Kriegsinvalidität und Körperbilder 1914–1923* (Paderborn: Schöningh, 2008), pp. 301–5 (quote on p. 303). On the politics of disabled veterans see Deborah Cohen, *The War Come Home: Disabled Veterans in Britain and Germany, 1914–1939* (Berkeley: University of California Press, 2001), pp. 88–97.

[42] Erich Kuttner, 'Vergessen! Die Kriegszermalmten in Berliner Lazaretten', *Vorwärts* no. 449, 8 September 1920, partly printed in Ulrich and Ziemann, *German Soldiers*, pp. 81f. (quote); see Ingenthron, *Kuttner*, p. 175.

veterans had no alternative associations at their disposal, the rate of non-disabled members stalled at a mere 12 per cent.[43]

No more war!

Despite the substantial strength of the Reichsbund and the considerable support for pacifist ideas from many POWs in the Reichsvereinigung, republican war remembrances in the years up till 1923 could not rely on a coherent organisational basis. What was lacking in terms of a clearly defined institution that could drive the politics of commemoration, however, was more than outweighed by the emotional power and popular support for a simple slogan that encapsulated the anti-militarist and pacifist sentiments of the masses: 'Nie wieder Krieg!' ('No more war!'). Hundreds of thousands of former soldiers rallied behind this slogan in the immediate post-war years, and it continued to resonate among Social Democrats throughout the 1920s.[44] When the Friedensbund der Kriegsteilnehmer was founded during a gathering in Berlin on 2 October 1919, Karl Vetter suggested that its main purpose should be to mark the importance of 1 August with an annual mass gathering on that date. Signifying the historical relevance of this 'black day' when the war had begun, these rallies would serve as a reminder about an era that nationalist discourse falsely dubbed the 'great time'. Collective remembrance of 1 August would not only be relevant for veterans, Vetter argued, but should also serve as a form of political education for the younger generation. All that was needed was a 'gripping, catchy' slogan to captivate the masses, and Vetter suggested 'Nie wieder Krieg!'.[45] This had, incidentally, been the headline of a special issue of the *BVZ* on 3 August 1919, with articles by Otto Nuschke, Minna Cauer – a leading member of the bourgeois women's movement – and Karl Vetter, who urged all 'comrades' to reject the 'idol of "heroic death"'. Instead of being an idol, he argued, death at the front had been the 'murder' of the enemy who fought and suffered alongside German soldiers, and its heroic representation was a 'poison for your souls'.[46]

[43] Diehl, 'The Organization of German Veterans', p. 179.

[44] For the organisational and political context of the 'no more war' movement see Reinhold Lütgemeier-Davin, 'Basismobilisierung gegen den Krieg: Die Nie-wieder-Krieg-Bewegung in der Weimarer Republik', in Karl Holl and Wolfram Wette (eds.), *Pazifismus in der Weimarer Republik* (Paderborn: Schöningh, 1981), pp. 47–76.

[45] See Ossietzky, 'Nie wieder Krieg', p. 268.

[46] 'Nie wieder Krieg!', *BVZ* no. 356, 3 August 1919.

The proposals to commemorate the beginning of the Great War were put into practice by an action committee, 'Nie wieder Krieg', which brought together representatives from various pacifist groups under the leadership of the FdK and Vetter. The first 'no more war' rally was staged at the Lustgarten in Berlin on 1 August 1920. Its biggest supporters were the Reichsbund and the Reichsvereinigung, while the two socialist parties and the socialist Free Trade Unions held a separate rally at a different venue. Both Vetter and Zickler were among the speakers when an estimated 50,000 people gathered at the Lustgarten, making this one of the largest demonstrations in early Weimar Berlin.[47] Turnout was even bigger in 1921 and 1922, with an estimated 100,000 people taking to the streets on 1 August 1921 in Berlin alone, and up to half a million across the Reich, where demonstrations took place in more than 200 cities. The peak of the movement in 1921 and 1922 was due to the additional support of both socialist parties and the Free Trade Unions, with the Independent Social Democrats of the USPD being the main driving force. Yet relations between these powerful players and the small pacifist groups such as the FdK were fraught from the beginning, and intensive competition for hegemony in this very fragile coalition accompanied its success from the start. When the remaining Independent Socialists reunited with the MSPD in September 1922, after their left wing had joined the German Communist Party (KPD) in December 1920, the 'no more war' movement declined rapidly. In 1923, the movement still managed to organise some rallies. But bowing to the widespread nationalist frenzy in the wake of the French occupation of the Ruhr, gatherings were only held behind closed doors, and were subject to relentless criticism both from the nationalist right and the KPD.[48]

Notwithstanding the back-room power struggles between the various organisers, the public appearance of the 'no more war' campaign from 1920 to 1922 was that of a powerful mass movement. It could indeed claim to represent the 'popular desire for peace', as *Vorwärts* suggested in its headline with regard to the 1921 rally in the Lustgarten. Both as a performative display of pacifist symbolism, and as a political demonstration, this mass gathering clearly expressed a set of ideas that resonated with many working-class people. In symbolic terms, a delegation from the socialist labour youth movement caught particular attention. Surrounded by groups of musicians who played socialist tunes, it

[47] 'Nach sechs Jahren', *BVZ* no. 358, 1 August 1920; see Lütgemeier-Davin, 'Basismobilisierung', pp. 54–56.

[48] Lütgemeier-Davin, 'Basismobilisierung', pp. 56–67.

featured a young girl in a white dress, symbolising the moral purity and innocence associated with childhood, holding a placard with the line: 'I will never let my father go to war again!'[49] Decked with flags in both red and black–red–gold, the gathering at the Lustgarten showed the strength of the two main socialist parties acting in unity. Gustav Heller, speaking for the MSPD, highlighted the significance of the anniversary by calling it a commemoration of the day when the 'murdering of the peoples' (*Völkermorden*) had begun. His use of the plural indicated his belief that the people in all belligerent nations were the victims of a war that the ruling elites had unleashed. Accordingly, Heller stressed that reconciliation between such nations was the paramount aim, and warned that right-wing circles wanted to stoke up a revanchist mood in the population.[50] As a *Vorwärts* journalist argued, hinting at the Treaty of Versailles, there were reasons why the Germans should not be 'cheerful' about the peace. But the mass gathering in the centre of the capital clearly dispelled any notional idea that Germany could resort to force in order to resolve international conflicts. Instead, it displayed the 'power of the idea of peace'.[51] Summing up the ideas behind the rally, the article stressed that it showed the extent to which a 'mental disarmament' had been achieved, not by an Allied *Diktat*, but internally, through a collective endeavour of the German people.[52]

Contemporary observers thus understood the public outings of the 'no more war' movement as a litmus test for the extent of cultural demobilisation among the German people. They showed that many Social Democrats embraced the end of the Great War as liberation from militarism even though it had brought defeat and a peace treaty with extremely harsh terms for the vanquished. When trade unionists, Social Democrats and pacifists gathered to commemorate the anniversary of 1 August 1914, they also gave voice to the hope that the remembrance of the horrors of war could bring about a new dawn for international solidarity and reconciliation. A pictorial expression for this hope can be found in the poster that advertised the 'commemoration ceremony for the dead' by the 'no more war' coalition in Munich in 1922. It shows the ruins of a house, an artillery canon and several corpses scattered

[49] 'Der Friedenswille des Volkes', *Vorwärts* no. 358, 1 August 1921. In the rally on 1 August 1920, the disabled veterans of the Reichsbund, in wheelchairs and on stretchers, took centre stage, carrying placards reading 'We hate genocide [*Völkermord*]!' or 'Do you want even more cripples?'. See the report by *Welt am Montag*, 2 August 1920, reprinted in Carl von Ossietzky, *Sämtliche Schriften*, 8 vols., Vol. VII (Reinbek: Rowohlt, 1994), pp. 151f.

[50] 'Der Friedenswille des Volkes', *Vorwärts* no. 358, 1 August 1921.

[51] *Ibid.* [52] *Ibid.*

around in the foreground. Behind such symbols of the utterly devastating consequences of war, the silhouettes of three larger-than-life-sized men shake hands above the clouds, with the sun rising in the background. The caption makes the political aims explicit: 'Against campaigning for war and murder. Against militarism and enmity between peoples'.[53]

Soldiers as victims

For obvious reasons, some symbolic elements of republican war narratives differed, depending on the context in which these recollections were situated, and on the group or individual who used them to highlight specific aspects of the war experience. But by and large, a number of clearly discernible interrelated themes dominated this field of remembrance in the early post-war years. The first relates to the dual role of the conscript soldier in times of war, drafted and employed to kill the enemy as effectively as possible, but also in constant danger of being injured or killed himself. In the rhetoric of the 'no more war' movement, the all-encompassing nature of the Great War was described with a terminology that highlighted its genocidal qualities. Usage of the term 'Völkermord' made it clear that it was perceived as large-scale murder, also implying a moral responsibility on the part of those who had acted as perpetrators in this carnage. But the republican portrayal of the front-line experience avoided discussing the fact that common soldiers might have been involved in the killing as well. Ordinary soldiers were always victims, never perpetrators. 'The Murderers Are Sitting in the Opera House!' Already the title of this poem by expressionist writer and playwright Walter Hasenclever highlights the central message of his moral indictment: the elites are to blame. The poem was written in 1917 and read in public to great acclaim on various occasions in post-war Berlin. Hasenclever dedicated it to the memory of Karl Liebknecht, who was murdered by the *Freikorps* in January 1919. Liebknecht is also mentioned in one verse, uttering his trademark slogan, 'Down with the war!'. In this nightmarish vision of slaughter and moral

[53] The 'no more war' movement is often associated with the activist image of an oath against war that Käthe Kollwitz created for a socialist youth gathering in 1924. But the iconography of the 'no more war' movement from 1920 to 1922 was dominated by visions of international reconciliation across the battlefield. See Annegret Jürgens-Kirchhoff, 'Kunst gegen den Krieg im Antikriegsjahr 1924', in Jost Dülffer and Gerd Krumeich (eds.), *Der verlorene Frieden: Politik und Kriegskultur nach 1918* (Essen: Klartext, 2002), pp. 287–310 (p. 296); picture postcards from 1921, and by the Friedensbund der Kriegsteilnehmer, n.d.: AdsD, 6/CARD000294; *ibid.*, 6/ CARD000561.

Figure 1 '"No more war": Commemoration Ceremony for the Dead', 31 July 1922, Munich. The programme included a brief tribute on behalf of women and mothers by the well-known British suffragette and pacifist Emmeline Pethick-Lawrence (1867–1954); a speech in tribute to the fallen by former army officer Hermann Schützinger, later a Reichsbanner luminary; and 'greetings from a former enemy country', delivered by Revd Holmes from New York.

decay where 'human life is cheap', ordinary soldiers are 'held in contempt' by their superiors. They appear either as corpses; 'lice-infested cripples'; or 'deserters', 'shot at dawn in the name of the supreme ruler', the Kaiser. In one way or another, soldiers are invariably described as passive victims of the military machine. Agency rests with the military commanders alone, and they were, from the low-ranking NCO with the 'distorted face of the ruler', to the generals who were 'resplendent' in the glory of their military decorations, the ones who drove and manipulated the machinery of destruction. In a reference to the set metaphor of the opera house, it was the 'conductor' who 'killed human beings' and taught others to do the same.[54]

One direct consequence of this emphasis on portraying soldiers as victims was a reluctance to depict battle scenes at the front in any great detail. What can be considered to be the very essence of war, the killing and dying at the front, did not loom large in republican recollections of the war. The self-stated 'duty' of these remembrances was to inject a 'deep-seated abhorrence' of war into the public mindset. But nonetheless, it seemed appropriate for Social Democrats to foreground the rare occasions of 'front-line peace', those quiet moments when shelling and other fire had stopped and soldiers could sit down and enjoy the first signs of spring.[55] Artur Zickler conjured up the image of a moment of reconciliation, when the German and British 'citizens of no man's land' met in a bomb crater between the trenches and grasped the 'sacred nature' of life.[56] One of the very rare depictions of battle in *Vorwärts* was published a few days after Ludendorff and von Hindenburg had first voiced their version of the *Dolchstoß* myth in public in November 1919. Only this appearance, the article claimed, had conjured up those 'images that the generals had not seen and about which one would not talk if it were unnecessary'. Yet after this political intervention, 'we have to!'. What followed was a deliberately gruesome recollection of the battle around Fort Vaux at Verdun in July 1916, which repeatedly mentioned how the advancing troops had stumbled over 'human bodies that had been crushed to mash'. But despite all its gory realism the article presented death as an aggregate state and did not describe how a soldier had killed others or been killed himself. The transition from life to death was signified only by the 'thundering' and 'howling' of shells.[57]

[54] Walter Hasenclever, 'Die Mörder sitzen in der Oper!', *Vorwärts* no. 296, 12 June 1919. Soldiers without cockade, who had been demoted for disciplinary offences, were 'victims of the system'; Vetter, *Zusammenbruch*, p. 11.

[55] Kurt Juliusburger, 'Front-Frieden', *Vorwärts* no. 101, 24 February 1919.

[56] Artur Zickler, 'Der Mann auf Niemandsland', *Vorwärts* no. 79, 12 February 1919.

[57] 'Heil dir im Siegerkranz!', *Vorwärts* no. 599, 23 November 1919.

In a number of cases, republican authors did spell out the fact that ordinary German soldiers had acted as perpetrators during the war. Yet these recollections were not an attempt to confront an inner demon and to work through the most complicated situation war presented for men in uniform. Rather, they served the clear-cut political aim of denouncing wartime German occupation policy in the West. A 1920 brochure on the *Etappensumpf*, the 'quagmire of the rear area', offered semi-documentary excerpts from the diary of a medical orderly who had worked in a Belgian military hospital. He notes how 'it was said that' early in the war 'hundreds of Belgians were killed for *franc-tireur* activities that had not been proven', even though he 'was not able to verify' this claim.[58] Even with these qualifications, this was a remarkably open reference to the large-scale atrocities that German troops had committed against civilians in August 1914. It was published at a time when the German public was in outright denial of these events while some of the responsible officers, whose extradition the Allies had demanded, prepared to stand in the dock in sham war crimes trials in Leipzig in 1921.[59] Writing in December 1916, at a time when thousands of Belgian civilians were deported to Germany as forced labourers, the anonymous author made it clear that he 'felt ashamed' about these 'brutal' acts, and could 'not defend' himself when confronted with these facts by his Belgian hosts.[60]

Indicting the *Etappensumpf*

Such a rare acknowledgement that German soldiers were not only victims of war, but had indeed acted as perpetrators, was part of a wider set of recollections that focused on the situation behind the front line. Technically speaking, the term *Etappe* – or 'rear area', to use the nearest equivalent that is available in English – could have at least two different meanings. In the wider sense, the *Etappe* encompassed all the territory that was out of the firing range of the enemy artillery. In a more narrow, administrative sense it was the territory between the operational area of the field army and the occupied territories or German territory, which was under the command of army rear area inspections and *Etappenkommandanturen* (rear area commands) in larger Belgian

[58] *Der Etappensumpf*, p. 7. The atrocities were also alluded to by Karl Vetter, 'Wie es kam: Ein Beitrag zur Geschichte des Zusammenbruchs', *BVZ* no. 129, 25 March 1919.

[59] See John Horne and Alan Kramer, *German Atrocities, 1914: A History of Denial* (New Haven; London: Yale University Press, 2001), pp. 345–55.

[60] *Der Etappensumpf*, p. 7.

cities. Already during the war, however, the term had begun to acquire another, more colloquial meaning that signified the deep-seated inequality within the German army. For a growing number of soldiers, *Etappe* epitomised the corruption of the Wilhelmine officer corps. *Etappe* served as symbol for all those who could exploit the war for their own benefit, without ever being exposed to enemy fire.[61]

Thus, republican war remembrances eagerly focused on an already well-established set of connotations and could try to maximise the negative image of the *Etappenschweine* (pigs of the rear area) for political purposes.[62] Placing the *Etappe* centre-stage in a narrative of the German war effort could serve a number of related purposes. First, gross material inequality between common soldiers and the officers could be highlighted as *the* endemic feature of German army organisation. Citing the popular slogan 'equal pay and equal food, and the war would be soon forgotten' not only conjured up the misery and hardship of life in the army. It also extended this class-based experience into the present, thus connecting the wartime past with the ongoing struggle for democratic rights.[63] The *Etappe* invariably signified the corruption and moral degradation of the Wilhelmine officer corps, particularly of its higher echelons. Secondly, painting a vivid and detailed picture of the widespread incompetence and cowardice among staff officers in great detail allowed republicans to portray the transformation of Germany into a 'people's state' (*Volksstaat*) as the only possible outcome of the war.[64] A third reason why the rear area played such a prominent role in republican war narratives was its relevance for contemporary struggles about the legitimacy of claims in this field of remembrance. In the preface to his book *Etappe Gent*, Heinrich Wandt ridiculed those who presented life at the front in nostalgic terms, as 'time of greatness', and who during the war had called on the soldiers in the trenches to 'hold out' while they were themselves situated in the 'bullet-proof' rear area. Those who now 'clamoured for revanche' and stood at the helm of the nationalist combat leagues, Wandt claimed, had to be recognised as the 'erstwhile *Etappenschweine*' who had undermined morale at the front with their 'life of debauchery'. 'In truth', he added, they were the ones

[61] See the documents in Ulrich and Ziemann, *German Soldiers*, pp. 120f., 123; for an attempt by a former staff officer to offer a balanced view see 'Das alte Heer', *Weltbühne* 16.I (1920), 325–9.

[62] See the popular poem 'Die Etappensäue', which had already circulated during the war; *Der Etappensumpf*, p. 5.

[63] *Ibid*., p. 6. Embezzlement and fraud by officers were also remembered in relation to the front. But the rear area epitomised these charges. See *Anklage der Gepeinigten*, pp. 8ff.

[64] *Der Etappensumpf*, p. 3.

who had perpetrated the *Dolchstoß* against those at the front.[65] This opportunity to deflect the stab-in-the-back charge onto those who had invented it in the first place was the fourth and ultimate advantage of the rear area as a trope of republican war remembrances. In a nutshell, the rear area signified how the front-line soldiers had been betrayed and abandoned by cowards.[66]

The portrayal of life in the rear area included all the key ingredients of a socialist trope. This portrayal brought class to the forefront, as it emphasised that the private soldiers and NCOs who had also served in the rear never took part in upper-class greed and corruption. It offered a stark moral dichotomy between the victimisation of the ordinary people and exploitation by the ruling elites. And it allowed hopes for international solidarity to enter into accounts of one of the darkest aspects of the wartime record of the German military: its occupation regime in Belgium and northern France. Precisely for these reasons, genre-pictures of life in the rear area were the most popular of all pro-republican memories in the early and mid 1920s. Two books in particular demonstrate the tremendous appeal of this topic.[67] In late 1919, the first edition of 'Charleville. Dark Aspects of Life in the Rear Area' appeared. The author, Wilhelm Appens, had served as an NCO with the food supply officer in Charleville during the war. Stocking up wine supplies from the cellars of local wholesale traders and private properties was one of his core duties, but he also worked as a billeting officer for the many members and guests of the German Army Headquarters, which was situated in the town from September 1914 until January 1916, replaced a few weeks later by the staff of the Army Group led by the German Crown Prince Wilhelm. Appens painted a vivid picture of the 'rear area militarism' that characterised German rule in this town, exemplified by a decree that demanded that all local citizens must raise their hat and step off the pavement when they pass a German officer. At the core of his narrative was the exploitation and robbery meted out by the system of requisitions. Appens detailed his feelings of anger and despair about these abuses. But the emphatic, if not pathetic, coda to his brief booklet indulged in hopes for reconciliation between France and Germany. The 'sounds of shawms' over northern France would call for peace while 'columns of workers'

[65] Heinrich Wandt, *Etappe Gent*, 2nd edn (Vienna; Berlin: Agis-Verlag, 1926 [1920]), p. 3; see *Anklage der Gepeinigten*, p. 5.

[66] Vetter, *Zusammenbruch*, p. 7.

[67] See in more detail Benjamin Ziemann, '"Charleville" und "Etappe Gent": Zwei kriegskritische Bestseller der Weimarer Republik', *Krieg und Literatur/War and Literature* 23 (2012), 59–82.

Figure 2 The *Etappe* was perceived as a site of sexual sleaziness, here pictured above the grey mass of ordinary, desperate victims of the war. Cover illustration from *Der Etappensumpf: Dokumente des Zusammenbruchs des deutschen Heeres aus den Jahren 1916/18. Aus dem Kriegstagebuch eines Gemeinen* (Jena: Verlag der Volksbuchhandlung, 1920).

marched onto the scene. 'We', he insisted, referring to German socialists, were 'innocent' of the death of the French 'fallen comrades'.[68]

Crucial for the appeal of this book was surely the strong element of soul-searching and self-examination it contained. Appens (1877–1947) had gained a Ph.D. in philosophy before the war, and, as a member of the educated middle class, he tended to believe in the phraseology of nationalism before the encounters in Charleville opened his eyes.[69] A teacher by training, he served as a district school inspector in the coal-mining city of Hörde, near Dortmund, after the war. During the Weimar Republic, Appens was a member of the SPD, the Liga für Menschenrechte and, from 1930, also the Reichsbanner.[70] His book was reprinted in a number of editions shortly after its release. When a slightly enlarged edition was published in 1927 under a different title, the overall print-run had reached 170,000 copies, turning 'Charleville' into one of the best-selling books of the Weimar period, though it has since been largely forgotten.[71] The same must be said about *Etappe Gent*, first published in two volumes in 1920. Reprinted in a single-volume version in 1926, it had by then already sold more than 100,000 copies. The author, Heinrich Wandt (1890–1965), was a socialist journalist who had spent some time in France before the war. No longer fit for front-line duty owing to an injury, he was commanded to serve with the rear-area inspection of the fourth army in Gent in 1915.[72] There he found plenty of examples for inclusion in his extended philippic tirade against the 'binging, greedy gobbling and whoring' of all those 'princes, counts and barons' who populated the rear area. Many members of the ruling houses were named and shamed with a detailed account of their worst exploits and acts of corruption. Wandt also included a detailed chapter on the plight of Belgian women who worked as prostitutes for the German military. Again, this topic was presented in the binary coding that characterised all critical accounts of the rear area. The hypocrisy and luxurious lifestyle of the officer

[68] Wilhelm Appens, *Charleville: Dunkle Punkte aus dem Etappenleben* (Dortmund: Gerisch, n.d. [1919]), pp. 6, 12, 23, quotes on pp. 25, 38.

[69] *Ibid.*, p. 10.

[70] On his biography see the extensive documentation in his personal file; on party membership see 'Fragebogen zur Durchführung des Gesetzes zur Wiederherstellung des Berufsbeamtentums vom 7.4.1933': NHStAH, Hann. 180, Hildesheim no. 11666, Vol. III.

[71] Wilhelm Appens, *Charleville: Ein trübes Kapitel aus der Etappen-Geschichte des Weltkrieges 1914/18* (Dortmund: Gerisch, 1927).

[72] For a brief biographical sketch see Heinrich Wandt, *Das Justizverbrechen des Reichsgerichts an dem Verfasser der 'Etappe Gent'* (Berlin: Der Syndikalist, 1926), pp. 6f.

caste, who could frequent separate designated brothels, were painted in dark colours, while the sexual encounters of ordinary soldiers were presented in a rather uncritical manner. Privates who met local women working as casual prostitutes in popular *estaminets* were introduced as 'decent soldiers in field-grey' (*biedere Feldgraue*). As Wandt explained, they were simply keen to have 'een groote pint Bier' and, in addition, 'something for their heart and soul'.[73]

Discipline and revolution

A systematic rejection of the stab-in-the-back myth was the foremost aim of all republican war remembrances in the immediate post-war years. To support this claim, however, it was necessary to offer a more detailed account of the endgame of the German army on the western front. How exactly could the predicament of the German troops in the final months of the war be explained, if not through the revolutionary agitation emanating from the home front? One obvious answer was to blame the 'inner decay' in the rear area as a 'decisive' reason for the collapse of the army.[74] Karl Vetter argued that 'hatred and emnity' against the officers had been 'systematically cultivated' through the class structure of the German army. In the very moment when only a final, 'fraternal' attempt could have rescued the situation, these seeds 'germinated' and shattered what little fighting power was left among the exhausted and decimated troops. Rather than blaming revolutionary propaganda, Vetter insisted, it was necessary to stress that the higher echelons were never informed about the widespread longing for peace. Among the war-weary and hungry troops, Allied leaflets, offering a reminder of all the promises the Prussian system had broken, had done more to convince the soldiers that the end was due than any leftist propaganda.[75] Timing was another crucial element in accounts that did not blame the revolutionary transformation at home for the defeat. Rather than existing as a strong and united force until the very end, troops were already showing symptoms of a 'disease' at the beginning of 1918, as increasing numbers of soldiers went AWOL, and performed self-mutilation and other acts of 'passive resistance'. When further German offensives did not seem to offer any hope for a swift conclusion to the war, and the Allied troops made rapid advances, 'morale was completely shattered'.

[73] Wandt, *Etappe Gent*, pp. 142–64 (quote on p. 153).
[74] *Der Etappensumpf*, p. 3.
[75] Vetter, *Zusammenbruch*, p. 9, quotes on pp. 13f.; cf. *Der 'Dolchstoß'*, p. 7; *Der Etappensumpf*, p. 16.

Thus, the turning point came in July and August 1918, and from that moment onwards, the German army disintegrated. The 'general strike' of the 'battle-weary millions' in the final weeks of the conflict sealed the end of the imperial system. Yet it did not come about as a result of top-down organised action, but rather through a final intensification of all the grievances that had already undermined military cohesion.[76]

Revolutionary agency did not play any role in republican recollections of the dying months of the Imperial Army. To be sure, some accounts stressed that a large majority of the soldiers had in principle been supporters of a revolutionary transformation.[77] However, stating that soldiers had actively revolutionised the army was an entirely different matter. In some accounts, the events of the final weeks were rendered as a kind of ordered surrender in which junior troop officers marched to the back, bringing their troops to safety, without waiting for any specific orders from the top.[78] Against the contemporary backdrop of revolutionary upheaval and street-fighting in many German cities, other versions of events stressed that the revolution had actually saved Germany from something worse. If Allied troops had pursued their enemy beyond the border, and had enacted revenge on behalf of Belgium, a much more devastating form of 'anarchy' would have ensued.[79] Representing the perspective of the MSPD, articles in *Vorwärts* were keen to mark offences against military discipline as a violation of moral rules. In a fictional story, for example, a group of soldiers in a train compartment expressed their hopes for the future while travelling back home after armistice. The main character, Heinrich, confronted two men who boasted that they had survived the last six months of the war as deserters. Heinrich felt the 'evil' in one of the shirkers when he justified his deed with the longing for freedom. Freedom, he lectured the two who had abandoned their unit, had always to be reconciled with a sense of duty.[80] Majority Social Democrats had to acknowledge that the value of discipline had lost any repute and that it was now seen as something that had only served the 'masters' in the bygone Imperial Army. Nonetheless, they were anxious to praise self-discipline as a requirement for labour-movement activism.[81]

[76] *Der 'Dolchstoß'*, pp. 7, 9 (quotes). See Vetter, *Zusammenbruch*, p. 5; Appens, *Charleville: Dunkle Punkte*, p. 13; Schützinger, *Zusammenbruch*, p. 4.
[77] *Der Zusammenbruch der Kriegspolitik*, p. 15.
[78] *Der Etappensumpf*, p. 27.
[79] Vetter, *Zusammenbruch*, p. 14.
[80] Walter Dornbusch, 'Die Heimkehr', *Vorwärts* no. 138/139, 27 and 28 March 1919.
[81] 'Disziplin', *Vorwärts* no. 280, 3 June 1919; see also 'Der 9. November im Ostheer', *Vorwärts* no. 576, 10 November 1919.

Radical Democrats and moderate socialists were rather evasive when they had to describe the extent of mass desertion and other forms of shirking in the final months of the war, and they had good reasons for this, as any mentioning of such incidents would have only played into the hands of those who denied the reality of the German defeat. Even so, all pro-republican accounts in the early post-war period were clear on one point: that the defeat had come for a reason, as the superiority of Allied manpower and weaponry overwhelmed exhausted and ultimately disappointed German soldiers who were sure that any further resistance was futile.[82] Moreover, the moment of defeat that the armistice on 11 November 1918 encapsulated was not remembered as a tragic moment of failure, when hopes for national grandeur were shattered. Rather, the defeat was described as something that the soldiers had embraced, as a moment of liberation both from the machinery of war and from the oppression they had endured under the imperial system. Karl Vetter recalled how young reservists from Pomerania had 'longed for a defeat with diabolical joy', claiming that 'the end could not come soon enough' anyway. He described Armistice Day, using religious language, as an 'hour of redemption', when soldiers rejoiced and commiserated at the same time. Everyone knew, Vetter claimed, that they could not have fought any further. While the Belgians celebrated, he and his comrades welcomed the news that Germany had become a republic, and the toast was to 'the fatherland of the free man'.[83] Elsewhere, the few remaining troops on the front line at a time when many companies consisted of no more than forty men received the news of the armistice and defeat 'as a matter of course'.[84] Guilt and remorse were not brushed under the carpet; rather responsibility was felt for the failure to prevent the war from happening in the first place.[85] Another booklet, published in 1919, described the ambivalent feelings of liberation and of nostalgia about futile sacrifices that the memory of the armistice conjured up:

> Nobody believed honestly in any military successes. Naturally, the resistance against the storm-like advance of the enemy was growing weaker. Thus, the lines were tottering at many points where they would probably have been able to hold in military terms … But nobody considered the defeat as his own defeat, but rather as a defeat of the old system. The withdrawal was welcomed as a march back home. There was just a wistful glance on some faces when they passed some famous places that were once conquered with the blood of many comrades.[86]

[82] Apart from the references cited above see Vetter, *Zusammenbruch*, p. 14.
[83] *Ibid.*, pp. 12f.; see *Der Etappensumpf*, p. 28; Schützinger, *Zusammenbruch*, pp. 78f.
[84] *Der 'Dolchstoß'*, pp. 10f. [85] Zickler, *Im Tollhause*, p. 60.
[86] *Der Zusammenbruch der Kriegspolitik*, p. 15.

The pestilence of war and the need for peace

For the survivors, the armistice had brought peace and, with the revolution, a new political settlement that promised to deliver freedom and an end to the oppression they had endured at the front. Yet it was felt that the fallen soldiers should not be forgotten. They emerged from the dark like 'millions of pale shadows'. Coming from an 'ice cold night', they deserved and indeed demanded to have the 'love' of the living, and affirmed, in return, to be 'eternally attached' to them.[87] The title of a poem by Karl Bröger, 'Self-Reflection' ('Einkehr'), suggests that feelings of loss and bereavement demanded contemplation. As they were about to usher in a new regime based on freedom and justice, it demanded that republicans should not forget the fate of the fallen soldiers who had not lived to see the arrival of this historic turning point.[88] Bröger (1886–1944) is nowadays largely unknown to a wider public, and is not a household name even among professional historians. Yet in many respects his biographical trajectory encapsulates both the significance and the political potential of war remembrance for Social Democrats in the Weimar period. Raised in a working-class family in Nuremberg, and from 1913 working as a journalist, he was already a distinguished labour movement poet before the war began. During the war, he rose to fame for his poem 'Bekenntnis' ('Confession'), published in January 1915. Its key line was the solemn oath that Germany's 'poorest son is also its most loyal one'.[89] More than any other text or gesture this line seemed to express the promise of the *Burgfrieden* in 1914, when the – on paper still revolutionary – Social Democrats had joined the national war effort. Such was the symbolic significance of this line that Chancellor Bethmann Hollweg quoted it in a Reichstag speech in February 1917. Yet during the war, Bröger had come out in support of an immediate peace. Returning home from the front, he resumed his work as a journalist for a Social Democrat newspaper in Nuremberg. In 1924 he was also one of the founding members of the Reichsbanner in Nuremberg, which he used as a platform to reflect upon the legacy of the fallen soldiers.[90]

[87] Karl Bröger, 'Einkehr', *Vorwärts* no. 599, 23 November 1919. See 'Den Gefallenen', *Vorwärts* no. 487, 23 September 1919; 'Unseren Toten', *Reichsbund* 2 (1919), no. 44.

[88] Bröger, 'Einkehr'.

[89] See Rolf Busch, 'Imperialismus und Arbeiterliteratur im Ersten Weltkrieg', *AfS* 14 (1974), 293–350 (pp. 298–302; 'Bekenntnis' on p. 298); and the biography by Gerhard Müller, *Für Vaterland und Republik: Monographie des Nürnberger Schriftstellers Karl Bröger* (Pfaffenweiler: Centaurus, 1985).

[90] On the style and significance of 'Bekenntnis' and other works by Bröger, see the perceptive remarks by Frank Trommler, *Sozialistische Literatur in Deutschland*

To be sure, Bröger was not the only Social Democrat to commemorate the fallen in the immediate post-war period. On *Totensonntag* in November 1919, hundreds of local Reichsbund branches across the country organised ceremonies of remembrance. Speaking to thousands of disabled veterans at the central rally in the Circus Busch in Berlin, Erich Roßmann, who had followed Erich Kuttner as the head of this organisation, asked why and for what reason millions had had to die. They had been sacrificed, he explained, because humankind had not yet learned to condemn war as a 'moral pestilence'. But they would not have died in vain if the survivors were now able to build a new social order 'without war and serfdom'. Introducing Reich president Friedrich Ebert as the next speaker, Roßmann reminded the audience that two of Ebert's sons had died at the front. Ebert urged the audience to remember both the fallen and those who had escaped the 'murder', but were no longer able to work. In no uncertain terms, he demanded that Germans, and indeed people of other nations, learn 'to detest and to combat war as the most gruesome crime against humanity'. After the ceremony had ended with the tunes of a dead march, several hundred people joined the procession that marched off to lay a wreath at a cemetery in the Hasenheide. On their way to the outskirts of town, the Social Democrat veterans experienced the difficulties of performing a republican war commemoration. A detachment of the *Sicherheitswehr* (Security Force), troops who would just a couple of months later support the reactionary Kapp Putsch, stood in their way and prevented them from marching in a closed formation.[91] Yet the Reich president's speech had been a powerful reminder of the destructive nature of war, in a stark contrast to the established image of Ebert as someone who had allegedly nurtured the *Dolchstoß* myth when he greeted the returning troops of the Garde Korps in Berlin on 10 December 1918.[92] This image, however, is wrong. It rests on a selective reading of Ebert's words on that earlier occasion. Then, he had explicitly admitted that the 'superior force' (*Übermacht*) of the Allied forces had motivated the revolutionary

(Stuttgart: Kröner, 1976), pp. 370–81. However, Trommler is wrong in assuming that Bröger's time 'was up' in 1923, when he lost his appeal to the youth; *ibid.*, p. 381. In many respects, his public impact vastly increased once he started to work for the Reichsbanner.

91 'Den Opfern des Krieges', *Vorwärts* no. 600, 24 November 1919; 'Die Gedächtnisfeier am Totensonntag', *Reichsbund* 2 (1919), no. 45; see Heinrich August Winkler, *Von der Revolution zur Stabilisierung: Arbeiter und Arbeiterbewegung in der Weimarer Republik 1918 bis 1924* (Berlin; Bonn: J. H.W. Dietz, 1984), p. 308.

92 For this image see for instance Winkler, *Von der Revolution*, p. 100; Bessel, *Germany*, pp. 85, 263.

government to stop fighting, and that it had been a patriotic 'duty' not to demand any further 'meaningless sacrifices'.[93]

As the members of the Reichsbund made abundantly clear, their fallen comrades would never have wanted a 'glorification of the battles' in which they had died. Nor, it was believed, should generals or other individual persons be idolised as heroes for their supposedly eminent contribution to the war effort. Whenever disabled veterans gathered to remember the war, they should renew their testimony 'against the war' and against the 'triumph of force'.[94] These Social Democratic veterans were wary of the many efforts to exploit ceremonies of mourning for the propagation of revanchist ideas, even more so as they consistently employed the rhetoric of the 'national' to stoke up hatred and enmity. What was needed was not a national day of mourning, but a 'popular holiday' for the celebration of republican citizenship that served to underpin and strengthen the new state and its constitution.[95] Inherent to this pacifist agenda was a commitment to international reconciliation and an international confederation of disabled veterans. The veterans of the Reichsbund were all too aware of how 'utopian' such a vision seemed to be at a time when the Treaty of Versailles caused widespread resentment. Public opinion among the former Allies was not favourable to the project either. Nevertheless, in the view of the Reichsbund, whenever a former '*Kriegsteilnehmer* of German nationality' conversed with one of his counterparts in other countries, he should do so not in the spirit of 'partisanship', but 'in the interests of humanity and culture'.[96]

'A short period of insight', 1918–1923

As the evidence in this chapter has amply demonstrated, nationalist mythologies of the war experience were anything but hegemonic in the immediate post-war period. On the contrary, an abundance of critical recollections of life at the front were published by radical democrats and moderate socialists in the first few years after the war, both as separate publications and in a number of newspapers. Through their portrayal of the corruption among the officer caste, particularly in the rear

93 For the full text of the speech see Lothar Berthold and Helmut Neef, *Militarismus und Opportunismus gegen die Novemberrevolution: Das Bündnis der rechten SPD-Führung mit der Obersten Heeresleitung November und Dezember 1918. Eine Dokumentation* (Berlin: Rütten & Loening, 1958), pp. 166–8 (quotes on p. 167).

94 'Wie ehren wir das Andenken der Toten?', *Reichsbund* 3 (1920), no. 21.

95 'Brauchen wir einen nationalen Trauertag?', *Reichsbund* 4 (1921), no. 4. See also 'Der Reichsbund grüßt die Heimkehrer!', *ibid.* 3 (1920), no. 8, against the abuse of returning POWs for chauvinistic revenge.

96 'Internationale Verbindungen', *ibid.* 3 (1920), no. 8.

area, and their focus on the exploitation of common soldiers as victims of a brutal war machinery, these memories were in many ways a corollary of the revolutionary mass movement that had swept the ruling houses aside in the autumn of 1918 and ushered in a new republican system that provided peace and freedom as its most important achievements.[97] Now, after censorship and military repression had been lifted, Social Democrats and other convinced republicans were free to speak out about the injustice and brutality they had experienced, and to use the worm's-eye perspective for a thorough indictment of the old system.[98] The fact that the former twin heads of the Third Army Supreme Command publicly endorsed the *Dolchstoß* myth in November 1919 provided another incentive to vent their anger about the recent past and its current falsification. It is simply not true, as historian Ulrich Heinemann has argued with regard to the *Dolchstoß* myth, that the republicans 'surrendered without a fight under the burden of the past'.[99] It seems much more appropriate to suggest, as the Social Democratic author of an anti-*Dolchstoß* brochure did in 1931, that the stab-in-the-back myth did not actually find much resonance in the immediate post-war years, least of all among war veterans. This was partly because the 'memory of the war years' was still fresh, and partly because millions of men who had served at the front 'kept their gruesome experiences alive' and were still aware of the inevitability of the German collapse.[100] There are enough reasons to challenge the lopsided claim by historian Hans Mommsen that large segments of the political left subscribed to the 'idea that Germany's defeat in World War I' was only 'a passing episode'. Rather, the 'inner rejection of the peace' – to quote Mommsen's phrase – among the German public was not shared by

[97] See Benjamin Ziemann, 'Germany 1914–1918: Total War as a Catalyst of Change', in Helmut Walser Smith (ed.), *The Oxford Handbook of Modern German History* (Oxford University Press, 2011), pp. 391f.

[98] See Ulrich, 'Perspektive'.

[99] Ulrich Heinemann, 'Die Last der Vergangenheit: Zur politischen Bedeutung der Kriegsschuld- und Dolchstoßdiskussion', in Karl-Dietrich Bracher, Manfred Funke and Hans-Adolf Jacobsen (eds.), *Die Weimarer Republik 1918–1933: Politik, Wirtschaft, Gesellschaft* (Düsseldorf: Droste, 1987), pp. 371–86 (p. 386). Even worse, Gerd Krumeich attributes a 'kernel of truth' to the myth: 'Die Dolchstoß-Legende', in Hagen Schulze and Etienne François (eds.), *Deutsche Erinnerungsorte*, 3 vols., Vol. I (Munich: C. H. Beck, 2001), pp. 585–99 (p. 586).

[100] Rolf Bathe, *Der Zusammenbruch: So war der Krieg! So war sein Ende!* (Wuppertal: Freie Presse, 1931), pp. 1f.; for a comparative perspective see Patrick J. Houlihan, 'Was There an Austrian Stab-in-the-Back Myth? Interwar Military Interpretations of Defeat', in Günter Bischof, Fritz Plasser and Peter Berger (eds.), *Postwar: Legacies of World War I in Interwar Austria* (University of New Orleans Press, 2010), pp. 67–89.

those radical democrats and socialists who, in the immediate post-war years, regarded the defeat of the imperial system as a liberation.[101]

Early republican war memories consistently employed a class-based binary coding, which contrasted the misery of the ordinary people with the selfish and reckless attitude of the masters in a system of 'class distinctions'.[102] In that sense, they supported the republican cause, as they insisted that military defeat had been a moment of liberation, that peace was paramount and that the Republic would serve a positive purpose.[103] In substance, however, these were socialist recollections of war, because the notion of class provided the core around which most aspects of the war experience were constructed. Most of these ideas also resonated with the members of two mass organisations, the Reichsbund and the Reichsvereinigung, and among the hundreds of thousands who attended the 'no more war' rallies from 1920 to 1922. In the immediate post-war years, a very large segment of German public opinion was indeed ready to evaluate the legacy of the war in a highly critical fashion, and to reject war as an instrument of politics, thus supporting the notion of cultural demobilisation. Franz Carl Endres (1878–1954), a Bavarian officer, had served on the general staff of the Ottoman Empire during the war before illness forced him to return to Germany in 1915. Now supporting a moderate pacifism, he wrote a series of books and articles on the legacy of the war, including a critique of the *Dolchstoß* myth.[104] Writing in 1924, Endres noted that the 'preparations for a persistent glorification of the war' were already under way. Nonetheless, he added in a footnote, it seemed justified to argue that the years from 1918 to 1922 had been a 'short period of insight', when critical recollections of the war experience did find substantial resonance in public opinion.[105] The perception of this major-turned-pacifist was indeed corroborated by another major who dealt with war remembrances in a professional capacity, George Soldan. Major Soldan was head of the department for 'popular writings' (*Volkstümliche Schriften*) in the Reichsarchiv in Potsdam, which

101 Hans Mommsen, *The Rise and Fall of Weimar Democracy* (Chapel Hill; London: University of North Carolina Press, 1996), pp. 89f.

102 Kurt Heilbut, 'Von hinten erdolcht', *Vorwärts* no. 59, 9 February 1920.

103 On the longing for defeat at the front in 1918 see also Karl Vetter, 'Wie es kam: Ein Beitrag zur Geschichte des Zusammenbruchs', *BVZ* no. 129, 25 March 1919.

104 See Simon Schaerer, 'Franz Carl Endres (1878–1954): Kaiserlich-osmanischer Major, Pazifist, Journalist, Schriftsteller', in Wette and Donat (eds.), *Pazifistische Offiziere*, pp. 231–45.

105 Franz Carl Endres, *Die Tragödie Deutschlands: Im Banne des Machtgedankens bis zum Zusammenbruch des Reiches. Von einem Deutschen*, 3rd edn (Stuttgart: Moritz, 1924 [1921]), pp. 289, 369.

will be discussed in more detail in Chapter 6. In a letter to his superior Hans von Haeften, director of the department for the history of war, Soldan explained in 1924 that not only newspapers on the left of the political spectrum, but also those that supported the Centre Party and the right-liberal German People's Party (DVP) were 'conspicuously negative' about printing articles on front-line experiences. Left liberal and Social Democrat dailies would only cover war experiences if they served to 'pursue a pacifist tendency'.[106]

This was a candid admission of the uphill struggle faced by nationalist circles within and outside the Reichswehr in 1924, when they aimed to circulate positive reminiscences of the war to a wider public. Any efforts to utilise war remembrances for 'nationalist publicity work' had in fact only increased the 'reluctance' of left-leaning and moderate newspaper editors to print them, as Soldan noted with regret.[107] But the backlash by nationalist circles and the Reichswehr began early. Immediately after the publication of his *Etappe Gent*, Heinrich Wandt became the target of repeated judicial attacks that effectively aimed to gag him. For libel against Prince Heinrich of Reuss, a criminal court in Berlin sentenced him in December 1920 to six months' imprisonment.[108] Another trial referred to an incident, detailed in *Etappe Gent*, in which a German sergeant had been executed by order of a court martial. This was a potentially damaging case for the Reichswehr, as throughout the 1920s it was insisted that only very few death sentences had been carried out during the war, particularly in comparison with the French and British armies.[109] Having been remanded in custody for almost four months, Wandt managed to reach a judicial settlement in this case.[110] The next trial, for high treason, took place in December 1923 at the Reichsgericht in Leipzig and amounted, as Wandt correctly stated, to nothing less than the charge of a 'judicial crime' against him. He was falsely accused of handing over a secret document from 1918 about a Flemish collaborator to someone in Belgium. Ernst Müsebeck, director of the archive department in the Reichsarchiv, and a Major Staehle from the Reichswehr ministry, were key witnesses for the prosecution. Although the evidence was thin and contradictory, Wandt was sentenced to six years'

[106] George Soldan to Hans von Haeften, 18 May 1924: BArch, R 1506, 326, fo. 219.
[107] *Ibid.*
[108] See the material in LAB, A Rep. 358-01, 2032.
[109] See *Gutachten des Sachverständigen Reichsarchivrat Volkmann, Soziale Heeresmißstände als Mitursache des deutschen Zusammenbruches von 1918*, *WUA* 11.2 (Berlin: Deutsche Verlagsgesellschaft für Politik und Geschichte, 1929), p. 63.
[110] Wandt, *Justizverbrechen*, pp. 9–11.

imprisonment, whilst the public was excluded from his trial. Only when the Social Democrat deputy Paul Levi raised this controversial, if not scandalous, sentence in the Reichstag in March 1925 did a wave of public indignation finally force the Reich Ministry of Justice to pardon Wandt in February 1926.[111]

Wandt was very aware of the peculiar irony that many of the judges and state prosecutors who exacted judicial revenge on him for publicising the exploits of high-ranking officers in occupied Belgium had served as officers – exactly there.[112] And Wandt was not the only pacifist who found himself in the dock. The Reichswehr received the support of a conservative judiciary when it cracked down on pacifist publications through judicial means. Between 1924 and 1927, it is estimated that 10,000 charges of treason or high treason were brought against pacifist or Social Democrat critics of the military, with 1,071 persons sentenced for these offences.[113] But it was not only political pressure and persecution by the Reichswehr and the judiciary that diminished the spread and impact of republican war memories in the years until 1923. The inherent weaknesses of the republican camp to which these authors and initiatives belonged outweighed any external pressure. Three shortcomings in particular stand out.

First, the coalition between left liberals and the two Social Democratic parties on which many of these commemorative initiatives rested was fragile. When the majority of Independent Social Democrats decided to join the KPD in December 1920, much momentum was lost simply because some of the most outspoken critics of the war abandoned the cooperation with the democratic camp. And the subsequent cooperation between bourgeois pacifists and the MSPD was not an easy one either. Secondly, critical memories of the war experience lost some of their potency when French and Belgian troops invaded the Ruhr in January 1923 in retaliation for delayed German reparation payments. The German public responded with an outpouring of jingoistic emotions. Some of those who had been among the most aggressive critics of the Imperial Army in 1919 joined in, and now honed their writing skills through vitriolic attacks against the French. Artur Zickler, for instance, wrote a series of articles about passive German resistance against the occupation for the right-wing *Deutsche Allgemeine Zeitung*,

[111] *Ibid.*, pp. 14–19, 24–6; Klaus Petersen, *Zensur in der Weimarer Republik* (Stuttgart: J. B. Metzler, 1995), pp. 178f.

[112] Wandt, *Justizverbrechen*, p. 8.

[113] Rainer Wohlfeil, 'Reichswehr und Republik', in Militärgeschichtliches Forschungsamt (ed.), *Handbuch zur deutschen Militärgeschichte*, 9 vols., Vol. VI (Frankfurt am Main: Bernard & Graefe, 1969), pp. 1–306 (p. 162).

which was affiliated with the DVP.[114] In spring 1923, he also joined a 'Freischar' group among the Jungsozialisten, which embraced, in the wake of the famous Hofgeismar meeting of the Young Socialists over the Easter holidays that year, an aggressive nationalism and a renewal of the nation through the *Führer* principle.[115]

A third weakness was the lack of a larger audience across the country for these critical recollections. We have seen that journalists writing for daily newspapers published in the capital played a crucial role in orchestrating and publicising a campaign against the *Dolchstoß* myth, based on the memories of former front-line soldiers. But the geographical reach of these publications was ultimately limited. As Kurt Tucholsky noted in a self-critical reflection, Berlin-based leader-writers often used the phrase 'out there in the country' when they talked about Germany. Thus, they tended to forget the limited resonance that republican ideas had in provincial towns and cities, particularly in the Prussian territories east of the River Elbe and, worse still, east of the River Oder.[116] To some extent, the Reichsbund could compensate for such a lack of coverage at least as far as the war memories of disabled veterans were concerned. Still missing, though, was an association of pro-republican war veterans that could systematically engage in the commemoration of war and reach out into even the most remote corners of the Reich. This gap, however, was only filled when a coalition of devoted republicans founded the Reichsbanner Black–Red–Gold in early 1924.

114 Artur Zickler, 'Ein Vierteljahr', *DAZ* no. 166, 11 April 1923; 'Der Ruhrkämpfer', *ibid.* no. 184, 23 April 1923, both in BArch, R 8034 III, 502, fo. 133. Zickler had started to work as a political informant for Reichswehr general Kurt von Schleicher in late 1922; see his autobiographical note, 3 August 1945: BArch, SAPMO, SgY 30, 1052, fo. 4. Wilhelm Appens claimed that he had supported German passive resistance at the Ruhr in 1923 in newspaper articles; see the report by Regierung Arnsberg to Prussian Ministry for Science, Arts and Education, 2 February 1930: NHStAH, Hann. 180, Hildesheim no. 11666, Vol. II, fos. 251–3.

115 Stefan Jax, *Der Hofgeismarkreis der Jungsozialisten und seine Nachwirkungen in der Weimarer Zeit* (Oer-Erkenschwick: Archiv der Arbeiterjugendbewegung, 1999), pp. 36–9; Franz Walter, *'Republik das ist nicht viel': Partei und Jugend in der Krise des Weimarer Sozialismus* (Bielefeld: Transkript, 2011), pp. 45–57.

116 Ignaz Wrobel, 'Berlin und die Provinz', *Weltbühne* 24.I (1928), 405.

2 Republican war memories: the Reichsbanner Black–Red–Gold

On 22 February 1924, a group of Social Democrats gathered in Magdeburg, capital of the Prussian province of Saxony, together with some representatives of the other two parties in the 'Weimar coalition' – not any longer active at the Reich level at this time, but still working in Prussia – the Catholic Centre Party and the left-liberal German Democratic Party (DDP). The meeting discussed plans for a republican defence league called the 'Reichsbanner Black–Red–Gold', which was formally established as a result. A number of Social Democratic functionaries were the driving force behind this venture. They included Otto Hörsing, the *Oberpräsident* (provincial governor), who also served as the chairman of the new association; Karl Höltermann, editor of the local Social Democratic newspaper *Madgeburger Volksstimme*, as Hörsing's deputy; and Dr Horst Bärensprung, who later held the office of police president in Magdeburg, and took the role of a secretary and keeper of the minutes in the new league. Walter Röber, who worked full-time as the regional head (*Gauleiter*) of the Reichsbund of war victims, served as Bärensprung's deputy, indicating that both organisations intended to cooperate closely.[1]

Highly industrialised and with a strong working-class presence, the Prussian province of Saxony was a stronghold of the reformist wing of the Social Democratic Party (SPD), but also the scene of deep political antagonisms between the nationalist right and the Communist left since 1919, culminating in bloody battles during the Kapp putsch in March 1920, and again during the Communist 'March Action' a year later. Since 1921, the situation had calmed, and the number of collective outbursts of political violence had dropped. But the Stahlhelm, the right-wing 'league of front line soldiers' founded in 1918, had its headquarters in Magdeburg, and it intensified efforts to occupy public space through flag consecrations and marches, to intimidate the political left.

[1] 'Kriegsteilnehmer, Republikaner!', *RB* no. 1, 15 April 1924; Rohe, *Reichsbanner*, pp. 55–65.

Already by 1922, the local SPD branch in Magdeburg had started to build up a Social Democratic defence league called the Republikanische Notwehr. As fears of a right-wing putsch loomed large from the beginning of 1923, the local Social Democrats decided to demonstrate their strength in public. On 15 April 1923, the 'Republican Self-Defence' had its first outing on the streets of Magdeburg, when 1,500 men paraded in a marching column through the streets of the city. They then gathered on the square in front of the cathedral, and Hörsing addressed them in a brief speech.[2] Across the province, the Notwehr had up to 25,000 members, who were registered as a possible auxiliary police force and called to service by Prussian Minister of the Interior Carl Severing on 7 November 1923.[3]

In other regions of Germany, Social Democrats and devoted republicans had also joined ranks and established associations that aimed to defend the Republic against political violence from the right. As the timing suggests, with most initiatives gathering pace since 1921/2, the experience of the Kapp putsch both prompted and encouraged these efforts. Supported by Free Corps units and parts of the Reichswehr, Wolfgang Kapp – during the war a cofounder of the extreme nationalist German Fatherland Party – had declared himself chancellor on 13 March 1920. But on the same day, Reich President Ebert and the Social Democrat government ministers called on the working class to support the constitutional order by means of a general strike. On the next day, the German Communist Party (KPD) supported this course of action, despite some reservations. On 17 March, the putschists gave up. Concerted efforts by trade unions and both leftist parties had thus demonstrated in 1920 that unified working-class action could indeed avert attempts to overthrow the Republic.[4] This success spurred many initiatives to establish defence leagues. Yet the names of these associations also hint at the cultural contexts in which they were situated, and at the symbolic aims they represented. In the town of Liegnitz, for instance, local trade union activists founded a group called Der Neue Stahlhelm: Bund republikanischer Frontkämpfer ('The New Steel Helmet: League of Republican Front-Line Fighters') in 1923. Thus, they responded to growing pressure from local branches of the Stahlhelm, which had proliferated rapidly in Silesia since 1922. It found substantial support from both industrial and agricultural employers,

2 Dirk Schumann, *Political Violence in the Weimar Republic 1918–1933: Battles for the Streets and Fears of Civil War* (New York: Berghahn, 2009), pp. 54–112, 151f.

3 Franz Osterroth, 'Vorläufer', n.d.: AdsD, NL Franz Osterroth, Mappe 138; see also 'Vorläufer des Reichsbanners', *RB* no. 8, 23 February 1929.

4 For a brief summary of events, see Mommsen, *The Rise and Fall of Weimar*, pp. 81–5.

and members of the right-wing veterans' league broke up trade union meetings of rural labourers. When news circulated that the nationalists planned to disrupt an event with the liberal pacifist Ludwig Quidde in Liegnitz, the defence league was established. The name indicated that the founders meant to counter the political and symbolic power of the Stahlhelm.[5] In the town of Cottbus, Social Democrats founded a 'League of Republican Front Fighters' (Republikanischer Frontkämpferbund) in 1922, also in an attempt to safeguard meetings from violent disruption. The same name was chosen when representatives of the Weimar coalition in East Prussia met in Königsberg on 25 November 1923 in a response to the Hitler putsch.[6]

Both the names and the historical contexts of these regional predecessors of the Reichsbanner emphasised their opposition to the Stahlhelm and the need to compete with its symbolic claim to represent the legacy of the war experience. In other regions, the immediate aim of safeguarding republican forces against violent attacks was paramount. In Munich, Social Democrats had founded a 'Security Section' ('Sicherheitsabteilung', or SA) by November 1921, which should not be confused with the 'Sturmabteilung', or SA of the Nazi Party, the infamous 'Brownshirts', to whose existence it clearly responded. In public, this defence formation was also known as the 'Auer Guard', named after the equally authoritarian and energetic head of the Bavarian SPD and member of the Bavarian diet, Erhard Auer.[7] Under the motto 'No power to despotism, all power to the law, all justice to the people', the new formation protected Social Democratic gatherings in the Bavarian capital.[8] In Saxony, the Proletarian Hundreds (Proletarische Hundertschaften) were the predecessors of the Reichsbanner. These proletarian self-defence formations were jointly established by Social Democrats and Communists in 1923 and served as auxiliary police forces for the short-lived coalition government formed by the two parties in March of that year.[9] As these local and regional initiatives indicate, many Social Democrats across the country were very aware of the need to pursue two aims: to shield their party members from right-wing attacks on the one hand, and on the other to demonstrate to a wider public that a large number of war veterans stood in the republican camp. These two aims were inherently linked, forming two sides of

[5] Franz Osterroth, 'Der schlesische "Neue Stahlhelm"', n.d.: AdsD, NL Franz Osterroth, Mappe 138.

[6] Osterroth, 'Vorläufer'.

[7] Gerstenberg, *Freiheit*, Vol. I, pp. 75ff., 87–97.

[8] See the undated poster [1922]: StAM, Pol. Dir. 6886.

[9] Voigt, *Kampfbünde*, pp. 83–95.

the same coin – especially but not only in the regions in which Social Democrats had to face a strong Stahlhelm presence.

A republican veterans' league

The founding of the Reichsbanner in February 1924 incorporated these earlier initiatives in two ways. First, the regional defence leagues were incorporated into the Reichsbanner, which now represented dedicated republicans across the Reich. And the twin objectives of defending the Republic and representing war veterans were inextricably entwined in the new organisation, as Otto Krille – Reichsbanner founding member in Munich and, from 1925, its *Gau* secretary in the city – stressed in a post-war testimony.[10] The founding appeal, published in the first issue of the league's journal, also drew attention to these connections. It introduced the organisation by its full name, Reichsbanner Black–Red–Gold: League of Republican Ex-Servicemen (Reichsbanner Schwarz–Rot–Gold: Bund der republikanischen Kriegsteilnehmer). Harking back to the founding of the Republic, the appeal described it as the work of 'men who did not lose their head amidst the collapse of imperial Germany'. In an attack on the 'unleashing of civil war' by those who claimed to pursue the best interests of the nation, the Reichsbanner described the young men in anti-republican paramilitary units as 'victims of wild demagogy' who abused concepts such as 'fatherland' or 'nation'. Turning against those circles that aimed to hide 'their own guilt' behind 'shameful Jew-baiting', the appeal made a direct reference to the war experience:

> We republicans will never forget that shoulder to shoulder with Catholics, Protestants and Free-Thinkers, Jewish soldiers fought and shed their blood. The number of dead and heavily wounded Jews is proof of that. This stupid anti-Semitism, which is even poisoning the souls of our children, is not only exposing Germany to ridicule in the world, but is also a danger in both domestic and foreign politics.[11]

The by-laws of the Reichsbanner made it equally clear that it had to be understood as a pro-republican veterans' association. The very first paragraph stated that the 'aim of the league' was the 'integration of all those Reich-German ex-servicemen of the World War and of men

[10] Otto Krille, 'Reichsbanner Schwarz–Rot–Gold', n.d. [1950?]: IfZ, F 86; on Krille see Gerstenberg, *Freiheit*, Vol. II, p. 275.

[11] 'Kriegsteilnehmer, Republikaner!' On Jewish support for the founding of the Reichsbanner see Jacob Toury, 'Die Judenfrage in der Entstehungsphase des Reichsbanners Schwarz–Rot–Gold', in Ludger Heid and Arnold Paucker (eds.), *Juden und deutsche Arbeiterbewegung bis 1933* (Tübingen: Mohr, 1992), pp. 215–35.

with military training who support the republican constitution without reservation'. The following paragraph highlighted the cultivation of 'comradeship and of a republican mindset' together with a defence of the republican constitutions in Reich and *Länder* as the key aims of the league. In addition, the organisation committed itself to supporting the interests of ex-servicemen, and disabled war veterans in particular.[12] A brief précis of the main nationalist combat leagues – including Stahlhelm and Jungdeutscher Orden or 'Jungdo' (Young German Order) – in the same issue outlined the political terrain in which the Reichsbanner situated itself.[13]

Mobilisation for the new league was initially stalled, as electioneering for the Reichstag elections in May 1924 absorbed the energies of the pro-republican forces in the early months of that year. With the elections out of the way, however, the founding of local branches gathered pace over the summer of 1924.[14] In many local branches, veterans of the Great War initially provided the overwhelming majority of all rank-and-file members.[15] That proportion was bound to decrease, as younger men without any experience of the draft joined the ranks over the years. From the beginning, the Reichsbanner also included male youths from the age of fourteen, who often socialised in separate youth groups within local branches, much to the chagrin of the Sozialistische Arbeiterjugend (SAJ), the official youth organisation of the SPD. In an attempt to boost the recruitment of young members and to cater for their needs, a separate Jungbanner was finally founded in 1926.[16] Yet the percentage of war veterans in the Reichsbanner remained high. Based on the details in application forms, the local branch in Munich estimated in autumn 1925 that about two-thirds of the members, or exactly 2,145 out of 3,000, had served in the army during the war. These men had been active for an average of 34.5 months, and 918 of them had been wounded.[17] In Barmen, slightly more than two-thirds of

[12] 'Die Bundessatzungen', *RB* no. 1, 15 April 1924. New by-laws, passed in May 1926, changed the aim to the integration of all 'Reich German men', thus dropping the exclusive focus on war veterans. See PND, 7 July 1926: StAM, Pol. Dir. 6889. See also 'Reichsbanner Schwarz–Rot–Gold', *Fränkische Tagespost* no. 87, 11 April 1924: StAM, Pol. Dir. 6890.

[13] 'Die Sturmhaufen gegen die Republik', *RB* no. 1, 15 April 1924.

[14] Voigt, *Kampfbünde*, pp. 98–114.

[15] See PND report, 14 August 1924; and a report on Würzburg, 10 July 1924: StAM, Pol. Dir. 6888; Dieter Gündisch, *Arbeiterbewegung und Bürgertum in Wetzlar 1918–1933* (Wetzlar: Geschichtsverein, 1992), p. 256; Rudolf Macht, *Niederlage: Geschichte der Hofer Arbeiterbewegung*, Vol. III.2: *1924–1945* (Hof: Selbstverlag, 1996), p. 102.

[16] Voigt, *Kampfbünde*, pp. 153–60.

[17] 'Der Dank des Vaterlandes und die Hetze gegen das Reichsbanner', *Münchener Post* no. 238, 15 October 1925: StAM, Pol. Dir. 6890; see Hans Harter, '"Das Bürgertum

the members were war veterans in 1925, and, perhaps more importantly, this figure remained high at 60 per cent in 1930.[18] These figures may not appear particularly impressive for a self-declared veterans' association. But by its own admission, the percentage of former front-line soldiers in the Stahlhelm was even lower, at least from the mid 1920s onwards. From 1924, members of a core group within the Stahlhelm named 'Kernstahlhelm' had to have served in the war for at least six months, while youths and men without wartime service were listed in separate branches. Only about half of the members were listed in the core, from a total that varied from 300,000 to 350,000 throughout the 1920s. Thus, the Stahlhelm hardly ever organised more than 175,000 war veterans.[19]

These figures were dwarfed by the huge organisational success that the Reichsbanner achieved within only a year of its foundation. By August 1924, the head office in Magdeburg reported that the league comprised 5,618 local branches, and boasted 1.26 million members. In the autumn of 1924, these figures were updated, with the organisation claiming that membership was as high as 2.2 million, even reaching 2.75 million members in early 1925.[20] During internal meetings, functionaries of the league also referred to the 'more than 2 million' members of the organisation.[21] These figures were obviously grossly exaggerated, at least as far as the number of individual members is concerned. This was part of a tactical 'numbers game', in which all combat leagues took part in the Weimar period, though they publicly condemned such actions. In May 1928, the Stahlhelm head office asked regional headquarters to gather and report data on the membership of the Reichsbanner. As the republican league still claimed to represent 'millions', this had to be 'proved' wrong.[22] It is thus quite difficult to arrive at conclusive

fehlt und überläßt dem Arbeiter den Schutz der Republik": Die Ortsgruppe Schiltach des Reichsbanners Schwarz–Rot–Gold', *Die Ortenau* 72 (1992), 271–302 (p. 277).

[18] Mintert, *Sturmtrupp*, p. 29.

[19] James M. Diehl, *Paramilitary Politics in Weimar Germany* (Bloomington; London: Indiana University Press, 1977), p. 294; Alois Klotzbücher, *Der politische Weg des Stahlhelm, Bund der Frontsoldaten, in der Weimarer Republik*, Ph.D. dissertation (University of Erlangen-Nuremberg, 1964), p. 42; reports by various mayors from cities in the Rhineland in 1929 to the *Regierungspräsident* in Düsseldorf: GStA, I. HA, Rep. 77, Tit. 4043, no. 351, fos. 19–22, 27.

[20] Helga Gotschlich, *Zwischen Kampf und Kapitulation: Zur Geschichte des Reichsbanners Schwarz–Rot–Gold* (Berlin: Dietz Verlag, 1987), pp. 32f.

[21] See PND report no. 489, 'Kameradschaftsabend des Reichsbanners', 20 December 1924: StAM, Pol. Dir. 6887.

[22] Stahlhelm Bundesleitung, 15 May 1928: BArch, R 72, 289, fo. 168; see 'Abstieg des Reichsbanners', *Welt am Abend*, 2 February 1925: LAB, A Pr. Br. Rep. 030, 7562, fo. 13.

estimates: even more so as a detailed breakdown of membership figures for the whole country was never published.[23] A somewhat plausible calculation was made by Franz Osterroth in his memoirs. Coming from the Hofgeismar Circle of Young Socialists, a group of Social Democrats who were influenced by the values of the youth movement, Osterroth had joined the head office of the Reichsbanner in Magdeburg in 1928 as one of the editors of the fortnightly membership journal of the league. He states that accurate membership statistics were never kept, and confirms that the published data were 'literally invented figures'. Osterroth estimated that the Reichsbanner had 'hardly more than a nominal 1 million members', based on the observation that he had never seen membership cards with a seven-digit number.[24]

It thus appears that the best available estimate for the overall strength of the Reichsbanner is just fewer than one million members. Less convincing, though, is Osterroth's guess that the membership of the league dropped towards the final years of the Republic to a maximum of 500,000 men.[25] One important indication that this estimate is most probably too pessimistic comes from Saxony, admittedly an important stronghold of the socialist labour movement. The number of Reichsbanner members in the various *Gaue* in Saxony was rising in 1929, and such a rise was described as 'like an explosion' in 1930. Many local branches in the Leipzig *Gau* tripled or even quadrupled their size by 1933, as did others in the Dresden and Chemnitz areas. Even then, the Reichsbanner had fewer members than the SPD in the region. It has to be noted, however, that the branches of the veterans' league in small provincial towns were larger than those of the local SPD, a finding that is matched in Bavaria and other states.[26] This is an indication that devoted supporters of Weimar democracy were more likely to rally and socialise in the republican defence league in those provincial towns, in which they could not rely on the organisational edifice of the SPD.

[23] Rohe, *Reichsbanner*, pp. 72–4.

[24] Franz Osterroth, 'Erinnerungen 1900–1934', AdsD, NL Franz Osterroth, 1/FOAC000001, p. 187. On Osterroth see Stefan Vogt, *Nationaler Sozialismus und Soziale Demokratie: Die sozialdemokratische Junge Rechte, 1918–1945* (Bonn: J. H. W. Dietz, 2006), pp. 83, 87, 98.

[25] Franz Osterroth, 'Erinnerungen 1900–1934', p. 187.

[26] Voigt, *Kampfbünde*, pp. 129–31, 446–50; see Rohe, *Reichsbanner*, p. 74; for Hanover see Harsch, *Social Democracy*, pp. 104, 285; for Bavaria: Anton Großmann, 'Milieubedingungen von Verfolgung und Widerstand am Beispiel ausgewählter Ortsvereine der SPD', in Martin Broszat and Hartmut Mehringer (eds.), *Bayern in der NS-Zeit*, 6 vols., Vol. V: *Die Parteien KPD, SPD, BVP in Verfolgung und Widerstand* (Munich; Vienna: Oldenbourg, 1983), pp. 433–540 (pp. 497, 499).

Overall, there can be no doubt that the founding of the Reichsbanner was one of the eminent organisational success stories of the Weimar period. While the number of actual war veterans in its ranks dwindled in the late 1920s – as was the case in all the other combat leagues founded in aftermath of the war – it is fair to assume that approximately 600,000 ex-servicemen were members of the pro-republican league in the mid 1920s. At this stage, it clearly outnumbered the self-declared custodians of the war experience on the political right, the Stahlhelm and the Young German Order, founded in 1920, who could never muster a combined membership of more than 500,000. And this figure, to be sure, included youths and older men who had not been conscripted during the war.[27] But it was not only the overall seize of the Reichsbanner that was impressive; its geographical range and depth across the country also stood out. The figure of more than 5,000 local branches, cited above, appears perfectly reasonable given the fact that the Reichsbanner attracted members literally 'almost up to the last village' and 'even ... where republican parties and trade unions had not yet had any local branches', as Franz Osterroth confirmed from his own in-depth knowledge.[28] By comparison, the Stahlhelm had only slightly more than 1,200 branches in 1923.[29] And the pro-republican league was not only present in traditional strongholds of the socialist labour movement such as Saxony, Berlin, Hamburg, Nuremberg and other industrial cities in Protestant regions; local branches were also immediately founded in small provincial towns in the predominantly agrarian Prussian province of Schleswig-Holstein, such as Eutin, and in regions that had not been known for a steady support of the republican constitution, such as East Prussia or Silesia.[30] In agrarian regions such as Pomerania, where the owners of large landed estates exerted political and social hegemony, Reichsbanner branches faced a constant uphill struggle. Yet here too they managed to make their presence

[27] On the membership figures of the Jungdo dropping to 100,000 from 1924, see Dieter Fricke (ed.), *Lexikon zur Parteiengeschichte: Die bürgerlichen und kleinbürgerlichen Parteien und Verbände in Deutschland (1789–1945)*, 4 vols. (Cologne: Pahl-Rugenstein, 1983–6), Vol. II, p. 138.

[28] Osterroth, 'Erinnerungen 1900–1934', p. 182. In the Franconian district of Hof, thirty-five local branches already existed by 1924. See Macht, *Niederlage*, p. 104.

[29] Schumann, *Political Violence*, p. 117.

[30] See Lawrence D. Stokes, 'Die Anfänge des Eutiner Reichsbanners (1924–1929/30)', *Demokratische Geschichte* 3 (1988), 335–43; Landespolizeistelle Wilhelmshaven, 20 June 1924: StA Bremen, 4, 65, 1026, fo. 80; 'Republikanischer Frontkämpfertag: Ein Kongress in Königsberg', *Berliner Tageblatt*, 17 April 1924: StA Bremen, 4, 65, 1026.

visible.[31] Even in the predominantly Catholic southern parts of Bavaria, which had functioned as a reactionary 'cell of order' during the revolutionary struggles in the immediate post-war period, Reichsbanner branches popped up almost everywhere, including in very small provincial towns.[32] Furthermore, some unaffiliated war veterans ultimately decided that the Reichsbanner had something to offer them. In the small town of Gauting in Upper Bavaria, the twenty-three members of a local independent '*Frontkämpfer* association' decided in May 1926 that the time had come for them to join the republican camp. Henceforth, they acted as the local branch of the Reichsbanner, with a worker as chairman.[33]

At least in numerical terms, there were enough reasons to claim that the Reichsbanner would act from a position of strength, as Karl Bröger, the *Gauleiter* in Franconia, stressed during the founding celebration of the neighbouring *Gau* in the Upper Palatinate in July 1924. There was no intention whatsoever to compete with the 'patriotic associations' in 'fooling around like soldiers'. Instead, Bröger insisted, the main aim was to demonstrate confidently and in public 'that the real ex-servicemen [*Kriegsteilnehmer*] stood in the republican camp' and were ready to support it actively, and that their strength was more than sufficient to defend the state against its enemies on the extreme right and left.[34] In September 1924, *Vorwärts* published a caricature that encapsulated the optimistic mood among Social Democrats. It was thought that the founding of the Reichsbanner would significantly shift the playing field between defenders and opponents of the Republic in their favour. It shows two Nazi Party members who were about to sabotage a train line with explosives. But from the background, a train with a steam locomotive labelled 'Reichsbanner Schwarz–Rot–Gold' approaches with high speed, forcing the two to contemplate with resignation whether 'we might blow up ourselves here'.[35] It was another question, though, whether and how the Reichsbanner was able to translate numerical strength into effective interventions in the contested field of war remembrances, and whether it could provide an integrative framework for the personal recollections of the many war veterans in its ranks. Before

[31] 'Aus dem finsteren Pommern', *RB* no. 14, 2 April 1932, Beilage; 'Ein Notruf aus dem Lande: Die Lage der ländlichen Ortsvereine', *RB* no. 2, 15 January 1928, Gaubeilage Berlin-Brandenburg.

[32] See the various examples in StAM, Pol. Dir. 6888. For the founding of new branches in later years, for instance in the small towns of Schliersee and Hausham: 'Halbmonatsbericht BA Miesbach', 15 January 1931: *ibid.*, Pol. Dir. 6892.

[33] PND report no. 48, 20 May 1926: *ibid.*, Pol. Dir. 6888.

[34] Police report, 25 July 1924: *ibid.*

[35] *Vorwärts* no. 426, 10 September 1924: *ibid.*, Pol. Dir. 6889.

„Egon, ich glaube, hierbei fliegen wir selbst in die Luft."

Figure 3 'Egon, I believe we might blow up ourselves here.' Caricature by Georg Wilke, *Vorwärts* no. 426, 10 September 1924.

addressing such matters, it is necessary to discuss some political, social and cultural aspects of the republican league in more detail.

The first is its claim to *Überparteilichkeit*, or to a position that transcended party divisions. When the Reichsbanner was founded in 1924, it was a joint endeavour of Social Democrats, members of the left-liberal DDP and of the Catholic Centre Party, thus reflecting the republican consensus of the Weimar coalition. Among the seventy-one members of the *Reichsausschuss*, a kind of non-executive board, prominent members of both the DDP – such as Ludwig Haas, from Baden – and the left wing of the Centre Party – such as the former chancellor Constantin Fehrenbach – represented this coalition.[36] Local and regional chapters also reserved places for members of the two bourgeois parties on their

[36] Rohe, *Reichsbanner*, pp. 69–72.

boards. But apart from some significant exceptions, members of the liberal and Catholic middle class were rather reluctant to join the league. When the number of violent clashes with the Nazi Stormtroopers increased in the late 1920s, many of the bourgeois members abandoned their seats on the executive boards of local branches.[37] For these reasons, the notion of a cross-party coalition was mostly a mere façade, even though it was real enough to trigger constant criticism from the radical left of the SPD. By 1924, 85 per cent of members were Social Democrats, and this proportion increased even further to 90 per cent over the next couple of years. As a police report in May 1932 concluded, the Reichsbanner was by then an 'almost purely SPD organisation'.[38] The social composition of the rank-and-file members reflected this situation; an overwhelming majority of them were workers. This did not imply, however, that all members were also SPD members. In Elberfeld, where the local Reichsbanner branch publicised party affiliation among its ranks in 1930, 59 per cent were also SPD members, and a slightly higher percentage also held membership in the socialist Free Trade Unions.[39] In what was often a rather complicated relationship with the SPD executive, the Reichsbanner could thus rightly claim that it was no direct competitor to the party, but would rather attract new supporters for the republican cause.[40]

A brief glance at the forms of sociability and the annual calendar of activities confirms that the Reichsbanner has to be seen as the Social Democratic veterans' association. It was thus part and parcel of a vast array of organisations that together formed the socialist working-class milieu. From joint hiking excursions and choirs and bands to the fielding of teams in football, handball or gymnastics, Reichsbanner members pursued a number of leisure activities that were popular among socialist workers. All these activities were deeply embedded in the cultural and social values of the socialist labour movement. One example was the constant attempts to curb alcohol consumption among its members, which occasionally provoked conflicts.[41] During the Kaiserreich, the SPD had

[37] Jürgen Weber, 'Das Reichsbanner im Norden: Ein Bollwerk der Demokratie?', *Demokratische Geschichte* 20 (2009), 127–46 (p. 130).

[38] Detlef Schmiechen-Ackermann, *Nationalsozialismus und Arbeitermilieus: Der nationalsozialistische Angriff auf die proletarischen Wohnquartiere und die Reaktion in den sozialistischen Vereinen* (Bonn: J. H. W. Dietz, 1998), quote on p. 400; for the figures see Gotschlich, *Kampf*, p. 33.

[39] Mintert, *Sturmtrupp*, pp. 29–31; see Voigt, *Kampfbünde*, p. 137.

[40] See PND no. 726, 21 February 1931: StAM, Pol. Dir. 6887; Rohe, *Reichsbanner*, pp. 314–20.

[41] 'Auszug aus N-Bericht', 31 October 1924: StAM, Pol. Dir. 6891; letter to the head of the local Reichsbanner branch in Hanover, 16 August 1925: NHStAH, Hann. 310

been somewhat ambivalent in its support for temperance, as the pub was an important site of labour movement sociability, and many local party functionaries earned their living as publicans. These attitudes persisted in Weimar, but the Reichsbanner reinforced a trend towards greater emphasis on curbing alcohol consumption.[42] Another example was the rejection of competitive elements in sports. When the Reichsbanner handball team from Hamburg was invited to play against a team from neighbouring Bremen in 1930, the *Gau* leadership in Hamburg would not allow this event to be flagged up as a '*Gau* championship'. As 'a matter of principle', they insisted, their team would never take part in 'any competitions'.[43] In their view, sports should not follow the competitive principle of winning/losing, but should rather be a means of fostering proletarian sociability and foster the bodily recreation of working-class men. The annual calendar of festivities included ceremonies for the fallen revolutionaries of March 1848; on the anniversary of Friedrich Ebert's death on 28 February, thus celebrating the first SPD president of the Republic; and Labour Day on 1 May. On paper, Reichsbanner branches were not supposed to celebrate Labour Day in closed formation to conform to the principle of non-partisanship. But most local branches ignored this policy, indicating how self-evident their socialist identity was.[44] On many occasions, local branches of the Reichsbund joined the Reichsbanner for these celebrations, and quite a number of individuals apparently held membership of both organisations.[45]

All in all, the Reichsbanner was clearly affiliated with the SPD, from the grass-roots level to the presence of many SPD luminaries on the non-exceutive board of the league. The close relationship between the two organisations was, however, never an easy one. Even leading SPD members in the Reichsbanner retained a distinctively sceptical attitude towards the league at least until the end of the 1920s. In their view, the Reichsbanner tended to dilute the socialist principles of the party and the notion of class struggle in particular, and the cooperation with the DDP and Centre Party made it difficult to maintain the distinctiveness

II C, no. 16, fos. 233–5; '2. Gaukonferenz am 21. und 22. September in München' (1929): BArch, SAPMO, Ry 12/II, 113, no. 2, fos. 8f.

[42] See Eve Rosenhaft, 'Working-Class Life and Working-Class Politics: Communists, Nazis and the State in the Battle for the Streets. Berlin, 1928–1932', in Richard Bessel and E. J. Feuchtwanger (eds.), *Social Change and Political Development in Weimar Germany* (London: Croom Helm, 1981), pp. 207–40 (pp. 211f.).

[43] Reichsbanner *Gau*, Hamburg, to Willy Dehnkamp, 17 April 1930: StA Bremen, 7, 88 (NL Willy Dehnkamp), 50/6.

[44] Mintert, *Sturmtrupp*, pp. 34–9; Voigt, *Kampfbünde*, pp. 303f.

[45] PND no. 466, 7 August 1924: StAM, Pol. Dir. 6887; *Reichsbund*, Beilage Heim und Garten, no. 16, 25 August 1929.

of Social Democrats in the league. Yet despite all these criticisms, the SPD leadership could not fail to support the Reichsbanner at least verbally; it had simply grown too fast and become too powerful to be ignored. And even critics of the Reichsbanner were always keen to rely on its services for purposes of campaigning or mobilisation.[46] Only in Saxony, in which the radical socialist wing of the party prevailed throughout the Republic, were relations with the regional Reichsbanner leadership severely strained, and the SPD left minced no words in their rejection of an alliance with liberal and Catholic democrats.[47]

A militarisation of the political culture?

Another important and controversial aspect of the Reichsbanner was its adoption of what appeared to be military principles in the training and organisation of its members. As historian Dirk Schumann has argued, the Reichsbanner did not differ much in this respect from other combat leagues such as the Stahlhelm, the Jungdo or the Communist Red Front Fighter's League (Rotfrontkämpferbund). Rather it was part and parcel of a broader 'militarization of political culture' that transcended the cleavages between the political camps. Employing 'similar forms of political self-representation' – namely an aggressive form of masculinity and military symbolism, such as uniforms and marching in closed formation – its practices fostered at least a 'partial adoption of military values' among the members of the Reichsbanner.[48] Any comprehensive investigation of the alleged militarist aspects of the political practice of the Reichsbanner must discuss both its form and, wherever possible, the meanings that were attached to it. Military categories surely played an important role in the internal organisation of the league. One of the basic distinctions many local branches applied was to keep *gediente* and *ungediente* members in separate formations, i.e. to differentiate between those who had served during the war and those who had not. Sometimes the latter category was divided further into young adults and youths. Ex-servicemen were kept together in 'comradeships' of 16 men each, and a 'platoon' of 100 men was supervised by a *Zeugmeister*, the equivalent of a sergeant who would oversee the provision of uniforms and handle financial transactions.[49] To a large extent, these practices simply

46 Rohe, *Reichsbanner*, pp. 314–21.
47 Voigt, *Kampfbünde*, pp. 201–19.
48 Schumann, *Political Violence*, pp. 186–206 (quotes on pp. 186, 191). For a similar argument, without any references, see Gerstenberg, *Freiheit*, Vol. I, p. 216.
49 Quotes: Pol. Dir. Nürnberg-Fürth, 9 July 1924: StAM, Pol. Dir. 6888; Macht, *Niederlage*, p. 104.

reflected the fact that the Reichsbanner was first and foremost meant to be a republican veterans' association, and that its symbolic capital relied on the visibility and coherent representation of these ex-servicemen. As the regulations stipulated, membership was not only open to 'front-line soldiers'. However, the application of a potential member who had not served during the war had to be supported and brought forward by two existing members, thus putting the veterans at least potentially in the position of gatekeepers.[50]

In the same vein, the executive board urged all members to display their military decorations in public, worn with a black–red–gold ribbon, particularly when war memorials were unveiled and during other festive occasions. Anticipating criticism from rank-and-file members who would argue that they 'objected in principle as socialists' to such a demand, the leadership used criticisms of nationalist combat leagues to support and provided a rationale for such measures. The nationalist camp would insist that the Reichsbanner had many 'deserters' and 'jailbirds' among its members; thus, it was necessary to demonstrate that these 'allegations' were not true. This was all the more urgent as many 'in the other camp' would wear 'orders and distinctions, but had never seen a trench during the whole course of the war'.[51] This argument brings one of the inherent ambivalences in the symbolic politics of the Reichsbanner to the fore. As the league aimed to intervene in the highly contested field of war remembrances, it had to adhere to the appropriate style of self-representation in this field, which inevitably included the adoption of military symbols. Yet for many of the socialist workers who had fought at the front, the war experience had either triggered or reinforced a strong anti-militarist and pacifist sentiment. Many Reichsbanner members wore their military decorations only with great reluctance. In the Franconian town of Hof, members of the local branch decided in October 1925 to reject any display of military decorations owing to their 'fundamental opposition to the imperialist war'.[52]

Both the rationale for wearing military decorations, and the partial reluctance to do so, indicate in themselves that the Reichsbanner did not make a substantial contribution to the militarisation of Weimar's political culture, at least not intentionally. The public display of military decorations did not necessarily imply an adoption of militarist values. A similar point can be made with regard to the wearing of uniforms and to paramilitary training. Reichsbanner members were supposed to wear

[50] Pol. Dir. Nürnberg-Fürth, 9 July 1924: StAM, Pol. Dir. 6888.
[51] PND no. 470, 5 September 1924: *ibid.*, Pol. Dir. 6887.
[52] Cited in Macht, *Niederlage*, p. 107. See PND no. 461, 18 July 1924; and PND no. 472, 5 September 1924, both in StAM, Pol. Dir. 6887.

a uniform – usually consisting of a windcheater and a cap, but many regional variations existed, and the uniform was thus never uniform – when they appeared in public as a group and for meetings. But during the early years of the association, many members were simply not willing or could not afford to buy a uniform. As late as 1930, the local branch in Schiltach (Baden) reckoned that uniforms were too expensive and hence not necessary for all of its seventy-three members, and decided to buy only one for each of the three flag-bearers.[53] Based on intelligence provided by the many informants it had placed within the Reichsbanner, an internal report by the KPD concluded in 1926 that any plans for a thorough paramilitary training of the members had so far been a failure. A substantial majority of the men in the Reichsbanner would disapprove of any 'Soldatenspielerei' (fooling around like soldiers) and understood the league as a basically pacifist organisation. Only a quarter of all members actually participated in any military instructions for self-defence purposes.[54] From 1925, the Reichsbanner made a sustained effort to introduce small-bore target practice for a certain number of members, leading to the introduction of the '*Reichskartell* Republic' in 1926, a separate branch that would offer systematic training in small-calibre rifles. These initiatives were prompted by a growing number of reports from local branches, who observed that the nationalist combat leagues had started to offer comprehensive small-bore training. But the *Reichskartell* never really gained any traction, and was almost forgotten by the early 1930s.[55] Discussions in a branch meeting in Munich in 1925, at which Dr Berthold Maurenbrecher, an academic and former Free Corps member, suggested the organisation should start small-bore practice, hint at the underlying reasons for this lack of success. He referred to the need for 'defence' (*Abwehr*), but admitted that 'we are, I am sure, all definite pacifists and supporters of the "no more war" movement', thus indicating why enthusiasm for any kind of weapons practice was not to be expected.[56] It is hence not plausible to assume that small-calibre shooting in the Reichsbanner did make a contribution 'to habituating people to violence as an element of political conflicts'.[57]

[53] See Gerstenberg, *Freiheit*, Vol. I, pp. 172f., 561; Harter, 'Bürgertum', p. 287; Macht, *Niederlage*, p. 107; PND no. 508, 18 May 1925: StAM, Pol. Dir. 6887; Polizeisekretär Hofmann to Pol. Dir. Munich, 14 June 1930: StAM, Pol. Dir. 6886.

[54] 'Reichsbanner Schwarz–Rot–Gold: Entwicklung im Jahre 1925', 1 February 1926: BArch, SAPMO, Ry 12/II, 113, no. 1, fos. 7f.

[55] Rohe, *Reichsbanner*, pp. 166–8; Voigt, *Kampfbünde*, pp. 281f.

[56] PND no. 508, 18 May 1925: StAM, Pol. Dir. 6887; on Maurenbrecher see Gerstenberg, *Freiheit*, Vol. II, p. 280.

[57] As claimed without any evidence by Schumann, *Political Violence*, p. 161.

Reichsbanner formations also paraded in public and marched in closed formation, particularly during the early 1930s, when a succession of Reichstag presidential and state elections intensified the frequency of campaigning. But the key aim of these outings was not to follow any military commands or drill, but to display a disciplined behaviour in public, which was in fact a traditional value of the socialist labour movement.[58] As the *Gau* secretary for Munich, Otto Krille, explained in 1926, the 'quasi-military' character of the Reichsbanner would simply require a 'compact and ponderous, uniform appearance' in public as the league aimed to present itself in the best light. Carrying *Masskrüge* (beer mugs), as members from Munich had done during a rally in Hamburg, was thus simply unacceptable.[59] It was not the Reichsbanner, though, but the Communist Red Front Fighters' League that adopted the regulations of the Reichswehr drill book.[60]

All in all, there was a clear understanding in the republican league that military insignia and marches in closed formation were only used as a means to an end, the effective public representation of one's own strength, and not as an intrinsic value or an end in itself.[61] Of all possible Reichsbanner leaders, it was the former Imperial Navy captain-at-sea Lothar Persius who insisted most vehemently that the organisation was anything but militaristic. A member of the non-executive board of the Reichsbanner, Persius was correctly described by police intelligence as a 'radical pacifist' who supported all sorts of left-leaning causes, including an obscure 'league against colonial atrocities'.[62] Writing in 1926, Persius offered a firm rebuttal of allegations that the Reichsbanner was so close in its militarist style to the nationalist combat leagues that it might even side with them at some point. Pacifist sentiments, not understood as sectarian principles such as in organised pacifism, but more broadly defined, formed for him the backbone and moral compass of the Reichsbanner. Giving a pertinent and vivid example, he pointed out that during his extensive speaking commitments at local branches across the country in the previous year, only in a single meeting had he

[58] See for instance Generalmajor a.D. von Bresler, 'Der Geist im Reichsbanner', *Berliner Tageblatt*, 14 August 1927: StA Bremen, 4, 65, 1032.

[59] PND no. 535, 30 March 1926: StAM, Pol. Dir. 6886.

[60] Kurt G. P. Schuster, *Der Rote Frontkämpferbund 1924–1929* (Düsseldorf: Droste, 1975), p. 67.

[61] See also Voigt, *Kampfbünde*, pp. 266–9.

[62] 'Der Reichsausschuß des Reichsbanners SRG: Anlage zu Pol. Dir. Nürnberg', 24 October 1929: StA Bremen, 4, 65, 1034; the biographical essay by Peter Steinkamp does not mention his Reichsbanner activism; see his 'Kapitän zur See a.D. Lothar Persius (1864–1944): Ein Seeoffizier als Kritiker der deutschen Flottenpolitik', in Wette and Donat (eds.), *Pazifistische Offiziere*, pp. 99–109.

encountered the 'tone of a Prussian NCO'. By that, to be sure, he did not mean to question the need for discipline and clear commands where they were deemed necessary, but rather the 'ugly dressing-down manners' (*Anschnauzermanieren*) that had been so common in the Imperial Army.[63]

Ambivalences of Reichsbanner sociability

As a radical pacifist, Persius was certainly not someone who would have glossed over persistent militarist values in the league, had he encountered them. Nonetheless, ambivalences emanating from the military style of organisation in the Reichsbanner remained, and they were discussed both by leading functionaries of the league itself, and by external critics. Among the league officials, Franz Osterroth reflected with hindsight on the somewhat contradictory expectations that the republican mass mobilisation in the Reichsbanner had raised. On the one hand, the mobilisation of many decorated former front-line soldiers triggered hopes that this potential could be used in the field of domestic politics, and would help Social Democracy to develop a coherent and strong position with regard to defence policies in particular. The many outright pacifists in the league, on the other hand, expected that the Reichsbanner would adopt their anti-militarist principles in its propaganda.[64] While this was a highly realistic assessment of the competing tendencies within the league, critics from the radical left did not mince their words. Writing in September 1924, radical pacifist Carl von Ossietzky attacked the apolitical sentiment that pervaded the Reichsbanner in his perception. 'Defence of the republic is good', he scorned, but it would be 'better to go beyond that to an understanding of what in the republic is worth defending and what should not be retained'. Yet the latter aim, he argued, 'evades the Reichsbanner'. Ossietzky took particular issue with the fortnightly membership journal *Das Reichsbanner*, which was edited in Magdeburg and circulated to individual subscribers, with a print-run of about 100,000 copies.[65] It

[63] Lothar Persius, 'Reichsbanner und Pazifismus', *RB* no. 1, 1 May 1926.

[64] Franz Osterroth, 'Erinnerungen 1900–1934', AdsD, NL Franz Osterroth, 1/FOAC000001, p. 182.

[65] Carl von Ossietzky, 'Defending the Republic: The Great Fashion', in Anton Kaes, Martin Jay and Edward Dimendberg (eds.), *The Weimar Republic Sourcebook* (Berkeley: University of California Press, 1994), pp. 110–12; translation amended from the German original: Carl von Ossietzky, 'Schutz der Republik: Die große Mode', in *Sämtliche Schriften*, 8 vols., Vol. II: *1922–1924* (Reinbek: Rowohlt, 1994), pp. 364–6. For a similar criiticism see Kurt Tucholsky, 'Der Sieg des republikanischen Gedankens' (1926), in *Gesammelte Werke*, 10 vols., ed. Mary Gerold-Tucholsky and

included sections headed 'Shell Splinter' and 'In the Canteen'. 'That, dear comrades', Ossietzky concluded, 'is body and soul the style of the justly slandered, old army newspaper', and would 'give the feeling in the republic of being in the canteen'. Instead of devoting mind and spirit to the republican cause, the Reichsbanner had turned itself into an organisation that pursued 'unadulterated veterans' association business'.[66]

In some respects, Ossietzky had identified a worthwhile point with his trenchant criticism. The *Reichsbanner* journal did indeed include a regular rubric headed 'In the Canteen'. It featured mostly humorous short anecdotes from the trenches that were primarily meant to entertain, with a focus on the inherent absurdity of army life. Some of them, however, directly targeted the *völkisch* right and tried to ridicule Hitler in particular.[67] Similar criticisms to Ossietzky's came also from within the ranks of the league. Based on letters by rank-and-file members, an article in the *Berliner Volks-Zeitung* concluded already in December 1925 that an 'intellectual will' was largely absent from the meetings in the local branches of the Reichsbanner. A 'refined republican intellectuality' was missing from an already firmly established, if not ossified, routine of convivial activities and public outings in the *Kameradschaften*.[68] To some extent, the excessive associational life in many local branches overshadowed the pursuit of the paramount political aim, the defence of the Republic. Sharing jocular and harmless army anecdotes from the Great War under the heading 'Shell Splinter' had, on the other hand, an important function. The exchange of such popular recollections was the glue that bound together the majority of those Reichsbanner members who had served at the front. At first glance, these patterns of sociability were similar to those of the associations of the nationalist Kyffhäuserbund, in which former conscripts and war veterans had traded in the citizenship status that had been a corollary of the draft since 1871.[69] In the context of the Social Democratic veterans' league, however, the exchange of unpolitical war recollections

Fritz J. Raddatz (Reinbek: Rowohlt, 1975), Vol. IV, pp. 495–9; the print-run is according to Osterroth, 'Erinnerungen 1900–1934', p. 188.

66 Ossietzky, 'Schutz der Republik', pp. 365f.

67 'In der Kantine', *RB* no. 3, 1 June 1924; no. 5, 15 July 1924.

68 Clipping from the *Berliner Volks-Zeitung*, 18 December 1925: BArch, R 1501, 113501, fo. 200.

69 For this interpretation see Robert von Friedeburg, 'Klassen-, Geschlechter- oder Nationalidentität? Handwerker und Tagelöhner in den Kriegervereinen der neupreußischen Provinz Hessen-Nassau 1890–1914', in Ute Frevert (ed.), *Militär und Gesellschaft im 19. und 20. Jahrhundert* (Stuttgart: Klett–Cotta, 1997), pp. 229–44; on the Kyffhäuserbund in the Weimar Republic see Christopher James Elliott, 'The Kriegervereine in the Weimar Republic', *JCH* 10 (1975), 109–29.

provided the framework for the peculiar combination of war remembrances and republican activism that characterised this league. In the city of Augsburg, some left-leaning workers left the Reichsbanner in 1926, perhaps influenced by Communist agitation. They accused the local leadership of lacking political energy, and scorned the league as a 'red veterans' association'.[70] The upshot of this episode was, however, that the overwhelming majority of all Reichsbanner members appreciated precisely this kind of sociability.

The everyday practices of associational life in the Reichsbanner were thus characterised by a certain ambivalence. Defending and representing the Republic – the declared aim of the league – required a coherent and uniform public presence, if not some basic training with small-bore rifles. But all attempts to develop these features were hampered by the instinctive suspicion of socialist working-class veterans towards everything that resembled the military drill of the Imperial Army, and any forms of *Soldatenspielerei* more generally. Yet these repercussions of the war experience had to be accommodated in a framework that characterised the Reichsbanner as a pro-republican veterans' association, where the thrust of political activism and the longing for convivial sociability among former front-line soldiers had to be balanced. These ambivalences also mark a final crucial element of the organisational framework of the Reichsbanner – its gendered nature. When the league was founded in 1924, there was apparently no discussion whatsoever as to whether women should be admitted as members. Female SPD members – providing no less than one-fifth of the overall membership in Weimar – repeatedly argued that the Reichsbanner acted like a *Männerbund*, an exclusively masculine form of bonding. But their complaints were brushed aside. During the annual general meeting in 1926, a motion to found a 'Women's League Black–Red–Gold' was brought forward, and then withdrawn without discussion.[71] As J. Kunzemann from Magdeburg had explained in Munich the year before, the federal executive board was convinced that women simply should not be admitted. 'In the hour of danger', the Reichsbanner had to 'act hands-on', and women had no business in that.[72] In practice, women were only involved during family events such as excursions in the nearby

[70] Pol. Dir. Munich, 15 November 1926: StAM, Pol. Dir. 6888.

[71] Gerstenberg, *Freiheit*, Vol. I, pp. 225–32 (quote on p. 267).

[72] *Münchener neueste Nachrichten* no. 276, 6 January 1925: BArch, R 1501, 113501, fo. 145; see *Wegweiser für Funktionäre, Führer und alle Bundeskameraden des Reichsbanners Schwarz–Rot–Gold*, 3rd edn (Magdeburg: Verlag des Bundesvorstandes, 1929), pp. 67f. J. Kunzemann was a county executive (*Landrat*) in the Magdeburg region, confidant to Otto Hörsing and an associate member of the Reichsbanner executive board; Schumann, *Political Violence*, pp. 58, 60.

Figure 4 Reichsbanner flag consecration in Unterföhring, 6 June 1926. Female *Ehrenjungfrauen* stand at the back, wearing white dresses.

countryside, or as honorary maids during flag consecrations.[73] The exclusively male character of the Reichsbanner reflected and reinforced its core quality of being a veterans' association. But it also contradicted its other core aim, namely to rally all available forces in defence of the Republic.

Recollections of war

So far we have outlined some key aspects of the organisation and public presence of the Reichsbanner – dimensions that had a bearing on its attempts to represent memories of the war experience to the general public. Now we will investigate which particular recollections of their front-line service the Reichsbanner members prioritised, mostly drawing on the membership journal. Almost every issue of the fortnightly journal contained short episodes and recollections that aimed to encapsulate crucial aspects of trench warfare. These war memories were

[73] 'Protokollbuch Ortsgruppe Schiltach', 15 January 1927, 8 June 1929: StA Schiltach, AS-2055a.

subject to a certain editorial control and selection, as Franz Osterroth outlined in his memoirs. The editorial team in Magdeburg agreed that the journal of a veterans' association had the duty to 'conjure up the true face of the war incessantly, without doing that in the black-and-white manner of the radical pacifists'.[74] Particularly during the economic crisis from 1929 onwards, the editors were inundated with submissions by ordinary Reichsbanner members, many of whom were now unemployed and had hence the time to write down their war memories and could also hope for a small honorarium. Recollections from all fronts and all branches of the military were selected for publication, based not on the literary quality of the pieces – which often required lengthy editing – but rather on the 'truth value' of their narrative. As rank-and-file members wrote the articles for their peers, these war memories were very well received by the readers of the journal.[75] They were not just pieces of propaganda or articulations of a preconceived ideology; they both reflected and shaped the remembrance of war in the Reichsbanner from a bottom-up perspective.

In their war memories, Reichsbanner members did not shy away from depicting the horrors of trench warfare in sometimes quite graphic detail. In that, they were hardly different from some of the most elaborate examples of the literature of soldierly nationalism, such as *Storm of Steel*, the heavily edited and stylised version of Ernst Jünger's war diaries. Differences between a nationalist and a socialist reading of the war experiences are apparent not at the level of realistic depictions of battle. Rather, what distinguishes them from each other is the use of different metaphors to endow individual episodes of destruction with meaning, and to relate particular incidents during which soldiers killed and died to the larger questions of the responsibility of certain groups for the war and its underlying causes. Ernst Jünger basically relied on two different sets of metaphors, both of which served to diffuse questions of responsibility and to evade questions of moral judgement. Describing war as a natural process in metaphors such as 'wave' or 'storm' suggested that it was, as a natural catastrophe, beyond the sphere of human agency. Metaphors of industrial production described the war as a 'crucible' in which large troops were reduced to melted 'slag' within hours. In any case, within the parameters of these metaphorical systems it was pointless to ask why the war was prolonged or how it could have been prevented.[76]

[74] Franz Osterroth, 'Erinnerungen 1900–1934', p. 192.
[75] *Ibid.*
[76] Helmuth Kiesel, *Ernst Jünger: Eine Biographie* (Munich: Pantheon, 2009), pp. 180–2.

One typical example of war memories by Reichsbanner members described the experiences of a 'gunner at Noyon'. When moving into a different position, his unit was shelled by French troops. In one of the gruesome scenes recalled, he watched comrades die and had to extinguish flames that surrounded soldiers who had been set on fire. Handling the corpse of a comrade in the aftermath of this attack was another horrific experience he faced, making him throw up. All this, however, was not described in metaphysical terms as the work of fate, but as a call for action. If he were to return home alive, the gunner swore to himself, he would fight against the 'juggernaut of war, which destroys us! Fight against all who preach war as a form of salvation to the youth! Fight against those scoundrels who want to satisfy their lust for power on the death-skulls of the coming generation!'.[77] The destructiveness of war was put in sharp relief, particularly through the use of the metaphor 'juggernaut'. However, the recollections also triggered a need for reflection on the causes of war, and these causes were clearly situated in the realm of human agency. Members of the Reichsbanner, though, were not always able to identify the culprits for the disaster of war in such a straightforward fashion, and to narrate the details of fighting as if they themselves had not had a stake in it. Another recollection focused on the minutes before an attack, and on the inner transformation the soldiers lived through during these moments. Preparing oneself for the very act of aggression, the contributor wrote, 'I was no longer a human being, I was a beast. I no longer saw friends or comrades, I only saw enemies.'[78] Writing in 1931, this veteran was still clearly terrified about the aggressive instincts that the battle had unleashed in him. As many leftist anti-war novelists, he used the metaphor of the animal and brute to highlight the destruction of humanity as an inherent part of the war's consequences for human beings.[79] And like other Reichsbanner soldiers, he mourned the loss of his comrades. But he could not endow their death with any higher meaning, as nowhere was there 'greater meaninglessness than in war.'[80]

The author of this recollection was not alone among the Reichsbanner veterans in his moral revulsion against the act of killing, and in his feelings of guilt about the fact that the war had so easily destroyed the inner restraints imposed by civilisation. In another episode, a Bavarian soldier told his comrades how he had been in French captivity. While he

[77] 'Kanonier bei Noyon', *RB* no. 17, 25 April 1931, Beilage.
[78] 'Der Angriff', *ibid.* no. 13, 28 March 1931, Beilage.
[79] See Vollmer, 'Imaginäre Schlachtfelder', pp. 158f.
[80] 'Der Angriff', *RB* no. 13, 28 March 1931, Beilage.

and his fellow POWs shovelled gravel into a field-railway lorry near the front line, a French NCO hurled verbal abuse at them. Apparently in an attempt to get a better view, he jumped on one of the lorries. When one of the POWs deliberately aimed a shovelful of gravel at his head, the French NCO fell unconscious to the ground. The German soldiers then continued their work in silence until the lorry was full, knowing that they had just buried the NCO alive. It was futile, the narrator summed up the upshot of this story, to speculate whether this should be classified as an act of murder or not. The bitter truth remained that all the German POWs who were working nearby this lorry had been 'carried away' by their collective action, and that the war had 'turned all of them together into animals'.[81] Reichsbanner veterans were thus clearly aware that the war had compromised the moral integrity of everyone who had participated in it, and they vividly remembered its brutalising effects as a very personal experience. Even a decade or more after the end of the war, Social Democrat war veterans were appalled and terrified by the 'stigma of violence' and their own involvement in the process of killing.[82] Ultimately, though, they blamed their own roles as perpetrators on those who had forced them to serve in the army – in their view the Wilhelmine elites, and nationalist pressure groups in particular.

One example was presented in 1928 by historian Martin Hobohm, whose Reichsbanner activism we will discuss in more detail in Chapter 6. In an article he introduced the unpublished war memoirs of Willibald Seemann. A Social Democrat and carpenter journeyman from Berlin, Seemann had served as a sapper at the western front, and had used a stay in a military hospital to write down his war experiences for the year 1915. Hobohm was convinced that the ability to express the 'terrible inner refusal against having-to-be-a-soldier, against being-obliged-to-fight-and-die' was one of the pre-eminent and utterly political qualities of Seemann's narrative. Such a testimony, he argued, was able to refute the claim often made that a 'mass instinct' had set the people of the belligerent nations on a collision course against each other during the war. And he quoted from Seemann's own formulation of this moral dilemma:

> Why, why was I forced to live in the mud, to be eaten by lice, and, among often morally and ethically dissipated human beings, to be the murderer of other human beings, whom I had never in my life seen before? I know for sure that the war is pitting nations against each other, nations that have never

[81] 'Das Tier im Menschen', *ibid.* no. 14, 2 April 1932, Beilage.

[82] See Michael Geyer, 'The Stigma of Violence: Nationalism and War in Twentieth-Century Germany', *German Studies Review* 15 (1992), 75–110.

encountered each other, but … why were those who saw the ideal of existence in it not expected to do the looting and murdering ad nauseam when it was ordered?[83]

Like other recollections in the Reichsbanner press, Seemann's war memoirs tapped into a victimisation narrative. Socialist war veterans were able to express the moral dilemmas that resulted from their own involvement in the large-scale destruction of industrial warfare. To some extent, they could do so because they were sure that the socialist labour movement had instilled a superior set of values into them, which distinguished class-conscious workers from the riff-raff that actually enjoyed life in the army. But all reflections on these dilemmas were cut short by an insistence on the key fact that working-class soldiers had been forced to serve in the military, and had thus merely been the victims of the military machinery of late imperial Germany. In this view, the subordination of ordinary soldiers and the repression of their ability to pursue legitimate aims was the key to an understanding of the war experience. Private soldiers had been 'jammed into the hell of mud and fire' that was the battle of Verdun, as they had been forced to serve everywhere else.[84]

The longing for peace

Against this backdrop, Reichsbanner activists foregrounded those rare instances where soldiers could display a certain degree of agency: mainly the Christmas truce that occurred in 1914 and on a lesser scale again in 1915, and other incidents of fraternisation with the enemy, also at the eastern front. Harking back to these moments, the veterans presented themselves as the true 'soldiers of peace'. On account of these moments of fraternisation, the veterans claimed that the war would have ended 'very quickly with a result that had satisfied all sides' if 'not the diplomats, but rather German, French and English soldiers' had been in a position to decide about the terms of peace.[85] Writing with hindsight in the 1920s, the veterans found this issue all the more pressing as they asked themselves whether their 'sacrifices' had had any positive results in the aftermath of the war.[86] But the memory of these

[83] Martin Hobohm, 'Soldat aus Berlin-Ost', *RB* no. 25, 5 August 1928. Ellipsis in the original.
[84] 'Das Kreuz vom Bois Hassoule', *ibid.* no. 10, 1 October 1924.
[85] 'Soldaten des Friedens', *ibid.* See 'Weihnachten draussen', *ibid.* no. 51, 21 December 1929, Beilage; 'Zwischen den Gräben: Eine Kriegserinnerung', *ibid.* no. 49, 8 November 1930, Beilage; 'Heiliger Abend im Niemandsland', *ibid.* no. 52, 24 December 1932.
[86] 'Soldaten des Friedens'.

temporary truces not only served to reinforce the juxtaposition between the innocent ordinary soldiers and the lust for war among the power elites in all belligerent countries; it also drove home one of the key messages of Reichsbanner activism: that the socialist veterans rejected the notion of enmity and national hatred. When they looked 'through the wire entanglements, the barrages, the clouds of gas and the uniforms', they did not see 'enemies', but rather 'the human being, the brother'. Referring to an instance of fraternisation at the Russian front during Easter 1915, this was described, in Christian terminology, as the 'resurrection' of the idea that a 'brotherhood of all human beings' existed.[87] As they explicitly took the perspective of the enemy into account, these texts emphasised their criticism of the war.[88] Incidents of fraternisation with the enemy were also a demonstration that socialist workers had always enjoyed those subtle acts of non-conformity that were 'contradictory to the principle of subordination'. Yet on occasion it had turned out that company commanders had no interest in court-martialling soldiers who sought peaceful contact with the enemy, as long as the overall framework of discipline was not affected.[89]

Another opportunity to cherish the agency of ordinary soldiers related to what historian Tony Ashworth has called the 'live and let live system'.[90] When troops on some of the quieter stretches of the western front opposed each other at close range, they were able mutually to diminish infantry fire by mutual agreement, or to reduce it to a ritualised exchange at predictable times. They thus created a stable environment that protected their lives, and sometimes they were even able to communicate across no man's land. Again, narrating these episodes invoked the notion of fraternity with the enemy, which was a highly delicate issue in the polarised political atmosphere of the early 1930s. When the Reichsbanner planned a meeting with French veterans at the Chemin des Dames in 1930, it had to face a flurry of aggressive attacks from the political right, including the charge of 'high treason'. But there had been a precedent, since the Chemin des Dames was, as one veteran recalled, the place of an extended period of 'live and let live' during the summer of 1917, which had lasted for weeks. With the sap-heads only a few metres apart, soldiers from both sides had fired no shots and had used the opportunity to exchange cigarettes and their respective views

87 'Auferstanden: Ein Ostererlebnis im Kriege', *RB* no. 13, 30 March 1929.

88 For Vollmer, 'Imaginäre Schlachtfelder', p. 161, this is one of the hard criteria that distinguish anti-war novels.

89 'Hallo Kamerad! Gazette des Ardennes!', *RB* no. 19, 18 July 1931.

90 Tony Ashworth, *Trench Warfare 1914–1918: The Live and Let Live System* (London: Macmillan, 1980).

of the war. Whenever French or German officers inspected the front line, the soldiers returned briefly to normal duty. Only when the regiment offered two weeks of extra holiday as a reward for any confirmed shooting of a French soldier, did an officer dare to leave his dug-out in the 'hinterland' and to kill a Frenchman like a 'head-hunter'. The immediate effect of this 'treacherous assassination' (*Meuchelmord*) was that the French troops had to retaliate. Re-enacting this moment of friendship amidst total war in 1930, though, French and German veterans were now confident that they could put checks on the 'warmongers of all countries'.[91]

As these episodes illustrate, the narrative elements of both tragedy and romance were equally relevant for the emplotment of war memories by Reichsbanner veterans. They minced no words in describing their own sacrifices as futile, and in condemning those whom they deemed responsible for the war and thus labelled as murderers. Yet the tragic aspects had a complement, and that was the equally important drama of self-discovery through war. Socialist veterans learned fully to appreciate their own peaceful aspirations through encounters with the alleged enemy. This allowed them to celebrate the victory of international brotherhood after the hardship and tribulations of military service during the Great War. As they were able to overcome national hatred and to turn their wartime suffering into evidence for the will to achieve peace, the republican veterans tapped into the socialist romance of international solidarity among working-class people.[92]

As such, there was an element of reconciliation and closure in the war remembrances of Reichsbanner members, which allowed them to come to terms with the difficult experiences they had had at the front. A set of other recollections, however, continued to stir up emotions and to agitate the socialist veterans, and this was an intrinsic part of their motivation to rally behind the republican cause. Most of these memories related to the injustice within the Wilhelmine military, with the privileges of the officer caste being at the top of a long list of complaints. These grievances, such as the meagre pay for private soldiers compared with the salary for a young lieutenant who had just left secondary school, were invariably described as a 'contribution to the stab-in-the-back'.[93]

91 'Reicht euch die Bruderhand! Das Treffen am Chemin des Dames', *RB* no. 4, 25 January 1930.

92 On the forms of emplotment see Benjamin Ziemann and Miriam Dobson, 'Introduction', in Miriam Dobson and Benjamin Ziemann (eds.), *Reading Primary Sources: The Interpretation of Texts from Nineteenth- and Twentieth-Century History* (London: Routledge, 2008), pp. 1–18 (pp. 10f.).

93 'Beitrag zum Dolchstoß', *RB* no. 2, 15 January 1926; see 'Wirkliche Dolchstöße', *ibid.* no. 4, 2 December 1928.

Such a claim was not only an ironical pun on the nationalist war mythology, but also served to drive home the important point that nothing had undermined the cohesion within the German army more than its inherent, and highly dysfunctional, gross inequality between the ranks. Allowing only officers to wear a small black crape when a close comrade had died served no particular purpose, other than to foster the self-conceit of a 'small caste' by symbolic means. At first glance seemingly banal recollections like these also reminded the Reichsbanner members why officers had thought so differently about the war, and how these differences fed into post-war politics.[94]

The class structure of the Wilhelmine army

According to Reichsbanner members, the officer corps completely alienated soldiers from the Wilhelmine state, and instilled proletarians with hatred against the imperial system. To be sure, this lasting enmity against the old system was not only fuelled by memories of material inequality and injustice. In line with socialist codes of personal integrity, the perceived moral degradation of the officer caste played an equally, if not more important, role, as two examples demonstrate. Alois Dichtl had served as an NCO during the war. A founding member and – from 1924 to 1930 – head of the Reichsbanner organisation in Munich, he died in 1933 in the Dachau concentration camp. When some recollections from his war diary were published in 1930, he was explicitly labelled as a 'worker-soldier', thus reinforcing the message that class was the key to an understanding of the war experience. Two incidents epitomised his resentment about everything that was wrong in the Imperial Army. The first came when a major handed out decorations on the Kaiser's birthday. Not only were most of them awarded to staff officers of the regiment, but the soldiers were also expected to shout a hooray, something Dichtl ordered his platoon not to do. The second came when the sergeant who gave out the pay during a roll call was accompanied by his French whore. Again, Dichtl insisted that he would not like to see that happening again.[95] This theme of corruption and moral sleaziness was echoed in one of the living pictures many Reichsbanner branches used to stage as part of their festive social events. In line with labour movement tradition, *tableaux vivants* provided an opportunity to express political ideas through the symbolism of theatrical play.[96] When

[94] 'Der Trauerflor', *ibid.* no. 2, 15 May 1924.

[95] 'Ein Arbeiter-Soldat im Weltkrieg', *ibid.* no. 8, 20 February 1932; on Dichtl see Gerstenberg, *Freiheit*, Vol. II, p. 260.

[96] See Gerstenberg, *Freiheit*, Vol. II, pp. 146f.

a branch in Nuremberg staged *tableaux vivants* in 1925, one of them showed, under the heading *Dolchstoß*, a group of officers in a fancy restaurant, each of them 'having a whore sitting on his lap'.[97]

In a certain sense, the alienation and deep resentment between working-class soldiers and their troop officers was presented as a tragedy, as the workers were in principle highly capable and also ready to excel in combat. But as the worker-soldier was steeped in the 'inherited consciousness of his class', he was not interested in status, and thus not keen to climb up the ladder of military ranks. In a story that was set in the battle of Verdun, a working-class soldier could not stop pointing out to his superiors instances of unfair treatment, and was treated with disregard. Like his comrades, he was not interested in conventional notions of heroism, but did not like to be called a coward by the company commander either. It took a joint trip through a difficult stretch of the front line to convince the lieutenant that the worker was no coward, and to promote him to lance corporal, a recognition that he finally accepted. But even this small and belated hint at a possible reconciliation between the classes came in vain, as the soldier was killed a few weeks later.[98] Alois Dichtl lamented just as much the impossibility of reconciling class and military performance. While at the front, private soldiers and NCOs were equally ready to sacrifice their lives 'for each other', but behind the lines, the power-system of the military had forced the latter to stress their status as superiors, and compelled the soldiers to acknowledge this difference.[99]

Reichsbanner veterans were unequivocal in their condemnation of the caste system within the Wilhelmine military, and of the acts of injustice it had meted out to ordinary soldiers. Hence, they were also highly critical of the myth of comradeship that all veterans' associations on the political right cultivated in equal measure. For the Stahlhelm, Jungdo and Kyffhäuserbund, the front-line community had transcended both class and military rank. Thus, it was an embryonic form of the *Volksgemeinschaft* that would halt the economic, power-political and moral decline in the aftermath of the war, and return the German nation to unity and strength.[100] Among Social Democrat veterans,

[97] Newspaper clipping, 24 March 1925: BArch, R 8034 II, 2870, fo. 25.

[98] 'Der Kompanieführer', *RB* no. 18, 3 May 1930, Beilage.

[99] 'Ein Arbeiter-Soldat im Weltkrieg'.

[100] See Günther Lutz, *Die Frontgemeinschaft: Das Gemeinschaftserlebnis in der Kriegsliteratur*, Ph.D. dissertation (University of Greifswald, 1936); Ann P. Linder, *Princes of the Trenches: Narrating the German Experience of the First World War* (Columbia: Camden House, 1996), pp. 74–85; Thomas Kühne, *Belonging and Genocide: Hitler's Community, 1918–1945* (New Haven; London: Yale University Press, 2010), pp. 21–6.

the notion of comradeship was not rejected out of hand. During the Depression of the early 1930s, members were urged to share meals with their unemployed comrades, and to reflect on how miserably the officers had failed in this respect during the war.[101] But the men in the Reichsbanner were keen to stress that they had never encountered superiors as comrades, and that the very few exceptions to this, usually active officers who had already served before the war, simply proved the rule. Those who currently held the notion of comradeship dearest were precisely those who had exploited their position most aggressively during the war. In their view, the myth of comradeship was simply a means to lure people into right-wing associations. Yet the alleged front-line community was not only rejected for ideological reasons. Working-class veterans clearly remembered that the word 'comrade' had generally lost much of its currency during the course of the war, and had hardly been used from 1917 onwards. To be sure, examples of 'real comrades' who sacrificed themselves for others without expecting any gratification had existed, and were 'gladly remembered'.[102] Over the course of four years, however, a growing number of private soldiers had pursued their own selfish interests in a more and more reckless manner, and – for instance – stole from their peers on a regular basis. As memories like these kept lingering in their minds, a mere 'fiction of comradeship' was what Reichsbanner members most strongly associated with their personal encounters at the front.[103]

Yet the Reichsbanner veterans not only rejected the nationalist mythology of a front-line community between soldiers and officers that could serve as a blueprint for the resolution of political problems in the Weimar Republic; they also differed in their concept of masculinity that underpinned the understanding of the military as an exclusively male site of sociability. The proponents of soldierly nationalism promoted an aggressive, hegemonic version of masculinity, in which men were supposed to show strength, and in which the in-group of male bonding had legitimate prevalence over the individual with his preferences and emotions. Individual soldiers who offended against the collective will of the 'we' were to be 'shamed and isolated'.[104] Reichsbanner veterans,

[101] 'Kameradschaft: Helft den notleidenden Kameraden!', *RB* no. 39, 26 September 1931.

[102] 'Kameradschaft', *ibid.* no. 11, 1 June 1926, Gaubeilage Berlin-Brandenburg.

[103] 'Das gestohlene Brot: Eine Kriegserinnerung', *ibid.* no. 41, 10 October 1931.

[104] Kühne, *Belonging*, p. 27; see Daniel Morat, 'Kalte Männlichkeit? Weimarer Verhaltenslehren im Spannungsfeld von Emotionen- und Geschlechtergeschichte', in Manuel Borutta and Nina Verheyen (eds.), *Die Präsenz der Gefühle: Männlichkeit und Emotion in der Moderne* (Bielefeld: Transkript, 2010), pp. 153–77.

by contrast, were prepared to accept the more sensitive and vulnerable aspects of masculine identity under the strains of war. Martin Hobohm explicitly highlighted one chapter in the war memoirs of the carpenter Willibald Seemann in which he detailed a period of 'inner despair' (*seelischen Verzagens*). Whereas members of the middle class would shy away from mentioning these issues, Hobohm argued, bound by their rigid conventions, Seemann was able to describe without any sense of shame how the compulsion of community had weighed upon him:

> Seemann is not embarrassed to indicate how military life [*Kommiß*] and trench warfare gradually wore him down, how this was noticed and how he was picked upon for it, how he finally lay down in a meadow pressing his face into the grass, and how he sobbed into his shaking hands. He is also not afraid to report how he made off on one occasion, running back full pelt after his first heavy barrage, until he was exhausted and out of his mind.[105]

Men in the Reichsbanner did admit to shedding tears during the war, and to moments of weakness. They were not necessarily proud to recall their war-weariness, but they had no problem talking about these feelings either. As the report on these episodes by Hobohm indicates, the articulation of these different forms of masculinity was closely connected to memories of cowardice.

In the pages of the Reichsbanner press, there was ample room for memories that detailed how Social Democrats had resented the war and the coercive structures of the Wilhelmine military, how they had sought to fraternise with their oppononents and had longed for peace from an early stage. Portraying the officers as a separate caste characterised by corruption and moral decay allowed them to counter the stab-in-the-back myth. The overall framework of these memories offered an explanation for the league's republican activism. Former ex-servicemen on the right of the political spectrum tended to claim that their associations had emerged from the *Fronterlebnis*, although it was, as the Reichsbanner insisted, a heavily stylised and mythologised version of that experience. The republican veterans, on the other hand, had developed their commitment from the direct 'experience of the most hideous bankruptcy in German and European history', as the former army major Karl Mayr put it in 1929.[106] It was the final collapse of the monarchical system in the autumn of 1918 that underpinned the war memories of the Reichsbanner members and fuelled their commitment to the republican polity. But the abdication of the Kaiser had also been the moment when the Imperial Army collapsed, a process that the socialist

105 Hobohm, 'Soldat aus Berlin-Ost'.
106 Karl Mayr, 'Reichsbanner vor die Front', *RB* no. 14, 6 April 1929.

veterans had personally witnessed. How exactly had it come about that the Germans had to sign an armistice even though their troops were still well advanced into enemy territory?

The road to armistice

This was an important but also highly problematic aspect of the republican remembrance of war, as it demanded a reflection on the individual and collective agency of the soldiers in the autumn of 1918, an issue that was highly charged with political implications. Over the years from 1924 to 1933, Reichsbanner members offered different recollections and readings of the situation at the front in autumn 1918, all of which ultimately tended to downplay or deny any collective agency of the troops, and insisted that they had succumbed to the overwhelming firepower and superior resources of the Allies. In 1931, the journalist and writer Alfred Kantorowicz (1899–1979) – by then already a member of the KPD, and later famous for his diary of the Spanish Civil War – described his impressions during the final weeks of the war in September and October 1918. The scattered 'fragments' of his battalion, after three weeks in the front line and down to forty men only, had been shelled by their own artillery, and did not stand a chance against fresh and well-equipped British units. Even the divisional headquarters did not really expect that any German troops were still left on the front line. But the few remaining soldiers defended their untenable position 'until the last moment' against this 'superior strength'.[107]

Already from the spring of 1918 onwards, Reichsbanner members had observed how the field army hospitals filled up with soldiers who had terrible, self-inflicted leg wounds, and how a growing percentage of transports absconded when units were shifted around at the western front. They also noticed that front-line soldiers sold their uniforms to French civilians, and tried everything to avoid rejoining their unit for one of the many offensives in the final summer of the war. Then and with hindsight, they clearly understood and respected that extreme war weariness had motivated these actions.[108] Reichsbanner veterans also remembered how the news of the declaration of a German Republic had been greeted with an 'enthusiastic' collective 'hoorah' when it reached the troops in the Belgian town of Leuven on 10 November. And they

[107] Alfred Kantorowicz, 'Die letzten Wochen', *ibid.* no. 45, 7 November 1931; see Wolfgang Gruner, *Ein Schicksal, das ich mit sehr vielen geteilt habe. Alfred Kantorowicz: Sein Leben und seine Zeit von 1899 bis 1935* (Kassel University Press, 2007), pp. 58–70 on his front service in 1918.

[108] 'Dolchstoß-Erinnerungen', *RB* no. 37, 14 September 1929.

recalled the concerted efforts of the revolutionary soldiers' councils to maintain order in the field army and to facilitate a swift return of the troops back home.[109] The revolutionary events of November 1918 and their connection with the unavoidable defeat of German troops thus had a clear presence in the recollection of Social Democrat veterans. But when they told the story of these momentous weeks, Reichsbanner members never used a first-person narrative to describe any revolutionary events. Thus, they carefully avoided anything that could hint at their own active contribution to the disintegration of the German field army and to the wave of politicisation that had swept the Wilhelmine system aside. Even as fierce critics of the Kaiserreich and its military, Social Democrats were bound by the 'language of national obligation' which was a corollary of universal conscription.[110] The Reichsbanner had set out to defend the new political system which was the direct result of the revolutionary upheaval in November 1918. But in the war remembrance of these dedicated republicans there was no space for any symbols or reminiscences of their own revolutionary agency. The revolution had occurred, and for good reasons, but it had been the work of others.

It should be clear by now that the Reichsbanner differed fundamentally from the right-wing veterans' associations in the ways in which it narrated and remembered the front-line experiences of the Great War. Instead of creating heroic war mythologies, Social Democrat veterans were keen to bring the destructive nature of war, the injustice within the Imperial Army and the victimisation of ordinary soldiers to the fore. Rather than employing a set of metaphors that characterised the war as an unavoidable and unexplainable fate, they pointed directly to the responsibility of the Wilhelmine elites and nationalist circles for the prolongation of the conflict and tried to reconstruct the hardship of front-line service in a realistic language. The discursive elements of this war remembrance were scattered across the pages of the *Reichsbanner* journal, provided by the many rank-and-file members who – along with some more well-known writers such as Kantorowicz – provided their own very personal recollections for publication. As these memories were one of the most popular features of the journal, there were repeated calls to publish them in more coherent form as a book.

[109] 'Erinnerungen eines Soldaten', *ibid.* no. 40, 18 November 1928; 'Der Umsturz bei der 6. Armee: Erinnerungen eines Soldatenrats' (quotes); *ibid.* no. 53, 21 December 1932.

[110] Michael Geyer, 'Eine Kriegsgeschichte, die vom Tod spricht', in Thomas Lindenberger and Alf Lüdtke (eds.), *Physische Gewalt: Studien zur Geschichte der Neuzeit* (Frankfurt am Main: Suhrkamp, 1995), pp. 136–61 (p. 148).

Owing to the lack of a separate Reichsbanner publishing house these plans never materialised. According to Franz Osterroth, those publishers who were affiliated with the Reichsbanner parties – and in particular, one can add, J. H. W. Dietz, the house publisher of the SPD since 1881 – would have objected to such a form of competition.[111]

Despite the lack of overall discursive coherence in the publication of these memories, the most important tropes of war remembrance in the Reichsbanner are clearly discernible. Their particular strength and appeal among the rank-and-file members did not rest on their specific form of presentation, but rather on the fact that they tapped into key interpretive elements of labour movement culture which had already informed and agitated male Social Democrats some time before the war. Criticising the privileges and better pay of the officer caste in some respects reiterated a commonplace Social Democrat agitation in Wilhelmine Germany, which had contrasted the poor living standards of the workers with the fact that only affluent people could indulge in nationalist thinking. Portraying ordinary soldiers as victims of a brutal military machine conjured up images of the class character of the Wilhelmine state and the ways in which it had deliberately harassed and excluded Social Democrats, particularly as conscripts in the army. Finally, the many recollections of fraternisation and the hopes for a brotherhood of soldiers from all belligerent nations tapped into the fierce anti-militarism and internationalism of the labour movement before 1914.[112] As we will explore in more detail in the next chapter, the published war remembrances of the Reichsbanner offered a convincing framework through which Social Democrat veterans could rework their own memories of front-line service. One important reason for this success was the class-based nature of this discursive framework. Quite deliberately, it gathered a number of important rhetoric set pieces that had already informed the socialist labour movement before the war, and thus linked the war experience to the cultural frames of civilian working-class life. In the historical context of the embattled Weimar Republic, this linkage can be interpreted both as a strength and as a

[111] Osterroth, 'Erinnerungen 1900–1934', pp. 192f.

[112] On these interpretive elements of labour movement culture before 1914 see Dieter Groh and Peter Brandt, *'Vaterlandslose Gesellen': Sozialdemokratie und Nation 1860–1990* (Munich: C. H. Beck, 1992), pp. 54–141; Alex Hall, *Scandal, Sensation and Social Democracy: The SPD Press and Wilhelmine Germany 1890–1914* (Cambridge University Press, 1977), pp. 116–42; Hartmut Wiedner, 'Soldatenmißhandlungen im Wilhelminischen Kaiserreich (1890–1914)', *AfS* 22 (1982), 159–99; and Nicholas Stargardt, *The German Idea of Militarism: Radical and Socialist Critics, 1866–1914* (Cambridge University Press, 1994), pp. 49–70, 127–41.

weakness. As they reinterpreted the disturbing experience of trench warfare in the time-honoured patterns of a precarious working-class culture, these memories offered an element of continuity and perhaps also stability. But as they focused on both the plight and the exemplary morality of socialist workers, it was highly unlikely that these memories could be shared beyond the Reichsbanner core constituency of Social Democrats and labour movement activists. Meant to support the new polity as republican war remembrances, they were in fact socialist remembrances, reflecting on the meaning of total war from a partisan political perspective. Thus, it could arguably be said that the Reichsbanner tried to counter the nationalist war mythologies of the political right with the class mythologies of the socialist labour movement.

Shortly after its inception in 1924, the Social Democrat war veterans of the Reichsbanner built up the impressive edifice of an organisation that was able to reach out into even the most remote corners of the Reich. In the first instance, it gathered those former soldiers of the Great War who were devoted republicans, and who supported the new state as a direct consequence of their war experiences in the Imperial Army. Writing in 1925, former Bavarian officer and Reichsbanner luminary, Hermann Schützinger – whose reasons for switching to a moderate pacifism we will analyse in Chapter 6 – could confidently compare the overall framework of veterans' associations in France and Germany. According to his estimate, about 60 per cent of all German war veterans were, as members of Reichsbund and Reichsbanner, firmly anchored in the republican camp, and represented a 'front of war refusal and reconciliation between the peoples'. Only 40 per cent of all German veterans were represented by the Kyffhäuserbund and the patriotic associations such as Stahlhelm and Jungdo. In France, by comparison, 70 per cent were supporters of the 'cartel of the left' in the Union fédérale, and just 20 per cent in the Union nationale des combattants, with only a minority supporting Communist or radical nationalist groups. But even the Union nationale – and this was the main difference – would not dare to deviate from the 'gospel of all French war veterans', namely support for the League of Nations in order to prevent another war.[113]

The institutional strength of the Reichsbanner, however, did not necessarily translate directly into a powerful position in symbolic

[113] Hermann Schützinger, 'Frankreichs Frontsoldaten', *Vorwärts* no. 258, 3 June 1925: BArch, R 8034 III, 432, fo. 167; and 'Das Friedenswerk der Frontsoldaten', *Die Glocke* 10 (1924), 1100–2. For the mid 1920s, this was a fair assessment of the French veterans' movement. In the early 1930s, however, the Union fédérale was only slightly stronger than the Union nationale. See Prost, *In the Wake of War*, pp. 35–41.

politics, including the representation of war memories. Contrary to claims by some historians, the Reichsbanner did not contribute to an overall militarisation of Weimar's political culture. But even though most of its members supported a moderate pacifism, they had to wear uniforms and military decorations in order to represent their claims as veterans in the public arena. Ambivalence also characterised the public narratives of war remembrance that the Reichsbanner cultivated in its membership journal. These highly popular pieces successfully tapped into key elements of socialist labour movement culture, such as anti-militarism and internationalism, or the notion of the Wilhelmine state and its military as instruments of class power. Nationalist mythologies of the war experience focused on the 'honour' of the veterans, understood as an equally exclusive and distinctive quality of the military that was closely associated with the principle of social stratification, and the privileges of an alleged 'elite' of aristocratic officers in particular. Recollections of the war experience in the Reichsbanner, on the other hand, aimed to retain the 'dignity' of the ordinary soldier amidst the inhumanity of the 'social order' that had brought the war about.[114] In line with the democratic principles of the league, this was an inclusive and egalitarian form of remembrance, which even took the suffering of the enemy into account. Within the framework of Reichsbanner war memories, however, it was not possible to resolve the conflict between a principled rejection of war and its destructive power, and the basic affirmation of wartime service.[115] While they were happy to describe themselves as reluctant soldiers with no interest in individual advancement, outright refusal, desertion or collective mutiny clearly had no place in the memory of Reichsbanner veterans. They recalled how the troops had greeted the armistice and the toppling of the monarchy in November 1918 with joy, but never claimed these political outcomes of the war were the result of their own collective agency.

[114] See Vollmer, 'Imaginäre Schlachtfelder', p. 128.

[115] On the representation of this conflict in anti-war novels by Remarque and Johannsen see *ibid.*, pp. 165f.

3 The personal microcosm of Reichsbanner activism

The Reichsbanner Black–Red–Gold was able to attract a mass following as the veterans' association of the moderate socialist camp, combining active support for the Republic with the provision of a framework of memories that endowed the wartime service of working-class men with meaning. It is possible to reconstruct the most important discursive elements of the war remembrances promoted by the Reichsbanner by studying the membership journal and reports of internal meetings. It is not sufficient, however, to analyse only the publicised versions of these war narratives, even though they were to a large extent based, as we have seen, on the contributions of Reichsbanner members, and thus had a bottom-up dynamic. In addition, it is also necessary to unearth the personal and political relevance and the particular contours of these memories within the individual microcosm of members of the league. How did their personal recollections of the Great War inform the political worldview and Reichsbanner activism of rank-and-file members? To what extent did they share these memories with other people in a local context or neighbourhood, thus contextualising their own perception of the past in a dense network of personal encounters and day-to-day interactions? Which social and political factors facilitated or impeded the public articulation of these war memories in the highly circumscribed setting of a local community?

In order to answer these questions, it is necessary to interrogate primary sources that shed light on the individual perception and formulation of war remembrances in a specified social context, i.e. some form of personal testimony. In this chapter, we will analyse and contextualise a significant piece of evidence that allows us to address these questions. Written in the mid 1920s, at some point after the founding of the Reichsbanner and well before the deepening of economic depression and political instability from 1930 onwards, this document offers a highly detailed glimpse into the personal life of a war veteran and Reichsbanner member, and into the connections between war experiences and pro-republican activism. As we will see, an external event prompted the author to feed this document into the ongoing struggle over the contested commemorations of the First World War. Yet it originated in the highly personal process in which an individual revisited and reassessed his own recollections of war and the military against the backdrop of the contemporary political setting in Weimar Germany.

Historian Ludwig Bergsträsser (1883–1960) worked from 1920 to 1933 in the research department of the Reichsarchiv in Potsdam and later in Frankfurt, where he conducted research on the Paulskirche, the revolutionary parliament in 1848/9. A Reichsbanner member from 1924, he began to serve as a Reichstag deputy for the left-liberal German Democractic Party (DDP) in the same year.[1] In that capacity, Bergsträsser was a member of the parliamentary subcommittee that investigated the 'causes of the German collapse' in 1918. Within this highly polarised forum, fierce battles raged between a majority of conservative deputies and their expert witnesses, who aimed to whitewash the Army Supreme Command from any responsibility for the German defeat in 1918. They were confronted by a small group of Democratic politicians and historians – also including fellow Reichsarchiv staff member and Reichsbanner activist Martin Hobohm – who sought to counter the *Dolchstoß* myth and other anti-republican narratives of the military endgame in 1918.[2] In this struggle about the recent past, each camp was eager to present and exploit a range of primary evidence that would corroborate their respective positions. The nationalist proponents of the *Dolchstoß* preferred to call former staff officers and generals as expert witnesses, whereas their republican counterparts aimed to provide documentation on the inevitability of defeat from a worm's-eye perspective. Bergsträsser in particular advocated the use of war letters written by soldiers. This first-hand evidence, he argued, would allow insights into the immediate 'psychological reality' of front-line soldiers, and thus into the factor of troop morale, which had not been accessible to the officers at the time.[3]

On 31 March 1926, Bergsträsser published a piece entitled 'Front and Peace' on the front page of the respected liberal broadsheet *Vossische*

[1] On his work and biography see Hans Schleier, *Die bürgerliche deutsche Geschichtsschreibung der Weimarer Republik* (Berlin: Akademie Verlag, 1975), pp. 303–45; Stephanie Zibell, *Politische Bildung und demokratische Verfassung: Ludwig Bergsträsser (1883–1960)* (Bonn: J. H. W. Dietz, 2006).

[2] Ulrich Heinemann, *Die verdrängte Niederlage: Politische Öffentlichkeit und Kriegsschuldfrage in der Weimarer Republik* (Göttingen: Vandenhoeck & Ruprecht, 1983), pp. 177–91.

[3] Ulrich, *Augenzeugen*, pp. 248–55 (quote on p. 248).

Zeitung.[4] The gist of his article was a firm rejection of the stab-in-the-back myth. Based on war letters that had been sent to him and his wife from the front, he sketched out a brief history of the changing expectations among the troops. Beginning in mid 1915, when leave was first granted on a regular basis, the soldiers perceived the war to be an 'instrument for peace', and believed that to 'fight was a chance to arrive at a peace'. Only by achieving a victory, according to such expectations, would it be possible to escape from the authoritarian straitjacket of life in the army and to return home. As such, longing for peace provided German soldiers with a crucial combat motivation. Yet as soon as the German offensives in spring 1918 stalled, the last hopes for victory were shattered. Eventually, combat no longer appeared to be a means for achieving peace, and morale deteriorated at a rapid rate. In order to substantiate this line of argument, Bergsträsser appealed for the help of the readers and asked them to send in war letters and diaries: materials that would help to counter the 'wicked slander' of the *Dolchstoß* myth. 'Thence, help!'[5]

Fritz Einert

On the very next day, a certain Fritz Einert responded to this call and wrote to Bergsträsser.[6] He had read the piece in the *Vossische* and was more than happy to help the historian with his 'task' – dispelling right-wing myths – by 'providing you with something from my experiences [*Erlebnissen*]' (p. 214). Some time previously, Einert had 'submitted himself to the trouble' of rereading all his surviving *Feldpostbriefe*, had transcribed all particularly 'critical' passages and collated them in chronological order. As his language indicates, conjuring up recollections of his front-line service had not been a pleasant task for Einert, but reasons for doing so were not just personal: 'Since I am a member of the Reichsbanner, I have combined my thoughts and experiences

[4] Ludwig Bergsträsser, 'Front und Frieden', *Vossische Zeitung*, 31 March 1926; the article was later reprinted as an appendix to the published proceedings of the subcommittee: *Verhandlungsbericht: Die allgemeinen Ursachen und Hergänge des inneren Zusammenbruches, 2. Teil, WUA* 5 (Berlin: Deutsche Verlagsgesellschaft für Politik und Geschichte, 1928), pp. 257–61.

[5] *Ibid*. For a later rebuttal of the *Dolchstoß* see Ludwig Bergsträsser, 'Das Ende der Dolchstoßlegende', *Berliner Tageblatt* no. 137, 21 March 1928.

[6] Fritz Einert to Ludwig Bergsträsser, 1 April 1926: BArch, R 9350, 275, fo. 23. For the full German text of this letter and of the attached manuscript, see my '"Gedanken eines Reichsbannermannes auf Grund von Erlebnissen und Erfahrungen": Politische Kultur, Flaggensymbolik und Kriegserinnerung in Schmalkalden 1926. Dokumentation', *Zeitschrift des Vereins für Thüringische Geschichte* 53 (1999), 214–32. In the following, all page numbers in brackets refer to this text.

with Reichsbanner ideas. After many years one can obviously not recall everything that one has experienced over four years, and I have based [the manuscript] only on those details of which I still have a very precise recollection' (p. 214). Einert had laid down his recollections and reflections on the front-line experience in a manuscript entitled 'Thoughts of a Reichsbanner Man Based on Impressions and Experiences', which he enclosed in his letter to Bergsträsser.[7] Both the content and context of this manuscript require detailed attention. But before we analyse them, it seems worthwhile to turn to an initial reflection on the more intricate mechanics of memory that can be illuminated through this document. Einert was clearly aware of the selective and unstable nature of his individual memory. As the member of a veterans' association, it seemed obvious to him to connect his own personal recollections with the wider framework of 'Reichsbanner ideas', and it is interesting to examine the extent to which both were entwined or even blended into one another. But the starting point for his endeavour of revisiting the war experience had been rereading his own war letters, most of which seem to have been addressed to his parents. Einert had not kept a war diary, as any 'appetite' for this type of autobiographical documentation had already 'worn off' during the first days of his wartime service (p. 214). Instead, he used his own war letters as a medium for autobiographical renegotiation and reflection, and as a reminder about specific situations where his personal memory of details had faded away quickly.

Such a use of *Feldpostbriefe* was not unusual in the broader context of post-war Germany. Throughout the 1920s, various edited collections of war letters had been a crucial reference point for public debates about the *Kriegserlebnis*, as these documents seemed to guarantee an immediate access point to the solders' inner selves.[8] And Einert was surely not the only war veteran who revisited his war experience through a rereading of his own letters from the front.[9] For Einert, his specific focus was on those passages 'that gave some vent to my heart during the war', even though postal censorship had often been able to suppress his urge to describe the bitter reality of war in more detail (p. 225). He included eight typewritten pages with these excerpts in his manuscript, covering

[7] The original of this manuscript, entitled 'Gedanken eines Reichsbannermannes auf Grund von Erlebnissen und Erfahrungen', n.d., neatly typrewritten on twenty-two pages, is located in BArch, R 9350, 275, fos. 1–22.

[8] Ulrich, *Augenzeugen*, pp. 228–44.

[9] Karl Dürkefälden suggested in May 1933 to his younger brother Willi, who had served at the front in 1917/18, that he might want to write his 'war memories' on the basis of his *Feldpostbriefe*. But Willi refused, claiming that this would be 'too tedious'. Herbert and Sybille Obenaus (eds.), *'Schreiben wie es wirklich war ...': Aufzeichnungen Karl Dürkefäldens aus den Jahren 1933–1945* (Hanover: Fackelträger, 1985), p. 53.

the period from February 1915 to May 1918 only, as he had misplaced the letters for the remaining period until the armistice. All in all, these letters were an almost perfect corroboration of Bergsträsser's argument, as Einert had noted his longing for peace as early as June 1915, and – despite a deep-felt war weariness – had kept his hopes alive until spring 1918. On 25 March 1918, four days into the German spring offensive, Einert was still hopeful that these 'colossal events' would finally 'really' bring about peace (p. 231).

War letters were thus a crucial medium of war remembrance for Einert. They allowed him to prop up and to corroborate his personal recollections in a way that also served the political aims of Bergsträsser's appeal. Einert expected that the historian could use some of his thoughts for his fight against the *Dolchstoß*. But in his covering letter, he was adamant in insisting that the document should not be used in public:

> The whole matter is a completely private affair of my own and has nothing to do with the public; also I do not wish to involve the latter. For this reason, I also ask you for complete discretion, because I am a salaried employee in a manufacturing business and – naturally – economically dependent. Unfortunately it is still the case that we are not yet free men, despite the Republic. The former *Feldgraue*, who was once so much glorified, is today again the subject [*Untertan*] of someone who is economically stronger. Nobody is interested in asking what the former front-line fighter once accomplished; he is nowadays again an object of exploitation, just as he was during the war. (p. 215)

Written by an active and devoted Reichsbanner member during Weimar's allegedly 'stable' or 'golden' years, this statement could be read as a devastating verdict on the achievements of the republican state. Einert explicitly employed the term *Untertan* to describe the current situation of war veterans. In his novel of the same title, published as a book in 1919 and an immediate runaway success, the writer Heinrich Mann had popularised its use as a generic term for the authoritarian political system of imperial Germany.[10] It would thus appear that not a lot had changed in the wake of the revolution, and that Weimar's democratic constitution was unable to safeguard the rights of its supporters among former front-line soldiers. In some respects, Einert's bitter résumé of power relations in German society was one of many examples of the huge gap between the expectations raised because of the

[10] Heinrich Mann, *Der Untertan: Roman* (Frankfurt am Main: Fischer Taschenbuch Verlag, 1991 [1919]). On contemporary reception see Rainer Rumold, 'Rereading Heinrich Mann's *Der Untertan*: The Seeds of Fascism, or Satire as Anticipation', in Volker Dürr, Kathy Harms and Peter Hayes (eds.), *Imperial Germany* (Madison: University of Wisconsin Press, 1985), pp. 168–81; and Reinhard Alter, 'Heinrich Manns *Untertan*: Prüfstein für die "Kaiserreich-Debatte"?', *GG* 17 (1991), 370–89.

transformation to a democratic system, and the almost inevitable disappointment about the failure of subsequent political action to transform social relations.[11] But as we will see, Einert's disappointment about the precarious state of war veterans was also motivated by specific incidents he had observed in his local community, and was to some extent balanced by the sense of entitlement the Reichsbanner ideas instilled in him. At any rate, Einert's insistence on the private character of his recollections prevented Ludwig Bergsträsser from using them for his public rebuttal of the *Dolchstoß* through an extensive documentation of war letters and other testimony.[12]

Fritz Einert (1893–1962) spent his whole life in Schmalkalden (Thuringia), a town with about 10,000 residents in 1925.[13] The son of an awl-maker, he married Luise Paula Bamberger in 1922, the daughter of a pliers-maker. As the parents of both were toolmakers, the family background of the couple was a perfect match to the economic structure of the town, which had been known as a centre for iron smelting and processing since the sixteenth century. From the late nineteenth century, iron production in Schmalkalden had been an industrial business, and Einert spent his working life with the H.-A. Erbe AG, which was, with 329 employees in 1926, the largest company in town. The firm was widely known by the colloquial name 'Löffelbude' ('Spoon Booth'), as cutlery was the main product. The Great War had – incidentally – presented the firm with the welcome opportunity to mass-produce knifes and forks for the army. Coming from an artisanal working-class background, Einert was a salaried employee and worked as a correspondence clerk, a fact that also explains his excellent and nuanced command of written German, which can be found in his typewritten manuscript. But Einert did not only depend economically on the H.-A. Erbe company – which thrived throughout the 1920s before the Depression forced the owners to make compulsory redundancies – he also lived in a house owned by his employer.

Most probably joining in 1921, Einert was a member of the Social Democrat Party (SPD) until it was disbanded by the Nazis in 1933.

[11] Thomas Mergel, 'High Expectations – Deep Disappointment: Structures of the Public Perception of Politics in the Weimar Republic', in Canning, Barndt and McGuire, *Weimar Publics*, pp. 192–210.

[12] This collection of extracts from war letters and diaries was published in the proceedings of the subcommittee: *WUA* 5, pp. 262–335. Bergsträsser did not, however, return the original of Einert's manuscript, as requested by the author.

[13] All following information on Einert and the local context is referenced in Ziemann, 'Gedanken', pp. 201–7. In administrative terms, Schmalkalden had, since 1866, actually been a Prussian exclave in Thuringia. Negotiations about a territorial transfer in 1919 had not led to any results.

According to his own testimony, he had not had any interest in politics before and during the war (p. 214). Describing his – in hindsight, for him, deplorable – political ignorance, Einert recalled how he had cheered some of his company comrades who tore down the red flag from a public building when the regiment marched home in November 1918. Arriving at the polling station for the January 1919 election to the National Assembly, he had to inquire about his options, not knowing any of the parties and candidates (p. 225). The town of Schmalkalden had already been a Social Democrat stronghold before 1914, and the SPD managed to expand its position as the strongest party at the ballot box in the 1920s before it was relegated to second place by the Nazis in the September 1930 Reichstag elections. As elsewhere, the local Reichsbanner branch was founded with some delay in August 1924 and, not surprisingly, the preparations were discussed in a meeting of the local SPD group in the context of a debate on 'upcoming tasks of the party'.[14] Einert may have been one of the founding members of the local Reichsbanner branch, and if not, he surely joined early on. For an extended period that cannot be established with certainty, he also served, using his professional skills, as the keeper of the minutes: a fact that indicates his practical commitment to Reichsbanner activism. As in many other towns across the country, the Schmalkalden branch of the republican defence league made regular public appearances on 1 May and on 11 August – constitution day – while the number of other public outings in the mid 1920s seems to have been rather limited. However, in September 1926, the local Reichsbanner members celebrated their flag consecration with a march through the town.

Einert's war experiences

Einert was drafted in 1914, but it was only in March 1915 that he moved to the front. He served in the 71st Infantry Regiment, a Thuringian unit, which had its garrison in Erfurt. It was first deployed at the eastern front, where Einert saw action in Russia, Serbia and Macedonia, before the regiment was transferred to the western front in spring 1916. There he served until the armistice, was decorated with the Iron Cross Second Class and with the Schwarzburger War Medal, and was discharged in the rank of an NCO (p. 214). In his manuscript, Einert was blunt in outlining his overall assessment of the military as an institution. 'Entry into the military', he wrote, 'was, for the common man, the beginning of a time of gagging and oppression.' The constant extended, useless

[14] Quoted in *Volksstimme: Schmalkalder Tageblatt*, 14 August 1924.

Figure 5 Reichsbanner flag consecration in Schmalkalden, 5 September 1926.

drill and grind were the prerogative of the superiors in the ‘Prussian military system’, meted out against the ‘sons of the working people’ who had ‘naturally’ to be at the receiving end of the ‘disciplinary rod’ (p. 216). He recalled a number of examples where NCOs and young lieutenants had inflicted the pain of endless drill on muddy ground upon the soldiers, and was particularly bitter about a sergeant who was already well known for his brutal exercise of power from the garrison, but was rarely ever seen close to the front line. Referring to this particular individual, but also summing up his experiences with superiors, he expected that ‘surely it should be possible to write books about the continuing drudgery exerted by these tormentors’ (p. 217).

This last remark is highly revealing for at least two reasons. First, it indicates that Einert longed for a more elaborate literary narrative that could do justice to the whole spectrum of negative experiences he and other ordinary men had accumulated in the Prussian army. Even though he recalled and described some of these incidents in great detail across several pages of his manuscript, he must have felt that his literary means were not sufficient to express the bitterness and humiliation soldiers had suffered at the hands of their superiors. Secondly, the figure of the brutal NCO who can terrorise private soldiers in the garrison and at the rearguard, but cannot cope with front-line action, is a crucial element of the narrative in Erich Maria Remarque's *All Quiet on the Western Front*. In the drill sergeant Himmelstoß, he epitomised this particular aspect of military life for many readers.[15] Einert's brief remark thus indicates an important element of the framing of popular expectations in the republican camp, expectations that helped to turn Remarque's novel into an immediate commercial success.

In Einert's description, the injustice and brutality of the power structures in the wartime army were a direct correlate of class rule, as the 'working people' had to endure maltreatment and abuse. His sentiment was widely shared by moderate socialist workers in the 1920s, as an academic inquiry revealed in 1923. This inquiry was based on many informal talks with and between miners at the Ruhr, and was thus a kind of early anthropological study, employing participatory observation as the main tool of data gathering. In these talks with the researcher, a Ph.D. student, the miners produced endless examples of young lieutenants who had behaved like 'masters' (*Herrenmenschen*), and had thus had a vested interest in the war.[16] Such a class-based explanation of the inherent cruelty of the Prussian military worked neatly as far as young officers with a middlle-class background were concerned. With regard to NCOs this approach was problematic, as Einert admitted, pre-empting the objection that they were in fact recruited from the 'lower people' (p. 217). His response was to describe the majority of the sergeants and NCOs as 'scum of the earth' (*Ausschuß der Menschheit*): as people who were not capable of earning their living through a 'peaceful craft' (p. 217).

Throughout his manuscript, Einert referred to many wartime episodes that further reinforced the overall message of how unjust and brutal the military machinery had been. One case in point was 'tying-up' (*Anbinden*) – the equivalent to Field Punishment No. 1 in the British army – where soldiers were tied to a wheel or tree in lieu of a detention room.[17] While the regiment was in Macedonia, one of his comrades had been punished for stealing some food. In blazing heat, he was tied up to the wheel of the field kitchen for three days – just long enough, as Einert commented with cynicism, 'to restore his patriotic feeling' (p. 224). But while the brutality of the class-based Prussian military system was one of the most deeply felt and enduring legacies of the war experience for Einert, his perception of

[15] See Erich Maria Remarque, *All Quiet on the Western Front* (London: Putnam, 1929), pp. 31–5, 54–9.

[16] Walter Friedrich, 'Die Ideenwelt der mehrheitssozialistischen Bergarbeiter des Ruhrgebiets', Ph.D. dissertation (University of Bonn, 1923), p. 54.

[17] For details, see Ziemann, *War Experiences*, pp. 59f.

the army had already been framed well before the war. His older brother, who was drafted in 1913, had told him often about 'the suffering under the Prussian military system, the oppression and the slave-like treatment by the superiors' (p. 219). Thus, the war experiences could to a large extent only confirm what he had already expected to be the predominant features of military service. Precisely at this point of his reflections, Einert also attacked the notion of a 'spirit of 1914'. He debunked nationalist mythologies of a rush to arms, explaining the readiness of young men to volunteer in August 1914 as an attempt to seek 'relief' from the oppression they had endured in the barracks (p. 219).[18]

Einert's text was an attempt to connect his front-line experiences with contemporary political struggles about the proper remembrance and overall meaning of the wartime past in Weimar Germany. He organised his core argument around a couple of related juxtapositions, which were repeated and slightly rephrased throughout his manuscript. Taken together, these juxtapositions not only reveal the core of his convictions as a 'Reichsbanner man' – a theme that the title of the piece had flagged up clearly – they were also meant to offer a comprehensive interpretation of the fault lines or cleavages that divided the political system of the Republic, as seen from the bottom-up perspective of a small provincial town. The first of these juxtapositions served to dispel the charge that the republican left, rallied and represented by the Reichsbanner, lacked patriotism. Einert first touched upon this topic when he discussed the fatal consequences of the pre-war arms trade and the vested interests manufacturers had in armed conflicts. He characterised the representatives of 'big industry' by their eagerness to make profits, thus tapping into a discourse that had already gained currency during the war.[19] But these 'war profiteers' would nowadays pretend to be the 'most nationalist men in the world', even though they had only 'robbed and deceived' both the ordinary people and their fatherland.[20] A case in point was the fact that German arms had been traded to prospective enemy countries before the war, although there had been a general knowledge – even in

[18] Socialist miners at the Ruhr also rejected the notion of unanimous enthusiasm in August 1914; Friedrich, 'Ideenwelt', p. 54. On the different popular responses in August 1914 see Jeffrey Verhey, *The Spirit of 1914: Militarism, Myth and Mobilization in Germany* (Cambridge University Press, 2000).

[19] See Martin H. Geyer, *Verkehrte Welt. Revolution, Inflation und Moderne: München 1914–1924* (Göttingen: Vandenhoeck & Ruprecht, 1998), pp. 243–8; and, in a comparative perspective, Jean-Louis Robert, 'The Image of the Profiteer', in Jay Winter and Jean-Louis Robert (eds.), *Capital Cities at War: Paris, London, Berlin 1914–1919* (Cambridge University Press, 1997), pp. 104–32.

[20] Throughout his text, Einert uses the term *national* to describe nationalist discourses and arguments.

Einert's school, conveyed through the teachers – that a war was imminent.[21] Einert recalled an incident in the summer of 1915 when his regiment had attacked a village in Serbia. When it finally managed to capture an abandoned Serbian artillery position, one of the cannon bore the sign of its manufacturer, the 'Krupp Company, Essen'.[22] Anyone claiming to be 'nationalist' would have refrained from delivering war materials to foreign countries, he maintained. But nowadays, Einert insisted, those who did so would claim to be 'much more "nationalist" than the front-line soldiers, who had their bones crushed by the fire' of exactly these cannon (p. 216).[23]

He returned to this theme in a deliberation on the rule of the officers and the changing social structure of the front-line army during the war. Once active, Einert claimed, pre-war officers had realised that the war would not be over within a few months, and as such, they started to withdraw from front-line service. Thus, teachers had to serve as troop officers in the final years of the war and, in terms of social strata, the front-line army more generally consisted of teachers as leaders, and 'of workers, salaried employees and lower civil servants as enlisted men'. High-ranking civil servants, industrialists, 'big landowners' (*Großagrarier*) and the higher strata of the military, conversely, ended up serving in the *Etappe*, or back home in Germany, and such men were precisely those who would, in the post-war period, exaggerate their claims to be 'nationalist' (p. 218). Thus, Einert followed the already well-developed pattern of socialist war remembrance, which contrasted the sacrifice of the ordinary people at the front with the past profiteering and current wealth of those who had sought a safe place behind the lines.

Delineating the republican camp

Einert presented this line of reasoning in a series of four rhetorical questions that juxtaposed the respective claims of being 'nationalist',

[21] This argument was common fare in the Reichsbanner. See Paul Freiherr von Schoenaich, 'Reichsbanner und Pazifismus' (1925), *Zehn Jahre Kampf für Frieden und Recht* (Hamburg: Fackelreiter, 1929), p. 116.

[22] Serbia had actually ordered only one small batch of cannon from Krupp in 1871. The ordnance Einert encountered must have been provided by Russia. See Zdeněk Jindra, 'Zur Entwicklung und Stellung der Kanonenausfuhr der Firma Friedrich Krupp/Essen 1854–1912', in Wilfried Feldenkirchen (ed.), *Wirtschaft, Gesellschaft, Unternehmen: Festschrift für Hans Pohl zum 60. Geburtstag* (Stuttgart: Steiner, 1995), pp. 956–76 (pp. 969, 974).

[23] For a similar indictment against the lack of patriotism by the Krupp firm in a Reichsbanner meeting in Bremen, see 'Eine Friedensreise über Frankreichs Schlachtfelder', *Bremer Volkszeitung*, 20 October 1928: StA Bremen, 7, 88, 50/2.

by those 'braggarts' who were now gathered in the right-wing combat leagues on the one hand, and by the 'working man' who 'had had for years to endure the suffering of this bloody war, but is nowadays a member of the Reichsbanner' on the other (pp. 218f.). In this rhetorical sweep, Einert associated wealth with a lack of patriotism, and in contrast characterised those who were on a 'meagre weekly wage' and also Reichsbanner members, as national (p. 218). With these rhetorical juxtapositions, Einert shifted his argument on the terrain of a discourse to what it meant to be nationalist. On the one hand, this was a smart move, as he could tap into the well-established Social Democrat argument that stated that only the wealthy few could afford to have pretensions about their nationalism. Unmasking the egoistic reasons for patriotic posturing, he effectively deconstructed a crucial element of nationalist discourse: the claim that only the right could legitimately speak about it. Every claim for a peculiar Reichsbanner patriotism was, on the other hand, tainted with the toxic legacy of service in the Imperial Army. Apart from that, Einert's claim was also tautological: in four consecutive rhetorical questions, he insisted that being a Reichsbanner member was the equivalent of being *national* – to use the German term – without ever qualifying this claim any further. As a positive assertion, it was an empty rhetorical gesture: convincing on a personal level bearing in mind his service record, but lacking firepower in the public arena. Throughout his text, Einert never detailed why he had a reason to be proud of the German nation. His Reichsbanner nationalism was like an empty shell.[24]

As we will discuss in more detail below, it was crucial for Einert's insistence on being part of the truly 'patriotic' political camp that he knew the members of both camps in person, owing to the small town setting of Schmalkalden. But such claims to be nationalist were quickly undermined, not least when doubts were cast on the front-line service of Reichsbanner activists. This happened in the small town of Eutin near the Baltic Sea when the local Reichsbanner branch was founded in July 1924. A secondary school teacher from nearby Kiel was scheduled to speak at the very first foundation gathering, but he had to be withdrawn and replaced by an SPD functionary from Hamburg because the local Stahlhelm had mocked the meagre front-line service record of the preferred speaker.[25] Einert himself was well aware that even extended

[24] On the difficulties of articulating progressive nationalism in official Reichsbanner rhetoric, see Rohe, *Reichsbanner*, pp. 245–7.

[25] Stokes, 'Anfänge', 335.

front-line service did not make Reichsbanner members immune against charges that the republican league and its members lacked patriotism:

A *Frontkämpfer* with many years of service, who has made sure that the German people were spared the misery of foreign occupation and who has also ensured that the pockets of these 'nationalist' heroes have been filled, but who nowadays wants nothing else than to live a well-ordered and peaceful life, is immediately branded an unpatriotic fellow [*vaterlandsloser Geselle*] as soon as he joins the Reichsbanner. (p. 218)

More than any other passage in his text, these lines indicate the contradictory nature of Einert's war memories, particularly the perennial tension between his personal wish to forget the past and the political need to remember it. Precisely because of the degradation, maltreatment and suffering he had had to endure during the war, Einert was keen to leave this world of misery behind and pursue his own personal advancement in a civilised social environment. But this urgent desire was hampered by his commitment to the Republic and to the veterans' league that defended it.[26] Via his Reichsbanner activism, Einert had entered the contested field of veterans' politics, and the continuing struggles between the right-wing associations and the republican league that shaped this field forced him to rework and articulate his war memories in a more coherent fashion. In that sense, Einert's manuscript did not present anything private or personal, since his own narrative of events was charged and suffused with the overarching pattern of 'Reichsbanner ideas', as he had explained in his covering letter (p. 214).

The first juxtaposition – between those who falsely claimed to be patriotic, and those who really had served their fatherland during the war – was thus complemented and expanded by a second juxtaposition, between those who were members of nationalist combat leagues – for which Einert invariably used the term 'right-wing leagues' (*Rechtsverbände*) – and those who had joined the Reichsbanner (pp. 218, 221). Einert insisted that it was easy to convey a correct picture of these competing organisations in a small town such as Schmalkalden, where he could know almost all local members of both Reichsbanner and Jungdo 'in person' (p. 220). Thuringia was one of the strongholds of this league, which adopted some of the principles of the bourgeois youth movement and combined an aggressive nationalism with an anti-democratic and anti-Semitic ideology. The political style of the Jungdo was political romanticism rather than fascism. Nevertheless,

[26] A similar tension characterises the war memoirs of Willibald Seemann; see Martin Hobohm, 'Soldat aus Berlin-Ost', *RB* no. 25, 5 August 1928.

Fritz Einert preferred to characterise Jungdo members as bearers of the 'swastika' (p. 221).[27] A local Jungdo branch had existed in Schmalkalden since 1920, and it was strong enough to publish a monthly newsletter in the latter half of the 1920s, and to gather 600 people for a festive event in the summer of 1927.[28] The relation between Reichsbanner and Jungdo might have been less confrontational in other regions and at other times, particularly during the late 1920s, when the Jungdo lost members and hence moved closer to the bourgeois parties, ultimately merging with the DDP to form the German State Party in July 1930. Yet also in Baden, where the political cleavages were less pronounced, Reichsbanner members in Schiltach 'raged' against the DDP in 1930, apparently agitated by the merger with the Jungdo, which had made the loss of any liberal substance in the DDP obvious.[29]

Reasons for joining a right-wing league

Obviously, the first point of Einert's juxtaposition regarded the claim to be a veterans' association. Only very few veterans had joined the Jungdo, Einert maintained.[30] He tried to refute the claim of a right-wing MP who had 'recently' argued in the Reichstag that no former front-line soldiers at all were represented in the Reichsbanner.[31] Quite to the contrary, Einert insisted, again referring to his own personal encounters, all those 'from my town and vicinity who were in the field together with me are without exception Reichsbanner members' (p. 220). Einert then offered a detailed survey of the different social strata and motives

27 Donald R. Tracey, 'Der Aufstieg der NSDAP bis 1930', in Detlev Heiden and Gunther Mai (eds.), *Thüringen auf dem Weg ins 'Dritte Reich'* (Erfurt: Landeszentrale für Politische Bildung, 1996), pp. 65–93 (pp. 75ff.).

28 Ziemann, 'Gedanken', 206.

29 'Protokollbuch Ortsgruppe Schiltach', 21 December 1930: StA Schiltach, AS-2055a.

30 Schumann, *Political Violence*, p. 117 argues that the Jungdo did not define itself 'as a veterans' organization'. But the founding manifesto had proclaimed the aim to educate the German youth 'in the spirit of the front line soldiers' (Fricke, *Lexikon*, Vol. II, p. 140), and Artur Mahraun, the Jungdo leader and former career officer, published a string of articles on the meaning of the front-line experience (Artur Mahraun, 'Das Martyrium der Frontsoldaten', *Der Meister: Jungdeutsche Monatsschrift für Führer und denkende Brüder* 1.2 (1925/6), 6–11; and 'Das Fronterlebnis', *ibid.* 3 (1927), 3–7). At any rate, Einert understood that the Jungdo claimed to be a veterans' association.

31 Incidentally, this remark allows us to narrow down the time when Einert wrote his manuscript to the period between July 1925 and March 1926. Einert most probably referred to an assertion by Jürgen von Ramin, a former career officer and MP for the Nationalsozialistische Freiheitspartei. In a Reichstag speech on 17 July 1925, Ramin had implied that, in contrast to the Kyffhäuserbund, the Reichsbanner had no war veterans among its members. See 'Deutscher Reichstag, 97. Sitzung', 17 July 1925: *Verhandlungen des Reichstags. Stenographische Berichte* 386 (1926), 3311.

for joining of those who were organised in the *Rechtsverbände*. The key categories of this analysis were economic advantage and status interest. Small artisans, for instance, would often join as they expected to gain business contracts, or in the belief that their property would be safer if they were *Hakenkreuzler*. Similar reasons motivated the broad category of the 'war and post-war profiteers' (p. 221). With the latter term, he was referring to those who had amassed a fortune during the inflationary period until 1923. Another category were businessmen who believed that, on average, the more affluent customers were to be found in the right-wing camp. Another group of joiners consisted of those with a secondary school diploma, *Abitur* or equivalent. These young men, Einert was convinced, believed that the reintroduction of a large 'standing army' would also bring the renewal of extra privileges for the *Einjährigen* (one-year volunteers) as in the imperial system, who were fast-tracked for promotion and could then abuse their authority and 'play the "lieutenant"' (p. 221).[32]

In a later passage, Einert returned to this theme and explained that these *Einjährigen* were usually members of the 'propertied class'. While their status had allowed quick advancement, the war had demonstrated that they were lacking 'aptitude' for military leadership. Long-serving men with a background in the 'working class' (*Arbeiterschaft*), on the other hand, had been denied advancement to the rank of a junior officer, even though they were 'proficient', as they did not match the status-centred promotion criteria (p. 222). This was a remarkably insightful deconstruction of the social dynamics of the *Einjährigen* privilege, and of the peculiar combination of class and estate (*Stand*) that underpinned its selection mechanism. In many ways, it bore a close resemblance to the equally sharp, seminal analysis of this military institution that the young leftist historian Eckart Kehr published only three years later in 1928.[33] In 1929, Einert's trenchant criticism of the lack of appropriate upward mobility in the wartime army was also repeated by Reichsbanner member and historian Martin Hobohm in his expert opinion on the causes of the German collapse.[34]

32 For a similar analysis in the Saxonian Reichsbanner see Voigt, *Kampfbünde*, pp. 348f.

33 Eckart Kehr, 'Zur Genesis des Königlich Preußischen Reserveoffiziers' (1928), in *Der Primat der Innenpolitik: Gesammelte Aufsätze zur preußisch-deutschen Sozialgeschichte im 19. und 20. Jahrhundert*, ed. Hans-Ulrich Wehler (Frankfurt am Main; Berlin; Vienna: Ullstein, 1976), pp. 53–63.

34 *Gutachten des Sachverständigen Dr. Hobohm, Soziale Heeresmißstände als Teilursache des deutschen Zusammenbruchs von 1918*, *WUA* 11.1 (Berlin: Deutsche Verlagsgesellschaft für Politik und Geschichte, 1929), pp. 104–10. In his often unreliable book, Alexander Watson falsely claims that the restrictive entry criteria for officers were 'discarded' in late 1917. Alexander Watson, *Enduring the Great War: Combat, Morale and Collapse*

According to Einert's observations, members of the lower and upper middle classes joined nationalist combat leagues primarily because of a set of different economic incentives. They all shared, however, an additional motive: their 'arrogant self-conceit' (*Hochmuts-Dünkel*). In the end, it was the 'delusion' of being something better and representing a higher status, and, on the flipside, fears of being stigmatised in social encounters that drove middle-class people into right-wing associations. But it was not only members of the middle class who joined nationalist leagues; so did working-class men. In order to account for their behaviour, Einert adopted a much more straightforward explanation that avoided any recourse to collective mentalities or issues of status interest.[35] Workers who joined the right-wing leagues were simply 'forced' to do so under 'economic pressure' (p. 221). Two categories in particular stood out here. There were, first, those long-term unemployed who – as a last resort – took the step of joining the Jungdo or Stahlhelm in order to get a job. Often, they did so with success, as many employers used these connections to hire reliable staff who did not support the political left. In doing so, they followed official Stahlhelm policy, as the league encouraged entrepreneurs to prioritise members when offering jobs, and in 1928 opened the Stahlhelm 'self-help', a special labour branch, in order to facilitate this process.[36]

The second category of workers had joined the right-wing leagues in the wake of industrial action. Some time before he wrote his manuscript, Einert had met a worker who was a Stahlhelm member, and who had told him about the circumstances of his entry. The workforce of one company had gone on strike, and once the dispute had ended, the 'factory masters' (*Fabrikherren*) only rehired those former staff who could legitimise themselves as members of a nationalist combat league (p. 221). Schmalkalden, to be sure, was not the only place where this occurred. It seems that it was the standard practice of Stahlhelm supporters among employers either to retain or rehire only those staff who were members of the combat league.[37] Einert himself drew two conclusions from these

in the German and British Armies, 1914–1918 (Cambridge University Press, 2008), p. 121.

35 Social Democrat critics of nationalist commemorations of war usually tried not to answer the question as to why ordinary people would join these events against their own very best interests. See Dieter Schott, *Die Konstanzer Gesellschaft 1918–1924: Der Kampf um Hegemonie zwischen Novemberrevolution und Inflation* (Constance: Stadler, 1989), p. 355.

36 Klotzbücher, *Der politische Weg des Stahlhelm*, pp. 44ff.; Schumann, *Political Violence*, p. 159.

37 Eric D. Weitz, *Creating German Communism, 1890–1990: From Popular Protests to Socialist State* (Princeton University Press, 1997), p. 145; Wolfgang Jäger, *Bergarbeitermilieus und Parteien im Ruhrgebiet: Zum Wahlverhalten des katholischen Bergarbeitermilieus bis 1933* (Munich: C. H. Beck, 1996), p. 276.

observations. First, it reinforced his own reluctance to use any of his recollections in the struggles on war remembrance that permeated the public arena. We do not know whether the owners of the H.-A. Erbe AG were organised in the Stahlhelm, but Einert's name is on a list of company employees who had gone on strike in 1924.[38] When he insisted in his covering letter to Ludwig Bergsträsser that, as an economically dependent person, he could not agree to the publication of his manuscript, Einert clearly knew what he was talking about. His case may not have been the only one where economic pressure prohibited the public dissemination of republican war memories. It is fair to assume, on the other hand, that Reichsbanner members in the more anonymous setting of big cities were less likely to face social control of their political activism, and if they did, then only by chance.[39]

Secondly, Einert was adamant in his insistence that any working-class members of right-wing leagues could never be deemed to be positively 'convinced supporters of nationalist ideas'. Only sheer economic pressure, rather than any idealist notions, drove them into the other camp. Einert was equally firm in his belief that the demarcation lines between the respective political camps were in principle well established. Anyone who crossed the divide between these camps apparently did so without proper conviction. Once, he had encountered some former Communists who had then joined the Jungdo. But such a 'strong change in the way of thinking' (*Gesinnungswechsel*), he wrote, was at least 'in my opinion, impossible' (p. 221). Einert did not mince his words when he accused the proponents of the nationalist camp of hypocrisy and of a misrepresentation of the wartime past. But as he tried the reasons for joining the right-wing camp, he never expressed any ideas that could be interpreted as a deliberate 'dehumanisation' of either the internal, political or external enemy. Yet such a 'dehumanisation' has been described by historian George Mosse as 'one of the most fateful consequences' of the alleged process of 'brutalisation'.[40] Like the majority of all Reichsbanner members, Einert was not at all interested in continuing the aggression and enmity of the war. Rather, his aim was to contribute to a cultural demobilisation and to settle peacefully in a civilian environment.

The first two juxtapositions – truly nationalist or not, Reichsbanner or right-wing league – were both reinforced and transcended by a third one, between 'black–red–gold' and 'black–white–red'. When the

[38] Ziemann, 'Gedanken', p. 202.

[39] See the example from Breslau in Hans Thomas, 'Mein politisches Leben' (1982): BArch, SAPMO, SgY 30, 2167, fo. 39.

[40] Mosse, *Fallen Soldiers*, p. 172.

National Assembly in Weimar had made decisions about the state symbols of the new Republic in July 1919, the search for a national flag had yielded only what the legal scholar Carl Schmitt later called a 'dilatory formula compromise' that carefully avoided and postponed a clear-cut decision.[41] Only the Majority Social Democrats (MSPD) had unanimously supported black–red–gold as the colours of the Republic, a choice that in their view stressed the emancipatory potential of German nationalism and harked back to the democratic heritage of the revolution in 1848/9. But it was not only the right-wing German People's Party (DVP) and German National People's Party (DNVP); a majority of the left-liberal DDP and many Centre deputies were also keen to retain black–white–red, which had only been the official national flag of the Kaiserreich since 1892.[42] A majority for black–red–gold was only secured when the deputies adopted a compromise that retained the old imperial colours for the flag of the merchant fleet, with the new *Reichsfarben* black–red–gold only visible in the upper-left corner of the flag.[43] From the early 1920s until 1933, symbolic conflicts between the two options black–red–gold and black–white–red not only permeated the political culture at the grassroots level; they also shaped high politics. Here, they took centre stage when the presidential elections in 1925 were fought between the 'people's bloc' – with Centre politician Wilhelm Marx as candidate, and rallying behind black–red–gold – and the 'Reich bloc', which supported former general Paul von Hindenburg in rallies that were decked in black–white–red.[44]

Black–red–gold and the flag controversy

Fritz Einert was clearly agitated by these conflicts. As a Reichsbanner man, he was passionate about black–red–gold, very much in accordance with the republican league, which already flagged up its unequivocal

[41] See Carl Schmitt, *Verfassungslehre* (Berlin: Duncker & Humblot, 1954 [1928]), pp. 31ff.

[42] On this and other often neglected technical details see Theodor Schieder, *Das Deutsche Kaiserreich von 1871 als Nationalstaat*, 2nd edn (Göttingen: Vandenhoeck & Ruprecht, 1992), p. 83. For the clear awareness of these details in the Reichsbanner see 'Fahnenweihe der Abteilung Brandenburg-Altstadt', *RB* no. 20, Gaubeilage Berlin-Brandenburg, 15 October 1927.

[43] See Buchner, *Um nationale Identität*, pp. 45–52; Winkler, *Von der Revolution*, p. 230.

[44] See Ziemann, 'Gedanken', 207f.; Buchner, *Um nationale Identität*, pp. 105–9; Nadine Rossol, 'Flaggenkrieg am Badestrand: Lokale Möglichkeiten repräsentativer Mitgestaltung in der Weimarer Republik', *Zeitschrift für Geschichtswissenschaft* 56 (2008), 617–37; Peter Fritzsche, 'Presidential Victory and Popular Festivity in Weimar Germany: Hindenburg's 1925 Election', *CEH* 23 (1990), 205–24 (pp. 212–15).

support for the new *Reichsfarben* in its name. It was one of the key characteristics of Reichsbanner mobilisation that it rallied hundreds of thousands of working-class Social Democrats behind the colours of the nineteenth-century national democratic movement, and not behind the traditional symbol of socialist labour, the red flag.[45] Einert touched upon the symbolism of these two competing flags when he discussed the banners that the troops had carried at the front. According to his recollection, black–white–red had been on display only during the very first battles, and was hardly ever seen in the following years.[46] More importantly, he insisted that these colours had not been 'chosen' by the army, but had rather been 'forced upon it'. It was hence wrong to claim that the soldiers had fought for black–white–red 'out of conviction' – even more so as the 'military system' that stood behind these colours had weighed upon their minds like a 'nightmare' (*Alp*; p. 220) With these remarks, Einert referred to a crucial element of the right-wing commemoration of war. In speeches at war memorials and on many other occasions, representatives of the nationalist camp stressed that the German army as a collective had fought for black–white–red. Einert tapped into the official Reichsbanner rhetoric, which aimed to refute this claim. During the founding celebration of the Reichsbanner *Gau* in Lower Bavaria in 1924, the poet Karl Bröger maintained, according to a police informer:

> Who of the servicemen had really gone to the front in order to fight for black–white–red? The two million dead soldiers had not fallen *for* black–white–red, but *under* black–white–red. Then, no defender of the fatherland used to bother about the colours. And who had actually seen black–white–red at the front? ... Nowadays, there is a lot of pretension in public as if all ex-servicemen are located in the black–white–red camp. Finally demonstrating that this is not the case is the actual aim of the Reichsbanner Black–Red–Gold (...).[47]

There is a remarkable, almost verbatim, resemblance in the ways in which both Fritz Einert and Karl Bröger connected the contested issue of the national flag with the legacy of the fallen soldiers. This is not a mere coincidence, but rather demonstrates that the need to reclaim the remembrance of front-line service for the republican camp stood at the

[45] Buchner, *Um nationale Identität*, pp. 99–101. In 1928, a Reichsbanner branch in the Saxonian city of Zwickau consecrated a new flag, black–red–gold on the one side, red on the other. This incident demonstrates how difficult it was for many socialists to abandon their colours for the national flag; Voigt, *Kampfbünde*, p. 288.

[46] Black–white–red had in fact only been introduced as the national cockade of German troops, alongside the traditional flags of their respective rulers, in 1897. See Schieder, *Kaiserreich*, p. 83.

[47] Pol. Dir., 25 July 1924: StAM, Pol. Dir. 6888. The italics are mine.

very heart of Reichsbanner activism. Einert, however, went one step even further as he not only put the alternative between the two flags in sharp relief, but also explained the underlying symbolism of both options. His choice of words to describe this mechanism indicates that Einert clearly recognised the fundamental significance of the flag issue as a symbolic conflict. This was not only a superficial struggle about the public display of politics. For him, it spoke to the core of his political beliefs, and in that sense it was the culmination of the four major juxtapositions that structured his attempt to reflect on Weimar politics in the light of his war experiences. Again highlighting that soldiers in the Imperial Army had not had any choice or agency of their own in reality, he couched this juxtaposition in the form of a hypothetical vote: 'If during the war someone had put the question to each soldier whether he would like to fight for the black–white–red ruler's flag [*Fürstenfahne*], which stood for "war", or for the black–red–gold people's flag [*Volksfahne*], which stood for "peace and reconciliation between the peoples", I know for sure what the result would have been' (p. 220). In the perception of this Reichsbanner activist, the flag colours black–red–gold did more than just delineate a particular camp that was interested in peace. They also emphatically represented the Republic as a legitimate state in its own right, based on the sovereignty of the people, rather than that of the rulers as in imperial Germany. Einert clearly associated black–white–red not only with – in his view – a misguided nationalism, but also with the authoritarian monarchical system.[48]

Only one month after Einert had sent his manuscript to Bergsträsser, the inconsistency of the 1919 flag compromise was laid bare when the Reich cabinet decided that all German consulates should hoist black–red–gold only in conjunction with the flag of the merchant navy, which was dominated by black–white–red. This decision triggered an outpouring of public protests by Social Democrats across the country. A mass rally in Bremen, staged by the local Reichsbanner branch, was attended by 2,000 people, and was followed by a number of verbal skirmishes with detachments of the Jungstahlhelm on the streets of the city.[49] But the cabinet decision also met resistance from the parliamentary group of the DDP and the Centre Party. In the short term, this 'flag struggle' (*Flaggenstreit*) led to the downfall of non-party chancellor Hans Luther, whose cabinet had been based on a bourgeois right-wing coalition and who had started the conflict when he tabled the proposal

[48] Rohe, *Reichsbanner*, p. 241, denies the prevalence of such a connection in the perception of Reichsbanner members.

[49] 'Bericht über die Protestkundgebung des Reichsbanners', 10 May 1926: StA Bremen, 4, 65, 1030; see Buchner, *Um nationale Identität*, pp. 109–15.

in late April.[50] Its medium-term consequences are more difficult to ascertain. As historian Heinrich August Winkler rightly states, the *Flaggenstreit* was indicative of the extent to which the Republic still lacked a 'strong political core consensus'.[51]

From the perspective of Reichsbanner activism, however, three other points need to be stressed. Black–red–gold were, first, not just the colours of a flag. These colours symbolised the legitimate claim of the Reichsbanner to situate the republican state in the *longue durée* of progressive currents and the longing for national unity in German history. In 1927, a certain professor Quenzer gave a talk in the Reichsbanner branch in the small town of Schiltach in Baden. He spoke about 'Black–red–gold in history', and explained to an attentive audience that this 'banner' had 'already been the imperial colour in earlier German histories'.[52] Apparently he referred to an oft-cited late medieval genealogy of the Reichsbanner, according to which, starting in the fourteenth century, depictions of the black imperial eagle coloured his beak and fangs in red, on a golden shield. Whatever the exact factual merits of this explanation, it could certainly claim a more pronounced historical heritage than the colours black–white–red. These had been 'artificially' cobbled together as late as 1867 from Prussian black–white and the white–red of the former Hanseatic League for the newly founded North German Federation.[53]

Secondly, it is necessary to emphasise that Reichsbanner members had already moved to the centre and contributed to a possible consensus with their support of the republican flag. Einert supported black–red–gold as the colours of peace, and not the red flag of the socialist labour movement, to which he also belonged as a party member. With the founding of the Reichsbanner, many socialists had deliberately abandoned the red flag, the dominant colour in the revolution of 1918/19.[54] Reichsbanner speakers also stressed adamantly that they would never disrespect or disparage black–white–red, not least because it had been used for the 'grave-clothes of two million German soldiers'.[55] Yet bourgeois observers still scorned black–red–gold as mere 'party colours', as a newspaper in the Franconian city of Hof suggested in 1927, thus indicating its own partisan stance.[56] Consensus, in other words, was not

[50] Heinrich August Winkler, *Der Schein der Normalität: Arbeiter und Arbeiterbewegung in der Weimarer Republik 1924 bis 1930* (Berlin; Bonn: J. H. W. Dietz, 1988), pp. 265–9.
[51] *Ibid.*, p. 267.
[52] 'Protokollbuch Ortsgruppe Schiltach', 19 February 1927: StA Schiltach, AS-2055a.
[53] Schieder, *Kaiserreich*, p. 83.
[54] Buchner, *Um nationale Identität*, pp. 52–8.
[55] 'Fahnenweihe der Abteilung Brandenburg-Altstadt', *RB* no. 20, Gaubeilage Berlin-Brandenburg, 15 October 1927; see Harter, 'Schiltach', p. 283.
[56] Cited in Macht, *Niederlage*, p. 108; see Stokes, 'Anfänge', p. 337.

lacking because the Republic did not offer grounds for it, but because its right-wing opponents rejected it out of hand.

Thirdly, it should be noted that the supporters of the republican flag were not simply propping up a lost cause. Einert's text indicates his confidence that the republican colours could muster stronger forces, and this sentiment was widely shared among Reichsbanner members in the mid 1920s. During a social event in a Reichsbanner section in Munich in early 1925, two boxers appeared on stage, wearing a black–red–gold and a black–white–red ribbon respectively, and battled the conflict over symbols out. To the 'stormy applause' of the audience, the former prevailed, driving home the message 'that the German Republic would hold the field and succeed'.[57] This was shadow-boxing of some kind. But it also shows the extent of the historical optimism that the Reichsbanner galvanised, at least during the first years of its existence, and the 'pride' and 'enthusiasm' they felt when they displayed their banners.[58] Optimism is a rather vague analytical category. Yet as a historical perception it is of utmost relevance, as it encapsulates the 'horizon of expectations' that was prevalent among contemporary actors.[59]

The fourth juxtaposition that structured Einert's exposition of his war memories was actually the first one in order of appearance. His text commenced with a reflection on the pre-war ideology that had justified the military as a means to defend the fatherland. 'But why', he asked in the kind of rhetorical question typical of his prose, 'can it happen that an attack [*Angriff*] by one country against the other occurs, and what are the causes [*Ursachen*] for this?' (p. 215). This issue had apparently been the topic of many previous discussions, as he referred to people who had 'on various occasions' told him that when a country was 'assaulted' [*angefallen*], it had to defend itself. This was the ideology of a defensive war that had stood at the heart of government rhetoric and nationalist discourse during the war. But Einert obviously did not buy into it. Quite on the contrary, his rhetorical question might suggest that he believed Germany had deliberately started a war of aggression in August 1914. Even if this was not the case, Einert had a strong point to make that the causes of war were not located in the need for defence, but rather in the vested interests of the capitalists. This insight

[57] PND no. 494, 7 February 1925: StAM, Pol. Dir. 6887.

[58] Kurt Hirche, *Immer in Bewegung: Lebensweg eines deutschen Sozialisten*, 3 vols., Vol. I: *Unruhe und Aufbruch* (Marburg: Schüren, 1994), p. 354.

[59] See Graf, *Die Zukunft der Weimarer Republik*, p. 83. On the 'horizon of expectation' see the seminal article by Reinhart Koselleck, '"Space of Experience" and "Horizon of Expectation": Two Historical Categories', in *Futures Past: On the Semantics of Historical Time* (New York: Columbia University Press, 2004), pp. 255–75.

was based on his 'experiences during the war', which had 'taught' him that 'the working people, thus the workers, salaried employees and civil servants, and these surely make up the by far largest part of a people, do not at all contemplate attacking each other and taking something away' from each other (p. 215).

Like so many other aspects of Einert's political worldview, this insight was based on personal encounters – in this case on discussions with the civilian population in those countries where he had fought during the war. He specifically referred to France, where people had told him they did not understand why the two countries were at war, 'as we [the people] were good together and would not harbour any enmity'. The French had always mentioned *capitalisme* as the true reason for the war, and Einert agreed with them that 'indeed a war is only a way to settle capitalist interests'. 'The people', on the other hand, and 'particularly the lower strata of the people, are only the instruments that are needed to settle these interests'. And the military system that Einert so much despised was in place precisely to make the ordinary people 'submissive' to this peculiar form of exploitation, war in the service of capitalism (p. 215). Einert knew the buzzwords of imperialist discourse all too well. Perhaps with a hint of irony, he referred to the famous dictum by former imperial chancellor Bernhard Count von Bülow, who had claimed in 1897 that Germany had to secure a 'place in the sun' (*Platz an der Sonne*) in competition with other imperialist powers. But provided there was a 'fair distribution', Einert opined, the produce of the world should be sufficient to feed all human beings. 'Economic reasons' were thus always only a pretence to wage war. In reality, apart from capitalist corporate interests, the 'ambitious drive' of the 'former rulers' and the higher echelons of the military were the driving forces behind wars (p. 216). The fourth juxtaposition Einert used to make sense of his war experiences was almost a perfect echo of the relevant parts of the Reichsbanner discourse to be found in the membership journal. It pitted the elementary solidarity of the ordinary people in all belligerent countries against the vested interests of the rulers, military leaders and capitalists, who were the driving forces behind the war. And the latter particularly, as Einert had shown with the Krupp example mentioned above, were always ready to betray the real interests of their country for short-term financial gain.

Armistice and defeat as a moment of liberation

Explaining the reasons for the Great War based on these premises, Einert had still to account for the fact that the German army had successfully fought until autumn 1918, and that he and other ordinary soldiers had continued to fulfil their orders up to that point. In some passages he had already offered the lust for power and status as the main motives of troop officers and NCOs. But what about the positive motivation of private soldiers to carry on fighting? They had not had any, Einert insisted. Tapping into the victimisation discourse that was widely used in the Reichsbanner to portray the troops as passive cogs in the workings of the war machine, he highlighted brute force, cheap incentives and censorship as the three main reasons why the soldiers had functioned. Contrary to the claims of right-wing commemorative speeches, the German soldiers had not willingly sacrificed their lives. Rather, they were 'driven into death like a flock' (p. 219).

'We know from the front line', Einert explained in one of the rare instances in which he used the plural to denote the front-line soldiers as a collective, 'that, once death was coming close, all options for a rescue were still tried out, but without will-power everyone had to succumb to his fate'. The bottom line was that once ordinary soldiers tried to escape to the rear, they were threatened with death by shooting (p. 219). In addition, the military provided extra rations and handed out schnapps as 'offensive-food' ahead of offensive action and major battles. Thus, many soldiers had actually died in a state of 'intoxication', rather than being driven by idealist motives (p. 223). Again speaking for a collective subject, he offered censorship as an additional explanation for why the right-wing rhetoric of a 'spirit' (*Geist*) that had motivated the 'fallen' was utterly wrong. Only 'we as front-line soldiers', who used to march next to the fallen, actually knew their motivation, Einert claimed. And he recalled how during marches, in dug-outs, trenches and rear-area quarters, all soldiers used to swear constantly 'not only against the war, but even more so against the oppressive system' they were in. But they made sure to keep their real thoughts among themselves, and not did let them be known to the officers.[60] In addition, a thorough censorship of their correspondence had made it virtually impossible to convey the real situation at the front to their relatives at home (p. 219). Oppression and censorship thus formed the third crucial factor that had concealed the fact that ordinary soldiers had not had any authentic combat motivation.

[60] To be sure, Einert did acknowledge that some troop officers – he explicitly mentioned company-commanders – had actually cared for their subordinates, and that some of these were still 'respected'. But, he added, not many had been like this, and most officers of this category were nowadays Reichsbanner members (p. 223). While he was keen to differentiate his assessment of the officer corps, Einert certainly did not buy into the idealist notion of an overarching front-line community.

They had fought, as Einert expressed this argument in symbolic terms, *under*, but not *for* the imperial flag.

Ultimately, though, the accumulation of 'tremendous physical hardship during the war, the mental suffering, the systematic oppression from above' and other factors led up to a point where the soldiers broke down in an 'inner collapse' and were absolutely 'indifferent' to whether they would achieve a 'victory' or not. The 'main issue', then, was that 'finally' the war had 'to come to an end' (p. 223). These remarks inaugurate the final section of Einert's manuscript, in which he detailed his account of the German endgame in 1918. It is worth quoting from this passage at some length, as it not only offers Einert's personal recollections, but has to be read – in the context of Weimar's contested war remembrances – as an eminently political statement with far-reaching implications. Throughout his manuscript, Einert had presented his rebuttal of nationalist discourse as something he could legitimately speak about, as he embodied and relied upon the worm's-eye perspective of the former soldier who had seen front-line action. This was, by implication, the only authentic and privileged position from to talk about the legacy of the war. Einert scorned Carl Günther Fürst zu Schwarzburg-Sondershausen, who had been the colonel-in-chief of his regiment from 1889. The 'tiny ruler', as he disparagingly called him, would always 'show off his chest full of gongs' when he talked about the war, but had never actually been with 'his' regiment during the war. Einert took the opportunity to criticise the *Dolchstoß* myth, which he directly mentioned only once, and rather in passing (p. 223). Thus, he made sure he stated that he had 'never noticed anything' about leaflets or other attempts coming from Germany which had aimed 'to influence' the soldiers at the front. At any rate, these would have been unnecessary 'machinations' as 'we were finished anyway' (p. 224). But his assessment of the German endgame was much more than a mere rebuttal of the stab-in-the-back accusation:

> From mid 1918 onwards it was over; everyone was completely shattered and tried as hard as possible to rescue his life after the long ordeal. Troops were hardly ever replaced, the [enemy] artillery became more terrifying by the minute, and the aircraft squadrons arrived in their droves. German soldiers came in captivity in divisional strength. Replacements who arrived at the front were totally exhausted and had already been shot into pieces; many were just a penny's worth and could hardly walk more than a few kilometres. The Americans went into battle in full marching columns. Thus, the end had to come if we should not totally collapse. Even before the armistice everyone was heading at full pace in a backward direction, sometimes six marching columns next to each other; nothing could stop this. The armistice was the hour of liberation from the yoke of the terrible sufferings and deprivations, but also

from the yoke of Prussian militarism. If someone claims that we could have battled on thence, this only goes to prove that he has seen absolutely nothing of the front line. Had the armistice not come, and so much the Army Supreme Command knew for sure, we would have been driven across the Rhine, and the Entente would have transformed our beautiful Rhineland into a wasteland, in order to make us feel the same suffering as those who lived in the occupied territory, since what the people living in the occupied territories of the enemy countries had to endure, those [Germans] who stayed at home do not know. It would have been a pleasure for the Entente if they could have marched through the Brandenburg Gate into Berlin. (p. 224)

Several elements of this comprehensive account of the dying months of imperial Germany are worth noting in particular. The first is the time-line Einert suggests. In his perception, the final collapse of the German field army had already commenced in the summer of 1918. That was at least two months before 29 September, when the Army Supreme Command finally called on the government to initiate negotiations about an armistice. German defeat was overdetermined, and had more than just one major cause: both the material superiority of the Allies and the lack of proper replacements contributed towards it. What military historian Wilhelm Deist has called the 'covert strike of the soldiers' added to these material factors, as front-line troops marched back home on their own in droves.[61] Now, as shirking and deserting had turned into a mass phenomenon, 'nothing could stop this' ('ein Halt gabs nicht mehr'). It is also worth pointing out again why Deist describes this mass movement as 'covert' (*verdeckt*).[62] In 1918 it was not covered in the media, and when Weimar contemporaries recalled it, as Einert did, they did not have a proper name for it, and would not dare to publicise their memories.

But Einert not only provided a comprehensive account of the reasons for German collapse from the worm's-eye perspective. He detailed a recollection that was in fact an utterly significant political statement: the armistice had not been the moment when defeat was ratified, but rather a moment of liberation and emancipation. Throughout his text, Einert explained the various social structures and organisational procedures that had turned the Prussian army into a 'total institution' (Erving Goffman), a place of unmitigated exercise of power. On 11 November 1918, the spell of this regime was broken. Finally, the Germans could usher in a new republican order that promised to end the degradation of human beings inherent in the now defunct imperial system. For an attentive reader of his text, the gist of Einert's stance vis-à-vis the

[61] See Deist, 'Military Collapse', 207.
[62] *Ibid.*, 206. Watson, *Enduring the Great War*, p. 206, misrepresents this argument.

military would not have required further explanation. Yet he employed the metaphor of a 'yoke' to summarise it again, thus comparing the soldiers to cattle harnessed to pull a plough. This demonstrates not only how deep-felt his emotional attachment to the armistice was, but also how political – in the widest sense of the word – this moment of emancipation appeared to be. But Einert not only recalled his own liberation; he also expressed his empathy with the plight of the civilians under German occupation. More than any other rhetorical device, this expression of understanding of the perspective of the other side marks his text as a truly pacifist document.[63] At the same time, it is also fair to assume that Einert was not particularly bothered about the terms of the Treaty of Versailles, and of its condemnation of German atrocities in particular. He knew that the armistice had averted foreign occupation of German territory – a possibility that he clearly resented – and that the German conduct of war went a long way to explain the harsh stance the Allies had taken.

Reichsbanner ideas as collective memory

Before we develop some more general conclusions based on Einert's text, it is worthwhile to consider the factors that shaped and framed his memories again. To begin with we have stressed the fact that – in the first instance – his manuscript was a conversation with himself, based on the rather painful process of rereading and collating his war letters, in the clear knowledge of the limits of this medium of self-reflection due to military censorship. Throughout his manuscript, another element of the way in which Einert developed and organised his recollections came to the fore. Whenever he pondered the details and the meaning of his own war experience, and its significance for his own Reichsbanner activism, Einert referred to personal encounters, both during and after the war. His text tried to make sense of the trajectory of his own service history and his post-war biography, and the 'Reichsbanner ideas', flagged up in his covering letter, were of importance as signposts and an overall memory framework for that endeavour (p. 214). In the manuscript, however, he often talked about the significance of this organisation, but never referred to any ideas for which the Reichsbanner positively stood.

It seems that something else was much more important for Einert as he embarked on the process of working through his recollections and presenting them in a coherent fashion. His recollections were

[63] See Vollmer, 'Imaginäre Schlachtfelder', p. 161.

of course unique, as his own personal war remembrances. Yet he had not been alone in facing these experiences, as he stressed time and again, but had rather shared them with many other ordinary working-class people from Schmalkalden and its vicinity. As he presented his memories in his manuscript and pondered their significance for the post-war period, Einert referred to them as part of a collective experience. This mechanism can be best described as a 'collective memory' in the way in which French sociologist Maurice Halbwachs used this term in his two seminal books on this topic from the 1920s. 'The individual', Halbwachs wrote, 'calls recollections to mind by relying on the frameworks of social memory'.[64] And these social or collective memories were nurtured in the setting of close encounters on a day-to-day basis, a mechanism Halbwachs described in more detail by taking the family as an example.[65] Einert foregrounded this collective framing of his own personal memories when he stressed the fact that he 'knew' both the members of the national camp and of the Reichsbanner 'in person', and insisted that 'all those from my town and vicinity who have been with me in the field' were Reichsbanner members (p. 220).

Remarks like these, however, do not only hint at the dense network of personal encounters and the many conversations that had nurtured, sustained and framed the range of collective memories Einert expressed in his manuscript. They also served a strategic function, which was to unmask the official rhetoric of nationalist commemorations as hollow phrases. In a scathing remark about right-wing circles he complained that they would always 'get worked up to commemorate the fallen soldiers during the unveiling of memorials', but would not know that the fallen, 'were they still alive, for the greatest part would not stand in their camp'. During his 'affiliation with an active unit at the front', Einert continued, 'I have got to know hundreds of comrades more closely', many of whom were killed. And 'from the personal attitude' of these fallen comrades, he insisted, 'I know for sure' that they would not have joined right-wing leagues, 'were they still alive' (p. 220). In his reference to an active field unit, Einert did not mean to invoke the culture of his former regiment as the framework for collective memory. Such a rose-tinted form of remembrance was championed by those nationalist circles that sought to preserve the collective honour and tradition

[64] Maurice Halbwachs, *On Collective Memory*, trans. and ed. Lewis A. Coser (Chicago; London: University of Chicago Press, 1992), p. 182; see Maurice Halbwachs, *La Mémoire collective*, ed. Gérard Namer (Paris: Albin Michel, 1997), pp. 51–96.

[65] Halbwachs, *Collective Memory*, pp. 54–83.

of imperial regiments into the post-war period.[66] For Einert, the regiment was only the institutional structure for his wartime memories, a frame that had to be filled with the sociability and solidarity among working-class conscripts. And with bitter irony, Einert identified one of the perennial contradictions of war memorials, which is, in the words of historian Reinhart Koselleck, 'The dead are supposed to have stood for the same cause as the surviving sponsors of memorials want to stand for. But the dead have no say in whether it is the same cause or not.'[67]

Maurice Halbwachs had analysed the family as an important site for the production of collective memories, and, in some respects, the process of retrieving and organising his memories of war and the military was for Einert a matter of kinship.[68] Right at the beginning – not of the text, but in chronological order – he referred to his older brother, who had already introduced him to the notion of Prussian militarism even before he himself had been drafted (p. 219). And at a later point in his narrative, he mentioned his first son, who had been born in 1923. In his sweep against the brutality of the NCOs and drill sergeants, he loathed the fact that, in the context of the military, this 'scum' could pretend to be the 'educator of other, more civilised human beings'. Resorting to sarcasm he added: 'I would say thank you if my son fell into the hands of such educators' (p. 217). For Einert, the process of memory was an element of kinship, as relatives conveyed to each other the most crucial insights they had gained in their life. And he was determined to make sure that the next generation would learn from the catastrophe that he had had to endure. Over decades, and well into the post-1945 period, Fritz Einert never tired of relaying his revulsion for the Prussian military when he talked to his sons. They knew the content of his manuscript by heart even though they had never had a chance to read it.[69] That the power of Prussian militarism over male adolescents had been broken, and that the memories of its destructiveness were kept alive, were for

66 See the sometimes uncritical analysis by Wencke Meteling, *Ehre, Einheit und Ordnung: Preußische und französische Städte und Regimenter im Krieg, 1870/71 und 1914/19* (Baden-Baden: Nomos, 2010), pp. 292–315, 375–411.

67 Reinhart Koselleck, 'War Memorials: Identity Formations of the Survivors', in *The Practice of Conceptual History: Timing History, Spacing Concepts* (Stanford University Press, 2002), pp. 285–326 (p. 288).

68 On memory as a form of kinship see the lucid remarks by Jay Winter, 'Forms of Kinship and Remembrance in the Aftermath of the Great War', in Jay Winter and Emmanuel Sivan (eds.), *War and Remembrance in the Twentieth Century* (Cambridge University Press, 1999), pp. 40–60.

69 Based on a telephone conversation with Helmut Einert, his younger son, in June 1998.

Einert crucial achievements of the Republic and of the veterans' league that defended it.

As a detailed, reflexive and highly personal piece of testimony on republican war remembrances in the Weimar Republic, Fritz Einert's manuscript is a unique document. It also has no parallel among the documentation that is available for nationalist veterans' and combat leagues, as one of the very few texts that were not written with immediate publication in mind. In 1938, American sociologist Theodore Abel published a small selection from more than 600 written autobiographies of early Nazi followers he had obtained via a call to submit manuscripts.[70] Many of these Stormtroopers and Nazi Party members were war veterans, and their front-line experiences and personal transformation through war played a crucial role in their autobiographical self-representation.[71] But the manuscripts were written in 1934, after the Nazi seizure of power. Thus, they can only partially be understood as contemporary interventions into the Weimar struggles over war remembrances. They were also, or perhaps even more so, individual attempts to tap into the then official mythological explanations for the motives of early Nazi Party followers.[72] Einert's manuscript, on the other hand, reflected his personal take on the significance of war memories for the political struggles in the embattled Republic, written down during Weimar's supposedly calm and stable middle years. But as his memories were nurtured and framed by the collective experience of class and his Reichsbanner membership, they have significance beyond the individual case. Some more general insights that can be drawn from his text will conclude this chapter.

Einert expressed his interpretation of the war experience in a pair of clearly distinguished sets of signifiers. On each side of the divide between the republican and the national camp, these signifiers formed an equation in which the meaning of each single signifier corroborated and enhanced that of the others. For the nationalist camp, the equation was '*Etappe* = falsely nationalist = right-wing leagues = pro-war = vested capitalist interests = black–white–red'.

[70] Theodore Abel, *Why Hitler Came into Power* (Cambridge, MA: Harvard University Press, 1986 [1938]).

[71] For a subtle interpretation of the narratives of war remembrance in this material see Patrick Krassnitzer, 'Die Geburt des Nationalsozialismus im Schützengraben: Formen der Brutalisierung in den Autobiographien von nationalsozialistischen Frontsoldaten', in Dülffer and Krumeich, *Der verlorene Frieden*, pp. 119–148; see Peter Fritzsche, 'The Economy of Experience in Weimar Germany', in Canning, Barndt and McGuire, *Weimar Publics*, pp. 360–83.

[72] Krassnitzer, 'Geburt', pp. 128f.

With regard to the republican camp, it was 'front = truly nationalist = Reichsbanner = peace = solidarity with the enemy = black–red–gold'. While every single element in these two chains of signifiers articulated the overall meaning of each set, two signifiers carried particular weight: the black–red–gold flag and the Reichsbanner were in essence synonyms, as the republican league had vowed to display and defend the colours of the Republic. Einert's juxtaposition between the two flag options emphasises the tremendous significance of this particular symbolic struggle for German history in the 1920s. It was one of the deepest and most enduring fissures in Weimar politics well before the 'flag controversy' in 1926 had raised the stakes even higher. This important point is not properly appreciated in those historiographical accounts that tend to downplay or ignore the relevance of symbolic politics.[73]

For Einert, the differences between the socialist and the nationalist or right-wing camp were clearly discernible. Their conflict permeated all levels of political engagement, from the circumscribed setting of a small provincial town such as Schmalkalden, all the way up to the Reichstag as the centre stage of national politics, whose debates Einert followed with close attention. There has been extensive historiographical debate on the internal organisational and ideological coherence of the moderate socialist camp between 1918 and 1933.[74] A particularly contentious point in this debate is the significance of nationalist ideologies and mythologies for socialist workers, and the extent to which Social Democrat voters defected to the nationalist camp.[75] Similar points have been raised with regard to the performative politics of the republican camp, for instance by historian Eric Weitz, who asked whether 'the similarity of demonstration forms' perhaps trumped 'the divergent ideological content'.[76] The highly detailed snapshot provided by Fritz Einert for the mid 1920s as the evidence presented in Chapter 2 allows us to answer the latter question with 'no'. There are also good reasons to doubt that the nationalist imaginary of a class-transcending community really appealed to Social Democrat workers, at least inasmuch as they were war veterans. Historians such as Heinrich August Winkler

[73] Schumann, *Political Violence*, p. 200, mentions the issue only in passing. Mommsen, *The Rise and Fall of Weimar*, p. 209, presents the *Flaggenstreit* as a mere cabinet crisis.

[74] Useful summaries are provided by Lösche and Walter, 'Organisationskultur'; Klaus Tenfelde, 'Historische Milieus: Erblichkeit und Konkurrenz', in Manfred Hettling and Paul Nolte (eds.), *Nation und Gesellschaft in Deutschland: Historische Essays* (Munich: C. H. Beck, 1996), pp. 247–68.

[75] Both points are emphasised by Fritzsche, 'Did Weimar Fail?', pp. 640–3, 647.

[76] Eric D. Weitz, 'Weimar Germany and Its Histories', *CEH* 43 (2010), 581–91 (p. 588).

have argued that the rhetoric of the *Volksgemeinschaft* had had a 'firm place in the everyday language' of the Reichsbanner.[77]

This is certainly true for the publications of the league, which frequently tapped into nationalist discourses of an overarching national community.[78] Yet many of these articles were written by the DDP and Centre Party members among the Reichsbanner leadership, or by Social Democrats with a bourgeois background. Such rhetoric was, however, rarely employed in speeches in local branches, as it contradicted the experiences working-class veterans had had in the Imperial Army.[79] Events in Berlin in 1932/3 corroborate the resistance among Reichsbanner rank-and-file members against excessive nationalist rhetoric. Hubertus Prince Löwenstein (1906–84), a member of the Centre Party and a journalist with an affluent family background, had joined the league in 1930, and quickly established himself as the leader of the 'Vanguard' (*Vortrupp*) – a special section for boys aged fourteen to seventeen.[80] But many parents and local functionaries in Berlin disliked his authoritarian leadership style. Even more, they openly criticised Löwenstein's promoting the notion of a '*Volksgemeinschaft* that encompassed all social strata'.[81] 'Patriotic speeches' and *Volksgemeinschaft* rhetoric from Reichsbanner leaders also met with opposition by leftist rank-and-file members in other cities.[82] Thus, together with evidence like this, Einert's repeated insistence on core ideological differences between the camps rather corroborates a point made by historian Karl Rohe. Based on both quantitative and qualitative data on voter fluctuation, Rohe argued that the Weimar years saw the 'climax of a three-camp system' in which the cleavages between the socialist, nationalist and Catholic camps further intensified, and realignment across the camps was a rare exception.[83]

But Fritz Einert's testimony does not only allow us to answer questions about the 'reception' of cultural forms such as the flag controversy,

[77] Winkler, *Schein der Normalität*, p. 383.

[78] See Rohe, *Reichsbanner*, pp. 245–58. But see the explicit critique by Dr Elling, 'Der Weg zur Volksgemeinschaft', *RB* no. 4, 15 February 1925.

[79] Based on evidence from Saxony, see Voigt, *Kampfbünde*, pp. 346f.

[80] See Rohe, *Reichsbanner*, pp. 121f.

[81] Gerhard Alt, *Vortrupp* leader in Berlin-Prenzlauer Berg, 9 February 1933 to Löwenstein: BArch, SAPMO, Ry 12/II, 113, 8, fo. 16f.; on the *Vortrupp* see the material in BArch, SAPMO, Ry 12/II, 113, 7. Löwenstein's own account glossed over these conflicts. See Prince Hubertus Löwenstein, *The Tragedy of a People: Germany, 1918–1934* (London: Faber & Faber, 1934), pp. 92–5.

[82] See Gündisch, *Wetzlar*, p. 259.

[83] See Karl Rohe, *Wahlen und Wählertraditionen in Deutschland: Kulturelle Grundlagen deutscher Parteien und Parteiensysteme im 19. und 20. Jahrhundert* (Frankfurt am Main: Suhrkamp, 1992), pp. 140–63.

and to highlight the fact that the Reichsbanner added another important pillar to the organisational framework of the socialist milieu.[84] Precisely because it offers unparalleled detailed insights into the factors that shaped the memory and political ideology of an ordinary war veteran, Einert's text invites reflections on wider conceptual issues in the debate on Weimar politics. Is it true, as historian Eric Weitz has argued, that the 'de-emphasis on political economy' has led to a 'narrowing of vision' for the historian? Are recent trends in historiography, and in particular the analysis of pro-republican cultural currents, really 'devoid of investigating and reflecting upon the real ... material conditions' in which ordinary people lived?[85] Or, in other words, is it necessary to reinstate the material dimension of and economic constraints on politics, as opposed to the symbolic dimension of the political?

It should be obvious why a thorough analysis of Einert's text has to eschew such a false alternative between the material and the symbolic. His narrative is saturated with references to the material circumstances of political action and everyday life, from the hardship and 'hunger' he had to endure at the front to the significance of affluence and social class for the setting of veterans' politics (p. 224). Not least, economic dependence hindered him from granting permission to Bergsträsser to publish his piece. But it would be wrong to understand these economic aspects of his recollections as set apart from the panorama of symbolic differences that Einert provided. Quite on the contrary, only the use of these signifiers allowed him to express the significance of those material factors that had a bearing on his war memories. The symbolic dimension was not something external, but rather intrinsic to the social terrain of these contested commemorations.

[84] Quote: Weitz, 'Weimar Germany', 589.
[85] *Ibid.*, 589.

4 Public commemorations and republican politics

The previous two chapters have analysed the set of ideas and recollections that framed the war remembrance of Reichsbanner members, and their significance within the wider associational culture of the republican veterans' league. It appeared that socialist working-class veterans were able to rework their front-line experiences, guided by the ideas of the Reichsbanner, and to situate the specific trajectory of their own wartime service and post-war reintegration in the larger framework of the competing veterans' leagues. In all these endeavours, however, the Reichsbanner members by and large kept to themselves. As the example of Fritz Einert demonstrates, socialist veterans had an in-depth knowledge of their counterparts in the nationalist camp, based on daily face-to-face encounters. But the speeches, talks and *tableaux vivants* presented in internal branch meetings and the contributions to the membership journal only spoke to those who already belonged to the socialist milieu. These cultural representations expressed the war memories, the *Kriegserinnerungen*, of Reichsbanner members. They did not directly, however, make claims in the wider sphere of commemorations of war, the rhetoric of *Kriegsgedenken*. In these public rituals and speeches, the death of the fallen soldiers was invoked as an example for the living, and more general conclusions about the current state of the German polity and the future of the German nation were drawn.

It was not only in Germany that the key sites for the public commemoration of the fallen soldiers were war memorials. These memorials contributed, as Reinhart Koselleck has argued in a seminal article, to the 'identity formation of the survivors', allowing them to frame the meaning of the past and to connect the fallen to political collectives in the present.[1] War memorials were a ubiquitous site in Weimar Germany, yet the pattern, political context and style of the memorial cult showed wide regional variations. As with regard to other aspects of Weimar's history, regional variety is a qualitative factor that has to

[1] Koselleck, 'War Memorials'.

be taken seriously.[2] In predominantly rural regions such as southern Bavaria, even very small villages had already unveiled a memorial of some kind by the early 1920s, before the hyper-inflation in 1923 eroded the available funds for larger figural sculptures.[3] For reasons outlined below, larger cities saw a proliferation of various memorial projects throughout the 1920s and early 1930s. In Bielefeld, an industrial city in Westphalia with a strong Social Democrat presence, more than 20 memorials were built from 1919 to 1933, commemorating the approximately 2,300 fallen soldiers from the city and its vicinity.[4] In Hanover, which had endured and needed to commemorate the violent deaths of 12,000 local citizens, a staggering 150 war memorials – including all memorial plaques – were planned and mostly also unveiled during the Republic.[5]

Given the sheer range and number of local memorial projects across Weimar Germany, this chapter can make no pretence at a comprehensive coverage of the artistic, symbolic and ritualistic aspects of the cult of the fallen soldiers in the period until 1933.[6] It rather aims to analyse the interventions of pro-republican forces, and of the socialist labour movement in particular, in the contested field of commemorations at war memorials. Were Social Democrat war veterans able to influence or even determine the figuration of war memorials, and thus the symbolism of their architecture? Was the socialist camp, and its veterans' associations in particular, an active participant in the public ceremonies that actualised and re-enacted the meaning of death year by year? How did moderate socialists articulate the meaning of war and violent death in their commemorative rhetoric? More generally, is it true that the cult of the fallen soldiers remained, despite the interventions from Reichsbund and Reichsbanner, a 'monopoly of the political right'?[7]

In the immediate post-war period, regimental associations were often the first to unveil commemorative plaques or even sculptured memorials. The cult of the fallen in the regimental associations was clearly

[2] See Ziemann, 'Weimar was Weimar', pp. 566f.
[3] Ziemann, *War Experiences*, pp. 252–68.
[4] Kruse and Kruse, 'Kriegerdenkmäler in Bielefeld', p. 106.
[5] Gerhard Schneider, *'Nicht umsonst gefallen'? Kriegerdenkmäler und Kriegstotenkult in Hannover* (Hanover: Hahn, 1991), p. 191.
[6] As an excellent short survey see Sabine Behrenbeck, 'Heldenkult oder Friedensmahnung? Kriegerdenkmale nach beiden Weltkriegen', in Gottfried Niedhart and Dieter Riesenberger (eds.), *Lernen aus dem Krieg? Deutsche Nachkriegszeiten 1918 und 1945* (Munich: C. H. Beck, 1992), pp. 344–64.
[7] Rohe, *Reichsbanner*, p. 156; see also Albrecht Lehmann, 'Militär und Militanz zwischen den Weltkriegen', in Dieter Langewiesche and Heinz-Elmar Tenorth (eds.), *Handbuch der deutschen Bildungsgeschichte*, 6 vols., Vol. V: *Die Weimarer Republik und die nationalsozialistische Diktatur* (Munich: C. H. Beck, 1989), pp. 407–29 (p. 420).

marked by a continuation of hierarchical patterns of differentiation, in which officers were honoured separately from their subaltern NCOs and soldiers.[8] During the early years of the Republic, Social Democrats usually watched these and other commemorative practices from the sidelines. In the town of Constance, a regimental association of the former 114th Infantry Regiment was established in early 1921, and shortly afterwards organised a regimental day, which was attended by more than 1,000 war veterans. As was the case during similar events in the following years, the commemorative speeches stressed the memory of comradeship in the wartime army, and praised the close community between the ranks as an example of attempts to heal the nation's woes in the post-war period. Local Social Democrats merely covered this event in a series of articles in their newspaper. They denounced the notion of comradeship as a myth, as the officers had always addressed private soldiers only with 'zoological epithets'. Portraying comradeship in nostalgic terms, the Social Democrat newspaper argued, only served to make people forget about the hatred against the officers that had pervaded the wartime army. As a consequence, workers were asked not to attend such regimental days. Thus, Social Democrats could only passively observe how the town was decked in black–white–red flags, which were even displayed at the local Reichswehr barracks.[9] Yet this was far from the only time that the army of the Republic took part in commemorative events that clearly served a monarchist or even revanchist tendency, and that were decorated in the old imperial colours. Leading Social Democrats such as Otto Braun, the Prussian prime minister, intervened to try to stop this practice, but to no avail.[10]

Nationalist ceremonies and their critics

Social Democrats had obvious reasons to be suspicious about the ideological agenda behind commemorations organised by regimental associations or by the local branches of the Kyffhäuserbund, the national-conservative league of veterans' associations. But in the early years of the Republic, there was another major reason why moderate socialists were reluctant to engage with public acts and symbols for the remembrance of the fallen soldiers. Their standard response was to denounce the huge sums that were spent on memorials at a time when hundreds of thousands of war widows, orphans and disabled veterans,

[8] See the critique in *BVZ*, 16 July 1919: BArch, R 8034 II, 7691, fo. 8.

[9] See Schott, *Konstanzer Gesellschaft*, pp. 352–5 (quote on p. 353).

[10] See Otto Braun to Chancellor Hans Luther, 19 November 1925: BArch, R 43/I, 710, fos. 248f.

living on meagre state pensions, were desperately trying to make ends meet. When preparations for a central municipal war memorial in Munich commenced in 1921, the Social Democrat *Münchener Post* resented the projected expenditure for a 'pile of stones worth millions' (*Millionensteinhaufen*). What was required was not a memorial that would 'boast' about the spilled blood of the fallen soldiers, but rather a 'memorial of charity' (*Denkmal der Nächstenliebe*) in the shape of financial aid and affordable food for the 'survivors'.[11]

Arguments like these were mirrored and reinforced by the Reichsbund of disabled veterans and war dependants. There is in fact reason to believe that the Social Democrat position with regard to the commemoration of the fallen was, until 1923, heavily influenced by the Reichsbund, which was not only a mass organisation, but also the most important stakeholder in this field within the socialist camp. As early as November 1919, the parameters of this discourse were established on the occasion of *Totensonntag*, the last Sunday before Advent, which had been traditionally used by German Protestants to commemorate the dead. As the *Reichsbund* journal stressed, 'all dying' was nothing else than a 'formidable indictment against war'. It was paramount to remember the 'sacrifice' of the fallen, but the members of the Reichsbund were sure that the 'fallen would not want memorials built of stone and iron ore, [and] did not want any glorification of the battles in which they had died'. What the fallen really demanded was 'justice' for their next-of-kin.[12] This call for justice was repeated in the following years, as the Reichsbund observed how commemorations were often abused to honour primarily generals and other high-ranking officers. Any participation of local Reichsbund branches in joint remembrance rituals was subject to another condition: they had to include a 'profession against war', as this was a statutory premise of the Reichsbund's activism based on the disastrous consequences of the First World War.[13]

Social Democrats did not simply watch from the sidelines as regimental associations and other nationalist organisations claimed to represent the legacy of the fallen soldiers in their commemorative practices. They also faced severe setbacks in any attempts to shape the design of the war memorials that were built during the 1920s. The reasons for this failure, however, differed in larger towns from those in the countryside. In the latter, decisions about the appropriate design and overall style

11 Article in the *Münchener Post*, 7 October 1921: BArch, R 8034 II, 7691, fo. 92.

12 'Unseren Toten: Zum Totensonntag am 23. November 1919', *Reichsbund* no. 44, 15 November 1919.

13 'Wie ehren wir das Andenken der Toten?', *Reichsbund* no. 21, 1 November 1920; see also 'Nie wieder Krieg!', *ibid.* 7 (1924), no. 7.

of a communal war memorial were based on a consensus, which was usually brought forward by the parish priest, or by the local branch of the Kyffhäuserbund, or by both working together. Other community representatives or the local council then usually rubberstamped the chosen design.[14] Even if local Social Democrats had wanted to suggest a different design, they were usually not in a strong enough position to challenge this consensus. In larger towns and cities, on the other hand, consensus was lacking from the outset, or complicated procedures and time-consuming competitions led to delays until any leeway for compromise had evaporated. The city of Bielefeld is a good example to illustrate these problems.

In Bielefeld, local politics were initially based on a cooperation between the Social Democrats and the moderate bourgeois parties. As early as 1920, the municipal authorities had agreed on the need to devise a central war memorial. After two time-consuming artistic competitions, the parties had finally settled in 1924 for the sculpture of a grieving woman, mourning the death of her relatives. This design had clear civic connotations, and disappointed those who hoped for an openly militaristic symbolism, in line with the hegemonic current in the German memorial cult. Local elections in 1924, however, produced a majority for a right-wing coalition against the Social Democrats. The design of the 'stern woman' was immediately abandoned, and in 1927 the city council launched a competition for a concert hall, which would also serve to memorialise Rudolf Oetker, who had died in Verdun in 1916, and his comrades. Private sponsorship by the Oetker family, who had based their fortune on the production of baking powder, thus allowed the opening of the 'Oetker Hall' in 1930, which henceforth served as a site for a nationalist commemoration of the fallen soldiers.[15] In Bielefeld and many other cities, the total lack or belated unveiling of a central memorial site contributed towards the proliferation of memorials that were designed and sponsored by firms, various local associations, schools and parish communities. Social Democrats made their voice heard in debates about municipal memorial projects, as for instance Social Democratic Party (SPD) Councillor Allenbach in Saarbrücken. When the debate started in 1928, he argued in favour of building a municipal welfare house for the 'poorest of the poor', and thus keeping the 'remembrance of the fallen of the World War' alive by serving 'living human beings'. Such a project, he argued, would also curb the 'spirit of war', and foster 'reconciliation between

[14] Ziemann, *War Experiences*, pp. 254f.

[15] Kruse and Kruse, 'Kriegerdenkmäler in Bielefeld', pp. 107–9 (quote on p. 108).

the peoples'.[16] Yet in Saarbrücken, as in other cities, such pacifist ideas did not materialise owing to the lack of a Social Democrat majority in the city council.[17]

Pacifist memorials

Consequently, only very few war memorials that were unveiled in Weimar Germany specifically displayed the intention to serve a pacifist cause. They were mostly situated in small towns in which a socialist majority was able to push through its preferences, or, alternatively, privately sponsored.[18] In either case, they rested on the strong presence and unified will of the socialist camp to defend such a design. In Annweiler in the Rhenish Palatinate, the inscription of the privately sponsored memorial, unveiled in 1922, read 'No more war'. It expressed, as a newspaper article explained, the deep-felt 'resentment against any war' amongst the local working-class population.[19] From its planning stage, the memorial had faced intensive criticism, but the socialist parties were able to withstand such pressure, and it was only after the Nazi seizure of power that the memorial was demolished in April 1933. As in other examples of memorials with an outright pacifist message, the chosen design was a simple pyramid.[20] This choice indicates another inherent problem in any attempts to encapsulate a pacifist commemoration of the fallen in stone: while traditional sculptural designs were deemed to be inappropriate for such an endeavour, modernist designs by Weimar's avant garde architects such as Walter Gropius or Mies van der Rohe were controversial even among labour movement activists. In addition, their artistic ideas did not necessarily have direct political implications. Architect Bruno Taut suggested in 1921 the building of public reading rooms that could serve as war memorials, but his designs

[16] Quoted in Ludwig Linsmayer, *Politische Kultur im Saargebiet 1920–1932: Symbolische Politik, verhinderte Demokratisierung, nationalisiertes Kulturleben in einer abgetrennten Region* (St Ingbert: Röhrig, 1992), pp. 75f.; see also Ute Scherb, 'Kriegerdenkmäler in Freiburg: Von der Gründerzeit bis nach dem Zweiten Weltkrieg', in Christian Geinitz, Volker Ilgen and Holger Skor, *Kriegsgedenken in Freiburg: Trauer–Kult–Verdrängung* (Freiburg: Haug, 1995), pp. 12–60 (pp. 41ff.).

[17] See Linsmayer, *Politische Kultur*, p. 77.

[18] See the example of Hörlitz-Flur, a brown coal-mining town, in which the socialist miners unveiled their memorial in July 1921, and invited the anarchist and pacifist Ernst Friedrich to speak at the unveiling ceremony. See the report in *Freiheit*, 6 July 1921: BArch, R 8034 II, 7691, fo. 79.

[19] *Münchener Morgenpost*, no. 140, 20 June 1922: BHStA/II, MK 51030.

[20] Jeismann and Westheider, 'Totenkult', p. 29; see Hans Joachim Teichler and Gerhard Hauk (eds.), *Illustrierte Geschichte des Arbeitersports* (Bonn: J. H. W. Dietz, 1987), pp. 82f.

remained a blueprint.[21] In the town of Völklingen in the Saar region, the local memorial displayed a female figure made of black marble in the pose of a *pietà*. The peaceful connotations of this design were emphasised by the inscription – 'To all victims' – which had been pushed through in the local assembly by the joint action of Social Democrats and Communists in 1925. This implied respect for the victims in other belligerent nations and thus had an internationalist appeal.[22]

Bielefeld was perhaps the only German city in which more than one pacifist sculptural design was realised during the Weimar Republic. Local war widows unveiled a 'peace fountain' as early as October 1919, and in 1931, the pacifist Vereinigung ehemaliger Kriegsgefangener (VeK) presented its own memorial. It was dedicated to those POWs who had not returned, and showed a group of three men embracing each other, in search of help, symbolising the suffering they had endured. In its funding appeal, the VeK branch had stressed the same thought, that those held in captivity and their tremendous 'suffering' should not be forgotten, and that those who had 'luckily returned home' had the duty to remember their comrades 'in the service of peace for mankind'.[23] The opening ceremony was attended by a vast crowd of mostly working-class people. A detachment of local Reichsbanner members was present, and the speeches drove home the key message: 'A new human right must emerge; not hatred, but love should reign the world.'[24]

For a number of reasons, Social Democrats were not actually willing and able to gain a stake in local commemorative practices during the early post-war years. A preference for welfare for the disabled veterans and a lack of consensus in city councils were the two most important of these reasons. As a result, commemoration remained by and large a monopoly of nationalist associations until 1923. In addition, the design of local war memorials in Weimar Germany had, despite many regional variations, a strong inclination towards a heroic nationalism that represented the serviceman as a warrior. Local war memorials in France, by comparison, stressed the civic qualities of the homecoming *poilu*, representing him as a *citoyen*, a citizen in uniform.[25] It should be stressed, however, that the overall lack of pacifist memorials was no German peculiarity. War memorials with an outright pacifist message such as 'No more war!' were never consensual in Germany, and were thus only realised in a very small number of towns; but the same applies to France.

21 See Behrenbeck, 'Heldenkult', pp. 351f.
22 Linsmayer, *Politische Kultur*, p. 45.
23 Kruse and Kruse, 'Kriegerdenkmäler in Bielefeld', p. 113.
24 *Ibid.*, p. 114.
25 See the comparison by Jeismann and Westheider, 'Totenkult', pp. 36–42.

As historian Annette Becker has noted, only six of the French local war memorials from the 1920s bear 'truly pacifist messages'.[26]

With the founding of the Reichsbanner in 1924, however, the field of commemorative practices was fundamentally changed. From its inception, the republican veterans' league made it clear that it wanted to have a stake in this field, and that it was determined not to leave the cult of the fallen soldiers to the political right. These interventions did not translate into a straightforward success story. But they demonstrate the drive and tenacity of the Reichsbanner in its attempts to claim the legacy of the fallen for the republican cause. Both the urgency of these endeavours and the obstacles they faced are highlighted by events that took place in Munich in 1924. On 7 July, the founding meeting of the Reichsbanner took place in the Bürgerbräukeller.[27] Adolf Dichtl, head of the association in Munich, alluded in his opening remarks to the symbolism of this particular place. Pointing to the bullet holes in the ceiling, he marked it as the site of the putsch staged by 'reactionary' elements in November 1923, which would now see the founding of a league 'of republican servicemen'.[28] Next on the agenda was a speech by Erhard Auer on the aims of the association. Highlighting the defence of the Republic as one main purpose, he metaphorically described the Reichsbanner as a 'dam' at which 'the spirit of dictatorship, of putsch and murder' would ultimately be 'shattered'. Auer also referred to the youth as the 'bearers of the future', and explained that social justice had to be injected into the republican state to secure its existence.[29]

The Reichsbanner and local commemorations

Yet this was only a brief rhetorical tribute to the possible future of the Republic as a 'horizon of expectation'.[30] Auer was in fact much more concerned with the past. As Reichsbanner members, he explained, 'we want to revitalise the spirit of the trenches'. The millions of fallen soldiers had 'not fought for kings and rulers, but for the German people and the fatherland'. Their legacy was at stake, and should guide the new

[26] Annette Becker, 'Der Kult der Erinnerung nach dem Grossen Krieg: Kriegerdenkmäler in Frankreich', in Koselleck and Jeismann, *Der politische Totenkult*, pp. 315–24 (p. 322).

[27] Speeches at the gathering are covered in 'Gründungsversammlung des Bundes Republikanischer Kriegsteilnehmer', PND no. 458, 7 July 1924: StAM, Pol. Dir. 6886; and in 'Reichsbanner Schwarz–Rot–Gold', *Münchener Post* no. 156, 8 July 1924.

[28] 'Gründungsversammlung des Bundes Republikanischer Kriegsteilnehmer'.

[29] Cited in *Münchener Post* no. 156, 8 July 1924.

[30] Koselleck, '"Space of Experience" and "Horizon of Expectation"'.

league. All the fallen who would 'rest in foreign soil', as those who lay in cemeteries at home, should be honoured. At this point, the audience members rose from their seats, 'paying tribute' to the fallen.[31] It was then left to Adolf Dichtl, lithographer by training and wartime NCO, to expand on the practical implications of these remarks. Dichtl received 'a stormy round of applause' when he demanded that the Reichsbanner should be an official participant at the unveiling of the central municipal war memorial, in order 'to honour its dead'. The possessive pronoun indicates that Dichtl was primarily interested in the symbolic capital of this commemorative ritual. Proponents of the opposite political camp, he explained, had 'no right to claim the fallen for themselves alone, and to use them for political bargaining'.[32]

On this occasion, however, the Reichsbanner failed in its attempt to be treated as a legitimate representative of the legacy of the fallen soldiers. The memorial for the approximately 12,000 fallen soldiers from Munich, situated in front of the army museum in the Hofgarten, displayed a recumbent 'sleeping warrior'. Notwithstanding the modern uniform and helmet, the sculpture conjured up reminiscences of the medieval greatness of the Holy Empire.[33] Yet despite repeated interventions, the Reichsbanner was not admitted to the unveiling of the monument, which took place on 14 December 1924. The Bayerischer Kriegerbund, the Bavarian section of the conservative Kyffhäuserbund, was in charge of the ceremony. It first did not respond, and then excluded the republican league from the ceremony on the grounds that it was a partisan organisation. Both local *Kameradschaften* and the leadership of the Reichsbanner in Munich discussed possible reactions and the fallout of this decision. One leader had suggested that individual Reichsbanner members should attend the ceremony on their own, but Dichtl strongly advised against such practice, as it could lead to verbal and physical confrontation and thus create a 'scandal'.[34]

Another setback was that the police had even prohibited attempts to hold a separate *Totenehrung*, or 'tribute to the fallen', in closed venues such as the Odeon or Tonhalle for Reichsbanner members only. This triggered the urge to sue the police for an offence against the 'Law for the Protection of the Republic', legislation enacted in July 1922 in the wake of public outrage over the assassination of Walther Rathenau.[35]

[31] 'Gründungsversammlung des Bundes Republikanischer Kriegsteilnehmer'.
[32] 'Reichsbanner Schwarz-Rot-Gold'.
[33] Goebel, *Great War*, pp. 261–3.
[34] PND report no. 488, 'Versammlung des Reichsbanners Schwarz-Rot-Gold, Kameradschaft Nordend', 12 December 1924: StAM, Pol. Dir. 6887.
[35] *Ibid.*; see Mommsen, *The Rise and Fall of Weimar*, pp. 125–7.

The whole course of events was disappointing for the Reichsbanner, yet in another branch meeting the speaker reassured the audience that it would remain an exception. Trying to inject some optimism, he admitted that the episode showed how everyone was keen to 'suppress' the league, 'but to no avail'. He was firmly convinced that the Reichsbanner would count four million members in the next year, and thus be more than able to overcome such problems.[36] This final remark is indicative of a widespread tendency in the Reichsbanner to measure strength and political success in numerical terms, and not as the product of convincing arguments or, with regard to the fallen soldiers, appropriate symbolism. But the episode in Munich also made clear that the Reichsbanner had to take the initiative, as former general Berthold von Deimling, whose Reichsbanner activism we will discuss in Chapter 6, concluded in a newspaper article. Citing a line from Ludwig Uhland's famous poem 'I had a comrade' (1809), the staple of every right-wing commemoration ceremony, Deimling scorned the Kyffhäuserbund for the exclusion of the republican veterans.[37]

The cult of the fallen in Weimar Germany was marked by many local variations, not only in the design of the memorial, but also with regard to the setting of the performative rituals that surrounded it. On a number of occasions, the Reichsbanner could either successfully challenge the hegemony of right-wing leagues or cooperate with them on equal terms in commemorative rituals. An example of the former was the town of Wetzlar in Hesse, where the Reichsbanner branch comprised many highly skilled and well-educated workers who manufactured optical instruments for local firms. They faced the first test of their determination to defend the Republic in public only a few months after the founding of their branch, when a memorial for the fallen Rhenish Jaeger was about to be unveiled in autumn 1924. Rumour had it that right-wing leagues – the Jungdo in particular – planned to transform this ceremony into a demonstrative 'anti-republican rally'. In direct response, the Reichsbanner announced it would celebrate its *Bannerweihe*, the formal consecration of the black–red–gold flag of the local chapter, on the very same day. The aim of this move was not to block the unveiling, which it supported in principle. Rather, the republican veterans aimed to put pressure on the local authorities and the ceremony's organising committee. And successfully so! After negotiations

[36] PND no. 489, 'Kameradschaftsabend des Reichsbanners', 20 December 1924: StAM, Pol. Dir. 6887.

[37] Berthold von Deimling, 'Die Verfemung des Reichsbanners', *Berliner Tageblatt* no. 18, 11 January 1925.

with the Reichsbanner, the invitations to the Stahlhelm and Jungdo were rescinded, and police hindered Jungdo members from joining the ceremony anyway. The unveiling of the memorial and the *Bannerweihe* went ahead on the same day, the latter including a tribute to the fallen, a festive concert and a procession through town.[38] This was a remarkable triumph for the local republicans, who had prevailed over attempts to hijack the memorial cult for right-wing purposes.

In other towns and cities, the Reichsbanner was able to cooperate with right-wing leagues. One example occurred in Halle in late December 1925. After a heated internal debate, the board of the Protestant Johannisgemeinde had taken a majority decision to invite representatives from the Reichsbanner alongside those of the Stahlhelm and the Kyffhäuserbund to the unveiling of a memorial plaque in their church. In order to avoid further conflicts, lots were cast to decide the order in which the three detachments should join the procession from the parish centre to the church.[39] In Vegesack, a suburb of Bremen, representatives of both Reichsbanner and Kyffhäuserbund gave speeches when the memorial was unveiled in June 1925. An article in the *Reichsbanner* journal used this opportunity to remind the members that a 'politics of abstinence' on these occasions would lead to nothing. Rather, republicans should ensure that right-wing circles could not claim the fallen for themselves alone.[40] Another turn of events occurred in Reutlingen in 1926. Here, as in many other towns, the building works subcommittee of the municipal authority was in charge of the planning process. It decided to invite the Reichsbanner to the opening ceremony, on the grounds that it was an 'association of republican front-line fighters'. In response, some of the right-wing military associations decided to boycott the unveiling of the memorial, and the bourgeois press commented that actually the Reichsbanner as a political group could not legitimately claim to be represented.[41]

Limits of republican representation

Overall, authorities in Bavaria took the most repressive stance against attempts by the Reichsbanner to commemorate the fallen soldiers. For a *Gau* meeting in Bamberg in 1924, a brief tribute to the fallen was

38 Gündisch, *Arbeiterbewegung*, pp. 257f.

39 'Monatsbericht Halle', n.d. [filed 4 January 1926]: StAM, Pol. Dir. 6888.

40 'Denkmalsweihe', *RB* no. 12, Beilage, 15 June 1925.

41 Paul Landmesser and Peter Päßler (eds.), *Wir lernen im Vorwärtsgehen! Dokumente zur Geschichte der Arbeiterbewegung in Reutlingen 1844–1949* (Heilbronn: Distel-Verlag, 1990), pp. 280–3 (quote on p. 281).

scheduled to take place in the local cemetery. Yet the local police prohibited this plan, and while the district government revoked this decision on appeal, this was not communicated in time, so the ceremony could not take place.[42] Explaining the decision, the Bavarian Ministry of the Interior pointed out that 'political gatherings' in open spaces were currently not allowed, following temporary regulations on a state of emergency.[43] While this position was formally correct, it revealed a similar point of view to the press reactions in Reutlingen. Although the sole purpose of the Reichsbanner was to support the Republic, even its commemorative activities were deemed to be 'political', a charge that was never levelled against comparable activities of the right-wing leagues. These interventions clearly reveal the hypocritical double standard applied by conservative civil servants and nationalist observers, and demonstrate the extent to which every act of war commemoration in Weimar Germany had – directly or indirectly – political implications.

Yet the exclusion of representatives of the left from the commemoration of the fallen was not only a deliberate strategy of the right-wing camp. To some extent, it was also the result of a self-exclusion, indicating that Reichsbanner functionaries and members were ambivalent about how to deal with moderate conservative veterans, and the Kyffhäuserbund in particular. In the Franconian town of Frankenwinheim, for instance, the local 'Krieger- und Kampfgenossenverein' explicitly invited the Reichsbanner branch in 1925 to attend the unveiling of the war memorial, a festive event that should also include the flag consecration of the conservative veterans' association. According to police informers, the leaders of the Reichsbanner *Gau* of Lower Franconia, who discussed the situation in a meeting, were not sure how to respond to this invitation. Some were sceptical about the prospect of a joint celebration with other 'black–white–red' organisations. Even more troubling was the prospect that 'a large part of those workers who have yet to be won over' for the Reichsbanner might be deterred by joint activities. Another consideration was the increased likelihood of violent brawls on such occasions.[44] Violent clashes could indeed occur when a strong labour movement presence was used to challenge public outings of the Kyffhäuserbund, as was the case in Neunkirchen in the Saar in July 1926.[45] In the case of

[42] Reichsbanner *Bundesvorstand* to Bavarian Ministry of the Interior, 30 October 1924: BArch, R 1501, 113501, fos. 46f.

[43] Bavarian Ministry of the Interior to Reich Ministry of the Interior, 10 January 1925: *ibid.*, fo. 49.

[44] Report dated 2 April 1925, n.a.: StAM, Pol. Dir. 6888.

[45] Linsmayer, *Politische Kultur*, p. 80.

Frankenwinheim, a decision was postponed until further inquiries into the local situation had been made.[46]

As this episode indicates, the joint presence of the Reichsbanner and right-wing associations at war memorials could put in jeopardy what was apparently the primary aim of the league in the eyes of many of its functionaries: to maximise mobilisation within the socialist camp, rather than trying to engage with war veterans in the moderate conservative camp and to relay the relevance of the Republic to them. This task was, ironically, left to individual Reichsbanner members. In Bavaria, as in other regions, quite a few members of the republican league also held membership in a local *Kriegerverein*. But shortly after the founding of the Reichsbanner, the Kyffhäuserbund declared a principled incompatibility between membership in the veterans' associations and in the republican league.[47] The Reichsbanner responded by formally recommending that individual rank-and-file members who were threatened with exclusion should fight it with all procedural means provided by the by-laws of the Kyffhäuserbund and its local branches. They should also try to engage the members in their local branch, and if possible win them over for the Reichsbanner. In public, however, the Reichsbanner would never pronounce opposition against the Kriegerbund, in order to uphold the façade of political neutrality.[48] This decision clearly left individual rank-and-file members in an untenable position. Rather than being able to rely on the collective might of the republican league, they were asked to drum up support for the Republic on their own. Ultimately, concerns about the internal strength and coherence of the socialist milieu trumped the Reichsbanner's interest in a mobilisation of all republican forces.

As the episode in Munich in 1924 had made clear, the Reichsbanner wanted to have a stake in official commemorations or, if that was not possible, stage its own ceremonies.[49] Decisions about the form and content of these ceremonies were left to those local or regional bodies who were responsible for setting them up. Only in the autumn of 1932 did the Reichsbanner executive board ask all branches to hold

[46] Report dated 2 April 1925, n.a.: StAM, Pol. Dir. 6888.

[47] 'Die Neutralität der Kriegervereine', *Vorwärts* no. 472, 7 October 1924.

[48] See the report on a decision taken by the Reichsbanner executive, 'Lagebericht', Pol. Dir. Munich, 5 February 1925: StAM, Pol. Dir. 6889. See also report, Pol. Dir. Munich, 9 October 1925 on a meeting of the Reichsbanner *Gau* leadership for Upper Bavaria: StAM, Pol. Dir. 6888.

[49] From 1927 onwards, joint commemorations of local branches with other veterans' leagues were only allowed with permission by the *Gau* executive; Rohe, *Reichsbanner*, p. 349. Individual members equally needed permission to join events staged by other combat leagues in uniform. See '2. Gaukonferenz am 21. und 22. September in München': BArch, SAPMO, Ry 12/II 113, 2, fos. 8f.

Totengedenkfeiern on All Saints' Day (1 November) or All Souls' Day (2 November) in Catholic or Protestant states respectively. On this occasion, it also issued detailed instructions on how to stage these ceremonies. First, they should involve mass demonstrations that would underscore the fact that many ex-servicemen stood in the republican camp. Secondly, speakers were meant to stress the patriotic attitude displayed by all 'democratic organisations' – i.e. the SPD – during the war. Yet the instructions stipulated that not only patriotic commitment and strength should be on display, but also the reasons why republicans were committed to honour the fallen soldiers. For this purpose, thirdly, the order of groups in a marching column was detailed: at the front, Reichsbanner members in uniform; in a second echelon, disabled war veterans; and in a third group, war widows and orphans in black clothes, followed again by uniformed Reichsbanner members.[50] Highlighting disabled veterans and widows, this particular marching order placed the themes of bereavement and trauma alongside those of patriotism and wartime service.

The Reichsbund as a stakeholder

Yet the inclusion of mutilated veterans and widows also suggests that these ceremonies were usually held in collaboration with the Social Democrat Reichsbund of disabled veterans and war dependants. From 1924 onwards, it was standard practice for these two mass organisations to stage joint rallies or commemorative events. In a less pronounced form of commemoration, a local Reichsbund functionary would speak at a ceremony for the fallen that was organised by the Reichsbanner.[51] But the Reichsbanner embraced a wider coalition of progressive and pacifist forces that also included the Deutsche Friedensgesellschaft (German Peace Society, or DFG). Founded in 1892, the DFG was the established core of the moderate bourgeois peace movement in Germany, with about 30,000 members in the mid 1920s. There was widespread consensus in the DFG that the Reichsbanner should find its unequivocal support, for instance among the representatives of local branches from Schleswig-Holstein who gathered in September 1924.[52] At this

[50] 'Rundschreiben des Gaus Oberbayern-Schwaben no. 22', 13 October 1932, referring to a directive of the *Bundesvorstand*: BArch, SAPMO, Ry 12/II 113, 3, fo. 99.

[51] 'Die Gefallenenehrung des Reichsbanners', *Münchener Post* no. 254, 2/3 November 1929; 'Totenehrungen zu Allerheiligen', *Münchener Post* no. 253, 3 November 1930. Both in StAM, Pol. Dir. 6886.

[52] Björn Marnau, '"Wir, die wir am Feuer von Chevreuse die Hand erhoben haben ...": Itzehoer Pazifisten in der Weimarer Republik', *Demokratische Geschichte* 10 (1996), 141–66 (pp. 144f.).

point, even the former captain-at-sea Heinz Kraschutzki (1891–1982), then head of the DFG branch in Itzehoe and, until his death, one of the most radical and outspoken German pacifists, was singing the praises of the Reichsbanner, which he had joined in 1925.[53] Writing in 1926, he commended the Reichsbanner as a 'bulwark of peace'. Some of the leaders of the republican league, he admitted, would overly stress its readiness to defend the fatherland. But the bulk of the rank-and-file members, Kraschutzki insisted, were deeply influenced by the horrors of the past war. Upon their return home in 1918 they 'had decided in their heart' that this had to be the last war, and almost unanimously joined in the call for 'no more war!'.[54]

Based on these perceptions among bourgeois pacifists and on overlapping aims, the DFG and the Reichsbanner co-organised a variety of public ceremonies throughout the mid 1920s in an alliance that often also included the Reichsbund. Some of these events were anti-war rallies such as a torchlight procession under the heading 'No more war!' in Itzehoe on Constitution Day, 11 August 1926.[55] Others directly confronted the right-wing rhetoric of commemoration used by 'nationalist-capitalist "benefactors of the people"' during the *Volkstrauertag*, or National Day of Mourning, in January, such as a jointly staged event in Hanover in 1926.[56] Yet as was the case during the 'no more war' movement in the early 1920s, this cooperation between bourgeois pacifists and Social Democrat Reichsbanner functionaries was never an easy one. Many of the latter were suspicious about the ulterior motives of the former, convinced that the DFG was simply desperate to drum up mass support for its cause, which it was so obviously lacking.[57] The simmering tensions could at first be contained,[58] but they did finally burst into the open in 1928, when the SPD – and the Reichsbanner in its wake – reluctantly supported the government decision to build the 'Battle Cruiser A' fleet. These were four armed ships, built within the limits on German armaments set by the Treaty of Versailles. Former general Paul von Schoenaich, a Reichsbanner member, was not the only pacifist who turned against the SPD government ministers, using aggressive rhetoric to accuse them of being influenced by financial circles. As

[53] See Helmut Donat, 'Kapitänleutnant a.D. Heinz Kraschutzki (1891–1982): Ein Offizier im Kampf für ein "anderes" Deutschland', in Wette and Donat, *Pazifistische Offiziere*, pp. 339–62 (p. 350).

[54] Cited in Marnau, 'Itzehoer Pazifisten', pp. 145–7.

[55] See *ibid.*, p. 149.

[56] Schneider, *'Nicht umsonst gefallen'?*, pp. 178f.

[57] See 'Friedlose Pazifisten', *RB* no. 21, 1 November 1925.

[58] See the conciliatory tone in the article by Paul Freiherr von Schoenaich, 'Reichsbanner und Pazifismus' (1925), in Schoenaich, *Zehn Jahre*, pp. 115–18.

he delivered his rant in mass meetings that were safeguarded by local Reichsbanner groups, members of the republican league were disappointed, to say the least.[59] Otto Hörsing used this opportunity to settle the scores with the radical pacifists in the Reichsbanner once and for all. During the AGM in 1928, he turned against draft resistance and other radical pacifist ideas, and against Otto Lehmann-Rußbüldt and Paul von Schoenaich in particular.[60] While these two pacifists remained in the republican league, Kraschutzki left both the Reichsbanner and the SPD, of which he had been a member since 1925.[61]

Severing the ties with radical pacifists?

Such a decisive severing of any ties with organised radical pacifism was, however, not necessarily implemented at the grassroots level. Even as late as 1927, the Reichsbanner executive was prohibiting local branches from staging joint events with the DFG,[62] but on a number of occasions Reichsbanner branches continued to cooperate not only with their regular partner, the Reichsbund, but with the DFG as well. One anti-war rally, jointly staged by these three organisations, took place in Hanover on 4 August 1929, and was attended by a crowd of 20,000 people. Both in its timing and symbolism, and with the broad coalition standing behind it, the rally continued the tradition of the 'no more war' movement during the early 1920s. The slogan itself was repeatedly used in the speeches, not least by a certain 'comrade' Elle, a war-blinded representative of the *Gau* executive of the Reichsbund. Elle urged the gathered crowd to join in the fight against those who portrayed the 'human mass murder' (*Massenmorden*) of war in a 'rose-tinted light', trying to seduce the youth in order to 'lead them as victims to the slaughter of the next war'. And he was keen for the people to empower themselves, not only to pay 'lip service' to the motto 'No more war!', but to work actively and with force towards it. Such activism, he was sure, could be fuelled by recollections of the autumn of 1918, 'when the people took their destiny in their own hands and crowns rolled into the dust'.[63]

59 For the example of a Schoenaich talk in Bremen on 26 September 1928, see 'Ausschnitt aus dem Lagebericht Nr. 12 vom 6.10.1928': StA Bremen, 4, 65, 1146, fos. 38f.

60 Rohe, *Reichsbanner*, pp. 182–8; on context, see Ursula Büttner, *Weimar: Die überforderte Republik 1918–1933. Leistung und Versagen in Staat, Gesellschaft, Wirtschaft und Kultur* (Stuttgart: Klett–Cotta, 2008), pp. 358–63.

61 See Donat, 'Kraschutzki', p. 352.

62 Rohe, *Reichsbanner*, p. 186.

63 'Denn die Menschen wollen Frieden, Frieden jedes Menschenherz', *Reichsbund* no. 16, 25 August 1929, Beilage Heim und Garten. This was only one of a number of similar events in August 1929 in Hanover. See Schneider, *'Nicht umsonst gefallen'?*, p. 179n98.

Figure 6 The Reichsbanner branch in Eberswalde, a town close to Berlin, displays the breaking of a sword as a symbol of proletarian anti-militarism, together with the slogan 'No more war!'. From the cover of *Himmelfahrt 1927: Reichsbanner Schwarz–Rot–Gold, Kameradschaft Eberswalde* (Eberswalde: n.p., 1927).

Elle's forceful invocation of the motto 'No more war!' was anything but exceptional. The slogan encapsulated the pacifist underpinnings of war commemorations by both Reichsbund and Reichsbanner, and was frequently used at all levels of these organisations and across the Reich.[64] Reichsbund members from Berlin adorned their lorry with the slogan when they took to the outskirts of the city on Constitution Day, 11 August 1931, in order to drum up support for their cause.[65] As these examples indicate, the two pro-republican veterans' associations

[64] For example in Stuttgart, with Kurt Schumacher, the post-1945 SPD leader, as a main speaker: 'Nie wieder Krieg! Die Gedächtnisfeier der Kriegsopfer Groß-Stuttgarts', *Schwäbische Tagwacht* no. 182, 5 August 1924: HStASt, E 130b, Bü 3846.

[65] See the photo in *Reichsbund* no. 17, 5 September 1931, p. 187. For the use of this slogan in the Reichsbund press see 'Die Kriegsopfer zum 11. August', *ibid.* no. 15, 1 August 1927, p. 147.

followed a different schedule in their invocation of the past war and their commemoration of fallen soldiers. Other stakeholders in the national discourse of commemoration had made their claims earlier and more forcefully, and had thus gained a head start. From its inception in 1919/20, the Volksbund deutsche Kriegsgräberfürsorge (People's League for German War Graves) had campaigned to celebrate a *Volkstrauertag* (national day of mourning) on Reminiscere, the second Sunday during Lent.[66] With a peak middle-class membership of 138,000 in 1930, mostly either war veterans or bereaved, the Volksbund was a powerful nationalist pressure group that successfully lobbied the Reich government to support a heroic style of commemoration.[67] The Reichsbund immediately recognised that the epithet 'national' for this holiday would only be a pretence to indulge in right-wing nationalism and revanchism. A national day of mourning, it argued, would only be justified once proper provision for disabled veterans had been guaranteed. Meanwhile, it was preferable to celebrate popular citizenship and a 'declaration of loyalty' to the new Republic, a demand that implied the form of a constitution day.[68] But nationalist circles clearly had much better leverage in the complicated negotiations about a national day of mourning, which had to take the interests of the *Länder* into account. From 1925 onwards, although not legally binding, *Volkstrauertag* was officially celebrated on Reminiscere across the Reich. Only Bavaria was an exception. Here, the Catholic majority continued to mourn the fallen on All Souls' Day.[69]

Throughout the Weimar Republic, the celebration of the *Volkstrauertag* employed a clearly discernible revanchist rhetoric, which also demanded that differences of class, party and confession be abandoned during the mourning, in favour of a unified people's community.[70] Social Democrat newspapers did not mince their words in their mockery of the – in their view pathetic – formulas that were used to conjure up the notion of

[66] Fritz Schellack, *Nationalfeiertage in Deutschland von 1871 bis 1945* (Frankfurt am Main: Lang, 1990), pp. 150f.

[67] See Goebel, *Great War*, p. 22; Alexandra Kaiser, *Von Helden und Opfern: Eine Geschichte des Volkstrauertags* (Frankfurt am Main: Campus, 2010), pp. 45–9 (figure on p. 47).

[68] 'Brauchen wir einen nationalen Trauertag?', *Reichsbund* no. 4, 15 February 1921; see 'Stellungnahme der Hinterbliebenen zum nationalen Trauertag', *ibid.* no. 7, 1 April 1921.

[69] Schellack, *Nationalfeiertage*, pp. 204, 231–41.

[70] See Janina Fuge, '"Ohne Tod und Sterben kein Sieg": Die gefallenen Soldaten des Ersten Weltkrieges in der Hamburger Erinnerungskultur der Weimarer Republik', *Historical Social Research* 34 (2009), 356–73 (pp. 360–7); Kaiser, *Von Helden und Opfern*, pp. 58–63.

national unity during the *Volkstrauertag*. Unity – 'in what spirit? That is the issue!' commented the *Volkswille* in Hanover in 1926. Any commemoration of the fallen would only make sense if it ensured that men were never again to die on the battlefield, and thus made days of mourning in the future superfluous.[71] In 1930, Otto Braun, the Social Democrat Prussian prime minister and Reichsbanner member, used a speech in remembrance of the successful popular fight against the Kapp putsch to lash out at the right-wing underpinnings of the *Volkstrauertag*. He would not accept a 'prescribed day and hour' at which he should mourn the fallen of the First World War, even less so as the ceremonies of the 'private association for *Kriegsgräberfürsorge*' would raise the 'suspicion that the remembrance of our dead was abused to nourish and keep alive a certain pernicious idea of revenge'.[72]

This critique was spot on, in particular as it highlighted the dubious way in which the organisation of a national holiday was left to a private pressure group. The Reichswehr minister, Wilhelm Groener, was furious, and complained in a letter to SPD chancellor Hermann Müller.[73] But both Reichswehr and Reich government supported the celebration of the *Volkstrauertag*. Republican activists thus had to look for alternative dates on which they could mourn and commemorate the fallen. A representative of the Reichsbanner head office hinted in 1925 that the league might throw its weight in support of 11 November into the debate on the national day of mourning.[74] But important as this date was as a day of liberation for republican veterans, among a wider public it was tainted with the stigma of defeat and hence impossible to implement. In practice, Reichsbanner activists thus had three options to celebrate the remembrance of their fallen comrades.

First, they included a brief tribute to the war dead whenever they celebrated a *Bannerweihe*, the festive event during which the red–black–gold banner of a local branch was consecrated. Secondly, Reichsbanner members mourned the fallen when they gathered for the annual celebration of the Republic on 11 August. As Constitution Day, this was an official holiday from 1921 onwards, which the government and all pro-republican organisations used to represent the inclusive citizenship

[71] Cited in Schneider, *'Nicht umsonst gefallen'?*, p. 177; see 'Totenfest in Magdeburg', *Volksstimme* no. 273, 22 November 1927; 'Eine "neutrale" Gedenkfeier', *Volksstimme*, no. 276, 26 November 1929; Fuge, 'Soldaten', pp. 368f.

[72] The speech was covered in *Vorwärts* on 17 March 1930, and is cited in a letter by Wilhelm Groener to Chancellor Hermann Müller, 24 March 1930: BArch, R 43/I, 712, fos. 54f.

[73] *Ibid.*

[74] 'Reichsbanner Schwarz–Rot–Gold', *Münchner Neueste Nachrichten* no. 276, 6 October 1925.

rights underpinned by the Weimar Republic by symbolic means.[75] Thirdly, Reichsbanner branches held separate events dedicated to the commemoration of the fallen on *Totensonntag*; another option was All Saints' Day, 1 November, in Catholic regions.[76] Both dates allowed the Reichsbanner to tap into the sombre autumn mood when the leaves were falling, and thus to foreground the earnest 'solemnity' of their commemorations as a key distinguishing feature.[77] Such rhetoric marked a direct contrast to the *Volkstrauertag*, situated in spring, which deliberately tied the remembrance to the need for a cyclical rebirth of the nation amidst its alleged post-Versailles despair.[78]

A fourth option was, to my knowledge, systematically used only by Social Democrats in the Saar region, and then only for the short period from 1925 to 1928. At any rate, the Saar was a special case, as the Treaty of Versailles had put it under a mandate of the League of Nations until a referendum would decide whether it be included in France or Germany. Meanwhile, the French could exploit the coal mines in the region, and integrated it into a customs union. This specific political setting and their undisputed strength encouraged the Social Democrats in the region to organise 'anti-war days' in various towns. They took place on 1 or 3 August, thus commemorating the onset of the Great War as a historical catastrophe. But it was not only the date that was meant to drive home frontal opposition to war; the speeches were too. What was special about these ceremonies was that Else Stratmann-Braun – the wife of Max Braun, later the head of the SPD in the Saar – gave speeches, in which she vividly described the horrors of war and highlighted females' mission to act as 'defenders of life'. The strong female presence during these events was also marked by the inclusion of mixed choirs, while all other elements of the ritual, including its situation in front of the local war memorial, closely resembled the pattern described below.[79]

Republican rituals of commemoration

Whenever local Reichsbanner branches mourned the fallen soldiers, often in conjunction with their Reichsbund comrades, their rituals followed a highly circumscribed pattern, which was repeated year after

[75] See Achilles, 'Celebrating'.

[76] See the sceptical commentary 'Der Totensonntag', *Lübecker Volksbote* no. 275, 25 November 1929.

[77] 'Totenehrungen zu Allerheiligen'; 'Novembergedanken', *RB* no. 22, Gaubeilage, 15 November 1927.

[78] Schellack, *Nationalfeiertage*, p. 192.

[79] Linsmayer, *Politische Kultur*, pp. 78f.

year.[80] In marching columns, the republican veterans would head towards a memorial stone or plaque in a local cemetery, or to the graves of soldiers who had died at the front. If the local branch had been able to set up a band, it would march in front of the column. The black–red–gold banners, carried in the midst of the detachment, were adorned with a black crape. Lined up in front of the memorial stone, those attending would then often listen to the tune of the 'Old Dutch Thanksgiving Prayer' ('Altniederländisches Dankgebet'). This song was originally written by Adrianus Valerius in the early seventeenth century, and referred to the Dutch campaign against the Spanish in 1597. In 1877, the Viennese Joseph Weyl translated the text into German, in a version that was later rendered as 'We Gather Together' by Theodore Baker in English. In the German text, the three verses invoke the notion of God's support for a righteous battle, and were thus a potent and widely used symbol of the close alliance between Protestant Church and the Hohenzollern in imperial Germany. Despite the collapse of the monarchy in 1918, the song retained its potency and was a staple of right-wing commemorations throughout Weimar, with clear anti-republican connotations.[81] Devoted republicans obviously did not share the political implications of the text. But they apparently liked the tune, written by the Viennese composer Eduard Kremser, which had been popular among front-line soldiers during the war, and which alone was played during Reichsbanner memorial ceremonies.[82]

Next on the agenda of a republican commemoration was often another brief musical interlude, usually presented by a choir of local *Arbeitersänger*. Founded in 1908, the Deutsche Arbeiter-Sängerbund

[80] For the following, see for instance the descriptions in 'Die Gefallenenehrung des Reichsbanners'; 'Totenehrungen zu Allerheiligen'; and 'Totenehrung in Karlshorst', *RB* no. 1, Gaubeilage Berlin-Brandenburg, 1 January 1927. For Saxony, see Voigt, *Kampfbünde*, p. 345; see also Harter, 'Bürgertum', pp. 281–3; and 'Totensonntag in Magdeburg', *Volksstimme* no. 278, 27 November 1928. For a slightly different procedure in a ritual that took place in the Protestant Martini Church in Bremen on 22 February 1925 – the first anniversary of the foundation of the Reichsbanner – see 'Bericht über die Veranstaltung des Reichsbanners', 23 February 1925: StA Bremen, 4, 65, 1028, fos. 75–7. On some occasions, the Reichsbund in Magdeburg organised commemorative events not in the cemetery, but in a banqueting hall, accompanied by classical music. See 'Totenfest in Magdeburg'; and 'Totensonntags-Feiern', *Volksstimme* no. 274, 24 November 1931.

[81] Kaiser, *Von Helden und Opfern*, pp. 39–41. The Nazis, to be sure, had to change the song, as it included as the final line the words 'God give us freedom'; George L. Mosse, *The Nationalization of the Masses: Political Symbolism and Mass Movements in Germany from the Napoleonic Wars through the Third Reich* (Ithaca, NY; London: Cornell University Press, 1991), p. 147.

[82] See explicitly 'Toten-Gedächtnisfeiern', *Münchener Post* no. 253, 2 November 1931; 'Totenehrungen zu Allerheiligen'.

was part and parcel of the socialist working-class milieu, with a peak membership of 263,000 during the Weimar years. Its main purpose was to foster the convivial practice of four-part singing in male choirs. To some extent, the artistic practice of the *Arbeitersänger* tried to emulate the highbrow ideals of German classical music, and idolised Beethoven in particular. Obviously, though, socialist proletarian choral singing also had a strong political impetus, and stood in direct competition to the male choirs in the nationalist camp. Throughout the Weimar Republic, the *Arbeitersänger* were immersed in attempts to express their ambivalent feelings about the Great War in verse and song. Their symbolic expressions of the war experience vacillated between praise and reverence for the sacrifice of the soldiers, and bitter indictments against the cruelty of a war machine driven by capitalist interests and Prussian militarism.[83] Socialist labour movement choirs understood themselves as opponents of war, and as such they were an almost natural ally for the Reichsbanner and its commemorative rituals.

Figure 7 Reichsbanner members in Weißenfels, a town in the Prussian province of Saxony, lower their banners during a commemorative ceremony (*c.* 1927).

[83] See Dietmar Klenke and Franz Walter, 'Der Deutsche Arbeiter-Sängerbund', in Dietmar Klenke, Peter Lilje and Franz Walter, *Arbeitersänger und Volksbühnen in der Weimarer Republik* (Bonn: J. H. W. Dietz, 1992), pp. 73–85, 91, 122–5, 153.

After the choral section, short speeches followed, usually delivered by a Reichsbund and a Reichsbanner representative. Then, a laurel wreath with black–red–gold ribbon was laid down at the memorial site, to which the banners of the Reichsbanner branch were lowered in honour of the fallen. This tribute was completed to the tune of 'I Had a Comrade'. Written by the Romantic poet Ludwig Uhland in 1809, the song encapsulated the grief caused by the death of a close comrade. It was a staple of all nationalist commemorative rituals throughout the Weimar Republic.[84] The fact that Reichsbanner rituals used it as well is indicative of the extent to which republican veterans also tapped into the discourse of comradeship, although they usually only sang the first stanza, which did not, as the second, invoke mythical comradeship even beyond the death of one comrade.[85] It should also not be overlooked that the Reichsbanner often used a slightly different version, which included the following lines:

> We had a comrade.
> He joined us on a hiking trip.
> He was with us.
> He gathered around the flag,
> Rallied around Black–Red–Gold.[86]

Rather than articulating the notion of male bonding in the wake of shared sacrifice in battle, as Uhland's version, this verse conjured up an entirely different set of connotations. Here, the accent was on shared activism and on peaceful convivial pastimes such as hiking, all meant to underpin the one thing that mattered most for Reichsbanner members: their unequivocal support for the republican colours. On some occasions, the song of the good comrade was followed by another performance by the *Arbeitersänger*. This was usually the funeral chorale 'Silent Sleeps the Singer', for which the original nineteenth-century lyrics by Thomas Moore had been adapted in a version that was widely used in the socialist choral movement.[87] After that, the ceremony was concluded, and the crowd dispersed.

These rituals were a crucial element of the cult of the fallen soldiers: an element whose significance and performative qualities are often

[84] Kühne, *Belonging*, p. 18.

[85] 'Gründungsfeier des Reichsbanners Schwarz–Rot–Gold, Ortsgruppe Hermelingen', *Bremer Volkszeitung* no. 255, 30 October 1924.

[86] 'Wir hatten einen Kameraden. / Er zog mit uns auf Fahrt. / Er war mit auf dem Plane. / Er stand mit um die Fahne, / um Schwarz–Rot–Gold geschart.' Cited by Mintert, *'Sturmtrupp'*, p. 17.

[87] See *Verzeichnis der im Bundesverlage erschienenen Männer-, Frauen-, gemischten und Kinderchöre* (Berlin: Deutscher Arbeiter-Sängerbund, n.d. [1930]), p. 17.

not fully appreciated.[88] As all rituals, they were repetitive, hardly ever changing their form over time, as their main purpose was to create a certainty that specific expectations were not going to be disappointed. This core function goes a long way to explain the apparent similarities between republican ceremonies for the mourning of the dead and those of the right-wing veterans' associations. Rituals cannot be understood in terms of a means–ends rationality. Rather, they helped to open up the participants for an emotional journey, to make them receptive to the experience of the sublime. In that perspective, even a song such as the 'Dutch Thanksgiving Prayer' could have its place in a republican and predominantly secular ceremony, as it brought back recollections and feelings the veterans had had on the battlefield. The bodily and sensual registers of experience were pivotal for the enactment of a ritual, and the music and choral singing served to support these elements. The content of the songs, however, was either firmly situated in the socialist camp, or had been, like the song of the 'good comrade', adapted for that context. While the mourning of dead comrades was the primary purpose of these ceremonies, they also served to 'endorse the valency' of specific values by symbolic means, and to translate mythological notions into a sequence of actions.[89] And in the context of Reichsbanner ceremonies, the core values were the rejection of war as a political means and the support for the Republic, also epitomised by the use of the republican colours.

Verbal elements of commemoration

In the context of the commemorative ritual, verbal elements apart from the chorales had only a limited space, and the speeches were thus usually short. In the most abridged form of delivery, they basically admonished the living not to forget the fallen.[90] In more elaborate versions, they drove home at least three major points. A Reichsbund representative would express the pain of losing a father, brother or son, and would describe how the 'scars' would 'bleed again' on a day that was devoted to their memory. Then, the Reichsbanner representative would invoke the 'horror' of war, highlight the mourning among the families, and stress that both losers and victors had been ravaged by the war. He would also insist that the struggle for peace was an obligation vis-à-vis

[88] See the pertinent remarks by Sabine Behrenbeck, *Der Kult um die toten Helden: Nationalsozialistische Mythen, Riten und Symbole 1923 bis 1945* (Vierow: SH-Verlag, 1996), pp. 50–7.

[89] *Ibid.*, pp. 51f.

[90] 'Die Gefallenenehrung des Reichsbanners'.

the fallen comrades and their sacrifice.[91] He would sometimes add that the remembrance of the war dead should include all those who had 'fallen for the German Republic', and close with the words that 'We declare our loyalty to the cause of peace!'[92] On most other occasions, the speaker would end with the call 'No more war!'.[93] Such a basic pacifist statement could be expanded or qualified in various directions. In cities where the Majority Social Democrats (MSPD) had been the stronger wing during the years from party break-up in 1917 to reunification with the Independent Social Democratic Party (USPD) in September 1922, some Reichsbanner speakers would stress that Social Democrats were in principle supporters of justified national defence. Yet in regions like Saxony, which had previously had a strong USPD tradition, the justification of national defence was never, ever mentioned, and speakers would instead focus on the need for international reconciliation as the key lesson of the Great War.[94] But even the Bavarian SPD leader Erhard Auer, firmly positioned on the right wing of the party, never highlighted the need for national defence as one of the key lessons of the Great War in his many speeches in remembrance of the fallen. At the founding meeting of the Munich branch in July 1924, those who attended rose from their seats when he paid tribute to the fallen, insisting that they had not fought for the 'rulers and kings, but for the German people'. On this occasion, Auer also argued that Germany had not lost the war alone, but in fact 'all of Europe' had, as governments were struggling to respond to the post-war crisis.[95] Speaking in 1927 at the flag consecration of a Reichsbanner *Kameradschaft* in Munich, Auer stressed that the fallen had sacrificed their lives 'for a Germany that was freer and more just in terms of social equality'.[96]

Quite often, strong rhetorical support for national defence in Reichsbanner ceremonies was actually offered by leading German Democratic Party (DDP) members of the republican league. During a tribute to the fallen in the Königsberg branch in 1924 for example, Ferdinand Friedensburg (1886–1972) spoke. Then a county executive (*Landrat*) in West Prussia, a Reichsbanner member and DDP candidate for the Reichstag election, Friedensburg later became a leading

[91] See the template speech provided for the Reichsbanner commemorative rituals: G. Wilke (ed.), *Reden für republikanische Gelegenheiten und für Reichsbanner-Veranstaltungen* (Berlin: Hoffmann, 1926), pp. 31f.

[92] 'Totenehrungen zu Allerheiligen'.

[93] 'Totensonntag in Magdeburg'; Wilke, *Reden*, p. 32.

[94] Voigt, *Kampfbünde*, pp. 345f.

[95] 'Gründungsversammlung des Bundes Republikanischer Kriegsteilnehmer'.

[96] See *Münchener Post*, no. 240, 17 October 1927: StAM, Pol. Dir. 6887.

Christian Democrat in the post-war Federal Republic. Speaking in 1924, he insisted that the moral 'corruption' of the German people during the war had only begun when the 'poison of greed for profit' had started to undermine the 'notion of defence' and the cohesion of the national community. Yet on the same occasion Horst Bärensprung, the Social Democrat Reichsbanner managing director from Magdeburg, steered clear of such blatantly nationalist rhetoric. In a tribute to the local giant of idealist philosophy, he instead referred to Kant's notion of 'perpetual peace' and insisted, in accordance with Kant's treatise on this topic, that 'the constitution of each state [had] to be republican' in order to abolish war for good.[97]

Repeatedly, speakers at Reichsbanner events turned the remembrance of the fallen into an elaborate and detailed rhetorical swipe against warmongers and the nationalist right. On Sunday 22 February 1925, a year after the founding call for the Reichsbanner had been issued, the branch in Bremen called for a festive celebration of republican values. The day began at 9am with a memorial service to the fallen in the Protestant Martini Church. After the first ritual elements – tribute to the black–red–gold banners that stood next to the altar, the chorus 'Silent Sleeps the Singer' – Emil Felden went up to the pulpit. Felden (1874–1959) was not only the pastor of St Martini, but also a libertarian, progressive theologian on the left wing of the Lutheran Church. In 1919, he had joined the SPD, for which he briefly served as Reichstag deputy in 1923/4.[98] Felden spoke only briefly to the 2,000 people who attended this ceremony, reciting a poem called 'No More War'. After another musical interlude, First Lieutenant Benno Georges of the Hamburg police mounted the pulpit as the main speaker. He denounced the 'black–white–red' camp as 'warmongers' who would never dare show the true face of war. To make his point, he mentioned those severely mutilated veterans with a face like a 'hole' who were still hidden in hospitals. It struck the police constable who filed a report on this gathering as particularly noteworthy that Georges claimed 'the dead of the World War for the labouring people alone', without ever mentioning that also 'other circles of the German people' had to mourn their dead.

[97] 'Fahnenweihe des Reichsbanners Schwarz–Rot–Gold in Königsberg', *Vossische Zeitung*, 24 November 1924: BArch, R 8034 II, 2869, fo. 133. In Magdeburg, Erich Roßmann, head of the Reichsbund, reminded the audience how, during the war, people had despaired about the notion of national defence; 'Totenfest in Magdeburg', *Volksstimme* no. 273, 22 November 1927.

[98] 'Bericht über die Veranstaltung des Reichsbanners', 23 February 1925: StA Bremen, 4, 65, 1028, fo. 75. On Felden see Horst Kalthoff, 'Felden, Emil', in *Biographisch-Bibliographisches Kirchenlexikon*, ed. Friedrich Wilhelm Bautz, 33 vols., Vol. XXII (Nordhausen: Bautz, 2003), pp. 316–19.

Georges thus invoked a higher, transcendent meaning for their death, but it was confined to the socialist working class. In the final section of his speech, Georges turned from commemoration to direct political indictment against the war profiteers, referring to industrial firms who had exported steel, but could not meet the demand for barbed wire as the war dragged on. This was a gap that the workers then 'had to fill with their bodies'.[99]

With their commemorative rituals, Reichsbund and Reichsbanner reaffirmed moderate pacifist values and claimed, as the example of Benno Georges demonstrates, the remembrance of the fallen soldiers for the labouring people. In some respects, such a rhetoric was more exclusive than that of right-wing commemorations. During these, the speakers always stressed that the fallen had made their sacrifice as part of a larger collective, the German nation, and that their example could thus help to overcome the deplorable fault-lines and political divisions within Germany. Yet on the other hand, republican commemorations were far more inclusive than their right-wing counterparts. They did not treat the ordinary soldiers as mere 'extras', as the right-wing camp did, in rituals that were dominated by former officers.[100] And they reached out to the former enemies and tried to foster international bonds of solidarity. These activities were an important part of what historian John Horne has described as 'cultural demobilisation'. In these endeavours, German war veterans tried to find appropriate 'gestures, words and practices of reconciliation' that would allow them to face their former enemies in personal encounters. Rather than continuing to dehumanise the enemies, as the radical proponents of the right-wing camp did, republican veterans tried to reach out to their counterparts in shared revulsion against war itself as the real atrocity.[101]

Reaching out to French war veterans

As such, bonds of solidarity and reconciliation between the former enemies could be extended to all the former belligerent nations. In practice, though, the Social Democrat war veterans in the Reichsbund and the Reichsbanner prioritised close relations with French veterans above everything else. The reasons for this preference were never explicitly mentioned, but it is fair to assume that one important point was

[99] 'Bericht über die Veranstaltung des Reichsbanners', fos. 75f. Georges had used similar pacifist rhetoric on an earlier occasion in Hermelingen; see 'Gründungsfeier des Reichsbanners Schwarz–Rot–Gold, Ortsgruppe Hermelingen'.
[100] Überegger, *Erinnerungskriege*, p. 152.
[101] See Horne, 'Kulturelle Demobilmachung', pp. 142f.

the availability of clearly defined counterparts on the other bank of the Rhine. With the mass mobilisation of French veterans who were – among others – organised in the Union fédérale, German republicans could rely on a partner to which they could address their hopes for reconciliation.[102] Attempts to understand the predicament of the French people during and after the war permeated the cultural practices and sociability of Reichsbund and Reichsbanner at all levels.

In the press of both leagues, many articles conveyed impressions of journeys to the former battlefields in France. Trying to raise empathy with the plight of the civilians who lived in the former war-zone, they detailed the devastation caused by the war, but also noted the fact that nature had, over time, been able to 'heal almost all wounds of the earth'.[103] Overall, the former battlefields 'symbolised the exhortation to gain peace'.[104] During their regular social events, local Reichsbanner chapters heard talks about the situation in France. On one occasion in Munich in 1929, a Reichsbanner member who had been living in France before the war was keen to debunk some of the most common myths. The French had not held any hatred against the Germans, he insisted, and had not prepared a war against them. Also, there had not been any displays of enthusiasm for war in August 1914. In the army, relations between privates and officers were characterised by mutual trust, and even service in the often loathed Foreign Legion was still better than the drill in German army barracks.[105]

In the Reichsbanner branch in Vegesack, Paul Günzel, a teacher from nearby Bremen, regularly gave talks on his war experiences, at which he showed photos using a reflecting projector. In 1928, he talked about a recent 'peace journey to French battlefields'. Among his audience were not only war veterans, but also women and children, and Günzel gave such a vivid description of the plight of the French population that the

[102] There had been initial contacts in 1924 with the Fédération Interalliée des Anciens Combattants (FIDAC), then headed by Sir Ian Hamilton, president of the British Legion. See 'Der Kongreß der FIDAC', *RB* no. 10, 1 October 1924. In 1927, the Reichsbanner accepted an official invitation to a FIDAC congress in Luxembourg, but that was a one-off, and was not followed up. See Rohe, *Reichsbanner*, pp. 147f.

[103] 'Auferstandenes Land: Verwischte Spuren', *Reichsbund* no. 8, 20 April 1931; see Walter Hammer, 'Verdun: Eine Woche in Frankreich, Juli 1926', *RB* no. 21, 1 November 1926; Ernst Glaeser, 'Im Lande der Gefallenen', *RB* no. 41, Beilage, 25 November 1928; 'Das größte Schlachtfeld des Krieges: Eine Verdun-Fahrt', *RB* no. 30, Beilage, 27 July 1929; and 'Zwischen Verdun und den Argonnen', *RB* no. 14, Beilage, 4 April 1930.

[104] B. Fehl, 'Auf den Schlachtfeldern von Verdun', *RB* no. 24, Gaubeilage Berlin-Brandenburg, 14 June 1930.

[105] 'Versammlung der Kameradschaft Schlachthausviertel', 13 March 1929: StAM, Pol. Dir. 6887.

latter also got an idea of the 'terror and horror' of war. Towards the end of his talk, Günzel referred to the brothers Fritz and Franz von Unruh as two exemplary role models for the necessary conversion to the cause of peace. Both had volunteered in August 1914, but had soon, under the impact of their war experiences, turned to outright 'proponents of the idea of peace'.[106]

Fritz von Unruh (1885–1970) in particular had a firm place in the list of authors who were associated with the ideas of the Reichsbanner. Coming from an aristocratic family with a long tradition of army service, Unruh served as an active cavalry officer before the war, while also kick-starting a career as a playwright, on which he focused after resigning from his military post in 1912. But in 1914 he joined the army again as a volunteer. His front-line experiences started a complicated and drawn-out process of disillusionment and inner reflection. Ultimately, the counter-revolutionary violence exerted by government troops in Berlin in January 1919 turned him into an outspoken pacifist, who devoted both some of his literary works and many speeches to the cause.[107] Unruh was also a Reichsbanner member, and served on the non-executive board of the league.[108] It was indeed highly pertinent to mention Fritz von Unruh in a talk about a journey to former battlefields in France, as Günzel had done. From the mid 1920s onwards, reconciliation with France stood at the heart of Unruh's pacifist writings, and he often referred to his 'Verdun oath' – 'returning from the trenches of death' – as the reason why he had been converted to the pacifist cause. It does not diminish his activism that his pretentious prose was loathed by critics, and that – according to the diplomat and writer Harry Count Kessler – the snobbish tone of his writings on France was not well received in Paris.[109]

At the official level of involvement in international veterans' politics, the two republican associations followed a different trajectory. First inaugurated by a conference in 1925, veterans' associations across Europe started to cooperate in a more formal manner with the founding of the CIAMAC (Conférence internationale des associations de victimes de la guerre et anciens combattants) in 1926. This network

[106] 'Eine Friedensreise über Frankreichs Schlachtfelder', *Bremer Volkszeitung*, 20 October 1928: StA Bremen, 7, 88, 50/2.

[107] See Hans-Joachim Schröder, 'Fritz von Unruh (1885–1970): Kavallerieoffizier, Dichter und Pazifist', in Wette and Donat, *Pazifistische Offiziere*, pp. 319–37.

[108] 'Polizeidirektion Nürnberg-Fürth, Sonderbericht Nr. 162/II/29, Anlage', 24 October 1929: StA Bremen, 4, 65, 1034; see his speech in Berlin, cited in *Vossische Zeitung*, 19 January 1932: GStA, I. HA, Rep. 77, Tit. 4043, no. 352, fo. 6.

[109] Schröder, 'Fritz von Unruh', pp. 331f.

included associations of both disabled soldiers and veterans, mostly from the moderate bourgeois and moderate socialist end of the political spectrum. Representing twenty-four associations from ten countries, it also included the Reichsbund.[110] Prior to these multilateral links, the disabled veterans of the Reichsbund had already been in contact with the French Union fédérale in 1921. The first meeting took place on neutral ground in Geneva, based on an initiative by Henri Pichot, the long-serving head of the Union fédérale. Pichot later recalled the awkward feelings among his delegation, as 'the war had not been over for so long'. In their view, 'the Germans were still the "boches"' and now 'they were supposed to shake their hands?'.[111] But the ice was broken, and even the Ruhr crisis in 1923 brought these contacts only to a temporary halt.

For the Reichsbanner, it was more difficult to become a regular member of the network of veterans provided by the CIAMAC. French veterans were initially reluctant to cooperate with the Reichsbanner, as they noted the paramilitary elements in its public appearance with some suspicion, and also perceived it as driven by the political interests of one particular party.[112] From the Reichsbanner's point of view, the CIAMAC was not a perfect match, as it was predominantly concerned with the more technical interests of disabled war veterans and war widows in welfare state provision. Nonetheless, the Reichsbanner was first invited to a CIAMAC meeting in Vienna in 1927. On this occasion, a representative from the Magdeburg head office renewed the commitment to international reconciliation in the framework of the League of Nations. The specific interests of the disabled veterans aside, the most important issue was 'to organise the peace'.[113] With observer status, Reichsbanner delegations attended subsequent meetings of the CIAMAC, before the league finally joined as a regular member in

[110] Christian Weiß, '"Soldaten des Friedens": Die pazifistischen Veteranen und Kriegsopfer des "Reichsbundes" und ihre Kontakte zu den französischen *anciens combattants* 1919–1933', in Hardtwig, *Politische Kulturgeschichte*, pp. 183–204 (pp. 190f.).

[111] See *ibid.*, pp. 188f. The quote is from an article by the conservative journalist Paul H. Distelbarth, who established his early contacts with France in the context of the Reichsbund. See Paul H. Distelbarth, 'Die Kriegsteilnehmer' (1936), in *Das andere Frankreich: Aufsätze zur Gesellschaft, Kultur und Politik Frankreichs und zu den deutsch–französischen Beziehungen 1932–1953*, ed. Hans Manfred Bock (Berne: Peter Lang, 1997), p. 216.

[112] Elliot Pennell Fagerberg, 'The "Anciens combattants" and French Foreign Policy', Ph.D. dissertation (University of Geneva, 1966), pp. 155, 170.

[113] Karl Mayr, 'Die "CIAMAC" in Wien: Auf dem Wege zu einer internationalen Einheitsfront der Kriegsteilnehmer', *RB* no. 20, 15 October 1927.

1932.[114] But the Reichsbanner also established direct links to French veterans' associations: to the Union fédérale and the much smaller Fédération nationale in particular. From the late 1920s, leading representatives of French veterans' leagues – including René Cassin and André Liautey, a member of the CIAMAC executive and head of its French committee – regularly appeared at Reichsbanner gatherings. In return, functionaries of the republican league travelled to France. The driving force behind these links, and their main representative, was the former staff officer Karl Mayr, who was ultimately recognised for these efforts with an honorary membership of the Fédération nationale.[115]

The various high-level contacts between representatives of the two German republican associations and the *anciens combattants* had at least three distinguishable aims: first, they provided a platform for the advancement of the pacifist ideas of socialist veterans; secondly, they allowed the Reichsbund in particular to stress that even disabled and severely mutilated veterans were not simply victims of war, but had also been soldiers;[116] and thirdly, they provided popular resonance for the politics of reconciliation between France and Germany that Gustav Stresemann and Aristide Briand had inaugurated in 1925. This support continued even during the early 1930s, at a time when the Brüning government pursued a tough stance vis-à-vis France and effectively abandoned the western orientation of German foreign politics.[117] Ultimately, though, the contacts between French and German war veterans served to drive home the key message that narrow-minded nationalist agendas were inadequate to shape a peaceful post-war world, and to emphasise the internationalism of the republican veterans on both sides.

The rhetoric of international reconciliation

As the members of Reichsbund and Reichsbanner were convinced, international reconciliation had to be built on respect for the war memories of the other side, and they thus enacted symbolic gestures encapsulating this respect. One example was the photo of a Reichsbund

[114] Rohe, *Reichsbanner*, p. 147; see Karl Mayr, 'Totengedächtnis und Wahlkampf: Reichsbanner tritt dem europäischen Kriegsteilnehmerbund Ciamac bei', *RB* no. 44, 29 October 1932.

[115] 'Französische Kameradenworte', *RB* no. 37, 14 September 1929; Rohe, *Reichsbanner*, pp. 151f. On Mayr's biography see Chapter 6. On Cassin and veterans' politics, see Antoine Prost and Jay Winter, *René Cassin et les droits de l'Homme: Le projet d'une génération* (Paris: Fayard, 2011), pp. 50–78, 88–93.

[116] Weiß, 'Soldaten des Friedens', pp. 195f.

[117] See for instance Karl Mayr, 'Hoch der Frieden! Hoch Briand!', *RB* no. 39, 26 September 1931; on context see Mommsen, *The Rise and Fall of Weimar*, pp. 381f.

delegation in Paris in 1930, paying tribute at the tomb of the *inconnu* under the Arc de Triomphe.[118] Another took place in Darmstadt the same year. The local Reichsbund branch had organised a screening of a film commissioned by the league, which first showed the horrors of trench warfare before illustrating the tireless efforts for the disabled veterans since the founding of the Reichsbund in 1917. Prior to the screening, a tribute to the fallen took place, and the wreaths were then placed in the local cemetery next to graves of both German and French soldiers. After a couple of days, however, the ribbons with the slogan 'No more war!' were cut out by unknown vandals, leaving only 'more war!' as a message. The *Reichsbund* journal described this act of vandalism as a 'disgrace' for Germany.[119] When the veterans' functionary and pacifist Henri Dumont, founder of the society Pour supprimer ce crime: la guerre, spoke in various German cities in spring 1929, the Reichsbund not only made sure that thousands listened to him; wherever he spoke, it also adorned the rostrum with a *tricolore*, and a 'republican' orchestra played the 'Marseillaise'. In the Saxonian city of Zwickau, a band accompanied him all along the way from the station to the meeting hall.[120]

In the eyes of republican war veterans, support for internationalism and reconciliation with France in memory of the horrors of war did not imply an outright rejection of patriotism. Rather, internationalism and patriotism had to be reconciled or, more precisely, the latter had to be turned into a springboard for the former, as various veterans' representatives tried to explain in language that was heavily loaded with metaphors. In July 1929, Erich Roßmann, head of the Reichsbund, spoke at the annual gathering of the Union fédérale in Brest. He rejected the revanchist notion that love for one's fatherland would necessarily imply deep-felt enmity towards other countries. The congress rose to a storm of applause when he explained his vision with the words: 'We do not want to get rid of the nations and the love of one's own fatherland; rather, we want to place them like gems in the central sun of mankind so that they can fully develop their gloss and their richness in colour and shape.'[121] The following year, René Cassin, university professor, French delegate to the League of Nations and leading member of

[118] 'Reichsbündler am Grab des unbekannten Soldaten in Paris', *Reichsbund* no. 15, 10 August 1930.
[119] 'Deutschlands Schmach: Schändung unserer gefallenen Kameraden', *Reichsbund* no. 23, 10 December 1930.
[120] Weiß, 'Soldaten des Friedens', p. 200.
[121] Erich Roßmann, 'Eine Friedensreise durch Frankreich', *Reichsbund* no. 14, 25 July 1929.

the Union fédérale came to the annual gathering of the Reichsbund in Mannheim. His visit was meant to stress the bonds of solidarity across the borders between war victims, Cassin explained. And he called for concerted efforts to tame the 'forces of hatred', both in material and in intellectual terms, and thus to develop an 'organised Europe'.[122]

In 1930, Martha Harnoß spoke as a German delegate at a meeting of veterans' representatives from twelve nations at the Chemin des Dames. She was the Reichsbund executive in charge of all issues relating to widows and orphans, and it was the first occasion on which a woman could address such a veterans' meeting. Her tribute to the French and German dead stressed that although they had died as 'enemies, representing these two great nations', they were now 'united as brothers in their graves'. And as such, they were the 'seed grains for a peaceful Europe'.[123] The rhetoric of these cross-border gatherings tapped into a humanist discourse, trying to reconcile it with respect for one's own fatherland. Such symbolic gestures of international reconciliation made an important contribution to the cultural demobilisation between former belligerent nations, even though they failed to convince the radical nationalist right in Germany. In early 1930, the Reichsbanner floated the idea of a peace gathering of French and German veterans on the battlefield at the Chemin des Dames. Karl Mayr was the driving force behind this venture, using his well-established contacts in the Fédération nationale. National Socialists and right-wing combat leagues loathed the plan as a betrayal of German interests.[124] Right-wing commentators considered the plan to be indicative of a grave lack of 'pride' and 'self-esteem' on behalf of the republican league.[125] The meeting was ultimately abandoned. Yet the failure to stage this event was at least partly the Reichsbanner's own fault. It had publicised its plans way ahead of the scheduled date, thus also allowing radical nationalist circles in France to drum up public sentiment against it, which forced the French government to intervene against the plan.[126]

[122] 'Das Parlament der Kriegsopfer', *Reichsbund* no. 11, 10 June 1930; see 'Um die Zukunft Europas', *Reichsbund* no. 21, 10 November 1930.

[123] 'Gelöbnis der Kriegerhinterbliebenen aller Länder: Die Rede unserer Kameradin Harnoß an den Gräbern von Soupir', *Reichsbund* no. 16, 25 August 1930.

[124] 'Reicht euch die Bruderhand! Das Treffen am Chemin des Dames', *RB* no. 4, 25 January 1930; 'Ein Verdunkämpfer über die Frankreich-Fahrt', *RB* no. 12, 22 March 1930; Rohe, *Reichsbanner*, p. 152.

[125] 'Des Reichsbanners Zug an die Westfront', *Fränkischer Kurier* no. 101, 11 April 1930: StAM, Pol. Dir. 6889.

[126] Osterroth, 'Erinnerungen 1900–1934', p. 196; 'Die Frankreichfahrt: Warum sie verschoben werden musste', *RB* no. 19, 10 May 1930.

The republican forces in Weimar Germany certainly did not leave the cult of the fallen to the political right, as Reinhart Koselleck and other historians have stated.[127] Yet they started to intervene in the contested field of public commemorations rather belatedly. Only once the Reichsbanner was established in 1924, five years after the ultimately short-lived Republic had been founded, did moderate socialists make concerted efforts to represent the meanings they attached to violent death in the Great War. These efforts were not in vain, and they changed the playing field of public rituals around war memorials. Republicans were rarely able to shape the architecture and iconographic symbolism of war memorials, and hence only very few memorials with an outright pacifist message were built. But they could represent republican values in the annual commemorative rituals around the memorials, sometimes in official municipal events. If that was not possible, they staged their own ceremonies. It is one of the arguments of this chapter that the repetitive rituals that were annually held at war memorials, and the rhetoric that was employed on these occasions, were centrally important elements of the cult of the fallen. They determined the overall symbolic function of these memorials at least as much as their iconography.[128]

Ultimately, the outcome of pro-republican commemorative efforts depended on the political landscape in a municipal context. Only where Social Democrats, sometimes jointly with Communists, held a majority in the local council, could they place a pacifist message at the centre of the cult of the fallen. Even such a majority, however, could not solve the underlying problem, which the architect Bruno Taut had already identified in 1922. 'A memorial is only possible', Taut argued, when it rests on a symbolic idea that has 'perfect and clear general validity … Yet the attitude of the German people to the past war is such a highly differentiated one, that the universal validity of a symbol' was impossible to ascertain.[129] Heroism and glorification of sacrifice on the one hand, and the gruesome memory of the horrors of war on the other, were strictly irreconcilable ideas. All that Social Democrats could do in such a situation was to develop a range of rhetorical patterns and ritual elements that could express their own interpretation of violent death. These republican commemorations included some elements that were also a staple of nationalist ceremonies, in particular music

[127] Koselleck, *Zur politischen Ikonologie*, p. 39; Lehmann, 'Militär', p. 420.

[128] A relative neglect of these ritualistic elements is one of the limitations of the iconographic approach by Koselleck and other scholars. See Koselleck, *Zur politischen Ikonologie*; and Goebel, *Great War*. For pertinent criticism and an excellent analysis of commemorative rituals see Überegger, *Erinnerungskriege*, pp. 144–80.

[129] Cited in Behrenbeck, 'Heldenkult', p. 345.

such as 'I Had a Comrade'. Yet despite these similarities, Reichsbanner rituals at war memorials did not simply copy those of the Stahlhelm and Kyffhäuserbund; they rather mirrored them. The latter used the remembrance of the fallen to compensate for German defeat.[130]

Ascribing meaning to violent death

Historians have argued that the socialist labour movement developed a highly rationalist and emotionally cold rhetoric that did not offer an answer to questions about the meaning of death, and was hence not able to satisfy the metaphysical needs of its rank-and-file members, and to accommodate the need for a reworking of war experiences.[131] For the Weimar Republic, this argument is not convincing. To be sure, Social Democrats were reluctant to ascribe any higher meaning to the horrors of violent death – not even the need for defence of their own country – and insisted that the main aim of many of the fallen had been to survive the war unharmed.[132] But despite this reluctance, they did ascribe some meaning to violent death, mostly the urgent need for international reconciliation as the key lesson. Karl Bröger insisted that the Reichsbanner not only remembered comrades in their own uniform, but also the dead of the 'other side' who shared a grave with them. Citing a stark metaphor coined by Henri Barbusse, Bröger declared as the real 'truth' that 'two belligerent armies are in fact one that is committing suicide'.[133]

Thus, the republican cult of the dead offered consolation and also encouragement. It tried to reinstate the dignity of the individual, which was a pertinent task, given the fact that the 'radical devaluation of the individual' was one of the most substantial effects of mass death in the First World War.[134] At the heart of the republican cult of the fallen stood the slogan 'No more war!'. With this motto, Reichsbund and Reichsbanner functionaries continued a pacifist tradition that had been inaugurated in the immediate post-war period by the Friedensbund der Kriegsteilnehmer. And they tapped into the anti-militarist and anti-war

[130] See *ibid.*, p. 357, and the critique by Erwin Frebe, 'Das Heer der Toten', *RB* no. 44, Beilage, 20 October 1932.

[131] Erhard Lucas, *Vom Scheitern der deutschen Arbeiterbewegung* (Frankfurt am Main: Roter Stern, 1983), pp. 96–100, 182–5.

[132] See the balanced reflection by Erwin Frebe, 'Die Toten Deutschlands: Gedanken zum Totensonntag', *RB* no. 47, 23 November 1929.

[133] Karl Bröger, 'Worte auf ein Massengrab: Allen Toten des Weltkrieges', *RB* no. 47, 22 November 1930.

[134] Michael Geyer, 'Das Stigma der Gewalt und das Problem der nationalen Identität in Deutschland', in Christian Jansen, Lutz Niethammer and Bernd Weisbrod (eds.), *Von der Aufgabe der Freiheit: Politische Verantwortung und bürgerliche Gesellschaft im 19. und 20. Jahrhundert* (Berlin: Akademie, 1995), pp. 673–98 (p. 679).

sentiment that was apparently still widespread among socialist workers even by the late 1920s. Yet snappy, emotional and confrontational as this slogan was, its widespread use in the republican remembrance of the fallen was not free of ambivalences. By the early 1930s, the constant repetition of 'No more war!' had turned the slogan into a set phrase that was full of pathos, but ran the risk of becoming the centrepiece of an empty, ossified ritual. On a rare occasion, critique of the annual calendar of commemorative events was voiced from within the Reichsbund. Writing during the autumn season of 1931, the deputy head of a local branch in the Rhineland argued that these events had to be rejected when they simply repeated 'the traditional, completely dated' sequence of ritual elements. In order to liven up the rigid formulaic pattern of events, he recommended the inclusion of poetic elements that were apparently designated to offer a much more diversified and reflexive pronunciation of socialist anti-militarist ideas. As possible examples, the Reichsbund functionary mentioned the recital of poems and spoken choruses by authors such as Ernst Toller – and here namely his *Hinkemann*, the play about the tragedy of a soldier who returned home with his genitals shot off – Heinrich Lersch, Ernst Preczang or Bruno Schönlank.[135]

Representing extremely diverse political positions and artistic ideas in the broad spectrum of Weimar's socialist literature, works of all four authors were widely read and performed in the socialist choral movement and the *Volksbühnen*, popular theatre companies that were supported by socialist trade unions and the SPD.[136] Thus, this critique pointed to the fact that the republican remembrance of the fallen could have included a much more differentiated set of artistic ideas. In different forms, poems and plays by these authors reflected and contemplated the existential problems of labouring men who had experienced the horror of trench warfare, the crucial role of technology for total war in the years from 1914 to 1918, or the longing for a peaceful life amidst the post-war class struggles. Yet while there was certainly potential for a much more elaborate symbolism of republican commemorations, there were also good reasons why they ultimately retained their rather formulaic character. The very purpose of rituals is to be ritualistic, as only their repetitive nature ensures that they perform their core function: to overcome the contingency of elaborate verbal communication with

[135] 'Festkultur der Kriegsopfer', *Reichsbund* no. 22, 20 November 1931.

[136] Trommler, *Sozialistische Literatur*, pp. 235f., 396–404, 450–3; see Ernst Toller, 'Der deutsche Hinkemann' (1923), in *Gesammelte Werke*, 5 vols., Vol. II (Munich: Carl Hanser, 1978), pp. 191–248.

a set sequence of mostly non-verbal gestures and actions.[137] Only as such, republican commemorative rituals conformed to the expectation of their participants that they might help to bring closure to a liminal experience. And apart from public recognition of their own suffering, closure was surely the most important effect republican war veterans expected from the memorial cult.

[137] Behrenbeck, *Der Kult um die toten Helden*, p. 50.

5 In search of a national symbol, 1924–1933

Weimar Germany was characterised by an abundance of physical spaces used to commemorate the fallen. By the late 1920s, even small villages usually had a memorial in honour of the soldiers of the Great War. In the cities, a large number of memorials by different sponsors and with a variety of designs and iconographical styles competed for the attention of those who wanted to mourn the dead. Regional variation characterised the rituals around the memorials, depending on the religious composition of the population and the relative strength of the socialist labour movement, to name only the two most important factors. This diversity of styles and rituals makes it hard, if not impossible, to make general statements about the prevalent message of the memorial cult in post-war Germany. What was missing, though, was a central site or unifying symbol that would represent the meaning of death on the battlefields for the German nation as a whole. Many belligerent countries used the notion of an 'Unknown Soldier' for precisely this purpose. On Armistice Day in 1920, Britain and France pioneered the burial of an unidentified corpse, at Westminster Abbey and the Arc de Triomphe respectively. These memorial practices were able to rally the nation – amidst political strife and social tensions created by post-war reconstruction – behind a single commemorative symbol.[1] In 1921, four other members of the victorious Entente – the USA, Italy, Belgium and Portugal – followed suit and unveiled their own memorials of the Unknown Soldier.[2]

[1] See Volker Ackermann, '"Ceux qui sont pieusement morts pour la France ...": Die Identität des Unbekannten Soldaten', in Koselleck and Jeismann, *Der politische Totenkult*, pp. 281–314; Gregory, *The Silence of Memory*.

[2] See Ken Inglis, 'Entombing Unknown Soldiers: From London and Paris to Baghdad', *History & Memory* 5 (1993), 7–31; for Poland, which followed in 1925 with an Unknown Soldier from the wars of independence in 1918–20, see the subtle analysis by Christof Mick, 'Der Kult um den "Unbekannten Soldaten" im Polen der Zwischenkriegszeit', in Martin Schulze-Wessel (ed.), *Nationalisierung der Nation und Sakralisierung der Religion im östlichen Europa* (Stuttgart: Steiner, 2006), pp. 181–200.

The power of the symbol of the Unknown Soldier was rooted in the very abstraction it encapsulated. In a quite literal sense, the Unknown Soldier was indeed unknown: it was the unidentified corpse of a person of unknown military rank, regional or social background, and unknown name. As such, it worked like an 'empty signifier': it could encapsulate or signify the usually contradictory meanings of dying in the Great War for a nation precisely because it was cleansed from any empirical specificity, apart from the fact that it was the corpse of a soldier. Only as an intrinsically empty signifier could the tomb of the Unknown Soldier be filled and enriched with the diverse imaginations of the nation it was meant to symbolise.[3] France and the United Kingdom led the way in employing this powerful symbol, and invented the accompanying annual ritual of the two minutes' silence during the hour of the armistice on 11 November, as the core of a patriotic cult that could reinvigorate and unify the national polity. Germany, though, was a rare exception from the rule that former belligerent countries used the burial of an Unknown Soldier as the centrepiece of a national memorial cult. This reluctance to embrace the symbol of the *inconnu* has often been noted, and various explanations have been suggested. German defeat and its specific 'origins', at the hands of those very powers who had invented this tradition, has been named as one particular reason why the Republic could not reach a consensus on a specific site at which an Unknown Soldier was to be buried.[4]

Constructing a *Reichsehrenmal*

That is certainly true, but should not be overstated, as various defeated countries adopted the ritual: Austria in 1927 and Hungary in 1929, while a monument to the Bulgarian 'Unknown Soldier' was unveiled in Sofia in 1928.[5] Perhaps more to the point is Reinhart Koselleck's hint at the 'federal structure' of the Reich, which allowed for a limited number of competing regional memorial sites.[6] Centrifugal tendencies were deeply embedded in the federal structure of the German

[3] Philipp Sarasin, *Geschichtswissenschaft und Diskursanalyse* (Frankfurt am Main: Suhrkamp, 2003), pp. 157, 169f., based on Ernesto Laclau, 'Why Do Empty Signifiers Matter to Politics?', in Jeffrey Weeks (ed.), *The Lesser Evil and the Greater Good* (London: Rivers Oram Press, 1994), pp. 167–78.

[4] Winter, *Sites of Memory*, p. 28.

[5] Snezhana Dimitrova, '"Taming the Death": The Culture of Death (1915–1918) and Its Remembering and Commemorating through First World War Soldier Monuments in Bulgaria (1917–1944)', *Social History* 30 (2005), 175–94 (p. 190).

[6] Reinhart Koselleck, 'Einleitung', in Koselleck and Jeismann, *Der politische Totenkult*, pp. 9–20 (p. 16).

polity. Although the republican constitution of Weimar Germany had diminished the institutional strength of regional powers, it had maintained their forum in the form of the Reichsrat, which represented the *Länder* as a legislature.[7] Ultimately, the project of a central national *Reichsehrenmal* (Reich memorial in honour of the dead) was also delayed and finally ground to a halt amidst the various competing claims and interests of the press, political parties and interest groups.[8]

While certainly acknowledging the relevance of these explanations, this chapter advances a different argument with regard to the search for a unifying symbol for the commemoration of the fallen in Germany. On the one hand, it will highlight that there was in fact quite substantial German interest in the notion of an 'Unknown Soldier' – an interest, though, that never materialised in a memorial built of stone. There were, on the other hand, also intrinsic artistic reasons for the failure of the *Reichsehrenmal* project, reasons that point to the ubiquity of the chosen core symbol. Only when these two strands of the debate are seen in conjunction is it possible to construct a coherent explanation for the failure to establish one unified national symbol for the fallen German soldiers. The search for such a symbol was the ultimate litmus test as to whether Germany could create its own national style of commemoration like France and the UK – a style that could integrate republicans and their opponents – or whether a contest over symbols and narratives remained the key defining issue. As we will see, the failure of this search was not a foregone conclusion. For once, veterans' associations from the left and right of the political spectrum could agree on a joint project, and there was wideapread consensus across the country on the style that was to be adopted. However, at the same time the extreme right adopted the notion of the 'Unknown Soldier', and thus expropriated a symbol that had initially found strong support by the left.

The starting point for a more concerted effort to find a national memorial was 3 August 1924. On this day, the Reich government conducted an official remembrance ceremony 'in honour of the victims of the World War' at the Reichstag in Berlin. Similar ceremonies were conducted in other cities across the Reich. This was in fact the only occasion on which the Republic celebrated the fallen in a unified, nationwide remembrance holiday. There was a strong Reichswehr presence during the ceremony, including speeches by the head and

[7] See Büttner, *Weimar*, pp. 116f.

[8] Winfried Speitkamp, '"Erziehung zur Nation": Reichskunstwart, Kulturpolitik und Identitätsstiftung im Staat von Weimar', in Helmut Berding (ed.), *Nationales Bewußtsein und kollektive Identität*, Studien zur Entwicklung des kollektiven Bewußtseins in der Neuzeit 2 (Frankfurt am Main: Suhrkamp, 1994), pp. 541–80 (p. 572).

the deputy head of the Protestant and Catholic military chaplaincies respectively. Nevertheless, the ritual also provided ample opportunity to mourn the fallen, not least through the inclusion of two minutes of silence across the country, adopting a central element of the British ritual for Armistice Day.[9] On the same day, Reich President Ebert – who had also given a speech in the Reichstag – and Chancellor Wilhelm Marx released a joint statement, which stressed the quest for the 'freedom and integrity of the fatherland' as the key 'legacy' of the fallen and their sacrifice. On a more civilian note, they also highlighted the plight of the war dependants and the 'hard destitution' that the hunger had brought to the home front. Ebert and Marx acknowledged that many memorials for the fallen had been built across the country. But still missing was the '*Ehrenmal* that the German people as a whole owes' to all those who had died at the front. Finally, they invited voluntary contributions for such a memorial, which, in a 'simple' shape, would embody 'mourning' for the fallen in the first instance.[10]

The terminology itself was already indicative of the specific parameters of this project. Throughout the nineteenth century, and particularly since the founding of the nation state in 1871, a whole raft of memorials had been designated to encapsulate the essence of German national identity, ranging from the reconstruction of the medieval cathedral in Cologne to the Völkerschlachtdenkmal near Leipzig, unveiled in 1913, which commemorated the Battle of the Nations against Napoleon in 1813. Following different artistic and iconographical ideas, and offering highly diverse interpretations of who and what constituted Germany, all these projects endeavoured to be the definitive *Nationaldenkmal*, a memorial that represented the German nation.[11] In the wake of the lost war, however, the focus had shifted. Reich government and Reichsrat agreed to pursue the project suggested by Ebert and Marx, and in October 1924, the latter set up a subcommittee for work on a *Nationaldenkmal* for the fallen of the First World War.[12] Yet this term was never used in the ensuing public debates, which instead tapped into the semantics used by Ebert and Marx, who had called the project a *Reichsehrenmal*. Instead of a *Denkmal*, which basically intended to commemorate the dead, the

[9] See the materials in BArch, R 32, 222; and Kaiser, *Von Helden und Opfern*, pp. 31–8.

[10] See the text in *Berliner Volkszeitung* no. 366, 3 August 1924: BArch R 8034 II, 7691, fo. 163.

[11] See the seminal article by Thomas Nipperdey, 'Nationalidee und Nationaldenkmal in Deutschland im 19. Jahrhundert', *HZ* 206 (1968), 529–85.

[12] Peter Bucher, 'Die Errichtung des Reichsehrenmals nach dem Ersten Weltkrieg', *Jahrbuch für westdeutsche Landesgeschichte* 7 (1981), 359–86 (p. 359).

Ehrenmal honoured the fallen, and thus implied that they and their deeds had been particularly noble.[13]

Initially, the response to the appeal was rather mixed. Many press comments were sceptical and questioned whether such a symbolic project was really necessary. Even with regard to the ceremony on 3 August 1924, *Vorwärts* had noted the refusal of the nationalist combat leagues to support the government, and had asked whether the differing visions of pacifist and militarist circles were at all reconcilable.[14] Professional commentators raised similar concerns. Bruno Taut (1880–1938), for instance, was one of the most prolific modernist architects of the Weimar era. Committed pacifist and activist of the revolution in 1918/19, he designed a string of innovative projects throughout the 1920s, most notably two landmark social housing developments in Berlin.[15] Writing in 1924, Taut noted the many contradictory opinions and symbolic ideas that had already been voiced. 'Even if it were possible at least to state the idea more precisely', he argued, 'it would remain absolutely insoluble for the artist' who was meant to implement it. Taut clearly situated the *Reichsehrenmal* in the tradition of the nineteenth-century *Nationaldenkmal* when he singled out the Völkerschlachtdenkmal as 'a monstrous ridiculousness and quixotism of our time'. Every similar 'attempt to honour the dead through *Wucht* [overwhelming power]' would fail in the same way, and would 'just smash them'. An appropriate commemoration rather had to keep the 'spirit' of the fallen alive, as the English had managed with the tomb of the Unknown Soldier and the ritual of two minutes' silence. But Taut was sure that the Germans would remain sceptical about a ritual that was not of their own making.[16]

Yet these and other critical arguments did not concern those who inundated the authorities with suggestions for an appropriate site for the *Reichsehrenmal* and detailed plans for its design. When the subcommittee met with considerable delay for its constitutive meeting on 21 November 1925, no fewer than 64 substantial blueprints had been submitted. By the autumn of 1928, this figure had risen to 300, mostly provided by towns and regional authorities across the Reich.[17]

13 Henrik Hilbig, *Das Reichsehrenmal bei Bad Berka: Entstehung und Entwicklung eines Denkmalprojekts der Weimarer Republik* (Aachen: Shaker, 2006), pp. 122f.

14 *Vorwärts* no. 363, 4 August 1924; Bucher, 'Errichtung', p. 361.

15 See Eric D. Weitz, *Weimar Germany: Promise and Tragedy* (Princeton University Press, 2007), pp. 170–83.

16 Bruno Taut, 'Das Reichsehrenmal für die Kriegsopfer', *Die Baugilde* 6 (1924), 590.

17 Bucher, 'Errichtung', 361; Reich Art Custodian to Reich Minister of the Interior, 10 October 1928: BArch, R 32, 353a, fo. 114.

Charged with the onerous task of collating and evaluating these proposals was the office of the Reichskunstwart, headed by the energetic and outspoken art historian Edwin Redslob. Established in 1920 and responsible for the symbolism and official pageantry of the Republic, the Reichskunstwart reported directly to the Reich Ministry of the Interior. Despite a shortage of financial means and frictions with other administrators at the Reich level, Redslob was a key player in government attempts to shape an appropriate iconography of war remembrance, and had already designed the ritual on 3 August 1924.[18]

Karl Bröger and the notion of the 'Unknown Soldier'

While the debate on the national memorial gathered pace, the republican veterans of the Reichsbanner expressed their own ideas on an appropriate symbolism for this project. In July 1924, the *Reichsbanner* journal reminded its readers that the notion of the 'Unknown Soldier' had been invented well before the memorials in Paris, Rome and London were unveiled; a German poet, 'risen from German labourers' and closely tied to their battles for recognition, had in fact invented this symbol. This was a reference to a short booklet in the popular series of mass novels published by the Reclam press in Leipzig, printed on low-quality 'war paper', which yellowed quickly.[19] The book in question was *The Unknown Soldier* by the worker-poet Karl Bröger, published in 1917. In a series of short vignettes, Bröger detailed the 'fate of the common man' at the front, highlighting how ordinary people from all belligerent countries were in fact the victims of the machinery of total war. But not all hope was lost, as working-class solidarity reached across borders. In one episode, two German soldiers visited one of the survivors of the major pit accident that had happened in Courrières in 1906. At the time, they had rushed to the help of their French comrades with a detachment of other miners from the Ruhr. Now, amidst the catastrophe of war, they wanted to reaffirm the bonds that had then been established.[20]

[18] Annegret Heffen, *Der Reichskunstwart: Kunstpolitik in den Jahren 1920–1933. Zu den Bemühungen um eine offizielle Reichskunstpolitik in der Weimarer Republik* (Essen: Die Blaue Eule, 1986), pp. 231–68; and the biography by Christian Welzbacher, *Edwin Redslob: Biografie eines unverbesserlichen Idealisten* (Berlin: Matthes & Seitz, 2009).

[19] 'Der unbekannte Soldat', *RB* no. 4, 1 July 1924.

[20] Karl Bröger, *Der unbekannte Soldat: Kriegstaten und Schicksale des kleinen Mannes* (Leipzig: Reclam, n.d. [1917]), pp. 77ff. It is indicative for the argument presented here that the second and third editions of this booklet were published in 1936 and 1937 respectively.

This reminder about the German genealogy of the term 'Unknown Soldier' was eagerly picked up across the Reichsbanner organisation. Several *Gaue* urged the executive to consider plans for a memorial for the German Unknown Soldier.[21] Yet these deliberations were almost immediately superseded by Ebert's call for a *Reichsehrenmal* on 3 August 1924, prompting the republican veterans not to pursue their idea any further. However, as frustration with the slow pace of the official project mounted, the Reichsbanner came back to its original idea. At some point in early 1925, the executive board charged a committee with the explicit task of finding an appropriate design for the memorial. After intensive debates, the committee settled for a garden landscape with the tomb of the Unknown Soldier in its midst, accompanied by a memorial stone.[22] On the eleventh anniversary of the beginning of the war, Karl Bröger had an opportunity to explain his choice of title for the booklet he had published in 1917. As he recalled, generals such as Hindenburg and Ludendorff had been celebrated as heroes and examples in so many speeches and publications. Against the backdrop of such hyperbolic nationalist glorification, Bröger was keen to single out the service of those ordinary soldiers who were never known or even mentioned by name. Any resentment against the alien origins of the Unknown Soldier was thus misguided, as 'the idea belongs to us'.[23] Subsequently, Reichsbanner publications never tired of driving home the key message of the 'army of the nameless' who made up the republican league: differences of rank should not matter, either in the commemoration of wartime service or in the inexhaustible fight for a democratic polity. Not deference, but altruism was key.[24]

Yet as in other areas of commemorative activity, the Reichsbanner was not the only veterans' league that had a stake in the debates on the *Reichsehrenmal*. Early on the Stahlhelm made clear why it unequivocally rejected the democratic symbol preferred by the Reichsbanner. It conceded that in a 'formally convincing manner', the Unknown Soldier was appropriate to epistomise the 'gigantic struggle of the masses and peoples', and the fact that it had absorbed and obliterated individuality. But whereas the former enemies sought to find the meaning of violent death in sacrifice for one's country, a German symbol would already presuppose such meaning. And this meaning was not to be found in any

[21] 'Der unbekannte Soldat', *RB* no. 5, 15 July 1924.
[22] 'Reichsehrenmal für die Gefallenen', *ibid.* no. 6, 15 March 1926.
[23] 'Der unbekannte Soldat', *ibid.* no. 15, 1 August 1925.
[24] Hermann Schützinger, 'Das Heer der Namenlosen', *ibid.* no. 5, 1 March 1925; 'Der unbekannte Soldat', *ibid.* no. 8, 15 April 1927; 'Der unbekannte Soldat', *ibid.* no. 42, 2 December 1928.

lofty 'ideals', but in the stubborn fight for the 'defence of the country' against enemy invasion.[25] At its core, this was a blunt reiteration of the pre-war notion of German encirclement, which alleged that Germany, situated in the middle of Europe, had to defend itself against enemies in the West and the East who were bent on destroying the newly established nation state. But the Stahlhelm connected this defensive ideology with the artistic idea of a 'sacred territory' that should be situated in Thuringia, as it was geographically in the midst of Germany. Thus the *Reichsehrenmal* should represent, in 'overwhelming simplicity', the natural 'beauty of the *Heimat*, which the fallen heroes had defended'. To a basically unchanged natural setting, only minimal sculptural elements were to be added, in the form of a sarcophagus with a sculpture of a reclining German soldier.[26]

This proposal successfully tapped into two cultural constructs that were intimately entwined and firmly embedded in the history of the nineteenth-century nationalist movement. The first construct cultivated the notion of a regionally and locally defined *Heimat* as the embodiment of everything that was peculiar and worthwhile about the Germans as a nation. It conjured up romantic and very intimate images of specific places and customs. Seen in conjunction, they constituted the wider realm of the nation. Ties to the *Heimat* – the term is untranslatable; rendering it as 'homeland' is grossly misleading – grounded and reinforced nationalist emotions in the concrete setting of a peculiar place.[27] The second construct glorified the forest as the key site that epitomised the primordial identity of the German people as a nation. Many nineteenth-century poets, painters and folklore writers had traded in those romantic connotations that turned the *deutscher Wald* into a powerful symbol of German identity. It was distinctive from the British notion of a 'landscape', which clearly showed the effects of centuries of human intervention. But the German forest, while it displayed the primal strength and rugged features of something that was distinctively nature, and not civilisation, was also no complete wilderness.[28] In his book *Crowds and Power*, a wide-ranging study of European nationalist and fascist cultural practices, Elias Canetti has offered a

[25] Stahlhelm Bundesleitung, 'Vorschlag für ein Reichs-Ehrenmal zum Gedächtnis der im Weltkriege gefallenen deutschen Soldaten', July 1925: BArch, R 43/I, 713, fos. 61f.

[26] *Ibid.*

[27] See the classic study by Celia Applegate, *A Nation of Provincials: The German Idea of Heimat* (Berkeley: University of California Press, 1990).

[28] Albrecht Lehmann, 'Der deutsche Wald', in Hagen Schulze and Etienne François (eds.), *Deutsche Erinnerungsorte*, 3 vols., Vol. III (Munich: C. H. Beck, 2001), pp. 187–200.

pertinent analysis of the 'marching forest' as the key 'mass symbol' of the Germans. With its clear vertical lines, thick trunks and geometrical order, the *Wald* symbolised 'steadfastness' and security, and was thus the embodiment of military strength, in many ways almost perceivable as an army of trees.[29]

Finding a 'sacred territory' in the German forest

When the Stahlhelm suggested in July 1925 that a 'sacred territory' in the midst of Germany should serve as the national memorial, it referred to an idea that had already emerged during the war. Landscape architect Willy Lange first suggested in 1915 the creation of *Ehrenhaine* ('heroes' groves') across Germany. At this point, they were primarily meant to provide a substitute for military cemeteries. Lange envisaged planting one tree for each fallen soldier, with a preference for oaks as the established symbol for national strength and endurance.[30] Writing to Otto Geßler as acting minister of the interior in December 1925, Stahlhelm leader Franz Seldte expanded on this idea. The German veterans insisted, he claimed, that the memorial should not be built in a 'big city'. Instead, they wanted to commemorate the fallen in 'God's free nature, where their fallen comrades rest'.[31] Using this rationale in the debate on the *Reichsehrenmal* Seldte deliberately tapped into strong anti-urbanist sentiments that were widely held and shared across the political spectrum. *Vorwärts* justified its rejection of plans to place the memorial in Berlin with the argument that the 'noisy hustle and bustle of the city of four million people, by far the most Americanised and surely the least primal' of all towns across the country, would not suit the remembrance. Only amidst the 'rustle of very old trees' could an appropriate, 'more poetic and meaningful' atmosphere be fostered.[32] An architect from Leipzig supported the view that the 'loud noise and soulless hustle' of the big city were inappropriate, and that the memorial should be situated in the German forest 'as the symbol of the essence of Germanness, of German manner and German power'.[33] Willy Lange himself, whom Redslob appointed in March 1926 as one of his official artistic advisers on the *Reichsehrenmal* project, obviously shared the widespread resentment against urbanism. His peculiar version of this

[29] Elias Canetti, *Masse und Macht* (Frankfurt am Main: Fischer, 1980), p. 190.
[30] Mosse, *Fallen Soldiers*, pp. 87f.
[31] Franz Seldte to Otto Geßler, 9 December 1925: BArch, R 32, 357, fos. 13f.
[32] 'Der Kampf um das Reichsehrenmal', *Vorwärts* no. 390, 20 August 1926: BArch, R 32, 358a, fo. 14.
[33] Hugo Koch to Edwin Redslob, 9 December 1925: BArch, R 32, 354, fos. 65ff.

dichotomy was presented in utterly racist terms, as he stipulated that a 'Nordic forest-folk culture' was threatened by the 'civilisation of a town-folk miscegenation [*Stadtvolk Rassenmischung*]'.[34]

Suggesting the 'sacred territory' as the most appropriate solution for the *Reichsehrenmal*, Stahlhelm leader Franz Seldte could also claim that the other 'large association of front-line fighters', the Reichsbanner, supported his plan.[35] At this point, in December 1925, the two veterans' associations had not yet settled for a single site and artistic idea,[36] but they both supported the notion of a memorial situated in the open countryside somewhere in Thuringia. This agreement between the two leagues is all the more surprising against the backdrop of their usually acrimonious relationship and the fact that the Reichsbanner presented itself as the democratic alternative to the right-wing combat league. On this occasion, however, the shared commonality of their status as being war veterans apparently outweighed the substantial political disagreement.[37] The archival evidence on the background of this cooperation is rather sparse, but according to the Reichsbanner's own account, the officials of the Weimar *Kreisdirektion* (district administration) were instrumental in facilitating it.

Following initial contacts, they first invited representatives of both leagues to a joint excursion to two alternative sites in the vicinity of Weimar: the Ettersberg, in walking distance from Weimar city centre, and a site near Bad Berka at the intersection of three valleys, which was eighteen kilometres away from Weimar, but connected to national rail traffic via a small-gauge railway.[38] Despite the railway link, the Reichsbanner deemed Bad Berka to be less suitable in terms of accessibility. Yet it was ready to leave the ultimate decision to artistic experts, i.e. to Edwin Redslob as the Reich Art Custodian. Then, secondly, the Weimar district officials approached other veterans' leagues, in particular the Kyffhäuserbund and the Reichsbund jüdischer Frontsoldaten

[34] Willy Lange to Edwin Redslob, 19 July 1926: BArch, R 32, 354, fos. 118–25 (quote on fo. 123).

[35] Franz Seldte to Otto Geßler, 9 December 1925: BArch, R 32, 357, fo. 13f.

[36] See Otto Hörsing to Reich Ministry of the Interior, 10 December 1925: BArch, R 32, 357, fo. 6.

[37] The associations of disabled veterans and former POWs, who mostly rejected any memorial in favour of material welfare, were sidelined throughout the whole process. See 'Protokoll über die auf Veranlassung des Herrn Ministers erfolgte Besprechung mit den Teilnehmern der mit der Frage der Kriegsopfer beschäftigten Verbände am 10. August 1926': BArch, R 32, 357, fos. 120f.

[38] Redslob to Reich Minister of the Interior, 26 March 1926: BArch, R 32, 357, fos. 22f.; on the Bad Berka site see the detailed description by Theodor Duesterberg, *Das Reichsehrenmal im Walde südlich Bad Berka: Gedanken und Anregungen für die Ausgestaltung* (Halle: Vaterländischer Verlag, 1931).

(Reich League of Jewish Front-Line Soldiers; RjF), and were soon able to rally veterans from across the political spectrum in support of the Bad Berka proposal.[39] The third and final step was to bring the Reich president on board. Paul von Hindenburg had so far supported the idea to convert the New Guard House (Neue Wache) into a memorial: a classicist building at Unter den Linden in the heart of the capital. But the four veterans' leagues successfully lobbied him in a meeting on 12 February 1926 to support a 'Holy Grove' (*Heiliger Hain*) at Bad Berka. This was the name and the place of the project on which the veterans had by then agreed.[40]

The cooperation between the veterans' associations was, to be sure, never an easy one. Both within the Reichsbanner and the Stahlhelm in particular, reservations about this course of action were voiced. Officially, the Reichsbanner claimed that it had no choice but to collaborate with right-wing organisations on this matter, and that the underlying political differences were not affected. In an apparent attempt to gloss over the difficulty of Reichsbanner support for the Bad Berka project, the journal of the republican league offered its close proximity to Weimar as a 'higher reason and angle' to legitimise this option. A memorial for those 'comrades' who had fallen for a 'freer Germany' could only be situated near the 'birthplace of the Weimar constitution'. The 'spirit' of that constitution, however, had also to be reflected in the design of the memorial, which should be a *Mahnmal* rather than a *Denkmal* – a memorial that not only served to commemorate the past, but rather admonished the living to heed the lessons of the past – hammering home the 'duty' to work towards a 'peaceful' cultural progress of all nations.[41] Written on behalf of the Reichsbanner executive, this statement made it clear that the functionaries in Magdeburg were keen not to repeat the mistake many Social Democrats had made in previous years, when they watched from the sidelines while municipal memorials were planned.

Limits of cooperation between Stahlhelm and Reichsbanner

Yet for many rank-and-file members of the republican league, even this limited cooperation with the political right was apparently not easy to

[39] 'Reichsehrenmal für die Gefallenen'; 'Das Reichsehrenmal', *RB* no. 14, 15 July 1926.

[40] 'Ein Ehrenmal für unsere Gefallenen: Die Frontkämpfer beim Reichspräsidenten', *Vossische Zeitung* no. 74, 13 February 1926; Hilbig, *Reichsehrenmal*, pp. 161–3.

[41] 'Reichsehrenmal für die Gefallenen'.

stomach. Some of the reasons for this discontent are illuminated in a letter by Paul Toller – a relative of the playwright Ernst Toller – to Paul Levi, member of parliament and a leading representative of the left wing of the Social Democratic Party (SPD). In April 1926, Toller informed Levi about his daily encounters with 'comrades' from all social strata, which had clearly revealed the extent of the 'gulf that exists between leadership and the masses'. A Reichsbanner activist himself, Toller seriously doubted whether it was shrewd political manoeuvering when Otto Hörsing joined the right-wing leagues in their recent meeting with Hindenburg on the *Reichsehrenmal* issue. Such public posturing was all the more detrimental to rank-and-file members' morale at a time when the Reichsbanner leadership demanded neutrality with regard to the ongoing debate on the expropriation of the former ruling houses.[42] This vexed issue of the expropriation of the former ruling houses, or *Fürstenenteignung*, which dominated German domestic politics in 1926, had already stretched the patience of Reichsbanner members to the limit.

Throughout the 1920s, former ruling houses had claimed the restitution of property that they had allegedly lost during the revolution. In an attempt to settle these claims once and for all, and to tap into the widespread anti-monarchist sentiment, the German Communist Party (KPD) had called for a referendum on this matter, which the SPD immediately supported, though both parties campaigned separately. A petition in favour of a referendum on expropriation without compensation – quite literally the seizing of assets – in March 1926 gathered 12.5 million votes, 2 million more than the combined vote for the SPD and KPD in the 1924 Reichstag elections. The actual referendum on 20 June 1926 drew even further support far beyond the socialist camp, with 14.5 million votes in favour.[43] This referendum on the *Fürstenenteignung* was the climax of pro-republican mobilisation in Weimar Germany, and its significance should not be overlooked. Thus, it was all the more problematic that the very organisation that had vowed to defend the Republic tied its hands in this matter. The Reichsbanner leadership decided not to campaign for the referendum in accordance with the principle of non-partisanship, as the German Democratic Party (DDP) and the Centre Party did not support it. However, it could not prevent many local branches from openly campaigning in favour of the referendum, not only in Saxony, where neutrality would have finished off any Social Democratic credibility among the many leftist socialist

[42] Paul Toller to Paul Levi, 9 April 1926: AdsD, NL Paul Levi, 1/PLAA000051.
[43] Mommsen, *The Rise and Fall of Weimar*, pp. 239–42.

workers, but for instance also in more moderate Schleswig-Holstein.[44] In Munich, a speaker in a local *Kameradschaft* demanded that members should come out in droves for a demonstration ahead of the referendum. Anticipating criticism about the fact that the Reichsbanner had nothing to offer but 'duty, duty', he reminded his audience about the war years, when they had had to fulfil their duty for a 'camarilla of monarchistic and big capitalist' interests.[45]

But such populist slogans could surely not close the gap between Reichsbanner leaders and rank-and-file members that had opened up in 1926. Many branches and some *Gaue* remained highly critical of the project. By and large, they voiced the same reservations that had, for instance, motivated Social Democrats in Württemberg to boycott the state ceremony on 3 August 1924 in Stuttgart altogether. On that occasion, local Social Democrats had highlighted the plight of the workers during the war, and of the war disabled in the present. They doubted the motives of those who talked of 'national freedom' during such ceremonies.[46] And they openly criticised the state president of Württemberg and member of the German National People's Party (DNVP) Wilhelm Bazille, who had identified 'discord' among the Germans as one major reason for defeat in 1918 in his official speech on 3 August 1924. Social Democrat newspapers juxtaposed this statement with the situation in the *Etappe* during the war.[47] Reinvigorating the notion of Social Democracy as an 'alternative culture', the Reichsbund in Stuttgart instead celebrated a summer fair under the motto 'No more war!' on 3 August 1924, with local Reichsbanner leader Dr Kurt Schumacher as the main speaker.[48] Reichsbanner officials had worked hard to overcome Social Democrat reluctance to engage with the commemoration of the fallen. But when discontent within the organisation about the alliance behind the 'Holy Grove' mounted, some regional branches fell back into their previous critical habits.[49]

44 Voigt, *Kampfbünde*, pp. 323–42; Stokes, 'Anfänge', pp. 338f.

45 'Kameradschaftsabend des Reichsbanners Schwarz–Rot–Gold, Schlachthausviertel', 18 June 1926: StAM, Pol. Dir. 6887.

46 'Die Sozialdemokratische Partei und die Ehrung der Toten des Weltkrieges', *Volkszeitung Esslingen* no. 180, 4 August 1924; 'Der Trauertag', *Schwäbische Tagwacht* no. 181, 4 August 1924 (quote); both in HStASt, E 130b, Bü 3846.

47 'Bazille's Dolchstoß', *Neckar-Echo Heilbronn* no. 181, 5 August 1924.

48 'Nie wieder Krieg! Die Gedächtnisfeier der Kriegsopfer Groß-Stuttgarts', *Schwäbische Tagwacht* no. 182, 5 August 1924. See Vernon L. Lidtke, *The Alternative Culture: Socialist Labor in Imperial Germany* (Oxford; New York: Oxford University Press, 1985).

49 See Hilbig, *Reichsehrenmal*, pp. 389ff.

Yet internal criticism of the collaboration between the veterans' leagues was not confined to the Reichsbanner alone. Simmering tensions also came to the fore in the Stahlhelm. Franz Seldte, the founder and head of the association, was ready to strike a rather conciliatory tone in his relations with the Reichsbanner if necessary. He was also on speaking terms with its leader, Otto Hörsing. The second Stahlhelm leader, however – Theodor Duesterberg, who had advanced quickly to the top of an organisation he had only joined in 1923 – took a rather hard-line stance, not only on this occasion. In July 1927, the Stahlhelm *Gau* in Thuringia forwarded a lengthy rant by a certain First Lieutenant Corsep from Erfurt. Corsep had, as he explained in his letter, voiced his resentment against any cooperation with the Reichsbanner and even more the RjF from the start. In explicitly anti-Semitic language, he railed against the alleged influence of 'Jewish' money on the design of this project; against Jewish 'hegemony' in national art more generally; and also against the 'superfluous post' of the Reich Art Custodian, a mere 'product of the revolution'. He was, however, not only driven by political antipathy towards the Republic and its supporters; Corsep had also strong misgivings about the chosen symbolism of a 'death memorial' in Bad Berka. Such a design struck him as wrong, as not the 'dead', but the heroic 'deeds' of all German soldiers – dead and alive – should be commemorated. He believed the Stahlhelm should dare to build its own project, not in a 'remote forest-valley', but as a 'stone colossus' right in the middle of Magdeburg, where it had been founded.[50] This is a clear indication that a memorial in the *Wald*, however closely that symbol was associated with the German nation, was deemed to be too inward-looking and contemplative by radical nationalists. Upon receiving Corsep's rant, Theodor Duesterberg noted that he had rejected any collaboration with the Reichsbanner and RjF all along, and decided that support for the project should be 'temporarily suspended'.[51]

The internal discontent in both major veterans' leagues contributed to the fact that the implementation of Bad Berka lost momentum in the late 1920s. In 1925, however, the strong initial support of four veterans' leagues for Bad Berka had secured a majority for that project in the first place, particularly when it was backed up by the highest state representative. Even Edwin Redslob changed tack almost immediately under the impression of the agreement reached between the leagues and Hindenburg. In June 1925, he had publicly come out in support of

[50] Corsep to the Erfurt Stahlhelm branch, 19 July 1927: BArch, R 72, 268, fos. 63–6.

[51] Note by Theodor Duesterberg, 23 July 1927, and Duesterberg to 'Stahlhelm, Landesverband Mitteldeutschland', 9 September 1927 (quote): BArch, R 72, 268, fos. 61f.

an idea to put the 'Unknown Soldier' centre stage: Redslob suggested building a bridge over the Rhine. In the middle, passers-by would be able to see the memorial to the Unknown Soldier, who would be buried in the river, hidden behind latticework. As Redslob explained, the grave of the Unknown Soldier would turn the bridge 'into the symbol of a time that wanted to overcome revenge and hatred through the power of the heart'.[52] Redslob's proposal, to be sure, tapped into the traditional mythology of the Rhine as a site of German identity. But his main inspiration had been a visit to Paris, where he had seen the burial site of the *inconnu* under the Arc de Triomphe, and the play *Heinrich of Andernach* by pacifist and Reichsbanner activist Fritz von Unruh.[53] In this play, the winegrower Heinrich is converted to the cause of reconciliation between France and Germany by an encounter with the Unknown Soldier, who has risen from his grave.[54] The Reich Art Custodian's idea received mostly welcome praise in newspaper articles and personal letters – not least by Fritz von Unruh himself, who saw an opportunity to promote his own work.[55]

But only a couple of months later, Redslob dropped his plan altogether. In a memorandum to the Reich Minister of the Interior, who was in charge of the whole process, Redslob supported the notion of the 'Holy Grove', referring to the 'united front-line fighters' expression of their will' as his main reason for doing so.[56] Shortly afterwards, the subcommittee of the Reichsrat, which tried to reconcile the interests of the *Länder*, followed suit. In January 1926, only the representatives for Bavaria and Thuringia had voted in favour of Bad Berka. By March 1926, only Prussia and Saxony were left as supporters of a memorial at the Neue Wache in Berlin, and Bad Berka had a clear majority among the Reichsrat.[57] Nonetheless, that still did not mean a swift decision in favour of Bad Berka. In the spring of 1926, two professors of the Art Academy in Düsseldorf submitted the design for a *Toteninsel*, or 'Island of the Dead', in the Rhine close to the town of Lorch. Connected by a footbridge made of stone, the first of

[52] Edwin Redslob, 'Das Soldatengrab am Rhein', *Berliner Tageblatt* no. 302, 28 June 1925.

[53] *Ibid.*

[54] Fritz von Unruh, 'Heinrich aus Andernach' (1925), in *Sämtliche Werke*, 13 vols., Vol. V (Berlin: Haude & Spener, 1991), pp. 7–64.

[55] Frankfurter Societäts-Druckerei to Redslob, 7 July 1925, and other materials in BArch, R 32, 361.

[56] Edwin Redslob, 'Denkschrift zu der Frage des Reichsehrenmales', 15 February 1926: BArch, R 43/I, 713, fos. 150–3 (quote on fo. 153). Welzbacher, *Redslob*, p. 179 wrongly asserts that Redslob sought out the veterans' leagues as allies in support of a design he had already developed.

[57] Bucher, 'Errichtung', pp. 363f.

two islands should serve as a gathering space, whereas the second should contain the memorial proper, a simple sarcophagus. The idea appealed to many politicians – including chancellors Hans Luther and Wilhelm Marx, who governed in 1926/7 – and members of the public, as the war had in their view been fought to protect the Rhine as a German river. Once the governor of the Prussian Rhineland province and other dignitaries from the region jumped on board, the campaign for Lorch gathered considerable momentum, and was able to rally the regional *Gaue* of both Stahlhelm and Reichsbanner to its cause.[58]

Ultimately, the campaign for a national memorial on the Rhine came to nothing. But it was strong enough to cause considerable delay a final decision, at a time when support for Bad Berka within the veterans' leagues was disputed, and when even the officials in charge had not finally agreed on procedural matters – for instance, whether the Reichsrat would also be part of the decision-making, or only the Reich government. Even in August 1926, the envoy of the state of Württemberg in Berlin anticipated that it could still 'take a long time' before a decision was made.[59] Four consecutive Reich Ministers of the Interior dealt with the issue, from Wilhelm Külz (DDP) to Joseph Wirth (Centre Party), before the Reich government finally decided in favour of Bad Berka in March 1931. By this time, however, two other projects had already sidelined the *Reichsehrenmal*. On 18 October 1927, the Tannenberg Memorial, a vast circular structure reminiscent of a medieval castle, with eight massive towers and a metal cross in its centre, was unveiled in East Prussia. Supported and erected by the private initiative of right-wing circles, it tapped into the myth of the medieval Teutonic Order. Its focus on German domination in the East was also connected with the glory of the victory in a 1914 battle against the Russians somewhere near this site, and with the myth of Hindenburg in particular, who was present at the unveiling ceremony.[60]

The Neue Wache in Berlin

Two years later, another sideline unfolded in Berlin. Partly frustrated by the slow progress of the decision-making process, and eager to demonstrate that Prussia could act quickly, the Social Democrat Prussian prime minister Otto Braun asked his officials in June 1929 to assess the option

[58] See the press clippings in BArch, R 32, 494; and Bucher, 'Errichtung', pp. 365–77.

[59] Württembergische Gesandschaft to Württembergisches Staatsministerium, 28 August 1926: HStASt, E 130b, Bü 3840.

[60] See Goebel, *Great War*, pp. 36–8, 127–32.

of converting the Neue Wache into a Prussian memorial for the fallen. This idea, to be sure, had already been floated during the meandering discussions on the *Reichsehrenmal*, and was thus nothing that required lengthy deliberation. Five months later, in November, the Prussian cabinet decided accordingly. After an artistic competition, the prize-winning design by architect Heinrich Tessenow was implemented. In minimalist fashion, it reduced the commemoration of the fallen to its abstract core, placing a simple granite cube in the centre of the room, illuminated by daylight flooding in from the ceiling. Only an oak wreath on top of the cube symbolised the link to the German nation, and a stone tablet with the inscription '1914–1918' made the reference to the war explicit.[61] Tessenow's design was a masterpiece of commemorative symbolism in Weimar Germany, and of twentieth-century modernist architecture more generally. Stripping the memorial of any political or monumentalist connotations, it forced the observer to focus on his or her grief and on the meaning of violent death alone. What has been said about the Cenotaph by Edwin Lutyens in London applied even more to Tessenow's design in Berlin: it was a 'work of genius largely because of its simplicity'.[62]

Yet in political terms, this was a missed opportunity. As Otto Braun stressed during the unveiling ceremony on 2 June 1931, the memorial was a deliberate attempt to demonstrate that a democratic Prussia, governed by Social Democrats, could work in altruistic service for the people and the nation. And he highlighted the symbolic fact that the fallen were commemorated at a place where the Prussian army used to house its guard. In his memoirs, Braun recalled that this war memorial for him also served as a symbolic tomb of the 'militaristic' traditions of the Prussian monarchy.[63] Braun was also personally concerned, as his son had died in the war, and he expressed his own grief. Nonetheless, many former Prussian generals refused to attend the ceremony, and the National Socialist press mocked the apparent inability of the Social Democrat Braun to reach out to nationalist circles. Even worse, though, he perceived the indifference of his own party, which did not send any official delegates, while *Vorwärts* covered the event only in a short notice on the back pages.[64]

[61] Bucher, 'Errichtung', p. 381; on the iconography see Sean A. Forner, 'War Commemoration and the Republic in Crisis: Weimar Germany and the Neue Wache', *CEH* 25 (2002), 513–49 (pp. 536–45). The oak wreath could also be read as the 'common symbol of reverence to the dead'. See the expert opinion of 'Ministerialrat Dr Behrendt', 'Niederschrift der Sitzung des Begutachtungsaussschusses für den Wettbewerb ..., Anlage 2', 15 July 1930: BArch, R 32, 358, fo. 38.

[62] Winter, *Sites of Memory*, p. 104.

[63] Otto Braun, *Von Weimar zu Hitler* (Hildesheim: Gerstenberg, 1979 [1940]), p. 335.

[64] Hagen Schulze, *Otto Braun oder Preußens demokratische Sendung* (Frankfurt am Main: Propyläen, 1977), p. 657.

These parallel developments were a major reason why the preparations for Bad Berka lost momentum, and why the memorial was never built even though the actual design competition began once the cabinet had finally approved of this site in 1931.[65] They were, however, not the only reasons why it was effectively impossible to implement a national memorial, at least when it was meant to commemorate the fallen in the context of the *deutscher Wald*. It should be clear by now that artistic, political, practical and symbolic considerations were deeply entwined in the protracted and wide-ranging search for an appropriate *Reichsehrenmal*. Arguments about the preferred symbolism of the memorial and its appropriate implementation were surely only one strand of the debate. Yet a closer look at the arguments in favour of a *Heiliger Hain* in the forest reveals the inherent problems and contradictions of this particular symbolic idea.

We have already highlighted anti-urbanist sentiment as one major reason why both active participants and observers of the debate on the *Reichsehrenmal* favoured a memorial in the German forest. According to one of the many architects who supplied Edwin Redslob with expert opinions on the preferred form and place of the *Reichsehrenmal*, the *Wald* was basically an ideal setting for a memorial site as it would allow visitors to gather in 'silent commemoration' and would also facilitate 'spiritual exchange'. The physical qualities of an environment dominated by huge trunks stood in direct correlation to the rituals of remembrance that were to take place in the shadow of the trees. Thus, the 'roaring of German male choirs' would subtly 'blend with the forest rustle of German oaks, and with the oath of allegiance and the solemn pledge for a strengthening of our people'.[66] Nature, in other words, nurtured and underscored the preferred mode of remembrance, which centred on the spiritual renewal of the nation after the catastrophe of war. Such a rendering of the *Wald* as *Reichsehrenmal* stressed the holiness of the site and by implication the religious qualities of remembrance it would foster. Not by chance, the memorial forest was often metaphorically described as a 'dome of nature'. And in the 'Most Holy' space of this dome, the 'grave of the unknown dead' could be situated, shaped by an artist, but embedded in an arrangement that relished the power of nature.[67]

[65] See Hilbig, *Reichsehrenmal*, pp. 243–52, 276–92.

[66] Architect Hugo Koch to Redslob, 9 December 1925: BArch, R 32, 354, fos. 65ff.

[67] *Ibid*. See also Alfred Bass to Redslob, n.d. [March 1926]: BArch, R 32, 355, fo. 10. Numerous suggestions for the centre of the Holy Grove were made. One example included a fountain design, adorned by a dying warrior who unbuttons his uniform, with a jet of water coming out of his chest collected in a bowl held by a women with two children. See memorandum by Edwin Redslob, 4 June 1926: BArch, R 32, 355, fo. 56. On the trope of the forest as a 'dome', conjuring up images of Gothic cathedrals,

The forest as a site of contemplation

Again combining practical and symbolic considerations, many commentators pointed to the fact that a memorial in the forest would not require extensive building work and was thus cost-effective. This would save funds that could be much better used for practical help to the war disabled and dependants. Such demonstrative restraint was all the more advisable as there was a broad agreement on the need to mark a fundamental break with the nineteenth-century tradition of erecting *Siegesmale*, or 'victory memorials', such as the Völkerschlachtdenkmal in Leipzig. Strictly focused on the remembrance of the fallen, a modest *Totengedenkmal* was envisaged.[68] In a remote place, far away from the hustle and bustle of the big cities, the 'Holy Grove' would allow for silent contemplation and would thus be a site of 'serious self-examination [*Einkehr*]', which was all the more needed as it was a constant reminder of the 'seriousness of the world-historical catastrophe' of the past First World War.[69] The list of arguments in favour of a Holy Grove did not stop here. Placing the national memorial in the midst of a German forest would not only foster the general mood of contemplation that was a key prerequisite of any meaningful commemoration; in addition, it would provide a rallying point in a time of bitter conflicts and general divisiveness. 'Nature was', after all, 'neutral, above party and confessional strife'.[70] The key to achieving this aim was the active participation such a memorial required. This was at least the opinion of architect Otto Bartning (1883–1959), who was affiliated with Bauhaus ideas and headed a school of architecture in Weimar once Bauhaus moved to Dessau in 1925. Himself an experienced designer of many Protestant churches in Austria and Germany, Bartning was convinced that any sculptural design was bound to fail, and that the memorial had to be situated in a wood. It had to be literally *erwandert*: requiring every visitor to walk through the forest in order to reach the actual memorial site: 'Everyone who is used to hiking through nature or has done so in the past knows that precisely through this very practice, step by step, the quarrelling of the present, whether it is based in politics

see Ursula Breymayer and Bernd Ulrich (eds.), *Unter Bäumen: Die Deutschen und der Wald* (Dresden: Sandstein, 2011), pp. 62, 135.

68 Fritz Hilpert, *Das Reichsehrenmal und die Frontkämpfer* (Berlin: Deutsche Verlagsgesellschaft für Politik und Geschichte, 1927), p. 8 (quotes); see also Hermann Kube and Karl Heicke, 'Kurze gutachtliche Äußerung über das Projekt der Schaffung eines Reichsehrenmals bei Weimar', 11 January 1926: BArch, R 32, 354, fos. 22–5; Ernst Boerschmann to Redslob, 20 April 1926: *ibid*., fo. 17.

69 Kube and Heicke, 'Kurze gutachtliche Äußerung', fos. 22–5.

70 Applegate, *Nation of Provincials*, p. 77.

or in aesthetics, ceases to exist, as does the inner conflict of the self.'[71] The veterans' associations insisted that designating a space in the forest as a memorial for the fallen would reveal the essence of the German nation. As 'Germany's heart is beating in its forests', it would be only appropriate 'to entrust the remembrance of the dead of the Great War to this heart'.[72] Expert opinions seconded this view and tapped into romanticist notions of the inward looking nature of German culture. A 'monumentalist construction' such as the Völkerschlachtdenkmal, one expert opined in 1925, would work well as a 'site for festivities'. But it would not be able to 'strike the deepest chords in the popular soul', the *Volksseele* of the Germans, as the Holy Grove in a forest would do.[73] The forest at Bad Berka was, to be sure, no *Forst* or cultivated woodland that had taken shape in order to maximise the number of logs that could be extracted. As the fallen had given what was 'most holy' to them – their lives – a space in the *deutscher Wald* was the 'most holy' the contemporaries could give in return to remember their deeds.[74]

There was, as these few examples from a large number of aide-memoires and opinion pieces confirm, widespread agreement that – in artistic terms – the *Reichsehrenmal* had to mark a decisive break with the monumentalist ambitions of Wilhelmine memorial art and what was often deemed to be its worst excess, the Völkerschlachtdenkmal. In the wake of military defeat, a more modest and humble approach seemed to be sensible. Most stakeholders in the process of establishing a *Reichsehrenmal* also agreed that architecture and sculptural art were simply not sufficient as a means to express the sheer magnitude of victims that the war had entailed. Even the sculptor and architect Hermann Hosaeus supported this line of reasoning, although he himself designed about forty local war memorials during the Weimar years and had had tremendous impact on many other projects through his work on the Kyffhäuserbund's advisory board on memorial art.[75] Hosaeus was also in line with many other commentators when he suggested that a grove of honour was by far the best option for the *Reichsehrenmal*. Revising his earlier criticism of the notion of an *Ehrenhain*, which he had voiced during the war, he described it as a truly 'romantic idea', and insisted that

[71] Otto Bartning, 'Gutachten zu der Frage des Reichsehrenmales', 30 March 1926: BArch, R 32, 354, fos. 7–9.

[72] Hilpert, *Reichsehrenmal*, p. 8.

[73] Harry Maaß to Redslob, 3 December 1925: BArch, R 32, 354, fo. 138.

[74] *Berkaer Blätter für den Reichsehrenhain* no. 1, 6 September 1926: HStASt, E 130b, Bü 3840.

[75] Hermann Hosaeus, 'Von der Anlage eines Ehrenhaines im allgemeinen', 9 July 1926: BArch, R 32, 354, fos. 52f.

the natural setting, an appropriate area of forest, should be subjected to only an absolute minimum of man-made interference.[76]

The notion of a Holy Grove had a number of other advantages that explain its popularity in the wide-ranging debates on a national memorial for the fallen. It did not express, as with the nineteenth-century *Nationaldenkmäler*, any specific conception of the German nation as a polity, be it a participatory, national democratic idea or the notion of 'national collection' in a people's community, which the Völkerschlachtdenkmal had encapsulated.[77] Thus, the Holy Grove did not suggest a statement against or in favour of the Republic, and was therefore agreeable across the political camps. In addition, the *Heiliger Hain* did not necessarily imply any specific reference to the military events of the past war, nor did it invoke any particular higher meaning of the sacrifice of the fallen, other than that it had indeed been a sacrifice. Positively speaking, a national memorial in the natural setting of the forest aimed to offer a space for a 'silent commemoration' of the fallen, as Edwin Redslob pointed out in May 1926 in a survey of the existing proposals. As such, it would foster a sense of the sheer 'scale of the suffering' during the war, and of the 'immortality' (*Unvergänglichkeit*) of the German people.[78] Remembering the fallen was thus contextualised in the inner spirituality of the people, conceived of as a community of the living and the dead. At a time when many medievalist and a few modernist designs for war memorials offered competing interpretations of the most recent past, the *Heiliger Hain* took a distinctively different approach: the specific trajectory of German history since 1914 was transferred into the indeterminate state of a natural setting. Nature, in other words, replaced history.[79] This focus on the *Unvergänglichkeit* of the German people was reinforced by a preference for the evergreen trees of a coniferous wood. Eschewing oak as the traditional symbol of German strength, most designs suggested the Holy Grove should consist of common spruce.[80] Set in a natural environment, the Holy Grove was sometimes also called the 'living *Ehrenmal*'.[81]

76 *Ibid.* On his earlier criticism see Goebel, *Great War*, p. 78.

77 See the analysis by Nipperdey, 'Nationalidee'.

78 Edwin Redslob, 'Nachtrag zur Denkschrift über das Ergebnis der Prüfung der Vorschläge zum Reichsehrenmal', 15 May 1926: BArch, R 32, 353a, fos. 46f.

79 On this shift see Wilfried Lipp, *Natur–Geschichte–Denkmal: Zur Entstehung des Denkmalbewußtseins der bürgerlichen Gesellschaft* (Frankfurt am Main; New York: Campus, 1987), pp. 264f.

80 Hilpert, *Reichsehrenmal*, p. 8; the core of the Bad Berka site consisted of fir trees: Duesterberg, *Reichsehrenmal*, p. 4.

81 Karl August Walther, 'Vom Reichsehrenmal', 4 January 1926: BArch, R 32, 355, fo. 105; see Karl August Walther, Cornelius Gurlitt and Johannes Keßler, *Vom Reichsehrenmal* (Munich: Callwey, 1926).

Yet in spite of these many qualities of the conceptual core idea, there was one major pitfall to designating a space in the *Wald* as the *Reichsehrenmal*: the sheer abundance of possible sites. While the forest was acknowledged as the very embodiment of the mythological qualities of the German nation, it had no specific place in the wider realm of the Reich. The inherent problem of the forest as a symbol was, in other words, its ubiquitous nature. Proponents of almost every coherent and well-matured stretch of forest could claim that 'theirs' was the most appropriate for the designated purpose. Hermann Kube and Karl Heicke were two of the experts involved in the assessment of suitable sites, and had – the former as municipal garden director in Hanover, the latter as managing director of the Deutsche Gesellschaft für Gartenkunst – intensive experience with landscaping issues. They expressed the dilemma in these words: 'Given the richness of our country in beautiful woods, which are our pride, it will not at all be difficult to find an appropriate site; rather, problems will emerge in choosing among the many places which might be suitable for this purpose.'[82] At this point, the two experts believed that, solely for practical reasons, Bad Berka was an 'ideal' site as it was situated in the midst of Germany and would thus facilitate access.[83] But only six months later, Hermann Kube had at least partly changed his mind. He inspected a site near Eisenach, which was deeply anchored in German national mythology owing to its proximity to the Wartburg, at which Martin Luther had sought refuge in 1521/2 during the early stages of his struggle for the Reformation. Kube had left with a very 'strong impression', and immediately reconsidered his position vis-à-vis the other proposals.[84] Summing up his inspection of eight forest sites altogether in the north of Germany, including Höxter in Westphalia and Goslar in the Harz mountain range, Kube expressed the inherent problem of any assessment. Faced with an 'abundance of magnificent landscape impressions'

[82] Hermann Kube and Karl Heicke, 'Gutachtliche Äußerung über das Projekt der Schaffung eines Reichsehrenhaines', 11 January 1926: BArch, R 32, 354, fos. 40f.

[83] *Ibid.* The same point was made by Bartning, 'Gutachten zu der Frage des Reichsehrenmales'.

[84] Hermann Kube to Redslob, 25 May 1926: BArch, R 32, 354, fo. 93. Redslob responded the next day, stating that the veterans' associations disliked the idea of a site near Eisenach as their members would be prone to leave it quickly for the Wartburg, thus destroying the contemplative atmosphere of the *Ehrenhain*; *ibid.*, fo. 94. Redslob himself reckoned that the vista to the Wartburg, which opened up on one of the footpaths, was 'a great symbol for the grappling power of German history'. He thus clearly situated the memorial in the Protestant teleology of the German nation state. See Edwin Redslob, 'Denkschrift über das Ergebnis der in Mitteldeutschland vorgenommenen Prüfung der Vorschläge zum Reichsehrenmal', 30 April 1926: BArch, R 32, 353a, fo. 25.

it was impossible to arrive at any 'precise statement' that avoided subjective bias. Any decision had to be based on the qualities of what was often called the 'most sacred' (*Allerheiligste*) ideal of the memorial site, preferably an 'absolutely reclusive' space in an appropriate woodland setting that alone fostered a 'serious, solemn mood'.[85]

Edwin Redslob, who had spent several months travelling across Germany, liaising with mayors and county representatives who all eagerly championed their local forest, shared the sense of exhaustion and frustration among the experts who were trying to identify the most suitable site.[86] Returning from an extended trip to Hesse, Saxony and Thuringia, he distinguished no less than six different potential forms that a Holy Grove in the woodland might take, including hilltops, the grove as an island, wide stretches of forest and those situated in a valley. Bad Berka belonged to the latter category, which was in his view able to draw every participant into a commemorative mood during the approach to the site. But it was disadvantageous that this design looked more like an amphitheatrical stage than an actual closed woodland.[87] In the end, Redslob's 'key criterion' for an overall assessment was that the preferential site have a 'connection to the whole of Germany', both in an 'idealistic' sense and with regard to geographical location and accessibility in terms of transport. But even when applying these strict criteria, Redslob was still able to endorse five sites, including woodland near Weimar, Eisenach, Coburg, Reinhardsbrunn and Augustusburg.[88]

Addressing the same dilemma, another expert suggested opting for Bad Berka, on the grounds that this site would complete the network of national memorials that had already been erected in the centre of Germany. Bad Berka, the argument went, was close to the Kyffhäuser and its memorial for the medieval imperial glory of Emperor Frederick Barbarossa. It also had to be seen in conjunction with the memorial for Hermann the Cheruscan, who had, according to legend, defeated the Romans in the Teutoburg Forest in 9 CE, and with the Niederwald memorial near the Rhine, which commemorated the founding of the Second Empire after the military victory against France in 1871. With the other three memorials, Bad Berka would constitute a 'rhythmic intersection of four' commemorative sites. Thus, it would be a symbol for the 'unity' and cohesiveness of the German manner.[89] The

85 Hermann Kube to Redslob, 11 June 1926: BArch, R 32, 354, fos. 98ff.
86 See for instance his itinerary for March 1926, in Hilbig, *Reichsehrenmal*, p. 168.
87 Redslob, 'Denkschrift über das Ergebnis', fos. 18–29. See the image of a design for Bad Berka by H. de Fries in Bucher, 'Errichtung', p. 372.
88 Redslob, 'Denkschrift über das Ergebnis', fo. 29.
89 Ernst Boerschmann to Redslob, 20 April 1926: BArch, R 32, 354, fos. 17–20.

dialectical nature of this kind of reasoning seems a bit far-fetched, and illuminates the tremendous problems contemporary supporters of the Bad Berka site had, even though its core symbol, the forest, undisputedly embodied 'Germanness'. Speaking in 1925 for the four main veterans' associations, Franz Seldte had established another, more straightforward reason why the site should be located in the 'heart' of Germany; using traditional terminology, he argued that 'all German tribes [*Stämme*]' had equally sacrificed their sons on the battlefield.[90]

As we know with hindsight, such arguments were not able to accelerate the search for a *Reichsehrenmal*. In the late 1920s, the years during which the whole process stalled, different responses to the stalemate emerged. In 1928, the journal of the Stahlhelm reported furiously a sketch on the 'memorial of the Unknown Soldier' that was performed in one of the many cabaret bars in the west of Berlin. On stage, three figures like 'caricatures', representing a mayor, a big industrialist and a military doctor, were about to unveil the statue of a soldier on a plinth. Suddenly, the soldier came to life, moaning and groaning. He started to hurl expletives against the three figures who symbolised the injustice of war, and accused them of war profiteering and hypocrisy. The journal of the nationalist combat league was clearly agitated by this performance, particularly in a city that had allegedly done nothing to honour the fallen, while it was busy renaming streets in a break with the imperial era, just stopping short of unveiling a 'Barmat Street' and a 'Kutisker Place'.[91] For the Stahlhelm, such sleaziness and disrespect for the fallen stood in stark contrast to the tomb of the *inconnu* in Paris. Here, the 'Comité de la Flamme', founded in 1924 to service the eternal flame under the Arc de Triomphe, even voiced the demand that every passer-by should bow his head in reverence to the Unknown Soldier.[92]

The Reichsbanner and its '*Ehrenmal* of the Republic'

Yet supporters of the Republic were also disappointed by the lack of progress in the search for a national memorial and decided to take things in their own hands, at least temporarily. On 11 August 1929,

90 Franz Seldte to Otto Geßler, 9 December 1925: BArch, R 32, 357, fos. 13f.

91 'Pariser und Berliner Heldenehrung', *Der Stahlhelm* no. 6, 5 February 1928. 'Barmat' and 'Kutisker', the names of two Jewish businessmen at the core of a widely publicised corruption scandal, were right-wing codewords for the moral decay of the republican system. See Martin H. Geyer, 'Contested Narratives of the Weimar Republic: The Case of the "Kutisker–Barmat Scandal"', in Canning, Barndt and McGuire, *Weimar Publics*, pp. 215–35.

92 'Pariser und Berliner Heldenehrung'; see Ackermann, 'Identität', p. 304.

Figure 8 Temporary memorial by the Reichsbanner for the celebration of Constitution Day in Berlin near the Brandenburg Gate, 11 August 1929.

the Reichsbanner was the key player in the central celebration of the tenth anniversary of the constitution on the streets of Berlin. To be sure, public rallies and other festivities took place in every major city in the country. But it was in the capital where the largest number of Reichsbanner activists took to the streets in a whole weekend of celebrations, which also included ordinary citizens and schools. The city was decked out in black–red–gold, and a heightened police presence ensured that brawls and open attacks on the republican symbols were kept to an absolute minimum.[93] Social Democrat newspapers hailed the occasion as a 'turning point in the history of Germany',[94] or as the 'great day of the Republic'. For hours, Reichsbanner detachments marched from the Lustgarten to the Brandenburg Gate, symbolising that 'the advance of the republican mindset is unstoppable' and truly 'inexhaustible like a flood'.[95] As the centrepiece of this performative display of republican

[93] Rossol, *Performing the Nation*, pp. 66–71.

[94] 'Triumph der Republik', *Lübecker Volksbote* no. 186, 12 August 1929.

[95] 'Der große Tag der Republik', *Volksstimme* no. 187, 13 August 1929. The Reichsbanner claimed 150,000 participants, but the most reliable estimate is 75,000; Rossol, *Performing the Nation*, p. 69.

Figure 9 '*Ehrenmal* der Republik' ('Monument of the Republic') in Berlin, 11 August 1929.

values, they passed by a temporary or 'ephemeral' memorial: a fleeting commemorative structure that was not made to last but rather to perish, not a monument, but a moment of remembrance.[96]

Designed by the sculptor Theodor Caspar Pilartz on behalf of the Reichsbanner, it was a wooden construction, the base covered in black–red–gold cloth, with three black pillars rising up seventeen metres. Three separate inscriptions drove home the key point: that the deaths of the fallen soldiers and the incessant struggle of the Reichsbanner activists for the Republic were intimately entwined. The first, 'Allen Toten des Weltkrieges' ('To all the dead of the World War'), again highlighted the genuinely inclusive nature of republican war commemorations. The second, 'Den Opfern der Republik und der Arbeit', was ambivalent.[97] It could be read as honouring the sacrifice of those who worked for the Republic. But in conjunction with the third, 'Den Toten des Reichbanners' ('To the dead of the Reichsbanner'), and given the

[96] On this type see Michael Diers (ed.), *Mo(nu)mente: Formen und Funktionen ephemerer Denkmäler* (Berlin: Akademie, 1993).

[97] On this and some other points, my interpretation differs from Rossol, *Performing the Nation*, p. 70.

double meaning of *Opfer* in German parlance, which can mean both sacrifice and victim, it could also imply that working-class people had been turned into the victims of those who attacked the democratic system and of the industrial labour process. As the commentator for the *Berliner Tageblatt* stressed, the 'daring, simple memorial' admonished all participants to mourn those who had lost their lives in the 'lunacy' of war.[98] The abstract, modernist design of the three black pillars with their constructivist shape was indeed striking, but its meaning remained contested. One SPD newspaper described it as a *Trauerkatafalk* – a 'catafalque of mourning'.[99] An illustrated journal was perhaps closer to the point when it referred to the memorial as the '*Ehrenmal* of the Republic', thus clearly associating it with the ongoing search for the *Reichsehrenmal*.[100]

The protracted search for a national memorial for the fallen reached no conclusion during the Weimar years, because regional interests and the right-wing initiative of the Tannenberg Memorial fragmented and thus delayed the decision-making process. Even the project of a Holy Grove in the heart of Germany came to nothing, after long delays in a design competition for Bad Berka, which was not completed until January 1933. While all of the main veterans' associations had supported the site since early 1926, the underlying idea itself remained inconclusive. When a stretch of forest could encapsulate the core qualities of the German nation, and allow for a reflection on the loss and sacrifice of the fallen, why take precisely this site, and not any other in the middle of Germany? Recourse to the immensity and immeasurability of the German people, which was founded and replenished through the forces of nature, was one possible strategy to signify the unity of the nation. But it was not the only one. Employing the 'Unknown Soldier' as an empty signifier was another. It had, as we have already seen, some proponents in the discourse on the *Reichsehrenmal*, including the prominent Reichsbanner members Karl Bröger and Fritz von Unruh.

Indeed, the Reich Art Custodian Edwin Redslob insisted that, far from being an alien invention that could never be adapted, the notion of an 'Unknown Soldier' was in fact deeply embedded in German cultural history. In 1925, he had himself promoted the idea of burying

[98] 'Die Parade des Volkes', *Berliner Tageblatt* no. 377, 12 August 1929.

[99] 'Der große Tag der Republik'.

[100] Cover of *Volk und Zeit* no. 34, 1929, printed in: Dorlis Blume, Ursula Breymayer and Bernd Ulrich (eds.), *Im Namen der Freiheit! Verfassung und Verfassungswirklichkeit in Deutschland* (Dresden: Sandstein, 2009), p. 238.

the Unknown Soldier in the midst of the river Rhine. The united front of the veterans' associations had soon forced him to drop this plan and to act as a liaison for the competing projects for a Holy Grove. But as an art historian and expert on German cultural history, Redslob continued to be committed to this idea in private, and summarised some of his findings in a memorandum written in 1931. According to his research, the formulation of 'An unknown soldier' had already been used on the graves of soldiers from the Napoleonic wars. Furthermore, a tombstone in the Berlin cemetery of the 'March fallen' for someone who had died in the barricade fights during the March revolution in 1848 was adorned with the words 'An unknown man'. Other examples included a resting place dedicated to 'the remains of the unknown', which Prince Hermann von Pückler-Muskau included in 1832 in the now world-famous English landscape park he designed in the meadowlands of the river Neisse near Cottbus. Burial crosses in some German towns during the Great War bore the inscription 'Unknown soldier'. Finally, Redslob was well aware of the fact that Karl Bröger had perhaps not coined but popularised the term with his book from 1917.[101]

The Unknown Soldier as a nationalist symbol

As these examples demonstrate, Redslob was not interested so much in the aspects of this concept specific to the First World War, particularly the fact that many corpses in no man's land had literally not been identified, and that the 'Unknown' had to be selected from a number of unidentified corpses. For Redslob, the use of the 'Unknown Soldier' was basically a fascinating way of avoiding the determination and thus limitation implied in every act of signification. In this perspective, the romantic notion of ineffability allowed an avoidance of the pitfalls of naming, which limited commemoration to one individual, or a multitude of them, without ever addressing the collective as a whole.[102] And this was precisely the reason why some right-wing authors adopted the notion of a nameless, 'unknown' soldier. One of them was Theodor Reismann-Grone, the publisher of the *Rheinisch-Westfälische Zeitung*, which acted as a mouthpiece for the interests of Rhenish heavy industry, who was himself a rabid

[101] Edwin Redslob, 'Aufzeichnungen über das Grab des Unbekannten Soldaten', 18 March 1931: BArch, R 32, 353a, fos. 130f. Redslob falsely situated the grave of the 'unknown' barricade fighter in the Invalidenfriedhof, and not in the 'Friedhof der Märzgefallenen'; for details see Manfred Hettling, *Totenkult statt Revolution: 1848 und seine Opfer* (Frankfurt am Main: S. Fischer, 1998), pp. 17–51.

[102] For Poland, see the quote in Mick, 'Kult', p. 195.

anti-Semite and proponent of *völkisch* nationalism.[103] Using a pseudonym, Reismann-Grone published a booklet in 1921 that the title dedicated 'To the Unknown Fallen Warrior'. A series of short poetic narratives, it contained some common tropes of radical nationalist war commemoration: the racist outcry about the use of non-white colonial soldiers by the Entente powers; the returning Stormtroop fighters who voiced their disgust about the moral decay at the home front; the idea that the inexhaustible forces of the German people would allow them to wage another fight for the glory of the Reich. The dedication of the text spoke on behalf of the 'truly poorest of all poor', in a clear allusion to the famous formulation in Karl Bröger's wartime poem 'Bekenntnis'. Yet this 'mute hero' had been silenced by the 'new rulers' of the Republic and, even worse, the enemies stole the 'ultimate glory' of being a nameless hero when they started to honour their own 'unknown heroism'.[104]

In Reismann-Grone's *völkisch* vision, the Unknown Soldier served as an indictment against the predominance of egoistic interests in the post-war period, which obliterated the altruistic sacrifice of the front-line soldiers and thus made national unity impossible. Other right-wing authors offered a similar reading of the Unknown Soldier as a cipher for the readiness to eradicate one's own subjectivity in the service of the nation.[105] An 'unknown war volunteer' who wrote to Redslob in 1925 wanted to adopt this principle for the *Reichsehrenmal*. All the artists and artisans who were involved in the building of the memorial, it was argued, should remain anonymous, because their names would contaminate the remembrance with their egoism. Ultimately, the memorial should serve only one aim: to commemorate the tremendous effort that 'the nameless', i.e. the 'German people themselves' had made at the battle and home fronts. Thus, it should be dedicated to 'the nameless of 1914'.[106] The Unknown Soldier was not necessarily always a 'victor type', as he was indeed in France, the UK and the USA.[107] In

103 Karl Mews, 'Dr. Theodor Reismann-Grone', *Beiträge zur Geschichte von Stadt und Stift Essen* 79 (1963), 5–32.

104 D[avid] Seeberg, *Dem unbekannt gefallenen Krieger* (Dortmund: Ruhfus, 1921), pp. 5f. On the pseudonym, see the materials in Stadtarchiv Essen, NL Reismann-Grone 652 192.

105 See Paul Beyer, *Düsseldorfer Passion: Ein deutsches National-Festspiel in zehn Bildern* (Munich: Eher, 1933), esp. p. 21; *Der unbekannte Soldat erzählt: Von* *** (Berlin: Mosse Stiftung, n.d. [1934]), p. 7; Wilhelm Becker, *Der unbekannte Soldat: Erlebnisse aus dem Weltkriege* (Paderborn: Schöningh, 1934).

106 Letter by 'an unknown war volunteer' to Edwin Redslob, 3 October 1925: BArch, R 32, 361, fos. 22f.

107 Rainer Rother, 'Der unbekannte Soldat', in Gerhard P. Groß (ed.), *Die vergessene Front: Der Osten 1914/15. Ereignis, Wirkung, Nachwirkung* (Paderborn: Schöningh, 2006), pp. 353–71 (p. 353).

its German right-wing permutation, the strength of this symbol rested precisely on the fact that the unknown, nameless soldier was distraught by defeat and the anomic tendencies of post-war society, but could rise from obscurity and humble origins to redeem the nation and to rescue it from domestic strife.

No one encapsulated this rendering of the Unknown Soldier better than Adolf Hitler. Referring to the British version, Hitler was in fact well acquainted with the notion of the Unknown Soldier, as notes for a speech given on 10 May 1922 confirm. He understood and appreciated it as a symbol for his own conviction that the single soldier was only an 'atom', whereas the army was an 'eternal' entity.[108] But it was apparently Joseph Goebbels who started to use the buzzword of the 'Unknown Stormtrooper' in 1927, trying to foreground the silent sacrifice of these 'party soldiers' for the National Socialist movement. In the same vein, Goebbels and other leading Nazis had referred to Hitler as the 'unknown soldier' since 1929.[109] Starting with the electoral breakthrough that saw the Nazis become a mass party in 1930, Hitler frequently used the cipher of the 'Unknown Soldier' to develop his own populist interpretation of radical nationalism. It marked a decisive break with the Wilhelmine understanding of nationalism and national commemoration, which Hitler repeatedly scorned as the mere formality of raising a toast to the Kaiser and singing the 'Watch at the Rhine', the anthem of traditional enmity towards the French.[110] In Hitler's view, the real challenge for nationalist politics was to overcome the deep cleavages in society and politics. And that could only be achieved through a sense of duty and commitment, not by a member of the bourgeoisie, but by someone who was intrinsically connected to the fate of the German people and to their suffering in the post-war period. No one other than a 'nameless individual' like the 'humble front-line soldier in the nameless army of twelve million people' could accomplish that.[111]

Healing the wounds of the German nation was what the Nazi mass movement had set out to achieve. In its initial version, Hitler tapped into the party legend of those 'seven unknown front-line fighters' who

[108] Eberhard Jäckel and Axel Kuhn (eds.), *Hitler: Sämtliche Aufzeichnungen 1905–1924* (Stuttgart: DVA, 1980), pp. 640f.

[109] See Vappu Tallgren, *Hitler und die Helden: Heroismus und Weltanschauung* (Helsinki: Suomaleinen Tiedeakatemia, 1981), pp. 222, 230–2, 234f.; Behrenbeck, *Der Kult um die toten Helden*, p. 154.

[110] See the speeches in Institut für Zeitgeschichte (ed.), *Hitler: Reden, Schriften, Anordnungen. Februar 1925 bis Januar 1933*, 6 vols., Vol. II.1 (Munich; New York: Saur, 1992–2003), pp. 176, 214.

[111] Speech on 7 December 1930, in *ibid.*, Vol. IV.1, p. 151.

had met in 1919 and who were 'miraculously' able to drum up support for a nationalist mass movement.[112] Campaigning in the spring of 1932, Hitler had narrowed this version down to praise for nationalist fervour which mainly focused on his own accomplishment. Speaking in Potsdam on 4 April 1932, he referred back to the humble origins of his struggle for the regeneration of the German nation: 'In the dying days of the World War, I was a nameless soldier and started the fight.'[113] A couple of days later, in another speech, Hitler recalled 'how difficult it had been to arrive at 11 million [voters], starting off as an unknown soldier with seven men'.[114] His populist appeal to the German people pitted himself, the 'unknown, nameless soldier' who had founded a nationalist mass movement in a time of political upheaval and national degradation, against the elites who 'ruled over Germany' and had betrayed their country.[115] Germany was indeed different, as a journal of the SA, the Nazi Stormtroopers, stressed in 1940. All belligerent nations of the First World War would 'pay homage to the Unknown Soldier'. Yet Germany was the 'only country in which the Unknown Soldier is not dead, but alive'.[116]

It was neither simply military defeat nor the centrifugal tendencies of the federal political system that caused the lack of a unifying national symbol as the centrepiece of German commemorations of the Great War. Both factors undoubtedly played a role, the latter actually much more so than the former. But they account for the failure to establish a *Reichsehrenmal* only in an analysis that is narrowly focused on the institutional parameters of the quite complicated decision-making process. For a full understanding of the underlying problems, however, it is necessary to consider the symbolic dimensions of this search for a national memorial. What was needed was a signifier that could function as a capstone for the diverse and often contradictory meanings attached to the war. That was indeed possible, through recourse to an intrinsically Germanic form of nature that signified the strength of the German people. Not least, the *Wald* had also been the site of the fiercest battles of the Great War, a place in which the forces of nature, technology and human willpower interacted. Ernst Jünger's novel *Das Wäldchen 125*,

112 Speech on 28 November 1930, in *ibid.*, p. 136.

113 *Ibid.*, Vol. V.1, p. 23.

114 Speech on 9 April 1932, in *ibid.*, p. 45.

115 Speech on 2 April 1932, in *ibid.*, p. 7. See also his speech on 5 March 1932, in *ibid.*, Vol. IV.3, p. 182.

116 *Die SA*, 21 June 1940, quoted in Behrenbeck, *Der Kult um die toten Helden*, p. 154; for similar quotes from Nazi Party members before 1933 see German Werth, *Verdun: Die Schlacht und der Mythos* (Bergisch Gladbach: Bastei Lübbe, 1982), pp. 521f.

published in 1925, updated the forest as a 'metaphor' for German 'identity' in the context of a battle in which it was not the outcome, but the very experience of the men who had fought in it, that mattered.[117] *Das Wäldchen 125* had been a German forest because German men battled in it. Back in Germany, it was anything but clear-cut which particular stretch of *Wald* was best suited to commemorate the sacrifice and suffering of German soldiers.

A *Reichsehrenhain* in the forest could have been the basis for a specific German style of commemoration. There was broad agreement on the pertinence of the symbol between the republican camp and those who despised the democratic state. Most of the experts who were involved agreed equally on the matter, from supporters of Bauhaus modernism on the left to a an utterly conservative architect such as Willy Lange. The recourse to nature depoliticised the search for a national symbol. Yet the forest as symbol for the root and core of the German manner was soon tangled up in the myriad woodland locations that could claim to have a deep historical connection to the 'heart' of the nation. In this matter, the centrifugal tendencies of German federalism could also prevail: a strong alliance between Redslob as the responsible civil servant and the Reichsbanner as the major democratic mass organisation did not materialise as it did, for instance, with regard to the celebration of Constitution Day.[118] Judging from the archival record, Redslob acted in rather opportunistic fashion in the matter of the *Reichsehrenmal*.

Many German observers were suspicious about the 'Unknown Soldier', as the Western Allies had quickly turned it into the centrepiece of a successful commemorative ritual in their respective capital cities. Simply emulating it in Berlin was deemed to be inappropriate, all the more so as anti-urbanist feelings were an important undercurrent in the debate on the national memorial. Yet a German Social Democrat war veteran, Karl Bröger, could justifiably claim that he was the first author who had popularised the notion of the Unknown Soldier, which also had precedent in German cultural history as a symbol for the dignity of the nameless humble patriot. In the footsteps of a number of right-wing authors, another war veteran, Adolf Hitler, adopted the

[117] See Ernst Jünger, *Das Wäldchen 125: Eine Chronik aus den Grabenkämpfen des Jahres 1918* (1925), in *Sämtliche Werke*, 23 vols., Vol. I.1 (Stuttgart: Klett–Cotta, 1978), pp. 301–438. It has been translated into English as Ernst Jünger, *Copse 125: A Chronicle from the Trench Warfare of 1918*, trans. Basil Creighton (London: Chatto & Windus, 1930). See the brilliant analysis by Heinz-Dieter Kittsteiner, 'Waldgänger ohne Wald: Bemerkungen zur politischen Metaphorik des deutschen Waldes', in Bernd Weyergraf (ed.), *Waldungen: Die Deutschen und ihr Wald. Ausstellungskatalog der Akademie der Künste* (Berlin: Nicolai, 1987), pp. 113–20 (p. 115).

[118] Rossol, *Performing the Nation*, pp. 18–33, 58–79.

name 'Unknown Soldier' for his populist agitation both against the Weimar Republic and against the shallow and meaningless patriotism of the Wilhelmine elites. The publicist Hans Schwarz, a proponent of the 'conservative revolution', rejected the 'Unknown Soldier' in 1930 as the 'magic coldness of conceptual thinking [*Begrifflichkeit*]', and as an egalitarian leveller. Instead of this abstract 'shadow', Schwarz argued, the Germans should rather commemorate those students who had sacrificed their lives in the battle of Langemarck in 1914. They were the prototype of a 'new aristocracy' that alone could rescue the German nation.[119] Hitler, however, was not concerned by these objections, and he had no use for the Langemarck myth with its elitist underpinnings. In his view, the self-determination of the German nation could only be accomplished through the self-denial of a nameless war veteran. Thus, the notion of the Unknown Soldier had travelled from the moderate left to the far right. In 1936, Joseph Goebbels publicly congratulated Karl Bröger on his fiftieth birthday, again referring to the famous words of Germany's 'poorest son'. In the same year, a second edition of Bröger's book on the Unknown Soldier was published.[120]

119 Hans Schwarz, *Die Wiedergeburt des heroischen Menschen: Eine Langemarck-Rede vor der Greifswalder Studentenschaft am 11. November 1928* (Berlin: Der Nahe Osten, 1930), pp. 12f.

120 Müller, *Für Vaterland und Republik*, p. 173.

6 Pacifist veterans and the politics of military history

In their symbolism and architectural design, and with all accompanying rituals, war memorials were 'realms of memory'.[1] At these sites, the impulse to mourn the fallen, to honour their sacrifice and to sketch out political consequences for the living were inseparably entwined. Ultimately, any commemoration of the dead around war memorials dealt with the sublime, and it was expected that all participants express their reverence towards the fallen. Political differences were not entirely suspended in the memorial cult, but they were much less pronounced than in other figurations of memory. Even though no ultimate consensus on a national symbol of commemoration could be reached, this was not due to political cleavages. Veterans from the left and right, as well as modernist and conservative architects, agreed that German national identity could be symbolised best through recourse to the *Wald*, and thus to the primordial power of nature.

Yet memories of the First World War were also expressed and elaborated in a more systematic engagement with the past – through history proper, so to speak, understood as the examination of sources that could shed light on perceptions and decisions that had shaped the course of events. To be sure, the Great War was only one of many periods and aspects of the more recent past that came under intensive scrutiny during the Weimar years.[2] But it was certainly a rather important one, as it was inextricably connected to the crucial question of the legitimacy of the republican system. Here, legitimacy was not understood in the legalese of constitutional deliberations, but rather in terms of a morality and necessity of certain actions. Had the war plans of the general staff offered a realistic basis for German success, taking all military and political factors into account? Had the Army Supreme Command with

[1] Pierre Nora, 'General Introduction: Between Memory and History', in Pierre Nora (ed.), *Realms of Memory: Rethinking the French Past*, 3 vols., Vol. I (New York: Columbia University Press, 1996), pp. 1–20.

[2] As a general reflection, see Robert Gerwart, 'The Past in Weimar History', *CEH* 15 (2006), 1–22.

its hyperbolic war aims caused the defeat, or the revolutionary agitation of socialist labour? These were some of the big questions that agitated a broad public throughout the 1920s. Seen in conjunction, they constituted what in German parlance is called *Geschichtspolitik*, the politics of history. It is best defined as a contested field in which 'competing interpretive elites' use the past as an instrument for the pursuit of political aims.[3]

One crucial element of this field was its relative openness. Professional academic historians were only one, and most often not the decisive, stakeholder in this arena.[4] Other interest groups included the Reichswehr as the official curator of the estate of the former wartime army; more generally former wartime officers; and, in a time when the mass media already shaped public opinion, all those who could mass-market popular genres of history writing. Again, these different forms of intervention in the politics of history were often closely related. Many former department heads in the Army Supreme Command, and heads of staff in the army groups and armies, for instance, were quick to publicise their version of events in memoirs. Most of these books were widely reviewed, not only in the specialist military press, but also in newspapers and other media outlets. Obviously, they were not simply literary works, but mainly driven by the 'strategic' interest to exonerate those who had been in charge of the German military machine from any responsibility for the defeat.[5] Generals and staff officers were not the only members of the military elite who publicised their own reading of the historical trajectory that had led to November 1918. Many other members of the old officer corps, most of whom were of aristocratic descent, contemplated the reasons for the German collapse in autobiographical accounts.[6]

But not all former members of the imperial officer corps were in some form of denial about the causes of German defeat, or even actively attempted to assign blame to the democratic politicians who had governed since October 1918. Either under the direct impact of the war

[3] For this definition see Markus Pöhlmann, *Kriegsgeschichte und Geschichtspolitik: Der Erste Weltkrieg. Die amtliche deutsche Militärgeschichtsschreibung 1914–1956* (Paderborn: Schöningh, 2002), p. 22.

[4] *Ibid.*, p. 23.

[5] See Markus Pöhlmann, '"Daß sich ein Sargdeckel über mir schlösse": Typen und Funktionen von Weltkriegserinnerungen militärischer Entscheidungsträger', in Dülffer and Krumeich, *Der verlorene Frieden*, pp. 149–70 (p. 170).

[6] Wencke Meteling, 'Der deutsche Zusammenbruch 1918 in den Selbstzeugnissen adeliger preußischer Offiziere', in Eckart Conze and Monika Wienfort (eds.), *Adel und Moderne: Deutschland im europäischen Vergleich im 19. und 20. Jahrhundert* (Cologne: Böhlau, 2004), pp. 289–321.

experience, or upon closer reflection at some point in its aftermath, a small group of officers formally abandoned their allegiance to the *esprit de corps* of the Wilhelmine military elite. They said farewell to active military service, if they had not already been discharged by the end of the war, and turned towards an active promotion of pacifist policies. The reasons for this decisive step were as diverse as the former military assignment and biographical trajectory of these pacifist officers. Abandoning the *esprit de corps* of the officer caste had made them homeless in a social and political sense, and leaning towards pacifism, with its highly disparate and divisive set of various small associations and factions, did not really change this situation. These pacifists remained, to be sure, a tiny minority among the approximately 24,000 wartime officers in the Prussian army and the 3,000 officers in the Imperial Navy.[7] The first more systematic effort to analyse the biographies of these individuals contains information on 15 officers who abandoned their career during or after the Great War, and henceforth actively engaged in pacifist circles.[8]

The significance of pacifist officers

Given the huge disparity between this figure and the overall number of officers in the German army, one might be tempted to discount pacifist officers as an entirely irrelevant phenomenon. That, however, would be wrong for at least three reasons. There was no common thread that characterised the decisive break of these men with the German military tradition; yet it is, firstly, significant that many of them joined the ranks of the Reichsbanner Black–Red–Gold and thus fused their tireless efforts to promote the democratic state and its colours with a mostly moderate pacifism. In contrast to the more radical versions of pacifism in the 1920s, these pacifist officers did not reject the notion of national defence outright, and accepted the existence of the Reichswehr in principle, while vehemently criticising the lack of democratic oversight and many other particular aspects of its policies. As a republican veterans' association, the Reichsbanner was in many respects the ideal political platform for these men, as it allowed them to work in an environment in which most members were familiar with the military. Moreover, secondly, some of these pacifist officers were not simply Reichsbanner members, but Reichsbanner luminaries. On the one hand, they took

[7] Figures in Wolfram Wette, 'Befreiung vom Schwertglauben: Pazifistische Offiziere in Deutschland 1871–1933', in Wette and Donat, *Pazifistische Offiziere*, pp. 9–39 (p. 11).
[8] See Wette and Donat, *Pazifistische Offiziere*.

a leading position in the republican league, and had a high profile as contributors to the *Reichsbanner* journal and as speakers at its mass rallies and branch meetings. On the other hand, the league systematically exploited the symbolic capital that their former service as officers brought to those political and historical topics in which military experience provided a particular competence.[9] As high-profile members and military experts of a mass organisation, this group of pacifist officers gained political significance way beyond their tiny numerical strength.

In addition it should, thirdly, be stressed that the Reichsbanner membership of many other former officers is a still largely unexplored phenomenon. Judging only from scattered evidence, it seems that a significant number of former officers in the wartime army, both from the reserve and from the active professional corps, joined the ranks of the republican league. One of them was the former major general Günther von Bresler (1867–1945), who served in 1929 on the non-executive board of the Reichsbanner, but who had also been the head of the Saxonian branch of the Deutsche Friedensgesellschaft (German Peace Society; DFG) since 1927.[10] In the same year, he reviewed the mass spectacle of up to 100,000 Reichsbanner members who had gathered in Leipzig for the celebration of Constitution Day on 11 August. On this and other occasions, von Bresler had met 'hundreds of former officers' who understood that the Republic provided the proper platform for the 'reconstruction' of the nation. Yet fears about a possible 'boycott' by their *Standesgenossen* – literally 'fellows in the officer estate', according to the feudal terminology still prevailing in the military – hindered many from openly declaring their support for the Republic.[11]

Certainly those who joined the league did not always bring the amount of publicity and controversy to the Reichsbanner as some of the former high-ranking professional officers. Nonetheless, they also contributed to the politics of military history from a leftist perspective. One example was Ludwig von Rudolph. During the war, he had served as a reserve lieutenant in various Bavarian regiments. Back at home in Nuremberg he worked as an elementary school teacher. As a Reichsbanner activist,

[9] The significance of these efforts is missed by Wette, 'Befreiung vom Schwertglauben', p. 33.

[10] Friedrich-Karl Scheer, *Die Deutsche Friedensgesellschaft (1892–1933): Organisation, Ideologie, politische Ziele. Ein Beitrag zur Geschichte des Pazifismus in Deutschland* (Frankfurt am Main: Haag und Herchen, 1981), p. 421; 'Der Reichsausschuß des Reichsbanners SRG: Anlage zu Pol. Dir. Nürnberg', 24 October 1929: StA Bremen, 4, 65, 1034; Generalmajor a.D. von Bresler, 'Wie ich Republikaner wurde', *RB* no. 8, 15 April 1927; see also his foreword to Schützinger, *Kampf um die Republik*, pp. 3f.

[11] Generalmajor a.D. von Bresler, 'Der Geist im Reichsbanner', *Berliner Tageblatt*, 14 August 1927: StA Bremen, 4, 65, 1032, fo. 242.

he occasionally gave talks on the history and significance of the Great War, such as a lecture on 'Ypern 1914 and 1926' at the local branch in the neighbouring town of Kronach.[12] Yet von Rudolph also publicly engaged with the politics of military history, for instance in the context of the *Dolchstoßprozeß*.

This trial, which took place in the autumn of 1925 in Munich, was in many respects a widely publicised version of the parallel proceedings of the parliamentary subcommittee on the 'causes of the German collapse' in 1918. Nicolaus Cossmann, national-conservative editor of the *Süddeutsche Monatshefte*, had published a special issue in 1924 that tried to underpin the allegation that the Social Democrats had systematically prepared a 'stab in the back' since the beginning of the war. When the Social Democrat newspaper *Münchener Post* heavily criticised this smear campaign, Cossmann sued the editor, Martin Gruber. Formally a libel process – which ended with Gruber being sentenced to a 3,000 mark fine – it was in fact another public controversy on the reasons for Germany's defeat. Both sides marshalled written evidence and presented expert witnesses to support their case.[13] Following extensive press coverage, von Rudolph volunteered to stand in the witness box for the *Münchener Post*. In a letter to Max Hirschberg, lawyer for the defendant, and himself a Reichsbanner member, von Rudolph explained his readiness to testify publicly about his experiences at the front. For him it was 'hard to bear' that 'the remembrance of the war and its final months deviate more and more from the reality' of these events.[14] As a highly decorated front-line officer, von Rudolph was ready to testify in public, something Fritz Einert for instance had not dared to do at about the same time. It was not only in the sense that the *Dolchstoßprozeß* became a success for the pacifist left, even though it was defeated in judicial terms. It was also a success for the majority wing of the Social Democratic Party (SPD), as, even before the sentence was announced, the legal representative for Cossmann declared that he had never intended to blame moderate Social Democrats for the defeat, but only the radical wing of the Independent Social Democratic Party (USPD).[15] By and large, the Reichsbanner had always justified

[12] 'Lagebericht der Polizei-Direktion Nürnberg Nr. 110/27', 13 June 1927: StAM, Pol. Dir. 6890.

[13] See Barth, *Dolchstoßlegenden*, pp. 510–15.

[14] See *Der Dolchstoß-Prozeß in München Oktober–November 1925: Eine Ehrenrettung des deutschen Volkes* (Munich: G. Birk, 1925), quote on p. 444, and his testimony on pp. 445–54. On Hirschberg see his memoirs: Max Hirschberg, *Jude und Demokrat: Erinnerungen eines Münchener Rechtsanwalts 1883 bis 1939* (Munich: Oldenbourg, 1998).

[15] See *Der Dolchstoß-Prozeß*, pp. 127f.

the politics of the majority wing of the SPD during the war, and was thus both relieved and exonerated by the outcome of this trial.

Before we analyse the republican politics of military history in more systematic fashion, it seems worthwhile to chart the biographical trajectory of some of these pacifist officers. They were in many ways significant actors on the political stage of imperial and Weimar Germany, and they certainly all had both turbulent and dissonant lives that are significant in their own right. From the small group of more prominent officers in the Reichsbanner – which also comprises the former captains-at-sea Lothar Persius and Heinz Kraschutzki, and the cavalry officer and playwright Fritz von Unruh – four individual biographies shall be scrutinised in some detail. The first is that of former general Paul Freiherr von Schoenaich (1866–1954).[16] When Schoenaich was sent into early retirement at the rank of major general on 1 April 1920, he looked back on thirty-seven years of distinguished service in the Prussian army. Even as late as 1949, he described these years as 'the best period of my life'.[17] After service in the navy and in a cavalry regiment, he worked in the Prussian War Ministry from 1907 before returning to the troops as a regimental commander in 1913. During the war, he first led a cavalry regiment, before serving as department head for railways and logistics in the War Ministry in Berlin.

Paul Freiherr von Schoenaich and Berthold von Deimling

By 1919, Schoenaich had joined the left-liberal German Democratic Party (DDP), presumably the main reason why he was sent into early retirement. During the revolution, he had worked well with the soldier's council for the War Ministry, which had sacked inefficient officers in cooperation with him. This gave Schoenaich the impression that the Republic would be based on principles of performance and duty, which he considered to be the authentic Prussian ethos. Support for the DDP had the immediate effect of his formal exclusion from the Deutscher Offiziersbund and the regimental association of the 2nd Guard Dragoon Regiment. Schoenaich also faced social ostracism from the affluent middle-class circles around the landed estate in

16 For the following, see Friederike Gräper, 'Die Deutsche Friedensgesellschaft und ihr General: Generalmajor a.D. Paul Freiherr von Schoenaich (1866–1954)', in Wette and Donat, *Pazifistische Offiziere*, pp. 201–17; Stefan Appelius, 'Der Friedensgeneral Paul Freiherr von Schoenaich: Demokrat und Pazifist in der Weimarer Republik', *Demokratische Geschichte* 7 (1992), 165–180.

17 Quoted in Gräper, 'Schoenaich', p. 201.

Holstein where he and his wife lived. In 1922, Schoenaich contacted the West German branch of the DFG and its head, the radical pacifist Fritz Küster. Soon after, the former general joined the DFG and promoted, among other pacifist ideas, disarmament and democratic reforms of the officer recruitment for the Reichswehr. From the mid 1920s, Schoenaich followed Küster in promoting more radical measures such as draft resistance. Thus, he also supported the so-called Ponsonby action in 1927/8. This transnational campaign adopted the call of Arthur Ponsonby MP to collect signatures in favour of draft resistance and the refusal to serve the country in case of a military conflict. While the radicals in the DFG around Küster adopted the call and collected signatures, moderates in the DFG remained sceptical, doubting the value of such a campaign at a time when the German military did not even have the draft.[18] Schoenaich's growing radicalism culminated in a clash with Otto Hörsing over 'Battle Cruiser A' in 1928. It was only in 1932, though, that Schoenaich was finally forced to leave the non-executive board of the Reichsbanner, much to the satisfaction of former general and Reichswehr minister Wilhelm Groener.[19]

Schoenaich had joined the Reichsbanner in 1924, and soon advanced to become one of the most active speakers of the league. When congratulating him on his sixtieth birthday in 1926, Ludwig Quidde, then head of the DFG and the prominent figurehead of liberal pacifism, described Schoenaich more generally as the 'most successful public speaker [*Versammlungs-Apostel*] of German pacifism'.[20] And that accolade was entirely justified. Schoenaich himself reckoned that he had spoken at about 1,000 public gatherings and rallies from the early 1920s to 1933.[21] Yet the increasingly bitter dispute between radical pacifists such as Schoenaich and the Reichsbanner leadership not only put a strain on relations at the top of the republican league; local Reichsbanner functionaries also felt increasingly uneasy about Schoenaich's appearances. Their reasons are illuminated in a letter by Willy Dehnkamp, then the head of the Reichsbanner branch in the Bremen suburb of Vegesack. In April 1929, Dehnkamp discussed his reasons for rejecting a planned event with another speaker from the DFG, just a few months after Schoenaich had railed against SPD support for Battle Cruiser A

[18] Scheer, *Friedensgesellschaft*, p. 513.

[19] See Gräper, 'Schoenaich', p. 211.

[20] Quoted in Thomas Lowry, 'Symbolische Gesten: Paul Freiherr von Schoenaich und die französischen Friedensgeneräle Martial-Justin Verraux (1855–1939) und Alexandre Percin (1846–1928)', in Wette and Donat, *Pazifistische Offiziere*, pp. 218–29 (p. 222).

[21] *Ibid.*

in front of a crowd of 1,800 people, in a gathering that was guarded by local Reichsbanner men. At the age of twenty-six, Dehnkamp (1903–85), a post-war mayor of Bremen and already a battle-hardened SPD functionary, simply could not understand, let alone condone, such undisciplined behaviour. Reflecting 'radical' discontent in his local Reichsbanner branch, Dehnkamp qualified Schoenaich's speech, which had immediately been exploited by the local Communisty Party (KPD) newspaper, as a 'great tactical imprudence', and explained the rationale for this hard judgement in the following:

> You might argue that I look at this issue far too much through the glasses of the organisational man, of the party secretary. Maybe. But precisely this is in my opinion the strength of our party, that in consideration of the movement or of a given target, criticism sometimes disappears or at least recedes in the background, in fact must recede if discipline and solidarity should not be empty words ... The existing external façade of party unity and unanimity despite inner antagonisms is exactly what no bourgeois party can emulate, and what provides the strength and the very foundation of our party. And because of this unanimity people such as Schoenaich can never work in the SPD, precisely because they are too much individualists.[22]

What is revealing about Dehnkamp's statement is not only the extent of open resentment towards an outspoken and utterly committed republican politician such as Schoenaich – who indeed was, as all pacifist officers, a highly idiosyncratic individualist, and necessarily all the more so as his former circles of sociability had turned their back on him – but that, furthermore, Dehnkamp did not hesitate to apply the same rather rigid organisational principles that governed the SPD to the Reichsbanner, without even noticing any possible difference between the two. Schoenaich himself, however, remained dedicated to the pacifist cause. From 1928 to its forced dissolution in 1933, he served as chairman of the DFG, and lived a reclusive life during the years of the Nazi dictatorship. After 1945, he again served as chairman of the newly founded DFG, but was forced out of this office in 1951 when he supported a referendum against West German rearmament that the Communists had initiated.

Another high-profile pacifist officer was the former general Berthold von Deimling (1853–1944).[23] During his military career, Deimling had been no stranger to controversy. Coming from a family of civil servants in liberal Baden, he joined the military in 1871 and advanced quickly

[22] Willy Dehnkamp to Paul Günzel, 4 April 1929: StA Bremen, 7, 88, 50/3.

[23] On Deimling, see Kirsten Zirkel, *General Berthold von Deimling: Eine politische Biographie* (Essen: Klartext, 2008).

as an officer in the Prussian army. His first controversial assignment came in 1904/5, when he was appointed as a regimental commander in the Schutztruppe for the German colony of South-West Africa. In that capacity, he took a leading role in the genocidal warfare against the Herero and Nama tribes, and commanded troops in the infamous battle at the Waterberg in August 1904, which initiated the genocide. During the campaign, Deimling alienated the civilian governor, Theodor Leutwein; sidelined his superior, General Lothar von Trotha; and pushed his inferiors around amid often frantic outbursts. Yet upon his return to Berlin in 1905, he was ennobled by Wilhelm II for his services. In May 1906, Deimling was appointed as commander of the Schutztruppe. Back in South-West Africa, he immediately halved the number of German troops and managed to settle the war with the Herero and Nama peoples. Yet before his departure Deimling presented himself on 26 May 1906, in a heated exchange with Matthias Erzberger and other critical deputies in the Reichstag, as a military hardliner full of contempt for the parliament as a legislature.[24]

From 1907, Deimling served in Alsace, first as a brigade commander, and then from 1 April 1913 as commanding general of the XV Army Corps in Strasbourg. When the Zabern Affair broke in November 1913, he had already made a name for himself as a ruthless supporter of German military superiority in the Reichsland, which was centrally controlled from Berlin. Following the verbal abuse of Alsatian civilians by a Lieutenant Günter von Forstner in the small garrison town of Zabern, the press and almost all parties in the Reichstag condemned this blatant abuse of military power. Deimling, however, covered Forstner's action up, and ordered a regimental commander to detain some civilians in Zabern, with full awareness of the illegality of his action. While the Zabern Affair evolved into *the* major constitutional crisis in late Wilhelmine Germany, Deimling's position was rather strengthened, despite widespread criticism in the media and in parliament, as he had the full support of the Kaiser.[25] During the war his fortunes eventually changed. Early on, other high-ranking officers criticised Deimling for acting alone and taking irrational decisions without proper strategic value. His reputation as a dare-devil commander who recklessly sacrificed the lives of his troops reached a first climax when Deimling ordered an attack against superior British forces at Ypres on 17 November 1914. It led to tremendous casualties among the German regiments.[26] Fifteen years later, as a highly popular Reichsbanner leader, Deimling still tried

[24] *Ibid.*, pp. 47–72. [25] *Ibid.*, pp. 74–91. [26] *Ibid.*, pp. 98f.

to counter the enduring negative reputation his actions on this day had engendered.[27]

Subsequent assignments at Verdun and the Somme in 1916 did not improve Deimling's fortunes as a military commander. In November 1916, he was sent to command troops on a very quiet stretch of the Vosges front and was thus informally demoted. In September 1917, he was finally forced to tender his resignation, and spent the remainder of the war as a pensioner in Baden-Baden. It is safe to assume that disappointment with this sudden end to a distinguished military career was one key factor in Deimling's incremental switch from a sabre-rattling arch-militarist to a devoted republican and moderate pacifist. At least equally important was the fundamentally altered political context after the departure of the Kaiser into his Dutch exile and the proclamation of the Republic, which spurred Deimling to work for the nation on the basis of the new political system.[28] Deimling himself described the recalibration of his political compass as a continuous process, turning him first into a *Vernunftrepublikaner* ('republican of convenience') who accepted the Republic on the grounds of reason, only gradually becoming a full-fledged 'democrat, heart and soul'.[29] At any rate, he also retained crucial elements of his soldierly worldview, for instance the tendency to obfuscate human agency through recourse to the contingency of greater powers. Writing his autobiography in 1928, he commented on the decision in 1917 that had forced him to resign with the words: 'Everything is fate. The soldier has not to ask for reasons, but has to obey.'[30]

Following German defeat, Deimling made a rapid career, first in the left-liberal DDP, and then in the Reichsbanner, which he joined immediately upon its foundation in 1924 as a member of the non-executive board. In both organisations, he advanced to become one of the most popular speakers. When the eighth anniversary of the Reichsbanner was celebrated on 22 February 1932, an enthusiastic crowd of 9,000 people squeezed into the hall in Magdeburg, eager to see the famous Reichsbanner luminary. In a 1924 DDP rally in the Sportpalast in Berlin, Deimling spoke in favour of international reconciliation in front of a crowd of 20,000.[31] Nothing in Deimling's agenda for a patriotic pacifism deviated from the most common features of this current: he

[27] Berthold von Deimling, 'Wie war es bei Ypern? Eine Abwehr', *RB* no. 44, 2 November 1929.

[28] Zirkel, *Berthold von Deimling*, pp. 102–10, 120–6.

[29] Berthold von Deimling, 'Lebenserinnerungen': BA/MA, N 559, 5, fo. 493.

[30] *Ibid.*, fo. 452.

[31] Zirkel, *Berthold von Deimling*, pp. 181f.

was in favour of coordinated disarmament and conflict resolution in the framework of the League of Nations, and strongly against conscription without supporting the more radical measure of draft resistance, but he insisted that nations had the right to maintain an army for self-defence.[32] The appeal of Deimling's pacifism and pro-republican commitment did not rest on the policies he suggested. Rather, it relied on the performative power of someone who could lend credibility to these policies as a highly decorated former officer – on 3 September 1916, Deimling had received the *Pour le Mérite*, the highest military distinction the Prussian king could award. Ludwig Quidde acknowledged this in 1924 when he wrote to Deimling that he had 'an authority that we as lay-people are lacking' when it came to convincing a larger public about the 'unimaginable horror of future wars'.[33] Deimling himself explicitly referred to the reasons for the persuasiveness of his convictions. Speaking in Paris on 3 October 1931 at a rally organised by the veterans of the 'Amitiés internationales', he expressed his 'pride' about being the 'first German general' who could condone peace in France 'in the aftermath of the war'.[34] Even political opponents grudgingly admitted the peculiar legitimacy of Deimling's engagement for a 'no more war' pacifism. Like articles by other pacifist officers, his statements were 'especially dangerous' as they were likely to 'confuse the minds of the readers'.[35]

Former police colonel Hermann Schützinger

Schoenaich and Deimling were high-ranking career officers who, with their flamboyant personalities, supported the struggle for international reconciliation, and the dignity of all individuals and democracy, and further increased their already high profile through relentless campaigning for DDP and Reichsbanner. The other two pacifist officers introduced here had a somewhat different profile. They were less well known among contemporaries, and their careers after the switch to republican pacifism are best described as those of two utterly loyal SPD soldiers. The first, Hermann Schützinger (1888–1962), came from a respected middle-class family in Bavarian Swabia. After leaving the *Gymnasium*

[32] *Ibid.*, pp. 197–210.
[33] Quidde to Deimling, 10 September 1924, cited in *ibid.*, p. 211.
[34] 'Ansprache des Generals v. Deimling bei der Kundgebung der "les Amitiés internationales" und "la ligue des Anciens Combattants Pacifistes"', 3 October 1931: BA/MA, N 559, 5.
[35] Werner von Heimburg, 'Nie wieder Krieg!', *Deutsche Tageszeitung* no. 153, 30 March 1924: BA/MA, N 559, 35.

(grammar school) with a high-school diploma, which was required for a career as an officer in the Bavarian army, he commenced service with the 11th Infantry Regiment in Regensburg in 1908, advancing to the rank of lieutenant in 1910.[36] Shortly before the outbreak of the war, Schützinger published a short novel with the title *Die Waffen hoch!* (*To arms!*) under a pseudonym. Already the title suggests the gist of the plot. It was a pun on *Die Waffen nieder!* (*Down with the Arms!*, 1889), the famous anti-war novel by Austrian pacifist Bertha von Suttner, who was the first woman to receive the Nobel Peace Prize in 1905. In his diatribe against organised pacifism, Schützinger reaffirmed the view that war is a law of nature, furthering the Social Darwinist principle of natural selection.[37]

During the war, Schützinger mostly served as a troop officer, first as a company commander, then a battalion commander in the 11th Bavarian Infantry Regiment. Unlike Deimling, he thus had first-hand experience of the destructive nature of machine warfare, and there can be no doubt that his impressions of the slaughter at the Ban de Sapt in 1915 were one particular turning point that fostered his critical attitude towards war, and instigated his post-war engagement in the peace movement.[38] Yet this was never a straightforward 'conversion' to pacifism, as war letters to his parents reveal. As early as August 1914, he noted with disappointment that the Iron Cross was mostly awarded to military staff in the rear area, but not to those who were actually 'smelling gunpowder'.[39] In October 1914, he observed, with critical undertones, the gruesome impression of swollen corpses in a 'field of death' at the front. But in the same letter, he also developed the paternalistic notion of his company as a 'family'. Schützinger conjured up the image of himself as the 'father' who would celebrate All Souls and later Christmas with his utterly pious Catholic Bavarian soldiers according to 'traditional German custom'.[40]

The turning point came in 1915, when his regiment prepared to storm a French position on the Ban de Sapt height in the Vosges. 'Do

[36] For a first sketch see Dieter Riesenberger, '"Soldat der Republik": Polizeioberst Hermann Schützinger (1888–*ca.* 1960)', in Wette and Donat, *Pazifistische Offiziere*, pp. 287–301. A more reliable, comprehensive outline of his biography is Heinrich Schützinger, 'Biographie von Dr. Hermann Schützinger', 13 August 2003: AdK, Kempowski-BIO, 6865/1; see also the scattered evidence in Gerstenberg, *Freiheit*, Vol. I, pp. 44f., 90, 112f., 249f.

[37] Riesenberger, 'Soldat', p. 289.

[38] See also the letter by his son, Heinrich Schützinger, to Walter Kempowski, 15 May 2003: AdK, Kempowski-BIO, 6865/1.

[39] Hermann Schützinger to his parents, 24 August 1914: *ibid.*

[40] Hermann Schützinger to his parents, 31 October 1914: *ibid.*

not publicise' – these words at the beginning of a letter to his parents in April 1915 indicate Schützinger's awareness that his impressions no longer fitted into the patterns of a patriotic discourse. Very often, excerpts from war letters were published in newspapers to foster an allegedly authentic image of the front.[41] A couple of weeks later, he 'openly' concluded that this 'brutal and beastly murdering' was no longer bearable.[42] And that was before the events on 22/3 June 1915, when his regiment attacked the Ban de Sapt and was almost wiped out. Among the most harrowing experiences of this day was an old friend's decision to have a photograph taken, in anticipation of his own death. When the news of his death came later that day, Schützinger assumed that his own 'foreboding of death' would 'have to be fulfilled for sure', as that of his friend had been. On top of that came the experience of face-to-face combat using hand grenades, bayonets and 'Bavarian knives'. Towards the end of the battle, three of the most reliable members of his company staff, a sergeant, an orderly and a hand-grenade thrower, died standing right next to him under artillery fire, leaving Schützinger with the 'uncanny' feeling of having survived among the dead.[43]

These two days were surely a turning point in Schützinger's life, but their significance was only realised later.[44] In another novel, published in 1918, he tried to express his feelings of despair about the deaths of his comrades and the underlying guilt about being a survivor, in a narrative that made explicit references to his own experiences at the Ban de Sapt.[45] But Schützinger continued to revel and excel in his army service. In October 1918, he was overjoyed to be promoted to the rank of captain, serving as a machine-gun officer in the 'Oberbau Stab' of the 5th Army. In that position, he was responsible for the development and fortification of machine-gun positions on a 45 km-long stretch of the western front, and he was proud to develop new procedures for machine-gun target finding and to get proper 'recognition' for it.[46] Only the revolution completed his switch to the SPD. Upon return to his garrison in Regensburg, he founded and commanded a 'Volkswehr'

[41] Hermann Schützinger to his parents, 14 April 1915: *ibid.*

[42] Hermann Schützinger to his parents, 5 May 1915: *ibid.*

[43] See the very detailed letter to his parents, 28 June 1915: *ibid.*

[44] Schoenaich had had a similar experience, but drowned his sorrows in alcohol, and acquired no pacifist feelings from it. See Paul Freiherr von Schoenaich, 'Soldat und Pazifist' (1924), in *Zehn Jahre*, p. 96.

[45] Hermann Schützinger, *Das Lied vom jungen Sterben: Kriegsroman aus dem Ban-de-Sapt* (Dresden; Leipzig: Pierson, 1918).

[46] Hermann Schützinger to his parents, 22 February (quote), 15 and 20 October 1918: AdK, Kempowski-BIO, 6865/1.

company in January 1919 – one of those units that served the Majority Social Democrat (MSPD) government. But Schützinger struggled to advance his unit against the Communist Council Republic in Munich in April, a disappointment that convinced him that Democratic troops also needed a strict chain of command.[47] From 1919 to 1921, Schützinger studied in Munich and completed a doctorate in economics, while also running a small pro-republican press agency, and publishing articles on – among other political topics – the strategic failures of the Army Supreme Command.[48]

An active member of the MSPD, he was involved in developing ideas for the safe-guarding of the Republic against the combat leagues of the *völkisch* right. On 28 June 1922, the Vaterländische Verbände (Nationalist Combat Leagues) had demonstrated their strength in a massive rally against the 'war guilt lie' on the Königsplatz. About 2,000 men of the 'Auer Guard', the SPD defence organisation, had tried to show strength and presence on the Odeonsplatz, but had been easily pushed aside by police units.[49] Just the next day, Schützinger submitted a detailed memorandum to the executive board of the local SPD, in which he suggested that much tighter administrative oversight and regular training in marching in closed columns for the republican self-defence formations were needed. Only such intensive efforts, he argued, would achieve the main aim of acting as a 'deterrent' against 'recklessness' from the right.[50] Written more than a year before the Hitler putsch, this was already an outline of the framework for republican defence work Schützinger later tried to implement as a Reichsbanner leader.[51] Soon after, Schützinger had the opportunity to put some of his ideas on policing public order into practice. In September 1922, he joined the Prussian police in Hamburg-Altona, advancing to the rank of a major. In May 1923, he was appointed as a police colonel in Dresden, serving the Saxonian government of Minister-President Erich Zeigner, who was elected by the combined vote of the SPD and KPD. In that function, Schützinger intended to use the so-called 'Proletarian Hundreds' – joint working-class self-defence units that in Saxony were the precursors of the Reichsbanner – as a tightly controlled auxiliary police in the case of a state of emergency.[52]

[47] Riesenberger, 'Soldat', p. 290.
[48] Heinrich Schützinger, 'Biographie von Dr. Hermann Schützinger'.
[49] Gerstenberg, *Freiheit*, Vol. I, p. 89.
[50] Hermann Schützinger, 'Denkschrift über die Organisation zum Schutz der Republik in München', 29 June 1922: StAM, Pol. Dir. 6878.
[51] See the outline in Schützinger, *Kampf um die Republik*.
[52] See Voigt, *Kampfbünde*, pp. 90f.

Figure 10 *Polizeioberst a.D. Dr. Schützinger, Mitglied des Reichsausschusses*, picture postcard, n.d. Schützinger is introduced as a member of the non-executive board of the Reichsbanner, but depicted in his uniform as police colonel.

When a Reich execution led by Reichswehr troops forced the Zeigner government out of office on 30 October 1923, Schützinger was sent into temporary retirement, and formally discharged in April 1925. At that time, he had already embarked on a very busy life as a public speaker and writer for the Reichsbanner, in which he was a leading member of the non-executive committee. Schützinger was also active in the pacifist Deutsche Liga für Menschenrechte (German League for Human

Rights), successor of the Bund Neues Vaterland (1914–22), which had directly opposed the war from the start, and participated in the 'no more war' movement during the early 1920s.[53] Another platform for his relentless activism was the Republikanischer Reichsbund, which had absorbed many former members of the Republikanischer Führerbund, a short-lived association of pro-republican Reichswehr officers. The funds for all political activities came from running a press agency that was accredited in Berlin at the Reichstag. During the years of the Nazi dictatorship, Schützinger first worked for a publisher and, from 1942 to 1945, for one of the state agencies that controlled the production of technical goods and iron materials. In the Federal Republic, he returned to work in journalism, covering debates in the Bundestag in Bonn for various media outlets until his death in 1962.[54]

It is impossible to do justice to the full range of topics and political issues that the pacifist officer Hermann Schützinger covered in his many writings and speeches during the Weimar Republic. He actively contributed to the politics of military history through his many articles in the *Sozialistische Monatshefte*, in which he rebutted the *Dolchstoß* myth, analysed the strategic shortcomings of the Army Supreme Command – and of Ludendorff and Hindenburg in particular – and openly criticised the fateful glorification of these generals among a bourgeois public.[55] One particular aspect of Schützinger's activism ought to be highlighted: his clear awareness of some of the ambivalences in the imposing edifice of the Reichsbanner organisation, ambivalences that in his view were necessary side-effects of the attempt to mobilise on a grand scale for the Republic. When the Reichsbanner – which was based, as we have seen, on his ideas at least with regard to the regular training and orderly discipline of its members – was founded in 1924, Schützinger travelled across Saxony and spoke during the founding meetings of various local branches. On one such occasion, in the town of Plauen, he justified the need for uniforms by arguing that they were needed to ensure popularity, but had to be balanced against the 'decidedly pacifist tendencies' of the league. The bottom line was, he insisted, that the Reichsbanner members reject any 'military humbug'.[56] In a similar vein, he insisted

[53] See 'Sonderbericht Pol. Dir. Nürnberg', 25 May 1925: StA Bremen, 4, 65, 1027.

[54] Heinrich Schützinger, 'Biographie von Dr. Hermann Schützinger'; on the Republikanischer Reichsbund see Geyer, *Verkehrte Welt*, pp. 119f.

[55] See for instance Hermann Schützinger, 'Die erdolchte Front', *Sozialistische Monatshefte* 27 (1921), 121–5; 'Feldherrnkult und militärische Kritik', *ibid.* 28 (1922), 88–96; 'Die neudeutsche Strategie im Weltkrieg', *ibid.* 28 (1922), 214–24; and 'Hindenburg und Ludendorff', *ibid.* 28 (1922), 726–35.

[56] Cited in Voigt, *Kampfbünde*, p. 268.

that the Reichsbanner try to tap into the pacifist idea of the 'Unknown Soldier' in its commemoration of the fallen. As such, they would only ever pay tribute to the 'soldiers', not to the 'war itself': would conduct *Kriegerehrung*, but not *Kriegsehrung*.[57]

Schützinger was also adamant in defending the Reichsbanner against aggressive criticism from the radical left. In 1926, for instance, Kurt Tucholsky launched another of his sweeping attacks on the mere *Realpolitik* of the republican league. Directly addressing one of Schützinger's articles, Tucholsky claimed that such an approach had so far yielded 'nothing, nothing and once again nothing'. He accused the Reichsbanner and the SPD more generally of not taking ownership of the revolution in 1918, and identified a 'misunderstood notion of discipline' as the root cause for the 'ruin of German Social Democracy'.[58] In his rebuttal, Schützinger acknowledged that 'revolutionary élan' was indeed often missing, and thanked Tucholsky for that reminder. He used the opportunity to illuminate the peculiar situation of the small bunch of officers who had come out in favour of pacifism and the left. In the past months, Schützinger explained, he had spent most of his time on paperwork for several court cases in which he had tried to restore his own personal integrity against hostile or libellous newspaper coverage. Meanwhile, the few republican ex-military had hardly any 'breathing space in their own camp'. Former captain-at-sea Lothar Persius had just telephoned, relaying the news that many people wondered why Persius and Schützinger endured such bad treatment by Otto Hörsing. Hans E. Lange had also been in touch with Schützinger. Lange (1871–1961) – lieutenant-colonel and commander of an infantry regiment during the war, and from 1919 to 1924 police colonel and head of the security force in Mecklenburg-Schwerin – was another pacifist officer and progressive multifunctionary: as an executive board member of the Deutsche Liga für Menschenrechte and – until 1929 – of the DFG, and as Reichsbanner leader in the Berlin-Brandenburg *Gau*. Temporarily frustrated by the internal workings of the Reichsbanner machine, Lange had told Schützinger that he wanted to retire to the countryside, and that Schoenaich said he wanted to move to Palestine.[59] He and other pacifist officers, Schützinger concluded, had 'sacrificed simply

[57] Cited in *ibid.*, p. 344; on the Unknown Soldier, see also Schützinger, *Kampf um die Republik*, p. 87.

[58] Kurt Tucholsky, 'Was brauchen wir – ?', *Weltbühne* 22.I (1926), 239–42.

[59] Hermann Schützinger, 'Kameraden', *ibid.*, 283f. These personal contacts suggest by the way that the pacifist officers in the Reichsbanner, while undoubtedly idiosyncratic individuals, kept close ties as an informal group. For a different view, see Zirkel, *Berthold von Deimling*, p. 137. On Lange, see 'Der Reichsausschuß des Reichsbanners SRG', and his few remaining personal papers in AdsD, NL Hans Emil Lange.

everything' for the pursuit of their ideas: 'family, former comrades, our whole existence'. And yet they were not only facing the 'roaring tide of nationalism' but also 'envy' within their own camp.[60]

Only a couple of months later, Schützinger had to refute yet another sweep by Tucholsky against the shallow 'Sunday republicans' of the Reichsbanner, who lacked any 'positive ideas'.[61] In his response, Schützinger admitted how hard it often was to slog on with the routine displays of Reichsbanner republicanism: just another Sunday spent at a local flag consecration, with the obligatory greetings by the branch leader and the mayor, the commemorative bit to the tune of 'I Had a Comrade' – 'often the most humanly touching scene of the whole theatre' – right up to the moment when the honorary maid forgot her few words as she handed over the black–red–gold banner, even though they were scribbled down in her 'shivering hands'. All that was a drudgery and an often tedious routine. But it was, Schützinger insisted, something he readily did again and again, simply because the question 'Republic or monarchy?' was not at all of secondary relevance as long as reactionary circles indulged in nostalgia for the past. And the left, he demanded, should pay respect to the 'endlessly devoted Reichsbanner *Muschkoten* ["humble foot-soldiers"]', who took to the streets in order to defend the Republic.[62] At any rate, Schützinger was a versatile and highly respected Social Democrat functionary and committed pacifist, who used the Reichsbanner as a platform for his many ideas on policing and other policy issues. Open-minded and reflexive, he also engaged in a meaningful dialogue with radical pacifists and critics on the left.

Karl Mayr: political maverick and Reichsbanner leader

These qualities were certainly not the strength of the final pacifist officer introduced here, former major Karl Mayr (1883–1945).[63] Throughout his lifetime, Mayr remained a political maverick, whose activities were

[60] Schützinger, 'Kameraden', 283.

[61] Kurt Tucholsky, 'Der Sieg des republikanischen Gedankens', *Weltbühne* 22.I (1926/II), 412–15 (quotes on pp. 412f.).

[62] Hermann Schützinger, 'Reichsbanner und republikanischer Gedanke', *Weltbühne* 22.II (1926), 494f.

[63] Aspects of Mayr's biography are often mentioned in studies on Hitler and the early Nazi Party. The account in Gerstenberg, *Freiheit*, Vol. I, pp. 283–97 is polemical; see my 'Wanderer zwischen den Welten: Der Militärkritiker und Gegner des entschiedenen Pazifismus Major a.D. Karl Mayr (1883–1945)', in Wette and Donat, *Pazifistische Offiziere*, pp. 273–85. Indispensable for the period from 1933 to 1945 is Olaf Schwede, *Karl Mayr: Frontsoldat, Förderer Hitlers, Kämpfer gegen den Nationalsozialismus*, M.A. dissertation (University of Hamburg, 2006).

often clouded in secrecy, and who alienated not only opponents but also his political friends. Communist historians in the German Democratic Republic alleged that he had joined the Reichsbanner only on behalf of the Reichswehr, in order to report on details of Social Democrat military policy.[64] In repeated libel trials, the radical pacifist Fritz Küster, who had gained influence in the DFG from the mid 1920s, tried to dig up dirt against Mayr. Küster accused Mayr, among other things, of having channelled French money into the hands of *völkisch* Bavarian separatists in the spring of 1923.[65] Social Democrats who knew him closely through long-term collaboration confirmed that Mayr retained the 'habit of a professional soldier', and even more so that of an 'intelligence officer'; that he was 'very close, very reticent'; and kept up close communication with personal contacts and acquaintances in the right-wing camp. Indeed, Mayr even had informants in the 'Braunes Haus' in Munich, the Nazi Party headquarters. Yet Franz Osterroth insisted that Mayr's activism in the SPD and the Reichsbanner was based on 'inner conviction', and that his fight against National Socialism was genuinely 'passionate'.[66] Walter Hammer, who knew Mayr from the Reichsbanner non-executive board, encountered him in the infamous prison cells in the basement of the Reich Main Security Office in Berlin in September 1940, and again in the Sachsenhausen concentration camp a year later. In post-war exchanges, Hammer also testified to Mayr's personal integrity.[67] Nevertheless, the trajectory of Mayr's biography is full of tragedy and ironical twists. From April 1943 until his death on 9 February 1945, Mayr worked in the Gustloff works in Weimar, a factory run by the SS that exploited his and other inmates' labour in the nearby Buchenwald concentration camp. When some Wehrmacht generals visited the factory, they clicked their heels in front of Mayr, whom they instantly recognised as their former superior in the wartime army.[68]

Coming from a respectable Catholic middle-class family in Mindelheim (Bavarian Swabia), Mayr commenced his career as an officer in 1901. Promoted to captain in June 1915, he served during the war at various fronts, becoming a general staff officer with the Bavarian Alpenkorps from September 1916 to January 1918. As head of the

[64] Gotschlich, *Kampf*, p. 139.

[65] 'Vom "Völkischen Beobachter" zur Reichsbannerzeitung', *Das andere Deutschland* no. 3, 18 January 1930; 'Die Wahrheit über Major a.D. Mayr', *ibid.* no. 32, 9 August 1930.

[66] Franz Osterroth to R. Vogel, 6 May 1969: AdsD, NL Franz Osterroth, 1/FOAC00000138.

[67] Walter Hammer to Rudolf Rothe, 11 November 1951: IfZ, ED 106, 54; see also the testimony in Viktor Korb von Koerber to Walter Hammer, 7 March 1954: *ibid.*

[68] Franz Osterroth, 'Erinnerungen 1900–1934', p. 198.

proganda office in the intelligence department of the Reichswehr Group Command 4 in Munich from May 1919, he employed Adolf Hitler as a 'V-man', or snitch. In early July 1920, Mayr left the Reichswehr at his own request having attained the rank of major and a pension entitlement. The most probable reason was his resentment of separatist plans formed in circles of the Catholic-conservative Bavarian People's Party (BVP), which governed Bavaria at the time.[69] In the following months, Mayr tried to gain influence in the Nazi Party, which he himself had helped to nurture. He had hoped that it could function as an equivalent to the short-lived party *Nationalsozialer Verein* (1896–1903), in which Friedrich Naumann, one of the most prominent liberals of late imperial Germany, had tried to reconcile national liberalism and attempts to better the condition of the working class.[70] But these hopes were disappointed, and Mayr left the Nazi Party in March 1921. Shortly afterwards, Mayr established contact with Erhard Auer, head of the SPD in Munich, whom he supplied with documents about the separatist ideas of Georg Heim and other leading BVP politicians. Auer used this information for articles in the *Münchener Post*.[71]

Starting with these contacts, Mayr subsequently moved closer to the republican camp. In a gradual process, he tried to 'accustom himself to the Social Democrat movement', and formally joined the party in 1924.[72] But the switch from active opponent of the democratic state – Mayr had supported the Kapp putsch in March 1920 while still a Reichswehr officer – to devoted supporter of the Republic took time. In a 1923 letter to Hans Delbrück, professor in Berlin and the liberal doyen of German military history, Mayr still described himself as a *Vernunftrepublikaner*, accepting the Republic merely out of reason, as a lesser evil.[73] Delbrück supported the plan to find a position in the Reichsarchiv for the former staff officer, but to no avail. Meanwhile, Mayr continued to study German strategy during the war in private, and published his first findings in article form.[74] It was only when he

[69] See his letter to Hans Delbrück, 24 March 1923, in which he also declared his principled opposition to Ludendorff's political ambitions: SBPK, NL Hans Delbrück, Mappe Karl Mayr, fos. 15f.

[70] According to conversations with Franz Osterroth. See Franz Osterroth, 'Erinnerungen 1900–1934', p. 197.

[71] For an example of such correspondence see Karl Mayr to Erhard Auer, 19 May 1922 (transcription): StAM, Pol. Dir. 6878.

[72] '"Wer ist Major Mayr?" Eine systematische Hetze', *RB* no. 9, 2 March 1929.

[73] Mayr to Delbrück, 6 April 1923: SBPK, NL Hans Delbrück, Mappe Karl Mayr, fos. 17f.

[74] Mayr to Delbrück, 26 April 1923: *ibid.*, fo. 19; see Karl Mayr, 'Die Deutsche Kriegs-Theorie und der Weltkrieg', *Die deutsche Nation: Eine Zeitschrift für Politik* 5 (1923), 193–210, 274–84.

Figure 11 Reichsbanner functionaries review a marching column on Prinzregentenstrasse in Munich, 26 May 1929. Standing in the front of the car is Karl Mayr, in the rear of the car Otto Hörsing. Adolf Dichtl, head of the Reichsbanner in Munich, is standing on the footboard.

joined the Reichsbanner in 1924 that Mayr became fully committed to the republican cause. During the first years of his engagement with the veterans' association, Mayr's sphere of activities was basically in and around Munich, giving speeches in local branches and at festivities, and writing articles for the *Münchener Post* and the *Reichsbanner* journal.[75] But soon his purview broadened, and he came into contact with Karl Höltermann, the deputy head of the Reichsbanner, who trusted him personally and was keen to employ his military expertise for the league. For a long time, it was planned that Mayr should be the deputy to Höltermann as editor-in-chief of the weekly *Reichsbanner* journal. It was only after a long delay, though, that he commenced working in this position in late 1928, and rented a flat in Magdeburg. Mayr soon clashed with Franz Osterroth, who had worked as acting deputy editor of the journal for a couple of months. Coming from the Jungsozialisten, the youth organisation of the SPD, Osterroth simply could not bear Mayr's 'glowing hatred against Soviet Russia'.[76]

[75] See Wolfgang Grammel, 'Das Reichsbanner Schwarz–Rot–Gold in Freising', *Amperland* 30 (1994), 325–31; PND report no. 560, 23 January 1927: StAM, Pol. Dir. 6888.

[76] Franz Osterroth, 'Erinnerungen 1900–1934', pp. 188, 195 (quote).

And anti-Bolshevism had indeed been one of the most persistent elements in Mayr's political worldview since his days as a counter-revolutionary army officer in post-war Munich. The ability to express these views was certainly one of the reasons why Mayr felt comfortable as a Social Democrat.[77] He was not a supporter of radical pacifism either. In 1922 he opined in a letter to Hans Delbrück that 'for the pacifist mentality, any fact-based critique of military affairs must already logically appear to be a sin against the spirit; from this mindset it is only those homicidal maniacs [*Amokläufer*], who have devastated the German army and who have lost the war, who profit'.[78] No love was lost between Mayr and Schoenaich once the latter started to support, in line with Fritz Küster, a more radical pacifist approach.[79]

Mayr was also critical with regard to the slogan 'No more war!', which, as we have seen, continued to be widely popular in the Reichsbanner even after the demise of the original 'no more war' movement of the early 1920s. Mayr fully respected and shared this emotional rejection of war, and agreed that only fascists like Mussolini would be unable to call the First World War a 'terrible disaster'. But he insisted that cultivating popular anti-war sentiment would not suffice, as the focus had to be on political decision-making that could lead to a renewed European conflict. The first pacifist demand thus had to be the call for total 'democratic openness' in international and defence politics, and armament politics in particular. The situation in 1914 provided a crucial historical example for Mayr's argument. Had the Reichstag known that the Schlieffen Plan necessarily involved a breach of Belgian neutrality, it should and would have turned against the war plans of the general staff, he was sure.[80] During the final years of the Republic, Mayr intensified his agitation against the Nazi Party. Immediately after the Nazi electoral breakthrough on 14 September 1930, he tried to uplift the mood in the republican camp. In a series of public appearances under the motto 'Adolf Hitler lying in prone position' ('Adolf Hitler auf dem Bauch'), peppered with revealing anecdotes about his former military subordinate, Mayr ridiculed the self-proclaimed Führer. This was a performance that clearly energised the depressed Reichsbanner members.[81] Shortly

[77] Rohe, *Reichsbanner*, p. 150.

[78] Mayr to Delbrück, 23 November 1922: SBPK, NL Hans Delbrück, Mappe Karl Mayr, fos. 4f.

[79] Karl Mayr, 'Aussprache unter Frontsoldaten', *RB* no. 2, 11 January 1930.

[80] Karl Mayr, '"Nie wieder Krieg"?', in *Republikanischer Volkskalender 1927* (Dillingen: Lange, 1927), pp. 63–6 (quotes on pp. 63, 66).

[81] Franz Osterroth, 'Erinnerungen 1900–1934', p. 198. See the report on a meeting in the Bürgerbräukeller on 22 February 1931: StAM, Pol. Dir. 6886.

after the Nazi seizure of power, Mayr fled to France, where he settled in a suburb of Paris, earning money with language tuition. In the wake of the German invasion, he was interned in southern France, and brought back to Germany in July 1940. Via Berlin and Sachsenhausen, Mayr arrived at Buchenwald in 1943, where he died in early 1945.[82]

Clearly, these high-profile pacifist officers in the Reichsbanner attracted the ire of the nationalist camp, and some aspects of their military track record came back to haunt them, as was particularly the case with Berthold von Deimling. Yet the right-wing press and patriotic associations had good reasons to attack this small group, as each of them brought invaluable symbolic capital to the republican camp. They had broken with the *esprit de corps* of the Imperial Army and were hence a vivid example that the elites of the defunct monarchy could indeed support the republican system. And as former military professionals, they could speak authoritatively about the German conduct of war in 1914 to 1918 and could thus address the most pertinent issues in the politics of military history. Their interventions in this field were as diverse as their former rank and military career. In 1921 and 1922, for instance, Deimling delivered a couple of public talks in Stuttgart, Tübingen and other cities, in which he presented the 'stab-in-the-back' myth as a smokescreen to divert attention from the real reasons for German defeat. During the *Dolchstoßprozeß* in Munich in 1925, he repeated this effort at a public gathering in Frankfurt, where he appeared together with Philipp Scheidemann.[83]

Meanwhile, Karl Mayr was directly involved in the trial. He offered his expertise to the defence counsel for the *Münchener Post*, Max Hirschberg, and made sure that the renowned military historian Hans Delbrück appeared as an expert witness for the Social Democrat newspaper. After the trial, he published articles that interpreted the trial as a clear-cut victory over the smear campaign of the nationalist right, and presented this reading in a series of extremely well attended Reichsbanner gatherings in various Bavarian cities.[84] As a former captain-at-sea, Lothar Persius focused on naval politics, on which he published, in addition to his many articles in the *Weltbühne* and various left-liberal newspapers, a number of short booklets. The thrust of Persius' argument was

[82] Schwede, *Karl Mayr*, pp. 59–75.

[83] Von Deimling, 'Lebenserinnerungen', fos. 528, 555.

[84] Karl Mayr to Delbrück, 10 and 29 November 1925, 2 January 1926: SBPK, NL Hans Delbrück, Mappe Karl Mayr, fos. 56, 59, 64; Karl Mayr, 'Die Dolchstoßlüge vor Gericht: Bemerkungen zum Münchener Dolchstoßprozeß', *RB* no. 24, 15 December 1925; 'Die Lehren des Dolchstoßprozesses: Protest des Münchener Reichsbanners', *Münchener Post* no. 274, 26 November 1925.

directed against the pre-war naval policies Admiral Alfred von Tirpitz had pursued and orchestrated since 1897 as head of the Reich Marine Office. Despite the best efforts of British diplomacy, Persius argued, the unmitigated Pan-German ambitions behind these armaments had driven Germany into a conflict it simply could not win. These pre-war policy mistakes had led to the catastrophic under-performance of the German navy during the war, and had forced it to watch idle in the harbours while the Royal Navy controlled the seas. No wonder, Persius insisted, that the revolution began in the high-sea fleet when the commanders ordered their troops to put out to sea in a last-ditch attempt in early November 1918. As the sailors knew for sure, at this point it would have been nothing but a 'useless sacrifice'.[85]

The Reichsarchiv and its popular war narratives

With their contributions to the politics of military history, Reichsbanner members covered a number of highly disputed topics. Yet wherever they intervened, they faced the substantial institutional and publicity-related firepower of the Reichsarchiv in Potsdam. Officially founded on 1 October 1919, the Reichsarchiv had the designated task of cataloguing and scrutinising the files of the wartime army and, on this basis, conducting research in preparation of an official history of the German military effort from 1914 to 1918. Behind this official façade, however, lurked two unofficial aims of this institution. First, that it should continue the work of the Kriegsgeschichtliche Abteilung (war history department) of the Prussian general staff, as the Western Allies had forced Germany in the Treaty of Versailles to disband the general staff altogether. Formally under the control of the Reich Minister of the Interior, the new civilian institution allowed the employment of most of the former officers in the war history department as civil servants, including the first president of the Reichsarchiv, former major general Hermann Ritter Mertz von Quirnheim.[86] Closely connected to the provision of institutional continuity was the second aim: a concerted effort to use military history to restore public recognition of the wartime army and its deeds.

The most ambitious, aggressive and manipulative formulation of this second aim was presented by Captain George Soldan in a lengthy memorandum. Colonel Theodor Jochim presented the work of his subordinate

[85] Lothar Persius, *Wie es kam daß der Anstoß zur Revolution von der Flotte ausging* (Berlin: Arbeitsgemeinschaft für staatsbürgerliche und wirtschaftliche Bildung, 1919), pp. 5f. (quote on p. 14); *Die Tirpitz-Legende* (Berlin: Engelmann, 1918).

[86] Pöhlmann, *Kriegsgeschichte*, pp. 79–104.

Soldan in May 1919 to Mertz von Quirnheim. Jochim, then the head of the Kriegsgeschichtliche Abteilung 4 in the general staff – nucleus of the subsequent archival department in the Reichsarchiv – described the memorandum as highly pertinent for the 'future' of the war history department.[87] On no fewer than forty-one typewritten pages, Soldan developed a detailed agenda for popular writings on the military history of the war. In its current state of mind the German people, he reasoned, suffering from the 'shivers' of revolutionary fever, were not susceptible to any form of systematic influence. Yet this momentary confusion would pass, Soldan was sure, and a time would come 'in which the recollections of the great experience in the field would resurface all by themselves'. Soon, the 'drawbacks' of the war would 'disappear from memory', and thoughts would turn to focus on the 'beautiful and edifying' moments that the war had provided 'in abundance'.[88] With a resurgence of such rose-tinted memories, Soldan reckoned, an increasing interest in readings that would 'refresh the memory' had to be satisfied. Different strata of society would respond to different forms of presentation, though: from objective, 'purely academic' works for the 'educated' people, to battlefield stories in 'dramatised' fashion and 'entertaining' delivery for the lower classes.[89] Hence, Soldan posited three major tasks for a 'historiography of the war':

> To encourage a devastated people; to reinject them with belief in themselves; to make sure that German nationalist sentiment can re-emerge from the shared experience of fortune and calamity, a sentiment that can guide the way to new ascent, beaming through the darkest present; and to utilise the great educational value of history, in order to bring a people who are apolitical to maturity in their thinking and feeling.[90]

In 1919, a large section of public opinion turned against the military and its conduct of war, as in the many booklets and newspaper articles analysed in Chapter 1. Against this backdrop, Soldan's strategy promised that the military could regain some degree of control over the interpretation of its own recent past. For Mertz von Quirnheim this was reason enough to promote Soldan to head of a department for

[87] Theodor Jochim to Oberquartiermeister Kriegsgeschichte, 22 May 1919: BArch, R 1506, 41, fo. 44.

[88] George Soldan, 'Die deutsche Geschichtsschreibung des Weltkrieges: Eine nationale Aufgabe', n.d. [1919]: BArch, R 1506, 41, fos. 49–90 (quotes on pp. 64f.).

[89] *Ibid.*

[90] *Ibid.*, fo. 64. For a similar memorandum by Max Leyh, head of the Bavarian Kriegsarchiv, from January 1919, see Hermann Rumschöttel, 'Kriegsgeschichtsschreibung als militärische Geschichtspolitik? Zur publizistischen Arbeit des Bayerischen Kriegsarchivs nach 1918', *Zeitschrift für Bayerische Landesgeschichte* 61 (1998), 233–54 (pp. 236f.).

'popular writings' (*volkstümliche Schriften*). Almost exclusively staffed with former officers who lacked any academic qualifications or training as professional historians, Soldan's department was responsible for two popular book series. Soon, they proved to be crucial outlets for his strategy to inundate the public with conveniently dramatised yet apolitical war memories. The first were the 'Schlachten des Weltkrieges', published in thirty-six volumes up to 1931. In a stark contrast to the dry presentation and top-down strategic perspective of the official history of the Great War, these books presented key battles in a popular narrative that was centred around the experiences of the front-line troops. They eschewed any overt political perspective or propaganda, and depicted death and defeat invariably as an inevitable 'tragedy'. On top of these activities, Soldan's department also coordinated the publication of regimental histories. By 1928, more than 250 of these had appeared for regiments of the former Prussian army alone.[91]

With their comprehensive coverage of events, the writings of the Reichsarchiv clearly had a hegemonic position in the popular historiography of the war, at least from the late 1920s. While regimental histories could foster personal attachment to one's former unit, the series of battlefield descriptions offered spotlights on the determination of the German soldier. It might be surprising that these books contained hardly any outright glorification of war. But that was part of their success, and a deliberate attempt to diffuse any remaining bitterness about the war experience, particularly among veterans. It was also an explicit recognition of their resentment against the embellishment of wartime propaganda.[92] There was not a lot the republican camp could do to counter the impact of this wave of popular history writings. In May 1924, Soldan still had reason to complain that even right-wing newspapers would not publish short 'notices' about a new instalment of Schlachten des Weltkrieges.[93] But as the output of publications gathered pace – by 1923, only seven books had been published in that series – Soldan had no reason to worry any longer. With increasing distance from the actual events, public demand for this kind of unassuming yet entertaining form of narrative turned out to be almost insatiable. In 1928, new volumes in the series regularly sold between 40,000 and 50,000 copies.[94] This trend stood in stark contrast to the situation in the UK, where the

[91] Pöhlmann, *Kriegsgeschichte*, pp. 194–216.

[92] See Rumschöttel, 'Kriegsgeschichtsschreibung', 238, 254.

[93] George Soldan to Hans von Haeften, 18 May 1924: BArch, R 1506, 326, fo. 219.

[94] Reinhard Brühl, *Militärgeschichte und Kriegspolitik: Zur Militärgeschichtsschreibung des preußisch–deutschen Generalstabes 1816–1945* (Berlin: Militärverlag der DDR, 1973), pp. 278f.

public of the late 1920s had a big appetite for books that exposed the 'mortal consequences of military blunders'.[95]

Originally, one particular area of concern was the lack of former military personnel who had the 'literary' capability to present their own impressions in an 'appealing form', as the Reichswehr ministry complained in 1924.[96] But Soldan found an ingenious way to solve even this problem. Only a few volumes were solely authored by staff in his department. Most were written or at least co-authored by professional writers. In Werner Beumelburg, Soldan even secured the services of the author of some of the best-selling nationalist war novels of the late 1920s.[97] In a rare intervention, Karl Mayr attacked the popular historiography of the Reichsarchiv head-on. He took issue with the way in which 'nationalist authors' such as Beumelberg had been employed to produce heavily 'stylised' accounts. But all Mayr had to offer by way of criticism was that the volumes of Schlachten des Weltkrieges lacked 'factual reliability'.[98] That was certainly true, but also off the mark. Mayr failed to recognise that this genre was not claiming to offer accurate accounts at all, and was not concerned with the 'truth' – as the title of his piece claimed – but rather with entertainment. Ultimately, Schlachten des Weltkrieges simply encouraged the readers to situate their own war memories in the complex dynamics of the major battles. Instead of pinpointing this form of emplotment, Mayr preferred to focus on his own personal interest in strategic issues. He offered a lengthy account of his – unsuccessful – attempts to obtain a copy of the revised attack plan for the German army in 1914 from the Reichsarchiv: the famous *Aufmarschplan*. As such he remained in his comfort zone, with a retrospective strategic critique of the Schlieffen Plan and its implementation.[99]

In the arena of popular military history, the republican camp suffered its first major setback in the contestation over the memory of the Great War. Against the tremendous publicity firepower and persuasive narratives of the popular history accounts published by the Reichsarchiv, a much more concerted critical effort would have been necessary. Or devoted republicans could have published military history accounts of

[95] George Robb, *British Culture and the First World War* (Basingstoke: Palgrave, 2002), p. 220.

[96] Nachrichtenstelle im Reichswehrministerium to Hans von Haeften, 3 May 1924: BArch, R 1506, 326, fos. 221f.

[97] Pöhlmann, *Kriegsgeschichte*, pp. 197, 214f.

[98] Karl Mayr, 'Reichsarchiv und Wahrheit', *RB* no. 12, 15 June 1927.

[99] *Ibid.*; see Karl Mayr, 'Der deutsche Einmarsch in Belgien', *Sozialistische Monatshefte* 34 (1928), 210–14; 'Kriegsplan und staatsmännische Voraussicht', *Zeitschrift für Politik* 14 (1925), 385–411.

their own, mixing an engaging narrative of individual units with pacifist statements. One such example had been published by Walter Hammer in 1919; the name was a pseudonym for Walter Hösterey (1888–1966). Hammer had been active in the pre-war youth movement, and was present in the famous gathering on the Hohen Meissner in 1913. His front-line experience had turned him into a pacifist, and he was appointed as an honorary member to the board of the Friedensbund der Kriegsteilnehmer in 1922. From 1925 onwards he served on the non-executive board of the Reichsbanner, by his own admission on the 'irksome radical-pacifist' wing of the league, and as an avid supporter of an *Einheitsfront*, i.e. joint working-class action with the KPD.[100] From 1922 to 1933, Hammer was also the owner and editor of the Fackelreiter Verlag in Hamburg. Pamphlets by renowned radical pacifists such as Hans Paasche – whom he had met at the Hohen Meissner – and Otto Lehmann-Rußbüldt figured on his list, along with pacifist anti-war novels by Ernst Johannsen and Peter Riss, and books by Reichsbanner luminaries such as the former general and pacifist Paul von Schoenaich.[101] In some respects, Fackelreiter served as the publishing house for books that expressed, in one way or another, Reichsbanner ideas.

In 1919, Hammer published a history of the 236th Infantry Division, in which he had served. It combined a chronological itinerary of the unit's wartime service with expressions of empathy with the fate of the Flemish people under German occupation. In his preface, Hammer stated his own pacifism outright as one possible consequence of the war experience. He combined it with a recognition of the 'pride' every member of the division could feel for his commitment to duty.[102] Yet this promising attempt to tap into sentimental attachments to regiment or division for pacifist purposes remained a rare exception that was not emulated by other republicans.

Investigating the 'causes of the inner collapse' in 1918

The republican camp intervened in the politics of military history with slightly more success in another arena, that of parliamentary scrutiny. In October 1919, the National Assembly set up a subcommittee on the 'causes of the inner collapse' of the German war effort in 1918. It was part of a broader parliamentary inquiry into the most controversial

100 Details and quotes are from his own CV in 'Zwecks Legitimation als "Opfer des Faschismus"', December 1949: IfZ, ED 106, 1.

101 See the materials in *ibid.*, 11.

102 Walter Hammer, *Das Buch der 236. I. D.* (Elberfeld: Baedecker, 1919), p. 10 (quote), pp. 209f., 217.

political aspects of the war, that also included subcommittees on the causes of war, on possible chances for peace and on breaches of international law by the German military. Of all subcommittees, the fourth attracted by far the largest public interest and newspaper coverage, not least because the controversial *Dolchstoß* issue was, by implication, part of its remit. The progress of its proceedings, which gathered pace only from 1924 onwards, was marred with obstacles, not the least of which was the collusion of the Reichswehr and Reichsmarine. Both were keen to slow down the work of the subcommittee, fearful that it would undermine the reverence of a bourgeois public for the Third Army Supreme Command under Hindenburg and Ludendorff. And both successfully lobbied the deputies to solicit expert reports from former military top brass. And so it transpired that of all people, Hermann von Kuhl, former chief of staff in the Heeresgruppe 'Kronprinz Rupprecht' ('Army Group "Crown Prince Rupprecht"') and avid proponent of the *Dolchstoß* myth, was called upon to report on the German spring offensive in 1918.[103] Quizzed by Deputy Joseph Joos as to whether he had failed to notice in 1918 how the troops had resented the hyper-nationalist agitation of the Fatherland Party, von Kuhl could only resort to recommending the books of Ernst Jünger. Jünger, Kuhl insisted, had been one of the lieutenants who really 'knew his men'.[104]

Yet not all deputies on the committee were as eager to unmask the blatant disregard of the Wilhelmine military for private soldiers as Joos (Centre Party), Ludwig Bergsträsser (DDP), and Simon Katzenstein and Wilhelm Dittmann (both SPD) were. Dittmann was himself a target of *Dolchstoß* agitation, as in 1917, then a leading USPD member, he had liaised with the navy mutineers. On the subcommittee, Dittmann was also one of the few champions of Martin Hobohm, the only expert witness with undoubted republican credentials. Hobohm (1883–1942) is one of the nowadays largely forgotten and unsung heroes – and this term is not used lightly here – of republican activism in Weimar Germany; it is thus necessary to detail at least some key aspects of his biography.[105] If Hobohm was a hero, he was certainly a troubled one. He was troubled, first of all, by his position as an extreme outsider in the German historical profession in the 1920s, as one of the very few dedicated supporters of the republican system. He was troubled, secondly, by the unfortunate psychological dynamics of his master–disciple

103 Heinemann, *Die verdrängte Niederlage*, pp. 177–9.

104 At the meeting on 4 February 1926: *Entschließung und Verhandlungsbericht: Die allgemeinen Ursachen und Hergänge des deutschen Zusammenbruches, 1. Teil*, *WUA* 4 (Berlin: Deutsche Verlagsgesellschaft für Politik und Geschichte, 1928), p. 174.

105 For an outline, see Schleier, *Die bürgerliche deutsche Geschichtsschreibung*, pp. 531–74.

relationship with Hans Delbrück, his Ph.D. supervisor. Delbrück, to be sure, was extremely supportive of Hobohm during the long delay of his dissertation – which he finally defended only in 1910 – as well as during subsequent years. Yet Hobohm was at the same time inextricably bound and utterly confused by the deferential terms of his relationship to his teacher, which were so typical of German academia in late imperial Germany – and beyond! A revealing document of this confusion is a letter to Delbrück from October 1920. On no fewer than thirty-five pages, Hobohm poured out his heart regarding their relationship, without asking himself whether it even mattered for the renowned professor at Berlin University. Hobohm explained how he, since first coming to Delbrück's seminar in 1905, had eagerly pounced on the professor's every word as revelatory, and how Delbrück appeared to be a teacher who would guide 'his disciples towards the great, eternal goal' in their intellectual development.[106] These were hopelessly idealistic terms for a historian who excelled in critical analysis much more than anyone else in his profession, and who was at the same time devastated whenever his admired teacher criticised him.

Hobohm was, thirdly, troubled by his extremely difficult professional situation. His academic career stalled. As an outspoken republican, he was not deemed to be acceptable for a full chair, and was only appointed as an adjunct professor without salary at Berlin University in 1923. Hence, he had to rely on his position in the Reichsarchiv, where he worked from 1920 as an *Archivrat* who conducted research with the available in-house files. As such, he belonged to a small group of only thirteen civilian historians, also including Veit Valentin and Ludwig Bergsträsser, who were confronted by a hostile majority of fifty-two former officers in the various research departments. The underlying tensions were both personal and institutional; they erupted in 1922/3. First, the Reichswehr ministry claimed the Reichsarchiv in quite drastic terms as its own domain, and described its work in the most traditional terms. Shortly afterwards, when hyper-inflation forced the government to implement staff reductions in the civil service, Reich Minister of the Interior Rudolf Oeser used the opportunity slightly to rebalance the proportion between former officers and civilians. In February 1923, he decreed that at least three of the latter should work in each research department.[107]

[106] Martin Hobohm to Delbrück, 27 October 1920: SBPK, NL Hans Delbrück, Briefe Martin Hobohm Mappe IV, fos. 26–61 (quote on fo. 27).

[107] Pöhlmann, *Kriegsgeschichte*, pp. 103f., 115–19.

In a direct response, five nationalist associations mounted pressure on the Reichsarchiv and demanded that military history should be left to former military persons as the 'only qualified' individuals for that role. Mertz von Quirnheim, as head of the Reichsarchiv, tried to defuse the situation, but to no avail. On 9 March 1923, four of his department heads, three of whom were former officers, drafted a protest letter against the involvement of any civilian historians in further research, which they sent to the Reich cabinet. Hobohm felt extremely pressurised when his own department head, former major general Hans von Haeften, presented him with the letter in order to obtain his signature – a request that he obviously refused.[108] From that point, Hobohm's position at the Reichsarchiv was totally untenable.[109] When von Haeften was promoted to president of the archive in October 1931, he tacitly approved another sweep against Hobohm, which this time came from historian Hans Rothfels, a member of the archive's academic advisory board. In June 1933, Hobohm was forced to take leave of absence, and in 1935 he was ultimately dismissed as a civil servant.[110]

All three factors clearly clouded Hobohm's life. Yet there were occasions when he was really content, and could forget about the dreadful encounters in the long corridors of the Reichsarchiv building on the Brauhausberg in Potsdam. This came once he had joined the Reichsbanner Black–Red–Gold. With hindsight, he described his involvement in the founding of the Potsdam branch in 1924 as 'the most enthusiastic period in my life'. At that time, he and his comrades had been sure 'to experience and to accomplish the most tremendous thing, the forging of a faithful fellowship between bourgeois and workers [daß Bürger und Arbeiter treue Kameradschaft schlössen], to overcome the unpleasant memories, each giving to the other what he had available.' As such, he and the other Reichsbanner members thought 'to put the national idea in Germany into practice, we believed that we could win the war belatedly in terms of our inner mental attitudes, by paying off the old social debt' of mutual class prejudice between bourgeois and workers.[111] In a similar manner to Schützinger, Hobohm had

[108] See 'Wachsende Krisis im Reichsarchiv: Vertrauliche Denkschrift von Archivrat Professor Martin Hobohm', 11 March 1923: BArch Koblenz, N 1017, 50, fos. 110–14 (quote on fo. 110).

[109] See his letter to Delbrück, 12 December 1923: SBPK, NL Hans Delbrück, Briefe Martin Hobohm Mappe V, fo. 11.

[110] Pöhlmann, *Kriegsgeschichte*, pp. 145–8.

[111] 'Wir dachten in Deutschland den nationalen Gedanken zu verwirklichen, wir glaubten den Krieg nachträglich seelisch zu gewinnen, indem wir die alte soziale Schuld tilgten.' Martin Hobohm to Dr Molinski, 23 August 1928: SBPK, NL Hans Delbrück, Briefe Martin Hobohm Mappe V, fos. 53–6 (fo. 55); see also Hobohm's

only the deepest, heartfelt respect for the inexhaustible 'enthusiasm' of the proletarian Reichsbanner members for the Republic and its colours. He admired their relentless sacrifice for the work of the league. Hobohm understood the tremendous amount of 'self-constraint' that working-class Reichsbanner members needed in daily confrontations with the political 'fanaticism' of the Communists and the extreme right.[112] Usually stifled by a lack of self-esteem in relation to his academic teacher, he confidently criticised Delbrück, who had claimed that the Republic was not popular among the masses. Delbrück simply knew 'nothing about the black–red–gold people's movement', he wrote, partly disappointed, partly in disdain for the dated political worldview of his teacher.[113] Delbrück, although no die-hard ultra-conservative, certainly had little enthusiasm for the Republic, and had signed a petition in May 1919, jointly with other high-profile academics, that basically exonerated imperial Germany from any war guilt. Thus, it was all the more remarkable that Karl Mayr had managed to get his support for the SPD in the *Dolchstoß* trial in 1925.

Martin Hobohm and the fight against the *Dolchstoß* myth

Hobohm's Reichsbanner activism and his academic work on the history of the wartime army had one core element in common. For him, part and parcel of republican 'citizenship' in Weimar had to be the full recognition of the corruption and ultimate 'bankruptcy' of a system that had relied on the exclusion of the proletarian masses from the state: a state that had been built on the deep 'social gulf between the propertied and the non-propertied classes, between the educated and those who were – through no fault of their own – uneducated'.[114] Politically, this insight impelled him actively to seek out the company of his proletarian Reichsbanner comrades, many of whom he knew very well. He also argued that the few bourgeois members of the league had an obligation to use their more advantageous background in an active, non-patronising contribution to the cultural enlightenment of their peers.[115] Both in political and in historical terms, Hobohm was adamant

chapter in Ortsgruppe Potsdam des Reichsbanners Schwarz–Rot–Gold (ed.), *Das Reichsbanner und Potsdam* (Berlin: Dr Hiehold, 1924), pp. 7–12.

112 Martin Hobohm to Dr Molinski, 23 August 1928, fo. 55.

113 Martin Hobohm to Dr Molinski, 21 August 1928: SBPK, NL Delbrück, Briefe Martin Hobohm Mappe V, fos. 50–2 (quote on fo. 51).

114 Martin Hobohm to Dr Molinski, 23 August 1928, fos. 54f.

115 *Ibid.*; see Martin Hobohm, 'Kulturarbeit im Reichsbanner', *RB* no. 23, Beilage, 1 December 1925.

that the *Dolchstoßlegende* amounted to much more than a simple falsification of the historical record. It was, he insisted, a grave 'moral crime' when the former elites aimed to shift their own responsibility for the 'calamity of the nation' onto the masses. He could only marvel at the 'proletarians' who, even though they had been gravely 'insulted' by the *Dolchstoß* allegation, had not 'smashed everything into pieces' in the immediate post-war period, but had continued to work tirelessly for the country.[116]

As a professional historian, Hobohm turned his ire against the *Dolchstoß* into one of the most important historical accounts of the German wartime army. It was produced as an expert report to the parliamentary subcommittee and published in the subcomittee's proceedings in 1929.[117] As early as 1920, when the fourth subcommittee had just begun its work, Hobohm was called to deliver an expert opinion. But he resigned from this assignment only a year later, citing both professional and political reasons.[118] Perhaps surprisingly, the political reasons were not related to the hostility he faced in the Reichsarchiv. Hobohm was rather deeply disappointed by those who represented the 'coalition of November '18'. Various deputies from pro-republican parties, presumably the SPD and perhaps the DDP, had told him they would 'expect simply nothing' from the parliamentary investigation. Such lack of 'energy' in the pursuit of the truth was all the more disappointing, as Hobohm knew that the radicals on the left and right would exploit these matters. And he was obviously convinced that much more was at stake than just insights into 'Ludendorff's fiasco'. It was no less than a battle over the 'inner legitimacy' of the new state, fought out through a historical investigation of the events that had led to the armistice in 1918.[119]

In February 1926, Hobohm was again called to provide an expert opinion for the subcommittee, following a proposal by Wilhelm Dittmann. He was asked to investigate the role of annexationist propaganda by the Pan-German League in the events of 1918, an issue he had already dealt with during the war when he had gathered material on behalf of the Zentralstelle für Auslandsdienst, a government agency for propaganda in foreign countries. At the same time, Erich Otto Volkmann was asked to report on the USPD and its position in national defence, thus tapping into the *Dolchstoß* theme. The appointment of Volkmann, a former major and Reichsarchiv staff member, clearly reflected the

[116] Martin Hobohm to Dr Molinski, 23 August 1928, fo. 53.
[117] *Gutachten des Sachverständigen Dr. Hobohm*, *WUA* 11.1.
[118] Pöhlmann, *Kriegsgeschichte*, p. 275.
[119] Martin Hobohm to Delbrück, n.d. [1920]: SBPK, NL Hans Delbrück, Briefe Martin Hobohm Mappe IV, fo. 65.

wish of the deputies for a somehow measured, proportional investigation of the extremes at both ends of the political spectrum.[120] Yet shortly afterwards, the committee also called upon Volkmann to write another report on annexationist propaganda. Hobohm immediately sensed that the main aim of this move was to undermine his position, and publicised the – in his view – scandalous developments in a brochure.[121] As an occasional leader writer for the *Vossische Zeitung*, Hobohm had already been in the public limelight for quite some time. In 1924, an article in the Hugenberg-owned daily *Der Tag* had criticised him as a 'new German *über*-republican' (*neudeutschen Überrepublikaner*).[122] A year later, a minor incident in a bar in Potsdam triggered even further hostile coverage in the *Deutsche Allgemeine Zeitung*.[123] Yet the climax was only reached when Hobohm publicised his critique of the parliamentary subcommittee. An article in the *Deutsche Zeitung* painted him in negative terms, as a 'professional pursuer of Pan-Germans and an excuser of Marxists', and alleged that Hobohm, like everyone who incited a vendetta against the imperial army, was connected to those of 'alien race', i.e. the Jews.[124]

Yet despite all this controversy, the subcommittee eventually accepted Hobohm's suggestion that he write another expert report, on 'social army grievances as a partial cause of the German collapse in 1918'. *Soziale Heeresmißstände* was the heading for a long list of complaints about the gross inequality in the wartime army, in terms of promotion, pay, food provision and the granting of leave. But Hobohm did more than just outline the nature and the extent of these grievances, something that many of the critical booklets published during the immediate post-war period had already done. In an extended chapter, he argued that these grievances were much more than the result of the 'egotism' and 'meanness' that were bound to flourish in a 'seven-million-strong army'.[125] This was the position of his critics, in this case Alexander Graf Brockdorff. They were eager to play down the extent of these grievances,

[120] Pöhlmann, *Kriegsgeschichte*, p. 275.

[121] Martin Hobohm, *Untersuchungsausschuß und Dolchstoßlegende* (Charlottenburg: Weltbühne, 1926), pp. 7–16; 'Reichsbanner und Dolchstoßlegende', *RB* no. 9, 1 May 1926.

[122] 'Schwarz–Rot–Gelbe Geschichtsphilosophie', *Der Tag* no. 257, 25 October 1924: BArch, R 8034 III, 201, fo. 27.

[123] Martin Hobohm to Delbrück, 27 October 1925: SBPK, NL Hans Delbrück, Briefe Martin Hobohm Mappe V, fos. 28f.

[124] Alexander Graf Brockdorff, 'Die Flucht des Martin Hobohm', *Deutsche Zeitung* no. 143, 22 June 1927. See Hobohm's ironical response in his 'Aus-, Durch- und Maulhalten!', *Weltbühne* 23.II (1927), 47–50.

[125] Brockdorff, 'Die Flucht des Martin Hobohm'.

and explained them as the unavoidable side-effects of a lengthy war, and the result of flaws in the characters of individuals. But in a meticulously researched argument, Hobohm demonstrated that the enduring nature and widespread extent of these grievances had been known to the highest military authorities early on, and that repeated warnings from high-ranking command units had pointed out how they undermined the cohesion of the army as whole. No serious action was ever taken, though, to remedy these problems, as such action would have compromised the privileged position of the officer caste.[126]

Hobohm was eager to acknowledge that not all officers had been complicit in the abuse and exploitation of the private soldiers, and that these differences had been very much appreciated by the troops.[127] Nevertheless, the social army grievances had been endemic, and were of a systematic nature. As the root cause of most of these problems lay in the separation of the different strata in the army (privates, NCOs, officers), 'the class army' was in fact 'a travesty [*Zerrbild*] of the class state'.[128] There was, to be sure, an inherent weakness in Hobohm's argument: if systematic and gross inequality had provided so many reasons for the troops to revolt, why on earth had the German army been capable of withstanding such powerful adversaries for four years, and why had it been capable of launching a major offensive in spring 1918?[129] Hobohm's report should thus not be misunderstood as a comprehensive history of the German wartime army. But it is, to this date, one of the most compelling analyses of the crucial underlying problems of the German war effort. One of the characteristic elements of his account was Hobohm's refusal to rely on personal testimony to corroborate his argument.

In the introduction to his report, he briefly mentioned the fact that he had served as a gunner from 1915 to 1917, before being discharged for medical reasons.[130] And indeed, critics seized upon the fact that he was not an officer, describing him as a 'shirker' (*Drückeberger*).[131] Ernst Müsebeck, head of the archive department in the Reichsarchiv, commended the use of *Feldpostbriefe* for a cultural history of the Great War.

126 *WUA* 11.1, pp. 195–255, 273–85.
127 *Ibid.*, pp. 219–25.
128 *Ibid.*, p. 264.
129 These were issues Ludwig Bergsträsser tried to address by taking the expectations among the troops into account. See Bergsträsser, 'Front und Frieden'. For brief and unconvincing remarks on the continuing battlefield performance of the troops, see *WUA* 11.1, pp. 297–9.
130 *Ibid.*, p. 11.
131 Martin Hobohm to Delbrück, 1 June 1926: SBPK, NL Hans Delbrück, Briefe Martin Hobohm, Mappe V, fo. 37.

But Hobohm mainly relied on documentary evidence from the internal workings of the military machine itself, i.e. dispatches and reports to high-level commanders. Using these types of documentation, he could underline his main point: how the cohesion of the German army had unravelled under the very eyes of the Army Supreme Command, which had nothing to offer as an antidote other than even more ideological indoctrination in the 'Patriotic Instruction Programme', started in 1917.[132]

Hobohm also chose this particular point – the fact that the Army Supreme Command had received repeated warnings about the deleterious impact of the army grievances but not acted upon them – when he publicised his findings in the *Reichsbanner* journal.[133] Yet while the pro-republican camp could employ Hobohm's report in its fight against the stab-in-the-back myth, it had to accept the fact that the subcommittee had chosen to mitigate its impact by soliciting another report on the same matter, again written by Erich Otto Volkmann.[134] In a confidential letter to a colleague at the Bavarian War Archive, the former major and Reichsarchiv staff member explicitly stated that the main purpose of his report would be to diffuse the criticism raised by 'circles that are hostile to the army'. Instead of denying the grievances, which was impossible, Volkmann tried to 'reduce' their significance by a distinction between 'inevitable' side-effects of the war, 'weaknesses' of the army organisation and the few 'outright mistakes'.[135] The result was a highly sanitised portrayal of the wartime army, in which the many tensions and conflicts within it did not feature at all.[136]

The pro-republican forces knew that the Reichsarchiv was a key player in the politics of military history, and that its version of events during the war had a tremendous impact. Speaking in 1925 during a Reichsbanner flag consecration in Munich, Erhard Auer made scathing remarks about Colonel Theodor Jochim, leading staff member of the Reichsarchiv. Called as a witness during the *Dolchstoß* trial, Jochim had publicly accused the German private soldiers of greed and mass theft.

[132] *WUA* 11.1, pp. 72–79, 377–420. For a similar use of official documents in the post-1918 booklets on the *Etappe*, see for example *Der Etappensumpf*, pp. 19–21. See Müsebeck, 'Vorwort'.

[133] Martin Hobohm, 'Warnrufe an die Oberste Heeresleitung', *RB* no. 30, 27 July 1929.

[134] *WUA* 11.2; see Pöhlmann, *Kriegsgeschichte*, p. 276.

[135] Erich Otto Volkmann to former lieutenant-colonel Schad at the Bayerisches Kriegsarchiv, 2 February 1928: Bayerisches Hauptstaatsarchiv München, Abt. IV, Kriegsarchiv, HS 2348.

[136] *WUA* 11.2; for a critique, see K. Kuhn, 'Soziale Mißstände im Weltkriegsheer', *RB* no. 18, 4 May 1929.

Amidst angry heckling from the clearly agitated audience, who insisted that 'the officers were the real thieves, sending home stuff in box-load quantities', Auer explained why such remarks were utterly detrimental, not least for the German image abroad.[137] Yet the Reichsbanner and its political allies, including the Reichstag deputies of the SPD, never developed a coherent strategy to counter the portrayal of the wartime army by the former officers of the Reichsarchiv, and by the right-wing authors who contributed to its more popular publications. To be sure, the Reichsbanner had attracted a number of mostly high-ranking former officers in the Wilhelmine army. Now dedicated supporters of the Republic, they brought their expertise and their symbolic capital as professional military personnel to the fight over the interpretation of the recent past. As such, they raised the profile of the Reichsbanner in its struggle against the instrumental nationalist use of the past, and energised the rank-and-file members of the league. Yet they also brought a more masculine political style and combative tone to moderate pacifism, which was perhaps a mixed blessing. In that respect, Schützinger for instance, had not really moved far away from his pre-war criticism of Bertha von Suttner and her sentimental pacifism.[138] Some of these officers, Hermann Schützinger and Karl Mayr in particular, were also keen to publicise their interpretation of responsibilities for the German defeat. But they were at best amateur historians, and could never match the publicity firepower of the Reichsarchiv with its many media outlets. In the field of academic military history, republican defence against the *Dolchstoß* myth and other distortions of the historical record was basically left to one individual, Martin Hobohm. Yet Hobohm was isolated at his workplace, lacked the prestige of a full university professor and was not a former officer either. His work was also hampered and often delayed by bouts of ill health and self-doubt.[139] Despite his best, and indeed heroic, efforts, Hobohm surely could not shoulder the burden of defending the legitimacy of the Republic in the field of military history on his own.

[137] PND report no. 522, 14 November 1925: StAM, Pol. Dir. 6887.

[138] See also Jennifer A. Davy '"Manly" and "Feminine" Antimilitarism: Perceptions of Gender in the Antimilitarist Wing of the Weimar Peace Movement', in Jennifer A. Davy, Karen Hagemann and Ute Kätzel (eds.), *Frieden, Gewalt, Geschlecht: Friedens- und Konfliktforschung als Geschlechterforschung* (Essen: Klartext, 2005), pp. 144–65.

[139] See the self-loathing remark on his own report on the *Heeresmißstände* as an 'average piece of work' in his letter to Delbrück of 26 September 1928, in which he insisted he had mainly drawn up the report out of a sense of 'duty': SBPK, NL Hans Delbrück, Briefe Martin Hobohm, Mappe V, fos. 57f.

7 Mass media and the changing texture of war remembrance, 1928–1933

In the years from 1928 to 1933, two seemingly contradictory tendencies affected the republican representation of the war experiences. On the one hand, the two main republican veterans' associations faced an increasingly difficult political situation that required their utmost attention. Soon after the onset of economic crisis in 1929, the frequency of political street violence increased, turning self-defence and the protection of Social Democratic Party (SPD) gatherings into the core activity of the Reichsbanner branches. Particularly in the wake of the Nazi success in the Reichstag elections of September 1930, the fascist Stormtroopers of the SA intensified their attacks against Reichsbanner members. Statistics about SA involvement in political violence across Germany during 1931 reveal that 55.2 per cent of all attacks by fascist perpetrators were directed at Reichsbanner members, whereas only 43.8 per cent of the victims were Communists. Violent confrontations between Stormtroopers and Communists were confined to the bigger industrial centres. In many smaller towns, especially in the Prussian East, in Pomerania, Silesia and East Prussia, which had hardly any Communist presence, Reichsbanner members bore the brunt of the relentless onslaught by Nazi Stormtroopers.[1] The disabled veterans of the Reichsbund faced an equally challenging situation. Starting in 1929/30, the Reich government implemented drastic cuts to the welfare provision for disabled former soldiers and their dependants, forcing the Reichsbund to stage public protests and intensify its lobbying activities.[2]

Yet while republican war veterans across Germany focused on the struggle to defend their pensions and the security of their meetings,

[1] Sven Reichardt, 'Totalitäre Gewaltpolitik? Überlegungen zum Verhältnis von nationalsozialistischer und kommunistischer Gewalt in der Weimarer Republik', in Wolfgang Hardtwig (ed.), *Ordnungen in der Krise: Zur politischen Kulturgeschichte Deutschlands 1900–1933* (Munich: Oldenbourg, 2007), pp. 377–402 (pp. 387f.; figures); Voigt, *Kampfbünde*, pp. 379–97.

[2] Whalen, *Bitter wounds*, pp. 168–76.

large sections of the public displayed, on the other hand, a renewed interest in the front-line experience. And this interest was mediated through artistic representations of the war experience in stage productions of plays, and in films and books, to name only the most significant media outlets. Thus, media representations increasingly shaped the texture of war remembrances, and realigned different threads that formed the fabric of private and public memories of the Great War. Media representations provided a lens through which the characteristic elements of trench warfare and its significance for the present could be observed. In principle, there was nothing new about this development. It is false to state that a 'return of the World War' in literature and film has occurred since the late 1920s, as literary scholars have done in their first serious engagement with these phenomena during the 1970s and 1980s.[3] As we have seen in the previous chapters, the Great War had been on the minds of most Germans since the armistice, and also during the so-called period of relative stabilisation from 1924 to 1928. Equally, fictional and semi-fictional accounts of front-line experiences had already been published in the immediate post-war period, a trend that continued in later years.[4]

In terms of the presence of the media in discourses on war remembrances, neither the existence of books and films per se, nor their mass circulation was new. Some nationalist fictional texts on the war had seen highly impressive print-runs well before 1928, such as Walter Flex's *Wanderer between Worlds*, first published in 1917, which sold 682,000 copies, or Günther Plüschow's *Abenteuer des Fliegers von Tsingtau* (*The Adventures of the Airman of Tsingtau*), which shifted 610,000 copies from 1916 to 1927 alone.[5] Key changes during the period from 1928 rather occurred in the structure of the literary field, which regulated the production and reception of literary texts. What was new was – first – the fact that the relative position of the author of books about the war in this field was no longer primarily determined by the reading habits of a rather small audience with an educated taste for certain styles. If at all, fictional texts about the war had been taken seriously for their literary qualities only for a short period in the mid 1920s, perhaps most

[3] Michael Gollbach, *Die Wiederkehr des Weltkrieges in der Literatur: Zu den Frontromanen der späten Zwanziger Jahre* (Kronberg: Scriptor, 1978); less pronounced in Hans Harald Müller, *Der Krieg und die Schriftsteller: Der Kriegsroman in der Weimarer Republik* (Stuttgart: Metzler, 1986), pp. 2, 36–9.

[4] For a comparative analysis of early post-war novels, see Nicolas Beaupré, *Ecrire en guerre, écrire la guerre: France, Allemagne 1914–1920* (Paris: CNRS, 2006).

[5] Sigrid Bock, 'Wirkungsbedingungen und Wirkungsweisen der Antikriegsliteratur in der Weimarer Republik', *Zeitschrift für Germanistik* 5 (1984), 19–32 (p. 21).

prominently Arnold Zweig's *Der Streit um den Sergeanten Grischa* (*The Case of Sergeant Grischa*), published in 1927.[6] Instead, the marketing strategies of publishing companies determined both the text and the author to an extent that was previously unseen in publishing history. The benchmark for this process was the publication of *All Quiet on the Western Front* by Erich Maria Remarque in 1928/9, not least because this book immediately became the key reference point for all subsequent publications in the field.[7]

The reception of Remarque's book also cemented a second crucial element of this segment of the literary field, which had already been present throughout the 1920s. The genre of books about the war, and by implication also the status of their authors, was a matter of dispute. In Remarque's case, the publisher, Ullstein, had deliberately decided not to flag up the book as a *Roman* (novel), something that the author had done in a typewritten draft. Instead, much effort was made to present Remarque as a simple war veteran who had written his book within a few weeks as a quasi-documentary text. By and large, reviewers bought into this marketing coup. From a comprehensive sample of reviews and opinion pieces published between 1928 and 1930, two-thirds described the text right away as 'literary', i.e. as a fictional text. However, many of these reviewers conceded that *All Quiet* had also a documentary character, i.e. it was a mixture between a literary text and a non-literary report of authentic events. And almost half of all reviews that touched upon these issues described the text as solely documentary or even non-literary, as the eyewitness account of a war veteran. Furthermore, as the debate over the book intensified, an increasing number of reviewers insisted that the alleged 'authenticity' of the account had to be the primary benchmark for any book about the Great War.[8] In addition, many reviews of war books took political factors, including the potential impact on the readership, into account, very often as the most important yardstick.[9] For these reasons, it would be problematic to label *All Quiet* and other textual accounts of the front-line experience simply as novels; the literary qualities of these books were very often of

[6] See Müller, *Der Krieg*, pp. 104–86.

[7] The most substantial analysis of the writing up, distribution, marketing and reception of *All Quiet* is Thomas F. Schneider, *Erich Maria Remarques Roman* Im Westen nichts Neues*: Test, Edition, Entstehung, Distribution und Rezeption* (Tübingen: Max Niemeyer, 2004); see also his '"Es ist ein Buch ohne Tendenz": *Im Westen nichts Neues* – Autor- und Textsysteme im Rahmen eines Konstitutions- und Wirkungsmodells für Literatur', *Krieg und Literatur/War and Literature* 1 (1989), 23–40; Vollmer, *Imaginäre Schlachtfelder*, pp. 172–90.

[8] Schneider, *Erich Maria Remarques Roman*, pp. 262f., 265–76, 359–64.

[9] Bock, 'Wirkungsbedingungen'.

secondary importance. What mattered most was whether the authors were genuine eyewitnesses of the war, or not. For these reasons, the texts by Remarque, Renn, Bosemüller and many other authors are here described as literary testimony, or simply as books.

Amidst these developments in the literary field, the pro-republican forces tried to maintain and defend their moderate pacifist commemoration of the war experience, while at the same time engaging with the renewed public interest in books and films about the war. In these fierce controversies over the reception and interpretation of allegedly authentic representations of war, the main focus of Reichsbund, Reichsbanner and other republicans quickly shifted to Remarque's *All Quiet on the Western Front*, both in its written version, published as a book in January 1929, and in the film adaption directed by Lewis Milestone, released in 1930. This focus was not only due to the tremendous popularity of the book, one of the biggest success stories in publishing history. More than that, it was a direct response to the fact that the radical-nationalist campaign against both book and film was conducted 'strategically', as an important part of the more general onslaught against the Republic and its institutions.[10] Particularly since the Nazi breakthrough in the September 1930 elections, Joseph Goebbels and other leading Nazi Party members had attempted to suppress the film adaptation by means of violence, vitriolic political attacks and censorship, and understood this attack as part and parcel of their general campaigning.[11] Defending the Republic thus meant defending *All Quiet on the Western Front*, whether one liked the book or not.

The changing demographics of war remembrance

Before we analyse these struggles and their structural parameters in more detail, though, it is necessary to address another, external factor that turned an engagement with media representations of the war into a challenging task for the two republican veterans' associations, and for the moderate socialist left more generally. This was the massive demographic shift in the composition of the German population that came

[10] Ulrich Baron and Hans Harald Müller, 'Die Weltkriege im Roman der Nachkriegszeiten', in Niedhart and Riesenberger, *Lernen aus dem Krieg?*, pp. 300–18 (p. 307).

[11] Thomas F. Schneider, 'Das virtuelle Denkmal des Unbekannten Soldaten: Erich Maria Remarques *Im Westen nichts Neues* und die Popularisierung des Ersten Weltkriegs', in Barbara Korte, Sylvia Paletschek and Wolfgang Hochbruck (eds.), *Der Erste Weltkrieg in der populären Erinnerungskultur* (Essen: Klartext, 2008), pp. 89–98 (p. 95).

to the fore in the post-war period. During the mid-to-late twenties, the age cohort of those born between 1900 – the first age group not affected by the draft for wartime service – and 1910 experienced the formative years of their youth. For the purposes of our inquiry, it seems justified to adopt a wide definition of youth, which ranges from the age of fourteen – when working-class boys and girls left elementary school – to the age of twenty-five, when still only 5.8 per cent of all male industrial and artisanal workers were married, according to figures for 1925.[12] The age group born between 1900 and 1910 had had the highest birth rate in modern German history, and the most dynamic population growth during these years occurred precisely in those cities and industrial conurbations with a high degree of employment in the heavy industries. Offspring of industrial workers was over-represented among those many children born between 1900 and 1910. As a knock-on effect, the proportion of youth among the male population thus increased from an already considerable 20.6 per cent in 1910 to 23.1 per cent in 1925.[13] To be sure, the overall percentage of male youth slightly decreased in the years until 1933, and the demographic 'front generation' – strictly speaking those males born between 1880 and 1899 – still comprised about 10 million men in 1932.[14]

Even a cursory glance at these data should suffice to convey the two problems that were induced by these demographic changes. First, from the almost seven million male youths in Germany in 1925, a large percentage grew up in working-class families. And during this period of adolescence, young people did not just have to face the usual problems of education and sexual development through puberty and beyond; from their late teens to their early twenties, the political worldviews of young workers also took shape, and it became clear whether they would follow their Social Democrat parents in their strict association with the socialist labour movement milieu, or whether they were receptive to a different set of values and convictions. These issues were compounded by a second, more time-specific effect of the demographic situation. When male working-class youths entered the job market in their droves during the late 1920s, they faced an increasingly difficult situation even before the onset of the Great Depression with its mass unemployment.

[12] Contemporary observers suggested a more narrow definition, ranging from fourteen to twenty. See Erich Ollenhauer in *Sozialdemokratischer Parteitag in Leipzig 1931 vom 31. Mai bis 5. Juni im Volkshaus: Protokoll* (Berlin: Dietz, 1931), p. 194. The statistic on marriage is in Detlev J. K. Peukert, *Jugend zwischen Krieg und Krise: Lebenswelten von Arbeiterjungen in der Weimarer Republik* (Cologne: Bund, 1987), pp. 14f.

[13] Peukert, *Jugend*, pp. 31–5.

[14] *Ibid.*, p. 35; Bessel, *Germany*, p. 270.

From 1927, youth unemployment had increased at a higher rate than that for adult workers. During the summer of 1932, an informed estimate put the number of male unemployed under twenty-five at about one million.[15] No wonder that historian Detlev Peukert, in his seminal work on young working-class people in the Weimar Republic, has aptly described the youth of the late 1920s as a 'superfluous generation'.[16] As the combined result of demographic and economic developments, a large age group grew up in a situation in which positive expectations for the future were basically marred by uncertainty and the depressing reality of reliance on meagre welfare state provision.

This complicated situation undoubtedly aggravated a problem that would have arisen even in a much more stable social and demographic environment. So far, until the late 1920s, the republican war veterans of the Reichsbanner and Reichsbund had quite successfully intervened in the contested field of war commemorations. Their war memories were, as the example of Fritz Einert had vividly demonstrated, a collective memory in the precise sense of Halbwachs' theory: to a large extent, their transmission and proliferation rested on the dense network of daily face-to-face encounters that existed in the labour movement milieu, and in the Reichsbanner branches in particular. In other words, the texture of these remembrances was shaped by the first-hand experiences of the veterans themselves. Other media – songs, poems, books and memorials – accompanied and further articulated the meaning of these memories. But their fabric was mainly created in the biographical trajectory of the veterans, and sustained in their sociability. Within the Reichsbanner, there was a clear understanding that conveying the meaning of an abhorrent war experience to a younger generation was a crucial part of the legacy of the war. At a 'republican day' in the town of Ettlingen in Baden in 1925, one of the speakers solemnly declared that as 'stern men' who had experienced the war at the front, the Reichsbanner members simply could not make it 'appear to youth as if modern war was something dignified and chivalrous'.[17]

Yet the members of the republican league were not blind to developments around them. In 1929 the *Reichsbanner* journal published a piece that acknowledged and analysed demographic change as a factor for shifting attitudes to war and peace. Under the somewhat glossy headline 'The war veterans are becoming extinct', it presented a graph with

[15] Peukert, *Jugend*, pp. 167–79.

[16] *Ibid.*, p. 29.

[17] Quoted in Cornelia Rauh-Kühne, *Katholisches Milieu und Kleinstadtgesellschaft: Ettlingen 1918–1939* (Sigmaringen: Thorbecke, 1991), p. 252.

three male population pyramids for the years 1919, 1928 and – projected – for 1932. To be sure, the death rate among war veterans was slightly exaggerated and the forecast for 1932 thus imprecise. But the forceful emergence of a younger generation was pinpointed with great clarity. The conclusions drawn from these demographic data were crucial: the political weight of the front-line generation was rapidly diminishing, and an increasing number of voters 'had no direct recollection' of the war. Thus, a decisive 'shift in attitudes towards peace' had to be expected.[18] Such aggregate statistical evidence was accompanied by qualitative insights into the widening chasm between the 'so-called front-line generation' and the mentalities of those 'who had been born in the years between 1900 and 1910'. Whereas the former had to live with their recollections of how they had killed out of a 'self-preservation instinct', the latter indulged in romanticist notions of heroism. Yet such an analysis mainly referred to the increasingly militarist and outright bellicose attitudes among middle-class youth and their associations.[19] In 1929, the *Reichsbund* journal was still adamant that proletarian youth would indeed 'guarantee' the prevalence of positive attitudes towards peace.[20]

Assessing the dangers of media consumption

In the early 1930s, however, concerns among Social Democrats about the cultural and political preferences of young workers increased. It was noticeable that the consumption of mass media such as film, radio and mass novels was a popular pastime among working-class youth, and that their preferences with regard to film and novel genres differed substantially from those of their parents. These perceptions were based on hearsay and casual observations, but they were also corroborated by empirical data. In 1930, a survey investigated the leisure activities of 5,000, mostly working-class, youths in Berlin. With regard to film, a clear hierarchy of genres emerged. Female teens preferred romantic films with cheesy plotlines, most of which were not even classified for viewers of their age group. Their male peers, on the other hand, listed films about the war and the navy on top of their personal charts,

[18] Wolfgang Seiferth, 'Die aussterbenden Kriegsteilnehmer: Kriegserlebnis und politische Willensbildung', *RB* no. 47, 23 November 1929.

[19] Heinrich Teipel, 'Jugend und Krieg', *RB* no. 23, 7 June 1930; on context, see Bernd-A. Rusinek, 'Der Kult der Jugend und des Krieges: Militärischer Stil als Phänomen der Jugendkultur in der Weimarer Zeit', in Dülffer and Krumeich, *Der verlorene Frieden*, pp. 171–97.

[20] 'Verbürgt die Jugend den Frieden?', *Reichsbund* no. 5, 10 March 1929.

followed by Westerns and crime movies. A similar picture emerged with regard to reading habits. Adventure stories, including accounts of the Great War, were again the top preference among working-class teenagers.[21]

Obviously, quantitative data of this kind can only offer a first glimpse into the highly complex process of media consumption, and for the evaluation of artistic and political preferences that are borne out by reading and viewing habits. Lists of the most popular titles provide at least some further evidence. Among male working-class youths in Berlin in 1930, *All Quiet on the Western Front* was ranked as the third most popular book behind the adventure stories of Karl May and Jack London.[22] More extensive data on loan frequencies in public libraries in Leipzig during the early 1930s reveal a somewhat more complicated picture. These figures do not take age groups into account, but they do differentiate between middle-class and working-class borrowers. Again, Remarque's book was the most widely read text in both groups. Yet workers not only read *Der Krieg* (1928) by former officer and Communist Ludwig Renn, but also Ernst Jünger's *Storm of Steel* and *Die Höhle von Beauregard* (1930) by Hans Henning von Grote, author of various books on the Great War from an extreme nationalist perspective.[23] This rather diverse list suggests that the reading of literary testimony about the war could transcend political cleavages, and that readers appreciated an appropriate – in their view – re-enactment of the war regardless of ideological differences. A contemporary report by a thirty-year-old Leipzig worker from 1930 on his reading preferences for this genre supports such an assumption. After detailing a long list of books about the war and their more specific topics, the worker stated his 'personal opinion' that 'apart from [Henri] Barbusse and [Theodor] Plievier, the authors are not sufficiently reckless in condemning war'.[24] But at the same time, he praised Wener Beumelburg's *Gruppe Bosemüller* (1930) as 'the best war book', because its portrayal of comradeship in the army was 'true to life' in each individual character. And he recommended that 'people should read' Franz Schauwecker's *Awakening of the Nation* (1929), one

[21] Winkler, *Schein der Normalität*, pp. 137f.; Peukert, *Jugend*, p. 211.

[22] Peukert, *Jugend*, p. 212.

[23] Gideon Reuveni, *Reading Germany: Literature and Consumer Culture in Germany before 1933* (New York: Berghahn, 2006), p. 236.

[24] *Ibid.*, p. 237. The quoted report is taken from Erich Thier, *Gestaltwandel des Arbeiters im Wandel seiner Lektüre: Ein Beitrag zu Volkskunde und Leserführung* (Leipzig: Harassowitz, 1939). The translation in Reuveni's book, however, is littered with mistakes: mostly the misspelling and false translation of authors and the titles of their novels.

of the key texts of an aggressive soldierly nationalism that had found another enthusiastic reader in Joseph Goebbels.[25]

In one way or another, SPD activists now started to realise that traditional ways of imparting pacifist values to young people no longer sufficed, and that books and films provided a different and highly attractive reading of the war experience. Economics professor and Reichsbanner activist Erik Nölting formulated a particularly snappy conception for the underlying dilemma during the 1931 party conference. Amidst heated debates about the party youth organisation Jungsozialisten, which was about to be closed down, Nölting reminded delegates that in the fight against radical nationalism it was no longer sufficient simply to declare 'No more war!'. This slogan, he was sure, 'makes only very little impression on the youth'.[26] The journal of the Reichsbund devoted particular attention to the detrimental effects of media consumption on the proliferation of pacifist values among the younger generation. In part, this focus reflected the situation of many a war widow who had to observe her children's genuine interest in realist or even affirmative depictions of the war, even though they had lost their father through it. It was not a coincidence that female authors had strong opinions on these issues. Some commentators simply assumed the solution was to make sure that youths did not watch any 'war-mongering films', and that the 'poisoning of their souls' could thus be prevented by simple admonishment.[27]

Other female Social Democrats were sceptical that simple parental guidance provided a straightforward way of dealing with the issue. One of them was Anna Siemsen (1882–1951), a renowned expert on pedagogical issues, progressive school reformer, and from 1928 to 1930 also Reichstag deputy for the SPD. Throughout the 1920s, peace pedagogy was an issue of particular concern for her.[28] As early as 1927, Siemsen had pointed out how film had become an important medium that could have political effects in a quasi-subconscious manner. Referring to a short film that was widely screened during Hindenburg's 1925 election

[25] Reuveni, *Reading Germany*, p. 236; see Ulrich Fröschle, '"Radikal im Denken aber schlapp im Handeln?" Franz Schauwecker: *Aufbruch der Nation* (1929)', in Schneider and Wagener, *Von Richthofen*, pp. 261–98.

[26] *Sozialdemokratischer Parteitag in Leipzig 1931*, p. 216; on context see Walter, *'Republik das ist nicht viel'*, pp. 330–8.

[27] Ida Schwarz, 'Erzieht die Jugend zu Friedenskämpfern!', *Reichsbund* no. 8, 20 April 1931.

[28] Ralf Schmölders, 'Anna Siemsen (1882–1951). Zwischen den Stühlen: Eine sozialdemokratische Pädagogin', in Peter Lösche, Michael Scholing and Franz Walter (eds.), *Vor dem Vergessen bewahren: Lebenswege Weimarer Sozialdemokraten* (Berlin: Colloquium, 1988), pp. 332–61.

campaign for the office of Reich president, Siemsen pointed out how a sequence of seemingly 'unpolitical' images of Hindenburg in uniform or in his private life had managed to influence the psyche of cinema-goers to an extent that they were finally *hindenburgreif* – 'ripe' to vote for the former general.[29]

Writing in 1930, Siemsen offered a detailed analysis of the current 'fashion' of war books, focusing on the social and psychological factors that made people inclined to consume these narratives of war. For the generation who had been children between 1914 and 1918, the war was something 'alien' but also 'interesting', and the few remaining memories whetted the appetite for more information about the 'adventurous' complement to the tedious routines at the home front. 'Explanations' were sought about what was already a distant past, but also 'liberation' from the drudgery of daily life during a deep economic crisis. Yet Siemsen stressed that the front-line generation also showed a huge interest in these books, a trend that required explanation. One answer was the simple fact that the 'gruesome reality of war' had 'faded' to a distant 'memory', which made revisiting war experiences less painful than it had been when the 'horror' was still present. Compensation for a blighted present provided another answer, an explanation also applicable to young people. Siemsen argued that the consumption of these fictional 'recollections is today an escape from the present and the re-experiencing of a time that can, with hindsight, be perceived as adventurous'. In accordance with historians' more recent arguments, Siemsen thus explained the massive popularity of war books mainly in terms of the deep crisis of the capitalist economy, which had affected the livelihood of white-collar employees and workers, civil servants and artisans alike.[30]

This attempt to explain the huge popularity of books about the war owed a lot to quite traditional Marxist approaches of accounting for ideologies using the base–superstructure model: false ideas were popular because they directly responded to social and economic developments, in this case in an escapist manner. To be fair, though, this rather mechanistic approach was not the last word of the Social Democrats concerned about this issue. A couple of months after Siemsen's article,

[29] Cited in Frank Heidenreich, *Arbeiterbildung und Politik: Kontroversen in der sozialdemokratischen Zeitschrift 'Kulturwille' 1924–1933* (Berlin: Argument, 1983), p. 94.

[30] Anna Siemsen, 'Zur Mode der Kriegsliteratur', *Reichsbund* no. 8, 25 April 1930; see Wolfram Wette, 'Ideologien, Propaganda und Innenpolitik als Voraussetzungen der Kriegspolitik des Dritten Reiches', in Wilhelm Deist, Manfred Messerschmidt and Hans-Erich Volkmann, *Ursachen und Voraussetzungen des Zweiten Weltkrieges* (Frankfurt am Main: Fischer, 1989) [1979], pp. 23–208 (p. 114).

Anna Würth discussed the same problem, taking as an example the film *Westfront 1918* by G. W. Pabst, which had been widely lauded for its highly realistic re-enactment of battlefield scenes through the sophisticated use of sound. For young men who had not experienced the war themselves, Würth admitted, it was easy to mistake these visual images of 'horror' as a form of 'romanticism'. Thus, they would situate their own 'pipe dreams' in the precise 'gap between reality and representation' that the film opened up, and would follow their 'subconscious imaginations'. As such films sparked the 'fantasies' of their viewers, a rethink of anti-war propaganda was needed, from a critique of war to a positive promotion of peace, pitting the ideal type of a 'good man' against heroic fantasies.[31]

It is difficult to ascertain whether the manifest references to Freudian terminology in this piece were deliberate or just the side-effect of a more complex argument that eschewed the trivia of Marxist thinking. At any rate, Würth was not the only socialist who was worried about the possibility that realistic depictions of war did not contribute to a progressive anti-war pedagogy. Among Social Democrats, school reformers and pedagogical experts, this was a hotly debated issue in the early 1930s. Empirical evidence gathered across Europe seemed to corroborate their worst fears. Asked about their impressions after a screening of films such as *Westfront 1918*, male working-class teenagers confirmed that they were highly interested in the depicted details of warfare. Realistic war films, it emerged, were consumed as adventure stories, and did not necessarily immunise the youth against militarist sentiments.[32]

Thus, a crucial problem emerged for those Social Democrats and moderate pacifists who wanted to engage with the tendency of the texture of war remembrance to become increasingly shaped by the narratives, metaphors and visual images provided by literary testimony and feature films about the front-line experience. By looking at the books and their position in the literary field for a moment, it was clear that outright anti-war texts and those with a critical tendency were marginal – in terms of sales figures – throughout the Weimar Republic. Despite the huge success of *All Quiet on the Western Front*, which alone sold 1.2 million copies in its original German version before the Nazi seizure of power, the circulation of war books by right-wing authors

[31] Alma Würth, 'Warum ist der Krieg – modern?', *Reichsbund* no. 19, 10 October 1930. On *Westfront 1918* see Garth Montgomery, '"Realistic" War Films in Weimar Germany: Entertainment as Education', *Historical Journal of Film, Radio and Television* 9 (1989), 115–33 (pp. 121–4).

[32] Anton Tesareck, 'Europas Jugend kriegsbereit? Gedanken zur Erziehung gegen den Krieg', *Die Sozialistische Erziehung* 11 (1931), no. 3, 49–52.

clearly outnumbered those few best-selling texts by authors such as Ludwig Renn, Karl Bröger or Leonhard Frank, who offered – at least in the perception of most reviewers – a critical portrayal of the war.[33] Based on the circulation figures compiled by Donald Day Richards, one estimate puts the share of pacifist texts among the overall sales of war books in the period from 1919 to 1939 at a mere 12 per cent.[34] At any rate, this estimate tends to exaggerate the success of right-wing and nationalist literary testimony during the years of the Weimar Republic. This is not so much because the list also includes books that were only published after 1933. Rather, the figure overestimates the popularity of key nationalist authors such as Werner Beumelburg, Paul Ettighofer or Edwin Erich Dwinger in the period before 1933.[35] Beumelberg's *Gruppe Bosemüller*, for instance, which drove home the notion of a front-line community in very aggressive fashion, shifted 65,000 copies from 1930 to 1933, and yet another 105,000 in the years from 1933 to 1940.[36] Sales figures for the whole period up to 1939 thus distort the picture. In the wake of 30 January 1933, the books by Remarque and other authors whom the Nazis deemed to be pacifists were forbidden, whereas the regime promoted and endorsed titles by Beumelburg and other right-wing authors, thus inflating sales.

The hegemony of nationalist war books

Despite these corrections, though, the fundamental point is valid: during the fierce ideological and political battles that followed the onset of the economic crisis, the moderate socialist left had to acknowledge the hegemony of the right-wing camp in the field of literary representations of war. This had indeed been the case ever since the 'short period of

[33] See the list of titles in Thomas F. Schneider and Hans Wagener, 'Einleitung', in *Von Richthofen*, pp. 11–16 (pp. 12–14). 'In the perception' has to be stressed, as the reception of war books was not straightforward. Ludwig Renn's *Krieg*, for instance, today usually recognised as a pacifist book, was also praised by right-wing journalists as a true and 'faithful' testimony, at least before the author outed himself as a Communist. See Herbert Kranz, 'Menschen des großen Krieges', *Die Tat* (1929/30), in Bärbel Schrader (ed.), *Der Fall Remarque:* Im Westen nichts Neues. *Eine Dokumentation* (Leipzig: Reclam, 1992), p. 49.

[34] Nicolas Beaupré, *Das Trauma des großen Krieges 1918–1932/33* (Darmstadt: Wissenschaftliche Buchgesellschaft, 2009), p. 185. In a footnote, Beaupré refers to Donald Day Richards, *The German Bestseller in the 20th Century: A Complete Bibliography and Analysis 1915–1940* (Berne: Herbert Lang, 1968), pp. 18–21. This reference is erroneous; he most probably refers to the titles listed in Table A, *ibid.*, pp. 55–93.

[35] Beaupré, *Das Trauma*, p. 185.

[36] See Wette, 'Ideologien', p. 112.

insight' (Franz Carl Endres) had come to an end in 1923. Yet the emergence of a youth that engaged with war memories only through the texture of allegedly authentic literary representations aggravated the situation. Republicans recognised the problem, and tried to remedy it. But the means at their own disposal were limited. Within the Reichsbund, Heinrich Hoffmann took a proactive stance. A disabled war veteran and former POW, he had worked his way up as a Reichsbund functionary. Finally, in 1930, he joined the federal executive board and also became an editor of its membership journal. Keen to inject a stronger political note into this publication, he used press conferences and other contacts to recruit left-leaning journalists and writers to present or discuss artistic representations of the meaning of the war.[37] Author and playwright Alfred Polgar, for instance, discussed the memorial for the *inconnu* in Paris, while Reichsbanner leader Hermann Schützinger introduced the 'Moral History of the World War' by the controversial sexologist and gay rights activist Magnus Hirschfeld.[38] The veteran of anti-war publishing Heinrich Wandt was also featured in the pages of the *Reichsbund* journal. He serialised a chapter from his sequel to *Etappe Gent*, first published in 1928. It told the judicial odyssey of Georg Niederländer, a young war volunteer from Lorraine who had shot his company commander during a drunken brawl. Following an original sentence of life imprisonment by court martial, the verdict was reversed until the third hearing returned the death penalty, which was carried out in February 1918.[39]

These were decent efforts, but they clearly lacked the means to influence a debate whose parameters were set by the huge success of *All Quiet on the Western Front*. To a large extent, this success was the result of a clever marketing strategy by the Ullstein publishing house, which presented Remarque as a disoriented drifter without substantial prior experience as a writer, and urged him to tone down many of the outright pacifist passages in the original manuscript version of the novel, thus streamlining the book for the mass market.[40] In a clever and unprecedented move, the publisher pre-empted

[37] 'Erinnerungen Heinrich Hoffmann', n.d. [*c.* 1965]: BArch, SAPMO, SgY 30, 1365/2, fos. 511f.

[38] Alfred Polgar, 'Der unbekannte Soldat', *Reichsbund* no. 5, 10 March 1930; Hermann Schützinger, 'Wie die Sittengeschichte des Weltkrieges entstand', *ibid.* no. 9, 10 May 1930.

[39] Heinrich Wandt, 'Die Tragödie eines Kriegsfreiwilligen', *Reichsbund* no. 22, 20 November 1931, to no. 3, 5 February 1932; see Heinrich Wandt, *Erotik und Spionage in der Etappe Gent* (Vienna; Berlin: Agis-Verlag, 1929 [1928]), pp. 159–62.

[40] Schneider, *Erich Maria Remarques Roman*, pp. 280f.; and 'Buch ohne Tendenz', pp. 32–6.

and prefigured the subsequent reception with a quote on the jacket by Walter von Molo, president of the literature department in the Prussian Academy of the Arts: 'Remarque's book is the memorial of our Unknown Soldier.'[41] Thus, the book was pitted against Adolf Hitler, who represented himself as the unknown soldier who would lead the German nation out of its current despair. As such, Remarque's book could be interpreted as the legitimate expression of the hopes and aspirations of all those republican war veterans who had themselves supported the notion of an 'Unkown Soldier'. With a clever interpretation of the political situation, Ullstein marketed its author and his text as the embodiment of a liberal-democratic reading of the war experience.[42]

Among the first to jump on the bandwagon was indeed Martin Hobohm, the war veteran and devoted Reichsbanner activist. In a brazen form of cross-marketing, the *Vossische Zeitung*, itself part of the Ullstein publishing house, had raised the expectations of the reading public through the serialisation of the novel, which appeared between 10 November and 9 December 1928, accompanied by advertisements that promoted the upcoming book version. Hobohm's letter to the editor was among the sample of unequivocally enthusiastic reactions that the *Vossische* presented to its readers a couple of days later. For Hobohm, this *Erzählung* (prose narrative) was:

> captivating, real and great. Authentic as a photographic document, felt and created by a poet. Art saves. Art makes indelible what human dullness threatens to hush up and bury: the mass fate of the soldiers, the most enormous part of the content of our time. Will the mature Zeitgeist eventually rediscover it properly with this book? ... Were there tragedies before 1914? They fade in comparison to this one, the tragedy of the common soldier in the World War. Lucky Dante, lucky Shakespeare, you never suspected anything like this piece of hell: *All Quiet on the Western Front*![43]

Hobohm's letter is a good example of the simultaneously contradictory and extremely high expectations that some devoted republicans associated with the novel. He clearly acknowledged the artistic power of the text and its ability to recalibrate the moral compass of a wider public. Yet at the same time, Hobohm invoked the metaphor of photographic representation to highlight authenticity as the benchmark for an assessment of the text. Thus, he tapped into a key category for the reception of war books that was equally applied by readers of nationalist texts

[41] Schneider, 'Buch ohne Tendenz'; and 'Das virtuelle Denkmal', p. 94 (quote).
[42] *Ibid.*
[43] *Vossische Zeitung* no. 300, 16 December 1928.

who claimed that their favourites were truly 'authentic'.[44] Hobohm's characterisation of the emplotment of the text was also problematic. Describing it as a tragedy of the grandest scale, he chose to highlight the seriousness of these events. Yet in his expert report for the parliamentary subcommittee, Hobohm had gone to great lengths in detailing the precise culpability of the higher echelons of the military. In that text, the horror of war was neither 'tragedy' nor 'fate', but only the predictable result of human action, which could be attributed to a handful of individuals. There was a clear tension between the many efforts by Reichsbanner members to pinpoint the causes of the catastrophe through documentary evidence, and their longing for an elaborate, gripping artistic representation of the Great War.

At the time, however, this contradiction was not noticed by the republican war veterans who were eagerly reading and promoting the book. The *Reichsbanner* journal set the tone in its review. It commended Remarque's text as an appropriate antidote to all those young people who were 'infected with nationalism', as if it were a disease.[45] Members of the local Reichsbanner branch in Schiltach in Baden read and discussed the text during their evening gatherings, and deemed it to be 'very interesting'.[46] The journal of the Reichsbund printed one of the rare interviews with the author, conducted by Henri Pichot, founder and leader of the left-leaning veterans' league Union fédérale, while Remarque was in Paris. As on other occasions, Remarque presented himself as the humble average veteran who by chance happened to be the mouthpiece of the ordinary front-line soldiers. And as proof, he pointed to the more than 30,000 positive letters he had received from his readers. Clearly pitching his message to the war veterans who read the journal, Remarque avoided any political statements and praised comradeship as the 'most beautiful gift' for their soldiers.[47]

The moderate pacifist left, and the two republican veterans' associations in particular, embraced Remarque's book as desperately needed ammunition in the struggle over the proper interpretation of the war experience. But the positive appraisal of the book tended to gloss over inherent problems of this artistic representation of war, problems that

44 Matthias Prangel, 'Das Geschäft mit der Wahrheit: Zu einer zentralen Kategorie der Rezeption von Kriegsromanen in der Weimarer Republik', in Jos Hoogeveen and Hans Würzner (eds.), *Ideologie und Literaturwissenschaft* (Amsterdam: Rodopi, 1986), pp. 47–78; see Schneider, *Erich Maria Remarques Roman*, pp. 373–84.

45 *RB*, 2 February 1929, printed in Schrader, *Der Fall Remarque*, p. 86.

46 'Protokollbuch Ortsgruppe Schiltach', 12 April 1930: StA Schiltach, AS-2055a.

47 Henri Pichot, 'Erich Maria Remarque und sein Buch', *Reichsbund* no. 24, 24 December 1930.

were quickly recognised by critics within the left. The first problem was that of bias. It was often asserted that the book could claim to offer an 'authentic' image of the front precisely because it lacked any bias or, even stronger, as the *Reichsbund* journal phrased it, because 'the book did not intend to have any biased effects' ('will nicht tedenziös wirken').[48] Yet for some socialist observers of the wave of literary representations of war, that was precisely the problem. They were concerned about the lack of a popular 'proletarian war book', as an article in the journal of the Socialist Labour Youth (SAJ), the youth organisation of the SPD, couched it.[49] And the 'proletarian' war book, to be sure, was not simply defined by the inclusion of working-class protagonists here: a problem that was not Remarque's in any case, as the group of soldiers in his text not only comprised middle-class war volunteers, but also Tjaden, an industrial worker and – often overlooked – Detering, a peasant farmer and Haie Westhus, a rural farm-hand. Leftists did not take issue with the social background of the key protagonists in *All Quiet on the Western Front*, but rather with the narrative strategy of the author, the plot. The author of a proletarian war book, the critics insisted, would never have chosen the motto 'My book shall not be an accusation' – as Remarque famously did, in slightly different wording.[50] Quite to the contrary, a truly socialist account 'had to be an indictment', had to lay bare and denounce the objective social background of the war in a crisis-ridden capitalism, something that was much more important than even a truly 'photographic depiction' of the front-line experience.[51]

All Quiet on the Western Front and its ambiguities

As this last remark indicates, socialist critics not only criticised the emplotment of Remarque's text, but also the 'extreme realism' of his literary re-enactment of life on the front line. Even an unmasked portrayal

[48] Max Mühlberger, 'Bedeutende Kriegsbücher', *Reichsbund* no. 23, 10 December 1930; see Schneider, *Erich Maria Remarques Roman*, pp. 364–72.

[49] Arthur Goldstein, 'Wo bleibt das proletarische Kriegsbuch?', *Arbeiter-Jugend* 21 (1929), 254f.

[50] *Ibid.*, p. 255. 'This book is to be neither an accusation, nor a confession' was the motto of his book. See Remarque, *All Quiet*, p. 5.

[51] Goldstein, 'Kriegsbuch', p. 255. A somewhat similar critique of the failure to understand the war as a cataclysmic societal event is Anna Siemsen, 'Kriegsbücher' (1929), in Schrader, *Der Fall Remarque*, pp. 63–9. Less aggressive, but pointing to the same problem, was socialist critic Karl Schröder, 'Erzählende Literatur' (1929), in *ibid.*, pp. 76f. On Communist critiques of the novel see Jens Ebert, 'Der Roman *Im Westen nichts Neues* im Spiegel der deutschsprachigen kommunistischen Literaturkritik der 20er und 30er Jahre', in Thomas F. Schneider (ed.), *Erich Maria Remarque: Leben, Werk und weltweite Wirkung* (Osnabrück: Rasch, 1998), pp. 99–108.

of the 'horrific scenes at the front' would only tend to increase the habitual tendency of the 'average reader' to acknowledge the underlying 'heroism' of those who had battled through such an ordeal. However gripping the depiction of disillusionment and despair in a literary testimony, readers took from it more than just a 'weak glimmer of romanticism'. Rather than denouncing war, it actually made it more 'lively'. And these ambivalences also had political implications, as the dominant focus on the psychology of the trench experience was bound to conjure up the 'spirit of comradeship' with its ideological implications, which only served the nationalist camp.[52] Radicalising this form of critique, an article in the *Weltbühne* described the books by Remarque and Ludwig Renn as 'pacifist war propaganda', using the oxymoron to highlight the fact that *All Quiet* could also be read as a pro-war book. This was a point borne out by positive responses from teachers and parents who confirmed that male youths who had read *All Quiet on the Western Front* were attracted by the adventurous aspects of life at the front, and confirmed that the 'more dangerous it was, the more interesting' it became.[53] In a contemporary interview, Remarque responded drily by stating that those who wanted to experience first-hand what he had described could 'not be helped'.[54]

Historian Thomas Kühne has asserted that the explicit praise of comradeship as 'the great experience of community' and 'fabric of military male bonding' in Remarque's text 'contributed to a moral conversion' in the early 1930s, 'which eventually became the cultural basis of the genocidal war Germany would wage on Europe ten years later'.[55] Such a claim is implausible if it is not backed up by a detailed inquiry into the reception of war books among the readership, and with the recognition that morality is a highly fluid medium and that it is near impossible to account for the impact of one text on the shaping of morality. Existing testimony about reading habits, to be sure, points in a different direction and confirms that ordinary Germans understood Remarque's novel as an example of precisely what the Nazis rejected as mere *Humanitätsduselei* ('exaggerated humanist concerns'). Franz Göll, born in 1899, though not a veteran of the Great War, maintained a clear sense of the distinction between empathy for the plight of the

[52] Goldstein, 'Kriegsbuch', p. 255.

[53] Karl Hugo Sclutius, 'Pazifistische Kriegspropaganda', *Weltbühne* I.25 (1929), 517–22; and 'Nochmals: Pazifistische Kriegspropaganda', *ibid.*, 826f. (quote). For a similar critique by Communist writers see Bock, 'Wirkungsbedingungen', p. 30.

[54] Cited in Günter Hartung, 'Gegenschriften zu *Im Westen nichts Neues* und *Der Weg zurück*', in Schneider, *Erich Maria Remarque*, pp. 109–50 (p. 117).

[55] Kühne, *Belonging*, pp. 10f.

soldiers and military male bonding. A visit to the exhibition of – in the view of the Nazis – 'degenerate' art (*entartete Kunst*) on 12 March 1938 prompted him to contemplate the significance of different literary testimony about the war. In his diary, he noted that Remarque – whose book he had read upon publication in 1929 – 'stands up for humanity and does not comport himself as a mass butcher like Zöberlein'. Göll had also read Hans Zöberlein's 1931 *Faith in Germany*, which depicted, much to Göll's chagrin, 'the enemy as "dogs" who need to be sent to their maker as fast as possible'.[56] Kühne's claim also grossly neglects the contemporary public reception of the Remarque's text, in which precisely those nationalist circles that supported military male bonding as preparation for another war were highly critical of what they perceived as the author's pacifism. The headteacher of a *Gymnasium* in Berlin epitomised this hostile reception in a piece entitled 'Education towards a Softening of the Bones' ('Erziehung zur Knochenerweichung'), detailing how the prevalence of disillusionment and the quest for self-preservation among Remarque's Paul Bäumer and his comrades undermined efforts to make the youth fit for another war.[57]

And, thirdly, Kühne's claim ignores the fact that only those aggressively nationalist war books that had appeared since 1929, often in direct response to Remarque, construed a hegemonic form of masculinity that foregrounded the new morality of the Nazi state. In these texts, by authors such as Werner Beumelburg and Franz Schauwecker, the gruesome reality of trench warfare triggered attempts to build a form of male bonding that could withstand such pressures.[58] This form of radical nationalism, however, required a masculinity that was characterised by a certain amount of masochism and the ability to overcome pain, surely not the key character traits of the fictional hero Paul Bäumer.[59] The ambivalences of Remarque's book and its reception must thus be taken seriously, but they certainly did not feed into the pre-history of the Holocaust. Rather, they laid bare some of the inherent ambiguities and problems of republican war remembrances in the early 1930s.

[56] Quoted in Peter Fritzsche, *The Turbulent World of Franz Göll: An Ordinary Berliner Writes the Twentieth Century* (Cambridge, MA; London: Harvard University Press, 2011), p. 163.

[57] Professor Pflug, 'Erziehung zur Knochenerweichung', *Berliner Börsen-Zeitung*, 16 May 1929, printed in Ulrich and Ziemann, *Krieg im Frieden*, pp. 186f. Many of the immediate right-wing rejoinders that appeared in book-length form also stressed this point; see Hartung, 'Gegenschriften', pp. 121–49.

[58] See Heidrun Ehrke-Rothermund, '"Durch die Erkenntnis des Schreckens zu seiner Überwindung"? Werner Beumelburg: *Gruppe Bosemüller*', in Schneider and Wagener, *Von Richthofen*, pp. 299–318; Gollbach, *Wiederkehr*, p. 302.

[59] Vollmer, *Imaginäre Schlachtfelder*, pp. 241–53.

There was, first of all, the growing gap between personal recollections of the war and the texture of remembrance provided by media representations such as literary testimony. This first problem was compounded by a second one: the fact that this gap was presented in terms of a generational hiatus between those who fought the war and those born after 1900. In the pro-republican reception of Remarque's work, this was a prominent feature of the reviews of his sequel, *Der Weg zurück*. First serialised and then published as a book in early 1931, the text focuses on the immediate post-war period from 1918 to 1920, and describes how a tightly knit group of soldiers is dispersed once they pursue different political and personal endeavours upon their return home.[60] A *Reichsbanner* reviewer described it as a melancholic farewell to the comradeship this age group had experienced at the front, and explicitly assessed its pedagogical value for peace politics from the perspective of the *Nachgeborenen*, the war youth who had been born after 1900.[61] That was not problematic per se. But it contributed towards a trend that presented generations as self-contained, mutually exclusive entities, rather than searching for common ground between age groups. Up to this point, the left had not tapped into the notion of the 'front generation', which so many right-wing authors eagerly exploited, often in a critical turn against the Weimar system.[62] Now, Social Democrats started to employ similar semantics of generation, even though they did not aim to undermine the Republic.[63]

The third problem concerned a fundamental shift in the relation between war remembrance and republican politics. For about a decade, from 1919 to 1929, republican war veterans had drawn direct political conclusions from their own war experiences. Their active support for the new democratic system was informed and shaped by their recollections of the war, and, of equal importance, they could themselves take ownership of their war memories and decide how they should inform their political activism. Some of them, like Fritz Einert, developed quite elaborate reflections on the intrinsic connections between

[60] Thomas F. Schneider, 'Die Revolution in der Provinz. Erich Maria Remarque: *Der Weg zurück* (1930/31)', in Ulrich Kittstein and Regine Zeller (eds.), *'Friede, Freiheit, Brot!' Romane zur deutschen Novemberrevolution* (New York; Amsterdam: Rodopi, 2009), pp. 255–67.

[61] Gustav Leuteritz, 'Wie eine Generation zerstört wurde: Gedanken über Remarques neues Buch', *RB* 30 June 1931; see Wilhelm Kuhlinski, '*Der Weg zurück – Frieden*: Zwei Romane aus der Revolutionszeit', *Reichsbund* no. 18, 20 January 1931.

[62] See the classic study by Robert Wohl, *The Generation of 1914* (Cambridge, MA: Harvard University Press, 1979), pp. 42–84.

[63] Otto Piper, 'Die Krise der Kriegsteilnehmergeneration', *Neue Blätter für den Sozialismus* 1 (1930), 441–51.

their wartime service and the political culture of post-war Germany. Many others were simply content to share their recollections in the local sociability of their Reichsbanner or Reichsbund branches, or to take part in the rituals of remembrance staged by the two organisations. With the upsurge of interest in war books and films after 1929, however, the terms of the debate on war remembrances were fundamentally altered. What took place was not a moral conversion, but rather a political one. Instead of articulating and defending their own war memories, republican war veterans were now forced to rally behind media releases whose success was to a large extent driven by the clever advertising campaign of a major publishing conglomerate. And, on top of that, they now faced an adversary whose interest in war remembrance was entirely driven by instrumental political motives, and who was extremely aggressive in the pursuit of this agenda: the Nazi Party.

Clashes over the Milestone film

These changes were brought to the fore in rather spectacular fashion by the bitter clashes over Lewis Milestone's film version of *All Quiet on the Western Front*, released in the USA in May 1930. Anticipating a backlash among the German public, Universal, the production company, deleted a couple of scenes in the version dubbed for the German market, including one in which the Kaiser was blamed for the war.[64] Despite concerns on the part of the Reichswehr ministry, the film passed the German censorship board, and was first screened to an invited audience in a cinema at the Nollendorfplatz in Berlin on 4 December 1930. Yet on the first public performance the following day, a group of National Socialists in the cinema created chaotic scenes when they threw stink bombs and released white mice, leading to the abandoning of the screening. Nazi demonstrations outside the theatre followed in subsequent days, supported by extremely hostile coverage, not only in the Nazi press, but also in conservative newspapers. After a discussion in the Reich cabinet on 9 December and another deliberation of the censorship board on 11 December, the film was banned, after no fewer than five *Länder* governments, the Reichswehr ministry and the Foreign Ministry had described it as a disgrace and a danger to Germany's prestige abroad. As Modris Eksteins has rightly stated in his

[64] Andrew Kelly, '*All Quiet on the Western Front*: "Brutal Cutting, Stupid Censors and Bigoted Politicos" (1930–1984)', *Historical Journal of Film, Radio and Television* 9 (1989), 135–50 (p. 138).

analysis of the scandal, 'the film was being rejected not as a statement on the war but as a political irritant'.[65]

Much more was at stake in this conflict than simply the 'integration of the "front generation" into the social and political landscape of Germany ten years after the Armistice'.[66] As we have seen throughout this book, the majority of German front-line soldiers had not only been surprisingly well integrated into post-war society, but had made an active contribution to the stability of the republican political system. When they rushed to the defence of Lewis Milestone's film in 1930/1, these republican veterans were not concerned about specific artistic imaginations of the Great War or their own position in the fabric of Weimar Germany, but about the very existence of the state that had been established in the wake of defeat and revolution. On the surface, pro-republican war veterans and socialist labour activists were again able to mount an impressive campaign against the political opponents of the film. Starting on the very day the film was banned, the Reichsbanner organised a whole series of public demonstrations and protest meetings that carried on for weeks, and the participants of which clearly outnumbered those of the initial Nazi protests against the film.[67] In addition, the *Reichsbanner* journal solicited a solidarity address by British war veterans and MPs who confirmed that not the film itself, but the politically motivated act of censorship, endangered Germany's reputation abroad.[68] Members of the SAJ in Baden found their own way of circumventing the ban. When the film was screened in France, they organised a joint trip to Strasbourg to watch it there. In an article that defiantly claimed 'We saw it anyway!', supported by stills from the movie, they informed their fellow members of the reasons why Milestone had created an impressive depiction of the 'mass murder of war'.[69]

Yet despite such acts of defiance, the mood in the republican camp was rather gloomy. An early response in the *Reichsbanner* journal clearly identified the ban as a 'great capitulation' of the republican state vis-à-vis a radical nationalist opposition. The ban epitomised the failure to bring key institutions such as the Reichswehr and Foreign Ministry under

[65] Modris Eksteins, 'War, Memory and Politics: The Fate of the Film *All Quiet on the Western Front*', *CEH* 13 (1980), 60–82 (p. 75). For right-wing press coverage, see Schrader, *Der Fall Remarque*, pp. 121–7, 134–8.

[66] Bessel, *Germany*, p. 268.

[67] Eksteins, 'War', 78.

[68] 'An unsere Freunde im Reichsbanner: Englische Frontsoldaten über den Remarque-Film', *RB* no. 13, 28 March 1931.

[69] Ernst Kerkow, 'Wir sahen ihn doch! Den Film *Im Westen nichts Neues*', *Arbeiter-Jugend* 23 (1931), no. 2, 43–6.

the strict control of devoted republicans. Without the republican failure to support the film, the nationalist campaign would never have succeeded. For the Reichsbanner this was a clear indication that core state institutions were systematically biased in favour of the extreme right, a fact that did not bode well for a democratic polity more generally. But it was not only support from supposedly democratic institutions that was lacking; the nature of political conflict over representations of the war had also changed. It was 'impossible' to reach any form of 'understanding' with those circles that had orchestrated the censorship of the Milestone film.[70] As long as the republican veterans had to deal with the Jungdo and the Stahlhelm only, at least a very basic level of mutual recognition among former soldiers could be maintained, as the joint support for the *Reichsehrenmal* in Bad Berka had demonstrated. The Nazi Party and the Stormtroopers of the SA were not bound by any such considerations, and were relentless in their attacks on the republican state and its symbols.

In the extremely hostile political situation of the final two years of the Republic, the recourse of republican war veterans to their own war remembrances turned into an increasingly empty but nevertheless defiant gesture. The ambivalence and problematic nature of such rhetoric were already clearly visible in the appeal against the censorship of the Milestone movie, which the executive board of the Reichsbund publicised in December 1930. In this appeal, the league insisted that the film was not at all biased against or in favour of any of the formerly belligerent nations, would depict 'the true face of the war' and simply offer a powerful praise of a comradeship based on 'sacrifice'. At the core of the appeal stood a highly pathetic and naïve attempt to construe a direct line of continuity between the collective memory of front-line service and the cinematographic version of Remarque's book, expressed in the statement that 'front-line war, front-line experience and the film *All Quiet on the Western Front* are an unbreakable, iron triad!'.[71] In a separate article, Christian Pfändner, the head of the Reichsbund, tried to underpin the legitimacy of this appeal through recourse to his own capacity as an eyewitness of battle at the western front, as someone who had – contrary to the nationalist myth – not heard the singing of the 'Deutschlandlied' during the battle of Langemarck in September 1914. As one of eight brothers who had served at the front, Pfändner

[70] 'Das Verbot des Remarque-Films: Die große Kapitulation', *RB* no. 51, 20 December 1930.

[71] 'Protest und Aufruf: Schützt die Jugend vor gewissenlosen Kriegshetzern', *Reichsbund* no. 24, 24 December 1930. See Eksteins, 'War', p 81 on the 'naïveté' of socialist praise for the film.

concluded, he was surely 'entitled' to offer his own criticism of the ban against the film.[72] Such an insistence on *Augenzeugenschaft* – on being an eyewitness of war as a prerequisite of any informed statement on artistic representations of the war experience – was an often repeated claim of the republican camp in the controversy over both the book and the film version of *All Quiet on the Western Front*.[73] It reflected the more general notion held among republican war veterans, that only they as *Kriegsteilnehmer* were in a position to make judgements about the political implications of the war experience.

Comprehensible as this claim was against the backdrop of the biographical trajectory of Reichsbanner and Reichsbund members, it tended to misread the political situation of the embattled Weimar Republic in the early 1930s. At this point, war veterans were no longer the only men who indulged in sentimental memories of the trench experience and its alleged heroism, and who based political claims on these memories. In the nationalist camp, a large cohort of young men embraced the myth of the front-line experience even though they had only experienced the war as 'victory watchers' while in school or working as apprentices.[74] This phenomenon found its most significant manifestation when the Nazi Stormtroopers of the SA turned into a mass organisation, surpassing 100,000 members in spring 1931. At that time, the overwhelming majority of the SA fighters were younger than thirty – one estimate puts the figure at 77 per cent – and had thus been too young to be subjected to the draft during the war. Yet heroic images of trench warfare formed an important part of the political iconography of these young SA members. They fantasised about the parallels between their own street-fighting against Communists and Social Democrats, and the struggle of their fathers and older brothers at the western front, imagining both practices as manifestations of the same wish to defend the German nation.[75]

Contemporary observers struggled to understand the underlying causes of this phenomenon, and offered a number of different explanations. They ranged from anger and frustration over German military defeat and the terms of the peace settlement to the idea that these young men tried to overcompensate for the lack of any proper fighting

[72] Christoph Pfändner, 'Zensurskandal: Der Streit um den Remarqueschen Film *Im Westen nichts Neues*', *Reichsbund* no. 24, 24 December 1930.

[73] See 'Der Kampf um den Remarque-Film: Von einem Zentrumskameraden', *RB* no. 51, 20 December 1930.

[74] Sven Reichardt, 'Die SA im "Nachkriegs-Krieg"', in Gerd Krumeich (ed.), *Nationalsozialismus und Erster Weltkrieg* (Essen: Klartext, 2010), pp. 243–59 (p. 251).

[75] *Ibid*., pp. 247–50.

credentials of their own, and thus to the dynamics of a generational conflict between the front generation and the war youth age group.[76] Historians have added the impact of wartime mobilisation, and particularly the nationalist underpinnings of war pedagogy, as other factors that might explain the right-wing radicalisation of the war youth generation and their readiness to indulge in militarist fantasies.[77] At any rate, one should be careful *not* to describe the shift of a younger age group towards the extreme nationalist right in the later years of the Republic as a generational phenomenon;[78] not all young men born between 1900 and 1910 were affected, and not even a majority of them. Re-enacting a heroic war experience and turning to the extreme right among male youth in the early 1930s was a matter of propensity, and not directly linked to or determined by certain age-specific experiences.

For the context of our inquiry, the most important aspect of the militarist fantasies of men from the war youth cohort is the concomitant change in the field of war memories and their artistic representations. In the early 1930s, remembering the Great War was no longer the domain of those who had served at the front. Extreme nationalists made claims about the legacy of the war regardless of whether they had fought in it or not. And both National Socialists, as the most radical representatives of the nationalist camp, and also the slightly more moderate members of the conservative German National People's Party (DNVP) and the Stahhelm, were increasingly hostile in their pursuit of those moderate socialists and republicans who still insisted on voicing their critical recollections of events at the front. One vivid example of the relentless aggression with which the extreme right tried to gain hegemony over the contested commemorations of the Great War played out in 1931. In a meeting in April that year, Wilhelm Hansmann (1886–1963), the Social Democrat county executive (*Landrat*) of the Ennepe-Ruhr county in Westphalia, had talked about his recollections of the front. The German people, he insisted, had had enough of military service and uniforms. He recalled how eighteen-year-old soldiers had been forced onto the battlefield during assaults like 'animals for slaughter', after they had been intoxicated with alcohol. Thus, these young soldiers had advanced totally 'drunk' to the French trenches.[79] Hansmann

[76] Friedrich Franz von Unruh, 'Nationalistische Jugend', *Die neue Rundschau* 43.5 (1932), 577–92 (pp. 591–2).

[77] Andrew Donson, *Youth in the Fatherless Land: War Pedagogy, Nationalism, and Authority, 1914–1918* (Cambridge, MA; London: Harvard University Press, 2010), esp. pp. 223–41.

[78] See *ibid*., p. 236.

[79] Quotes in *Der Tag*, 7 November 1931: BArch, R 72, 682.

had served during the war, and had returned as a committed pacifist. In essence, he publicly reiterated the claim Fritz Einert had made in his manuscript in 1926, that the German army had used alcohol as 'offensive-food'.

Yet in the heated political atmosphere of the early 1930s, such a claim would not go unchallenged. Immediately, Dr Hans Bernd Gisevius, a jurist and member of both the DNVP and the Stahlhelm, deliberately insulted Hansmann in order to enforce a legal clarification. In the first instance, he was sentenced for libel. But in the appeal procedure, even the state attorney conceded that Gisevius had good reason to be outraged, as Hansmann's words had been a 'grave insult against the front-line soldiers and the fallen'.[80] The nationalist press extensively covered the trial, and the Stahlhelm demanded that the Prussian Ministry of the Interior should remove Hansmann's parliamentary immunity as a member of the Prussian diet.[81] And this was not the end of the story. After the Nazi seizure of power, twenty members of the SS used the opportunity to avenge what they had perceived as an insult against the honour of the war veterans. On 17 March 1933, they abducted Hansmann from his house in Dortmund, and brutalised and assaulted him repeatedly. Hansmann had to flee into exile, first to France, then to Switzerland.[82]

In a highly influential interpretation, historian Hans Mommsen has characterised the political stance of German Social Democracy during the final years of the Republic as one of 'immobility', 'passivity' or even 'paralysis'. Mommsen claims that Social Democrats were unable to respond effectively to the fascist challenge, yet he fails to explain what such an effective response should have looked like. The Reichsbanner figures in his reflections only insofar as it was criticised, from a normative point of view, for its 'questionable outward style' of political representation, i.e. its allegedly paramilitary form of mobilisation.[83] Any sober assessment of the political situation from 1930 to 1933 has

[80] *Ibid.* For a satirical comment on the trial see Peter Scher, 'Immer mal wieder', *Simplicissimus* 36.5 (1931), 58.

[81] See the materials in BArch, R 72, 682.

[82] Kurt Klotzbach, *Gegen den Nationalsozialismus: Widerstand und Verfolgung in Dortmund 1930–1945* (Hanover: Verlag für Literatur und Zeitgeschehen, 1969), pp. 108f., 269.

[83] Hans Mommsen, 'Social Democracy on the Defensive: The Immobility of the SPD and the Rise of National Socialism', in *From Weimar to Auschwitz: Essays in German History* (Cambridge: Polity, 1991), pp. 39–61 (pp. 41, 52). For a more balanced, positive view of SPD politics in this period see Eberhard Kolb, 'Rettung der Republik: Die Politik der SPD in den Jahren 1930 bis 1933', in Heinrich August Winkler (ed.), *Weimar im Widerstreit: Deutungen der ersten deutschen Republik im geteilten Deutschland* (Munich: Oldenbourg, 2002), pp. 85–104.

to recognise that the SPD was on the defensive. But that is not the same as 'passivity' or 'paralysis'. Far from being paralysed, hundreds of thousands Reichsbanner members engaged in an incessant struggle against the Nazi presence in their communities. From late 1931, the Iron Front combined SPD, Reichsbanner, Free Trade Unions and workers' sports associations in a joint effort to stave off the Nazi challenge and to develop new forms of political propaganda.[84] In August 1932, the Reichsbanner circulated materials that rebutted the claim of the Nazis to be nationalist, while at the same stressing the Social Democrat anti-war credentials for the time since 1914, and blaming the devastation and cost of the war on the radical nationalists.[85]

From the vantage point of the republican veterans of the Reichsbanner, the situation in 1931/2 is best described as an 'insoluble dilemma', a no-win situation. Any offensive against the Nazi Stormtroopers would have abandoned the legalist principles on which the socialist labour movement was based. Hence, Reichsbanner activists opted for an even closer alignment with the SPD, which allowed them to hold on to the democratic norms of the league. But such an approach offered no sufficient basis to counter the 'terror and violence' of the extreme right.[86] In the wake of the September 1930 Reichstag elections, Karl Höltermann had pushed for the founding of the Schutzformationen, or Schufo, a core of those physically robust Reichsbanner members who should bear the brunt of daily street encounters with the Brownshirts, and who received extra training in preparation for an eventual right-wing coup. Yet in the summer of 1932 about 600 Schufo members in the capital Berlin faced the presence of 15,000 Stormtroopers, even though Berlin was a socialist stronghold and had been a notoriously difficult territory for Nazi Party mobilisation.[87]

The fate of the Republic was not decided in the contested field of war remembrances, but by the readiness of conservative elites to hand over power to the Nazi movement. Social Democrat war veterans had shown tremendous persistence in their attempts to elaborate a coherent set of republican war remembrances. Ultimately, these attempts were defeated with the Nazi seizure of power in January 1933. In the remaining weeks until the Reichstag elections on 5 March 1933, which cemented the Nazi *Machtergreifung*, Reichsbanner functionaries continued to show defiance in the face of an insurmountable opponent. On

[84] Voigt, *Kampfbünde*, pp. 456–82.
[85] Reichsbanner *Gau* executive Hanover, 28 August 1932: NHStAH, Hann. 310 II C, no. 25, fos. 125–9.
[86] Schmiechen-Ackermann, *Nationalsozialismus*, p. 402.
[87] *Ibid.*, p. 401; see Voigt, *Kampfbünde*, pp. 450–5.

26 February 1933, Karl Höltermann, head of the Reichsbanner since July 1932, when he had replaced the idiosyncratic Otto Hörsing who was subsequently expelled from the SPD, spoke to a large crowd in the jam-packed Circus Krone in Munich. Höltermann offered a lengthy swipe against the Nazi Party, effectively destroying their credentials and unmasking the cynical basis of the fascist approach to politics. And he insisted that republicans and workers had indeed rescued and reconstructed the German nation after the defeat in 1918. Thus, he linked the republican citizenship of Weimar Germany once again to the outcome of the First World War. When they had returned from the front in 1918, he reminded his audience, 'we brought nothing home but mud, lice, discharge clothing and a fee of 50 marks, but also the entitlement to be a free citizen in a free Germany'.[88] A couple of weeks later, in the north of Germany, a Social Democrat newspaper tried to rebut the slanderous accusation that the party leaders were 'traitors of the fatherland' and 'war shirkers'. It printed the military rank of each of the sixteen – out of seventeen – male SPD deputies in the regional parliament of Mecklenburg-Vorpommern who had served in the war, and added the total of twenty-three decorations they had received.[89]

Defections from the republican camp

These were acts of defiance, performed by Social Democrats who continued to insist that they had drawn the right conclusions from their experiences on the battlefields of the Great War. Yet not all those war veterans who had contributed to the republican commemoration of war were as stubborn and defiant as the many members of Reichsbund and Reichsbanner who went into exile or joined the resistance against the Nazi regime once the state authorities had forced their leagues into illegality across Germany. Some of the high-profile figures who had previously promoted and performed republican war memories had already defected to the right-wing camp before 1933, or did so in the wake of the Nazi seizure of power. They were only few, but their examples should be mentioned nevertheless, as they are indicative of the problem of sustaining an effective front against the glorification of war in Weimar. The journalist Karl Vetter, for instance, had been one of the founders of the Friedensbund der Kriegsteilnehmer (FdK), and

[88] 'Bericht über die Wahlversammlung des Reichsbanners am 26. Februar 1933': StAM, Pol. Dir. 6886.

[89] 'Tatsachen über sozialdemokratische Führer', *Mecklenburgische Volkszeitung*, 2 April 1933; see Meik Woyke, *Albert Schulz (1895–1974): Ein sozialdemokratischer Regionalpolitiker* (Bonn: J. H. W. Dietz, 2006), pp. 78–84.

had organised the 'no more war' rallies in the early 1920s. Vetter had left the *Berliner Volks-Zeitung* in 1924 and started a successful career in advertising – reason enough for the Mosse publishing company to bring him back to the *Berliner Tageblatt* in a senior position. His pacifist credentials were long forgotten when Vetter organised the smooth transition of the *Tageblatt* to the new regime in 1933, covering for Jewish journalists, but also publishing an infamous 'Frontschwein' article on 4 April 1933. In this piece, Vetter argued that he, as a former front-line soldier, could not have any sentimental feelings amidst the necessary Nazi revolution.[90]

From the crew of war veterans and pacifist journalists who drove the 'no more war' movement, Henning Duderstadt had subsequently joined the Reichsbanner. Shortly after the Nazi seizure of power in 1933, Duderstadt published a 'confession' giving reasons why his conversion to Nazism was an inevitable move.[91] Artur Zickler had abandoned progressive politics even earlier. *Vorwärts* editor, author of anti-militarist pamphlets and leading member of the FdK, he had started publicly to support nationalist politics during the occupation of the Ruhr in 1923. In 1926, his former comrades among the Jungsozialisten denounced him as a 'renegade of the labour movement' and one of the 'first' who had defected to the reactionary right. In the late 1920s, Zickler joined the circle of radical conservatives who were affiliated with the journal *Die Tat*.[92]

In 1929, Erich Weniger published a piece on the changing image of the war in 'experience, remembrance' and cultural 'tradition'.[93] Himself a war veteran, Weniger (1894–1961) taught as a professor of pedagogy and the didactics of history teaching. Weniger was interested in two related questions. What did the upsurge of interest in war books during these years mean for the 'real remembrance' and the 'real tradition' of the war? And why was it so difficult to convey the meaning of the front-line experience to the 'next generation': those of the 'class of 1902', as he formulated it in a clear reference to Ernst Glaeser's famous 1928 novel of the same title, which told the story of the war from the

[90] See Boveri, *Wir lügen alle*, pp. 39f., 86–9, article on pp. 95–7.

[91] Henning Duderstadt, *Vom Reichsbanner zum Hakenkreuz. Wie es kommen musste: Ein Bekenntnis* (Stuttgart: Union, 1933).

[92] Otto Lamm, 'Renegaten der Arbeiterbewegung', *Jungsozialistische Blätter* 5 (1926), no. 1, 29–31; Otto Ernst Schüddekopf, *Linke Leute von rechts: Die nationalrevolutionären Minderheiten und der Kommunismus in der Weimarer Republik* (Stuttgart: W. Kohlhammer, 1960), p. 451. His own post-war testimony did not mention this shift. See Zickler's autobiographical note, 3 August 1945: BArch, SAPMO, SgY 30, 1052.

[93] Erich Weniger, 'Das Bild des Krieges: Erlebnis, Erinnerung, Überlieferung', *Die Erziehung* 5 (1929), 1–21.

perspective of a year group who had been too young to be called to the draft.[94] In his assessment of the situation, Weniger struck a sceptical, if not outright melancholic tone. He noted that both in the public remembrances of the various political camps, but also in the 'personal recollection' of each individual, 'certain moments of the war experience were receding' into the background. Moments of 'weakness, horror, despair' diminished among those who glorified war, while moments of 'heroism, humour and the satisfaction brought by a soldierly existence' diminished among the pacifists. Such a lopsided approach had to be addressed, and Weniger was convinced that the 'festivals of remembrance in the present' could at least partly be explained as compensation for the gaps and imbalances in the collective recollection.[95] Using a French term, he concluded that there was a broad current of *fausse reconnaissance*, to an extent that it was highly doubtful whether there was any 'true memory' of the war. But when the trench experience could only be conveyed in a multiplicity of different 'readings', where would that leave the 'truth about the war [*Wahrheit über den Krieg*]'?[96]

Weniger's answer was negative: there was no overarching truth about the war. And that was not only due to the divergent perspectives that the war experience itself had offered, differing between military ranks and assignments during the war, observed by individuals with different backgrounds in terms of class, education and political viewpoint. It was compounded by the huge discrepancies between different age groups and the ways in which they dealt with the transition from war to civilian life. Weniger also discussed how each of the various literary representations of the war only ever offered one particular and hence relative perspective on the front-line experience, often with political underpinnings that were actually taken from the 'post-war situation'.[97] With his insistence on the relativity and ambivalence of war remembrances, and of their literary representations in particular, Weniger was a lone voice in the discourse on media representations of the front-line experience between 1928 and 1933. Across the board, the substantial 'truth' of their narratives was a key criterion for the assessment of war books. The reception of these pieces of literary testimony was shaped by highly

[94] *Ibid.*, p. 1; see Ernst Glaeser, *Class of 1902* (London: Martin Secker, 1929).

[95] Weniger, 'Bild', pp. 4f.

[96] *Ibid.*, 5. Incidentally, this was also the title of the German translation of Jean Norton Cru's second book *Du témoignage* (1930), which appeared as Jean Norton Cru, *Wo ist die Wahrheit über den Krieg? Eine kritische Studie mit Berichten von Augenzeugen* (Potsdam: Müller & Kiepenheuer, 1932). Weniger referred to 'Wahrheit über den Krieg' in inverted commas, but he must have taken the quote from another contemporary German publication that I am not able to identify.

[97] Weniger, 'Bild', pp. 6–19 (quote on p. 8).

divergent and contradictory political and ideological positions. That was, to be sure, not in itself remarkable, as contestation had been the pre-eminent feature of war remembrances in Weimar Germany from the start. Yet in the reception of war books from 1928 onwards, and particularly in the struggle over *All Quiet on the Western Front*, these positions were presented with 'totalising claims for validity', mutually denying each other any relative 'truth' in their portrayal of specific war experiences.[98]

Amidst this hardening of the battle fronts over the reception of media representations, the republican camp leapt almost instinctively to the defence of Remarque's text and its film version, even though many socialists had reservations about what they perceived as a lack of partisanship and structural analysis of the causes of war in the book. But as the only war book identified by the mainstream public as 'pacifist' with a mass circulation, it was the best ammunition they had at their disposal. When the film was banned in December 1930, the battle in support of republican war remembrances was almost lost. A shortened and slightly sanitised version of the Milestone film was actually re-released in September 1931.[99] Yet Social Democrat commentators were right when they described the initial ban as a 'great capitulation' of the republican state. As we have seen throughout this book, the republican camp lagged behind in the field of media representations of the war from the mid 1920s at the latest. Concerted efforts to promote anti-war novels were left to one individual: Walter Hammer and his Fackelreiter publishing house. No serious attempts were made to counter the flood of popular media outlets released by the Reichsarchiv. Only belatedly – too late in fact – did republican critics clearly pinpoint and attack the ideologies of the right-wing soldierly nationalism that the former Stormtroop leader Ernst Jünger had promoted since the early 1920s.[100] When the film version of the only piece of fiction that could compete with the huge popularity of heroic war stories was banned, the fate of republican war narratives was basically sealed. The Nazi seizure of power in January 1933 did the rest, silencing critics, banning most anti-war texts including *All Quiet on the Western Front*, and motivating individuals to abandon their previous critical attitudes to war and its representation. Erich Weniger was actually one of them. In 1935, when the Nazi regime reintroduced general conscription, he declared

[98] Prangel, 'Das Geschäft mit der Wahrheit', p. 76.
[99] Eksteins, 'War', p. 82.
[100] See for instance Alfred Kantorowicz, 'Krieg und Krieger: Eine Auseinandersetzung mit dem neuen Nationalismus', *RB* no. 46, 15 November 1930.

that 'the time of arbitrary war remembrances is over'. What he meant was that the *Gleichschaltung* also had to be completed in this field, as German re-armament was now the key 'task'.[101]

[101] Erich Weniger, 'Kriegserinnerung und Kriegserfahrung' (1935), in Ulrich and Ziemann, *Krieg im Frieden*, p. 195. See Kurt Beutler, 'Der Militärpädagoge Erich Weniger', in Martina Tschirner and Heinz-Werner Göbel (eds.), *Wissenschaft im Krieg – Krieg in der Wissenschaft* (Marburg: Eigenverlag AMW, 1990), pp. 293–304.

Conclusion

It is a staple of historical scholarship on inter-war Europe to argue that German war veterans were, at least in comparison with their peers in France, overwhelmingly nationalist or reactionary, and that their war experience had turned them into natural supporters of right-wing or extreme right-wing political parties. Such a comparison is problematic with regard to the chosen reference point, the veterans' movement in the French Third Republic up to 1933/4. To be sure, none of the main veterans' leagues in France 'explicitly condemned the Republic as a regime'. But they consistently voiced their reservations about key institutions of parliamentary democracy, not least parliament itself, and developed a discourse that portrayed themselves as the flag-bearers of a 'true' republican spirit against the backdrop of the perceived deficiencies and corruption of the political system. As political instability persisted throughout the 1920s, with many short-lived governments following each other in quick succession, the main French veterans' leagues demanded a move towards a 'strong government', and developed a clear preference for a more authoritarian style of politics.[1] Such an interpretation does not deny the relevance of their patriotic pacifism for the collective identity of French veterans of the Great War. But it points out that the political repercussions of their activism were much more fluid and ambivalent than their republican public rhetoric suggests.

The standard comparison between French and German war veterans, and between the commemoration of war in these two countries more generally, is also problematic in that it grossly underestimates the presence and activism of pro-republican war veterans in Germany. Throughout this book, we have seen how moderate socialist war veterans in the Social Democratic Party (SPD), sometimes in collaboration with more radical pacifists and left-liberal democrats, developed republican memories and narratives of the war experience. These veterans

[1] See Millington, *From victory to Vichy*, pp. 220f.

intervened at all levels of the debate over the meaning and legacy of the war: staging public mass rallies and commemorative rituals at war memorials; contemplating the meaning of their war memories in newspaper and journal articles, booklets and novels, as well as in personal documents of self-reflection; rejecting right-wing mythologies such as the *Dolchstoß* myth. They also held the radical nationalist purveyors of heroic war narratives to account, while at the same time establishing international contacts with French war veterans in the pursuit of reconciliation and disarmament; and, last but not least, republican veterans pointed out the strategic blunders of the Imperial Army leadership, and of Hindenburg and Ludendorff in particular.

In all these different endeavours, the German republican war veterans were driven by a set of moral values that reflected both their socialist worldview and the key lessons they had drawn from their war experiences. They were committed to a basic humanism that condemned the destructive consequences of the war; refused to accept that national enmity had to be its natural consequence, even in the light of the terms of the Treaty of Versailles; and concluded that a moderate pacifism was the key lesson to be learnt from the militarism and chauvinism that had driven Germany into the war. Most importantly, these war veterans were adamant that the democratic system of the Weimar Republic was the logical consequence of the corruption and incompetence of the Wilhelmine elites for which they had seen tangible evidence both at the front and, perhaps even more so, in the *Etappe*. The republicanism of these veterans resulted from their first-hand knowledge about the moral and political bankruptcy of the imperial system in the autumn of 1918.

Not all republican war veterans felt the need to engage with these issues in a more coherent fashion, or to feed their recollections into an organisational framework of remembrance by joining one of the veterans' leagues. But the level of mobilisation among them was high, and while the size of the different leagues is no exact measure for the success of one of the contested commemorations, it is certainly more than just a vague indication of their relative strength. And on that count, the fact that pro-republican veterans in Weimar were at least as numerous as their conservative and reactionary counterparts cannot be overlooked. The Social Democrat Reichsbund was by far the largest representation of disabled veterans, war widows and orphans. Among former POWs, the breakaway group of the Vereinigung ehemaliger Kriegsgefangener (VeK) established itself in 1925 as a pro-republican alternative to the more conservative Reichsvereinigung. While the exact strength of these associations cannot be established, it seems obvious that both faced dwindling membership figures during the late 1920s, with the Reichsvereinigung stabilising at about 30,000.[2] And despite being a latecomer on the scene of veterans' leagues, the Reichsbanner was one of the often forgotten success stories of the Weimar Republic, clearly outnumbering its immediate competitors in the right-wing camp: the Stahlhelm and Jungdo.

It has been suggested that we should conceptualise the alleged 'brutalisation' of German society through the war experience using a broader approach, which looks beyond the immediate effects on the veterans and takes more general changes in the political culture into account.[3] But even if we accept his proposition – and there are many good reasons to do so – the brutalisation thesis is unconvincing as a substantial historical argument about Weimar Germany. Republican war remembrances had a tremendous presence at least until the late 1920s, and their humanist and internationalist values had repercussions throughout German society, affecting many working-class youth until the Great Depression and, considerably less so, in the following years. In a variety of cultural forms and practices, these remembrances de-legitimised the notion of a heroic sacrifice for the nation as the cornerstone of the 'war cultures' that had fostered mobilisation during the war.[4] Thus, they contributed to a substantial cultural demobilisation of German post-war society.

Commemoration also had, to be sure, another important element to it, as it expressed the meaning of violent death and offered consolation to grieving relatives and comrades of the fallen soldiers. In his seminal book *Sites of Memory*, Jay Winter has forcefully argued that war memorials and other commemorative practices have to be seen as expressions of bereavement and as 'sites of mourning'.[5] Grief and mourning were not entirely absent from the republican cult of the fallen soldiers. In their rituals at war memorials, Reichsbund and Reichsbanner paid tribute to the fallen, and tried to interpret their death as a call for international reconciliation. In the Reichsbund, the bereaved families of the fallen soldiers also had their place and their say, and, particularly during the final years of the Republic, female functionaries of the league stressed the significance of mourning for their work. Yet overall, the more intimate aspects of remembrance – the need to come to terms with the loss of friends and relatives – played a much less prominent role in the republican disourse of the Reichsbanner than one might have expected. As the written recollections by Fritz Einert demonstrate, personal relations and the loss of

[2] Pöppinghege, 'Kriegsteilnehmer', p. 405.
[3] Beaupré, *Das Trauma*, pp. 230–6.
[4] Horne, 'Kulturelle Demobilmachung', p. 132.
[5] Winter, *Sites of Memory*, pp. 78–116.

former friends and comrades did indeed matter for republican veterans. But their absence was not primarily perceived as a reason to mourn their death. At least for Einert, much more important about the fallen soldiers was that they were missing in his political struggle against the nationalist camp, and that he had to speak out on their behalf in order to prevent their legacy from being distorted. In that perspective, mourning was almost a luxurious indulgence.

The public commemoration of war by Reichsbund and Reichsbanner was first of all a performative celebration of republican citizenship. Thus, it made a tangible contribution to this important field of politics, which underpinned and strengthened the new democratic polity.[6] Yet despite all these efforts, the National Socialist onslaught on the Republic finally prevailed. Even before the Nazi seizure of power in January 1933, radical nationalist representations of the front-line experience had become hegemonic, as is clearly evidenced by the sales figures of war books that presented heroic narratives. How can we understand the relation between the relative strength of republican war memories and their ultimate failure to offer a hegemonic reading of the war amidst the intensive political battles of the 1930s? Any more systematic attempt to address this issue has to go beyond a mere quantitative roll call of the pro- and anti-republican forces. It makes perfect sense to gauge the relative strength of the respective camps through an assessment of membership figures and organisational capacities, but ultimately, the appeal and success of republican commemorations of war did not depend on whether the Reichsbanner staged more rallies or commemorative rituals than the Stahlhelm and Jungdo.[7] Such an approach would demonstrate a lack of understanding of how the use of symbolic politics is able to frame popular expectations and to shape politics in the age of mass democracy.[8] Thus, a proper historical analysis of republican war remembrances has to scrutinise the inherent strengths and weaknesses of the symbols and narratives different collective actors employed. Weimar society is best described as a forest of symbols, which were used to mark, elaborate and support competing political positions, and to accumulate symbolic capital that could be translated into power.[9] And in this regard, not only the quantity

[6] Rossol, *Performing the Nation*; Achilles, 'Performing the Reich'.

[7] This is, however, *mutatis mutandis* the argument suggested by Weitz, 'Weimar Germany', p. 588.

[8] Thomas Mergel, 'Überlegungen zu einer Kulturgeschichte der Politik', *GG* 28 (2002), 574–606.

[9] Andreas Dörner, *Politischer Mythos und symbolische Politik. Der Hermannmythos: Zur Entstehung des Nationalbewußtseins der Deutschen* (Reinbek: Rowohlt, 1996), pp. 13–62.

but also the inherent qualities of these symbols mattered. This was highlighted in the final years of the Republic, when the intensive political struggles also led to renewed conflicts over symbols. The Iron Front adopted the symbol of three downward-facing arrows, literally crushing National Socialist symbols such as the swastika. This symbolism was used in posters, graffiti and other outlets.[10] When National Socialists turned these arrows into umbrellas, or mocked them by other symbolic means, the Reichsbanner devised detailed measures to counter this effect.[11]

Any convincing answer to this conundrum of symbolic politics requires both a systematic and a chronological approach. Some of the more systematic ambivalences of the republican commemorations of the Reichsbanner have already been highlighted in previous chapters. They include the fact that the Reichsbanner aimed to offer an inclusive, egalitarian form of republican activism, but did not admit women as members, and also marginalised female experiences in the representation of the war. The situation differed in the other big veterans' league of the republican camp, the Reichsbund. Not only did it include war widows and female orphans as a matter of course but, particularly during the early 1930s, it also gave female functionaries, of whom it had a considerable number, a clearly distinguishable voice in its commemorative rituals. Nevertheless, the basic fact remains that the republican camp did not systematically engage women in the commemoration of war, despite its inclusive rhetoric. Such a self-imposed limitation stood in stark contrast to the right-wing camp, in which an intrinsic female contribution to the renewal of the nation was part and parcel of nationalist politics, and in which the Stahlhelm – to give just one example – made sure to organise women in a separate, highly successful Bund Königin Luise.[12] To be sure, representations of wartime masculinity among republican veterans differed from the hegemonic forms of the nationalist right. But the self-imposed neglect of female participation weakened the republican appropriation of war remembrances, and thus republican activism more generally.[13]

[10] Voigt, *Kampfbünde*, pp. 459–61.

[11] Reichsbanner *Gau* Hanover to all local branches, 5 July 1932, appendix: NHStAH, Hann. 310 II, no. 25, fo. 143.

[12] Ziemann, 'Weimar was Weimar', pp. 551f.; Christiane Streubel, *Radikale Nationalistinnen: Agitation und Programmatik rechter Frauen in der Weimarer Republik* (Frankfurt am Main; New York: Campus, 2006), pp. 114f.

[13] As a self-critical acknowledgement of this negligence, in direct comparison with the Bund Königin Luise, see Berta Jourdan, 'Frauen an die Front!', *RB* no. 34, 22 August 1931.

Another, second ambivalence stemmed from the use of military symbols by republican veterans. Contrary to the claims by some historians, the Reichsbanner did not contribute to an overall militarisation of Weimar's political culture. Even though most of its members supported a moderate pacifism, they had to wear uniforms and military decorations in order to represent their claims. It was nigh impossible to make claims with regard to one's own military service in the public arena without displaying at least some military insignia. Yet even the moderate and rather subdued way in which the Reichsbanner members presented themselves in marching columns and wore their military decorations still alienated radical pacifists and socialist working-class youth in the Socialist Labour Youth (SAJ) in equal measure. The latter by and large felt that the *Soldatenspielerei* of the Reichsbanner directly contradicted their well-established patterns of peace pedagogy.[14] At the same time, these paramilitary elements did not prevent nationalist observers from claiming that the pacifist Reichsbanner veterans weakened the overall readiness for defence, or *Wehrhaftigkeit*. And even the introduction of the more intensively trained Schutzformationen in late 1930 did nothing to improve the actual ability of the Reichsbanner to withstand or even stop any coordinated attack against the republican institutions by the Nazi Stormtroopers and the Reichswehr. In such a case, it would be simply 'impotent', as critical observers from the radical left of the SPD correctly concluded.[15]

These two ambivalences in the symbolic representation of republican war narratives already weakened any attempt to maximise their thrust in the political arena. Two further, even more general inherent problems of republican war remembrances came on top of that. The first relates to the ways in which the wartime soldiers were presented as individual and collective actors in the recollections of the front-line experience, and how these recollections were connected to the kind of citizenship that the republican veterans aimed to foster after 1918. The key tenet of Reichsbanner and Reichsbund members was that they supported the new republican polity precisely because they had observed the corruption and ultimate collapse of the imperial system

[14] See Hirche, *Immer in Bewegung*, p. 357 (Hirche was himself a committed Reichsbanner activist); and the exchange in 'Wir und "Reichsbanner Schwarz–Rot–Gold"', *Sozialistische Jugend: Mitteilungsblatt der Sozialistischen Arbeiter-Jugend West-Sachsen* 1 (1924), pp. 58f., 72–4. Other SAJ members greeted the Reichsbanner's focus on 'symbols' and 'outward appearance' (*Äußerlichkeiten*), because working-class youth embraced it, and the Republic had neglected it so far. See 'Noch einmal: Reichsbanner Schwarz–Rot–Gold', *Jugend-Echo Mittelelbe* 8 (1924), no. 8, 37f.

[15] Helmut Wagner, 'Das Reichsbanner: Die proletarische Wehrorganisation?', *Jungsozialistische Blätter* 8 (1929), no. 2, 39–42 (quote on p. 40).

first-hand. In that sense, even Social Democrats on the right wing of the party such as Erhard Auer claimed collective ownership of the revolution in 1918. As late as December 1932, a Catholic observer could correctly state that 'millions of front-line soldiers' would 'still own up to the November revolution'.[16] But in their war remembrances, these republican veterans never claimed any collective agency for themselves in their roles as front-line soldiers, apart from the Christmas truces in 1914 and 1915 when they had actively engaged with their counterparts on the other side of no man's land. Rather, they consistently tapped into a victimisation narrative that portrayed ordinary soldiers as the overpowered, innocent victims of a brutal war machine reliant on technology and oppression to keep checks on the men in the front line. In many respects, these narratives were similar to those used in the publicised eyewitness accounts of French veterans during the inter-war period, except that the Germans could not close their narratives with at least some sort of vindication through military victory.[17]

Like their counterparts among the French war veterans, the socialist veterans of the Reichsbanner were particularly eager to highlight the plight of those soldiers who had become the victims of the court-martial system. There was no significant German equivalent to the spectacular case of the *fusillés*, those *poilus* who had been sentenced to death and executed mostly in the wake of the mutinies that had laid bare a major crisis of motivation in the French army in the spring of 1917.[18] Nevertheless, the *Reichsbanner* journal paid particular attention to the court-martial system as a gross example of how 'militarism' had victimised ordinary people. The court martial had not only been a 'remnant of the darkest medieval age': like French socialist veterans, Reichsbanner members highlighted its arbitrary nature, which reflected the fact that its wilful and relentless use was meant to cement the class rule of the elites. In their indictment of victimisation through court martial, the German veterans also directly referred to the French debates on this issue during the 1920s.[19] Even a centrist Social Democrat such as Philipp Scheidemann, who had announced the Republic from the

[16] Ferdinand Muralt, 'Der "Stahlhelm" und die Große Politik', *Hochland: Monatsschrift für alle Gebiete des Wissens, der Literatur und der Kunst* 30 (1932/3), 193–204 (p. 198).

[17] Leonard V. Smith, *The Embattled Self: French Soldiers' Testimony of the Great War* (Ithaca, NY: Cornell University Press, 2007), pp. 106–47.

[18] Nicolas Offenstadt, *Les Fusillés de la Grande Guerre et la mémoire collective (1914–1999)* (Paris: Editions Odile Jacob, 1999), pp. 17–46, 110–17.

[19] 'Die Verbrechen der Kriegsgerichte', *RB* no. 46, 30 December 1928; Hans Reich, 'Exekution: Eine Kriegserinnerung', *RB* no. 40, 5 October 1929; see Offenstadt, *Les Fusillés*, pp. 73–8.

balcony of the Reichstag on 9 November 1918, denounced the death sentences against the mutineers in the German navy in the summer of 1917 as a case of 'judicial murder'.[20] Writing in the *Reichsbanner* journal in 1926, he thus took up a cause that was usually associated with the Independent Social Democratic Party (USPD), whose founding member, Wilhelm Dittmann, had used similar rhetoric during the war.

Victimisation narratives were not only prevalent in the publicised war remembrances of the republican war veterans; they also pervaded the personal recollections of Reichsbanner members, as the example of Fritz Einert demonstrates. In letters to his parents during the war, Einert had repeatedly conveyed his despair about the ways in which the lives of so many young people 'are sacrificed' as mere 'cannon fodder'. For his own – and at the end of the war quite downtrodden – sense of victimisation he used the metaphor of life in a 'Prussian prison'.[21] Throughout the self-reflexive recollections he penned in 1926, Einert returned to this theme, stressing in a variety of ways how oppression through the military system and its disciplinary apparatus had turned front-line soldiers into slaves. These examples should suffice to illustrate the point that the almost exclusive focus among the Reichsbanner members on victimisation narratives certainly reflected one of the dominant motives of their own war experiences. Yet this focus on the soldier as a victim of overwhelming external forces made it difficult, if not impossible, to employ wartime memories as a springboard for the empowerment of these republican veterans. Basically remembered as someone who was fenced in by a rigid, oppressive system, the front-line soldier could not serve as a role model for the collective agency of democratic citizens in the Weimar Republic. Thus, in the wider field of Reichsbanner *Geschichtspolitik*, the barricade fighters of the democratic revolution in March 1848 had to fulfil this role. They were remembered as heroes and martyrs, whose example served to inspire Reichsbanner members for their fight in defence of the Republic.[22] The victimisation narratives of war remembrance helped to fuel popular resentment against the Hohenzollern monarchy and thus underscored the legitimacy of the Republic. But they did not inject a strong sense of agency and historical optimism into Reichsbanner members, who, as the case of Fritz Einert shows, felt they had reasons to complain that economic dependency had turned them again into *Untertanen*.

[20] Philipp Scheidemann, 'Justizmorde im Kriege', *RB* no. 4, 15 February 1926.

[21] Letters dated 6 October and 22 November 1916, 11 May 1918, quoted in Ziemann, 'Gedanken', pp. 227, 232

[22] Eric Bryden, 'Heroes and Martyrs of the Republic: Reichsbanner *Geschichtspolitik* in Weimar Germany', *CEH* 43 (2010), 639–65.

A final systematic ambivalence of republican war remembrances was the imprecise nature of their republicanism itself. In its celebration of Constitution Day on 11 August, the Reichsbanner employed a rhetoric that was intended to be as inclusive as possible, stressing the equality and active participation of all citizens of the Republic. Particularly on the tenth anniversary of the constitution on 11 August 1929, the spatial integration of the nation was highlighted as well: the Reich, as the Republic was still called, consisted of people from all districts, including the border regions in the East and West. Ultimately, integration was also celebrated in terms of social cohesion. Based on the cooperation between Edwin Redslob as Reich Art Custodian and the Reichsbanner, which provided the participants for mass gatherings and demonstrations, Constitution Day celebrated the unity of the Republic in terms of a *Volksgemeinschaft*, in the inclusive, egalitarian reading of the term.[23] Yet in the commemorative celebrations at war memorials, and on all the other occasions at which the Reichsbanner remembered the war, the rhetoric differed quite fundamentally from that employed on Constitution Day. Some bourgeois representatives of the league, to be sure – usually members of the liberal German Democratic Party (DDP) – also invoked the notion of a *Volksgemeinschaft*, as did Social Democrat mavericks on the right wing of the party, such as former major Karl Mayr.[24] But these were rare exceptions.

More generally, the war narratives of the Reichsbanner and Reichsbund were confrontational, not integrative. They denied the legitimacy of some of the most pertinent nationalist war narratives; they described the situation in the wartime army basically as a class confrontation between the officer corps, which was recruited from the Wilhelmine elites, and working-class private soldiers; and they claimed the legacy of the fallen for socialist labour, including its quest for a positive internationalism in exchanges with the former enemies. While firmly supporting the Republic, these were basically moderate socialist war remembrances. And as the organisational history of the Reichsbanner illustrates, the Social Democrat underpinnings of this commemorative discourse became even more pronounced over the years. Socialist rhetoric offered a firm basis for the thorough inclusion of Social Democrat workers into this discourse, and as such certainly explains the huge organisational success of the Reichsbanner. However, such a focus on the socialist rhetoric of class was also bound to exclude

[23] Rossol, *Performing the Nation*, pp. 60, 62, 70, 75.

[24] 'Bericht über den Verlauf der Kundgebung des Reichsbanners', 22 February 1931: StAM, Pol. Dir. 6886.

sizeable groups of potential supporters, not least Catholic workers, who would have surely expected a Christian symbolism of consolation and redemption alongside the republican elements of commemoration.[25] In that sense, the massive organisational edifice of the Reichsbanner, one of the biggest success stories of the Weimar Republic, also included a substantial failure. It failed to deliver on one of its core promises: to strengthen and protect the Republic from a non-partisan perspective of *Überparteilichkeit*. And nowhere in the political discourse of Reichsbanner ideas was this failure more obvious and tangible than in its performative display of war remembrances.

After this brief résumé of the most important shortcomings and ambivalences of leftist anti-war remembrances, their relative strength should also be assessed in a chronological overview. In the immediate aftermath of the war, nationalist–revisionist narratives of the war experience had very little traction. When Franz Seldte gathered a circle of like-minded former army comrades in Magdeburg in December 1918 to found the Stahlhelm, they agreed basically to support the new republican system. Only after the terms of the Treaty of Versailles were announced in May 1919, and the government accepted them in June, did the Stahlhelm swiftly move to the anti-republican right.[26] Surely, the harsh terms of the treaty had a considerable impact on the national camp, and locked it into a revisionist mindset.[27] Yet the progressive democrats and moderate socialists among the veterans were not agitated or even severely disappointed by the Treaty of Versailles. They accepted it as a payment for the underlying catastrophe they had experienced first-hand: the utter failure of the expansionist ambitions of imperial Germany, and the brutal treatment it had meted out against civilians in the occupied territories and its own working-class subjects alike. Fuelled by their ire against the lost years of wartime service, republican war veterans drove home their own version of the 'stab-in-the-back' myth: corruption and betrayal of the Wilhelmine elite had turned defeat into political liberation, and rightly so, as the Kaiser – going into exile in the Netherlands – had committed an act of desertion

[25] Catholic war remembrances in Weimar Germany have yet to be studied in detail. For Austria, see the important study by Überegger, *Erinnerungskriege*, pp. 127–80, 203–18. For a comparative perspective, see the forthcoming monograph by Patrick Houlihan.

[26] Volker R. Berghahn, *Der Stahlhelm: Bund der Frontsoldaten 1918–1935* (Düsseldorf: Droste, 1966), pp. 13f., 18ff. Writing in 1932, Muralt, 'Stahlhelm', p. 193, was astonished by the early commitment of the Stahlhelm to the new state.

[27] Judith Voelker, '"Unerträglich, unerfüllbar und deshalb unannehmbar": Kollektiver Protest gegen Versailles im Rheinland in den Monaten Mai und Juni 1919', in Dülffer and Krumeich, *Der verlorene Frieden*, pp. 229–41.

in a difficult moment for the nation. During the 'short period of insight' (Franz Carl Endres) from 1919 to 1922, these ideas resonated widely not only among committed Social Democrats, but also among many left-liberal bourgeois democrats.

French and Belgian occupation of the Ruhr, the industrial heart of Germany, in January 1923 shifted the terms of the debate to the right. While the government proclaimed a policy of passive resistance, it was not only the right-wing media that whipped up a frenzy of national enmity against the French. Young Socialists and left-liberals, who had previously been busy indicting the moral decay in the Imperial Army, also now praised the superior values of the German nation. The political upheaval of 1923, culminating in the Hitler putsch in November, prompted Social Democrats to pursue an approach that had already been practised at a local level since the Kapp putsch in 1920. They aimed to gather committed war veterans in self-defence leagues against the street politics of the right-wing combat leagues, and the Stahlhelm in particular. The founding of the Reichsbanner in 1924 fundamentally consolidated the representation of republican war remembrances. Quickly, a coherent set of narratives, symbols and performative rituals for the commemoration of the war was established. Even political setbacks, such as the election of former general Paul von Hindenburg as Reich president in April 1925, did not negatively affect these war remembrances. When it was mentioned during a Reichsbanner meeting in Munich that Hindenburg had sworn his oath on the constitution, rank-and-file members heckled, accusing him of perjury.[28] As the former head of the Third Army Supreme Command, Hindenburg could not command respect among Social Democrats, and particularly not among Reichsbanner members.[29]

The republican war remembrances of the Reichsbund and Reichsbanner were fostered and transmitted as a form of collective memory as defined by Maurice Halbwachs. Their strength rested on the tightly knit sociability among working-class people in local communities: on the daily interactions and conversations between Social Democrats who had themselves experienced the war, and who – contrary to some intellectual commentators at the time – never really

[28] 'Mitgliederversammlung des Reichsbanners Schwarz–Rot–Gold am 8.6.1925 im Kolosseum', PND no. 509: StAM, Pol. Dir. 6886. The Reichsbanner certainly did not claim 'ownership of the Hindenburg myth', as Goltz, *Hindenburg* asserts (p. 126), based on a single pictorial source.

[29] Hirche, *Immer in Bewegung*, p. 361.

stopped talking about it.[30] Yet there were clear limits to this form of sustaining recollections of front-line service. As the war youth generation, those born between 1900 and 1910, reached the age of adulthood and entered the political scene in their droves in the late 1920s, a new challenge for the anti-war discourse of moderate socialists arose. Simply reiterating the popular catchphrase 'No more war!' ad nauseam no longer sufficed. Even male working-class youths from socialist households proved susceptible to the allure of novels and films that represented the war as a big adventure story.

The intensive public debate about first the book and then the film *All Quiet on the Western Front* from late 1928 to 1930 laid bare the problems of the republican camp in its relation to media representations of the war. Republicans rushed to the defence of Remarque's work, even though the book itself carefully avoided any explicit political statement and could be also read, with its praise for the comradeship among the soldiers, as a nationalist war novel. With the massive presence of books and films on the war since the late 1920s, the texture of war remembrance had changed, forcing the republican camp to embark on an uphill struggle in the defence of those few releases that they could identify with their cause. The overall political circumstances of the years from 1930 to 1933 – economic crisis, political instability and the rise of the Nazis to a mass movement – obviously did not help Social Democrats in their attempts to maintain the thrust of their war remembrances in the public sphere. More and more often, they were forced to defend their wartime record in acts of defiance against slander by ruthless radical nationalists, rather than to elaborate in a more complex manner on the meaning of the war experience. Yet only with the Nazi seizure of power in early 1933 were republican war memories effectively silenced and suppressed.

Throughout this book, I have described the representation of republican war remembrances as an intervention in a highly contested field. Moderate pacifists and socialists developed their narratives of the war experience in direct confrontation with the nationalist right-wing camp. The Weimar Republic never developed a national style of war remembrance, and that is, after all, the biggest comparative difference

[30] See for example Walter Benjamin's famous remark that 'men who returned from the battlefield had grown silent – not richer but poorer in communicable experience'; Walter Benjamin, 'The Storyteller: Observations on the Works of Nikolai Leskow' (1936), in *Selected Writings*, 4 vols., Vol. III, ed. Howard Eiland and Michael W. Jennings (Cambridge, MA; London: Belknap Press, 2002), pp. 143–66 (pp. 143f.). See Chapter 3 in this book.

to countries such as France or the UK. Thus, contestation is surely the most relevant aspect of war remembrances in post-war Germany. But there is also another important story to be told, which is perhaps best described as expropriation by stealth. We have analysed key elements of this process in previous chapters, but never brought them to the forefront. Now is the time to do this. When pacifists, Social Democrats and radical democrats started in early 1919 to offer relentless criticism of the injustice and mendacity of the Imperial Army, they employed the 'worm's-eye perspective' as their default point of view. The inevitable and liberating nature of the military collapse was told from the perspective of the ordinary front-line soldier, and this vantage point was defended as the best position for an assessment of all aspects of the war.[31] At this time, the political right still privileged the perspective of generals and high-ranking officers.

Yet in subsequent years, the nationalist camp learned to adopt the worm's-eye view for its own political purposes. Confronted with the hegemony of leftist anti-war remembrances in the early 1920s, the Reichsarchiv devised a series of popular battlefield narratives that privileged the soldier's perspective. In *Mein Kampf*, Hitler presented himself as a battle-hardened soldier, even though he saw battle action only once and subsequently served as a dispatch-runner. More importantly, he used the worm's-eye view to criticise the 'big-mouths' of the parliamentary elites, as if his humble position had offered him any privileged insights into the nature of politics, which he claimed to despise.[32] In his speeches and election campaigns from the late 1920s onwards, Hitler went even one step further in the expropriation of the worm's-eye view for political purposes, which the left had pioneered. Presenting himself in populist fashion as the 'unknown soldier' who had come to save the nation, Hitler imagined himself as the living embodiment and epitome of the German war remembrance. In 1933, the expropriation of the worm's-eye view by the extreme nationalist right had come full circle. Speaking in public on 10 May 1933, Hitler explicitly referred to Karl Bröger's famous words about the 'poorest citizens' who are also the 'most loyal ones' of the German nation, and stressed that he had closely encountered these 'poorest sons' of the nation for four years during the war.[33] Meanwhile, Bröger himself, the worker, poet, prolific journalist, Social Democrat and tireless Reichsbanner leader, was violently

[31] Ulrich, 'Perspektive'.

[32] Adolf Hitler, *Mein Kampf* (London: Hutchinson, 1969), p. 152; see Thomas Weber, *Hitler's First War: Adolf Hitler, the Men of the List Regiment, and the First World War* (Oxford University Press, 2010), p. 156.

[33] Quoted in Müller, *Für Vaterland und Republik*, p. 159.

removed as a city councillor in his native Nuremberg by Nazi thugs on 28 April 1933. On 30 June, he was detained in the Dachau concentration camp.[34]

Overall, the republican war veterans of the Reichsbund and Reichsbanner have a more general significance for our understanding of the Weimar Republic. Not many historians would today support the notion that Weimar was a 'Republic without republicans'. Yet there is an ongoing debate over the extent and nature of pro-republican engagement from 1918 to 1933.[35] Based on the evidence presented in this book, there are many reasons to stress the extent to which the republican system could rely on the massive presence of people who supported it not merely out of reason, but with their hearts and souls. These devoted republicans and moderate socialists injected a strong sense of historical optimism into the new polity.[36] And they did not only do so during the allegedly stable period of the Republic from 1924 to 1928, but were also keen to keep up their commitment during the following turbulent years. The future of the Republic was not sealed before the Nazis employed brutal force and physical violence to destroy its political system in 1933.

34 *Ibid.*, pp. 158, 160.

35 Ziemann, 'Weimar was Weimar', p. 568.

36 On journalists and highbrow intellectuals see Graf, *Die Zukunft der Weimarer Republik*.

Bibliography

ARCHIVAL SOURCES

Bundesarchiv Berlin-Lichterfelde (BArch)

R 32: Reichskunstwart
221, 222, 353, 353a, 354, 355, 357, 357a, 358, 358a, 361, 364, 366, 494, 496

R 43/I: Reichskanzlei
710, 712, 713, 714

R 72: Stahlhelm. Bund der Frontsoldaten
268, 289, 682

R 1501: Reichsministerium des Innern
113501, 113502, 125965

R 1506: Reichsarchiv
41, 48, 97, 193, 323, 326

R 8034 II: Reichslandbund Pressearchiv
2869, 2870, 7690–2

R 8034 III: Reichslandbund Pressearchiv, Personen
201, 432, 502

R 9350 Sachthematische Sammlung
262, 275

Bundesarchiv Berlin-Lichterfelde-SAPMO

Ry 12/II, 113
1, 2, 3, 7, 8

SgY 30
1052, 1365/2, 2167

Akademie der Künste, Berlin (AdK)

Kempowski-Biographienarchiv (Kempowski-BIO)
6865/1, 6865/2, 6865/3, 6865/4, 6865/5

Geheimes Staatsarchiv Preußischer Kulturbesitz Berlin (GStA)

Rep. 77
Tit. 1137, no. 50; Tit. 4043, nos. 351, 352

Landesarchiv Berlin (LAB)

A Pr. Br. Rep. 030 Polizeipräsidium Berlin
7532, 7562, 7562/1, 21600, 21643

A Rep. 358–01 Generalstaatsanwaltschaft bei dem Landgericht Berlin: Strafverfahren 1919–1933
2032, 2033, 2057

Staatsbibliothek Preußischer Kulturbesitz zu Berlin, Handschriftenabteilung (SBPK)

NL Hans Delbrück
Mappe Karl Mayr; Briefe Martin Hobohm Mappe IV, Mappe V

Archiv der sozialen Demokratie Bonn (AdsD)

NL Karl Höltermann
Box 1, 2, 5, 6

NL Otto Hörsing
Mappe 24, 25

NL Hans Emil Lange
Karton I, Karton II

NL Paul Levi
1/PLAA000051, 1/PLAA0000296

NL Franz Osterroth
1/FOAC000001, 1/FOAC00000138, 1/FOAC00000193, 1/FOAC00000195, 1/FOAC00000206

Postkartensammlung
6/CARD000294, 6/CARD000561

Staatsarchiv Bremen (StA Bremen)

4, 65 Nachrichtenstelle der Polizeidirektion Bremen
1026–36, 1146, 1157

7, 88 Nachlass Willy Dehnkamp
50/2, 50/3, 50/6

Stadtarchiv Essen

NL Reismann-Grone
652 192

Bundesarchiv/Militärarchiv Freiburg im Breisgau (BA/MA)

N 559 (NL Berthold von Deimling)
5, 35

Niedersächsisches Hauptstaatsarchiv Hannover (NHStAH)

Hann. 310 II C
2–25

Hann. 180, Hildesheim
11666, Vols. I–III

Bundesarchiv Koblenz

N 1017 (NL Hans Delbrück)
50

Bayerisches Hauptstaatsarchiv München (BHStA), Abt. II

MK Ministerium für Unterricht und Kultus
51030

Institut für Zeitgeschichte München, Archiv (IfZ)

ED 106
1, 11, 38, 41, 49, 54

F 86

Bayerisches Hauptstaatsarchiv München, Abt. IV: Kriegsarchiv

HS 2348

Staatsarchiv München (StAM)

Polizei-Direktion München (Pol. Dir.)
6878, 6886–92

Archiv der Arbeiterjugend, Oer-Erkenschwick

PB Siemsen, Anna 22
Anna Siemsen, *Mein Leben in Deutschland vor und nach 1933*
Various journals of the socialist labour youth movement

Stadtarchiv Schiltach (StA Schiltach)

AS-2055a Protokollbuch Ortsgruppe Schiltach

Hauptstaatsarchiv Stuttgart (HStASt)

E 130b Staatsministerium
Bü 3840, Bü 3846

PUBLISHED SOURCES

Newspapers and journals

Das andere Deutschland
Arbeiter-Jugend
Berliner Tageblatt
Berliner Volks-Zeitung
Bremer Volkszeitung
Deutsche Allgemeine Zeitung
Deutsche Tageszeitung
Deutsche Zeitung
Fränkische Tagespost
Freiheit
Illustrierte Reichsbanner-Zeitung (from 6 (1929): *Illustrierte republikanische Zeitung)*
Jugend-Echo Mittelelbe
Jungsozialistische Blätter
Lübecker Volksbote
Mecklenburgische Volkszeitung
Münchener Post
Münchner Neueste Nachrichten
Neckar-Echo Heilbronn
Das Reichsbanner: Zeitung des Reichsbanner Schwarz–Rot–Gold
Reichsbund: Mitteilungen des Reichsbundes der Kriegsbeschädigten, Kriegsteilnehmer und Kriegshinterbliebenen
Schwäbische Tagwacht
Die Sozialistische Erziehung
Sozialistische Jugend: Mitteilungsblatt der Sozialistischen Arbeiter-Jugend West-Sachsen
Sozialistische Monatshefte
Der Stahlhelm
Volksstimme: Schmalkalder Tageblatt
Volksstimme: Tageszeitung der sozialdemokratischen Partei im Regierungsbezirk Magdeburg
Volkszeitung Esslingen
Vorwärts
Vossische Zeitung
Weltbühne

Parliamentary Proceedings

Verhandlungen des Reichstages: Stenographische Berichte, 386 (1926)

SOURCE COLLECTIONS

Berthold, Lothar and Helmut Neef, *Militarismus und Opportunismus gegen die Novemberrevolution: Das Bündnis der rechten SPD-Führung mit der Obersten Heeresleitung November und Dezember 1918. Eine Dokumentation* (Berlin: Rütten & Loening, 1958).

Institut für Zeitgeschichte (ed.), *Hitler: Reden, Schriften, Anordnungen. Februar 1925 bis Januar 1933*, 6 vols. (Munich; New York: Saur, 1992–2003).

Jäckel, Eberhard and Axel Kuhn (eds.), *Hitler: Sämtliche Aufzeichnungen 1905–1924* (Stuttgart: DVA, 1980).

Kaes, Anton, Martin Jay and Edward Dimendberg (eds.), *The Weimar Republic Sourcebook* (Berkeley: University of California Press, 1994).

Landmesser, Paul and Peter Päßler (eds.), *Wir lernen im Vorwärtsgehen! Dokumente zur Geschichte der Arbeiterbewegung in Reutlingen 1844–1949* (Heilbronn: Distel-Verlag, 1990).

Obenaus, Herbert and Sybille (eds.), *'Schreiben wie es wirklich war …': Aufzeichnungen Karl Dürkefäldens aus den Jahren 1933–1945* (Hanover: Fackelträger, 1985).

Schrader, Bärbel (ed.), *Der Fall Remarque:* Im Westen nichts Neues. *Eine Dokumentation* (Leipzig: Reclam, 1992).

Ulrich, Bernd and Benjamin Ziemann (eds.), *Krieg im Frieden: Die umkämpfte Erinnerung an den Ersten Weltkrieg* (Frankfurt am Main: Fischer, 1997).

Ulrich, Bernd and Benjamin Ziemann (eds.), *German Soldiers in the Great War. Letters and Eyewitness Accounts* (Barnsley: Pern & Sword, 2010).

BOOKS AND ARTICLES

Abel, Theodore, *Why Hitler Came into Power* (Cambridge, MA: Harvard University Press, 1986 [1938]).

Anklage der Gepeinigten! Geschichte eines Feldlazarettes: Aus den Tagebüchern eines Sanitäts-Feldwebels (Berlin: Firn-Verlag, 1919).

Appens, Wilhelm, *Charleville: Dunkle Punkte aus dem Etappenleben* (Dortmund: Gerisch, n.d. [1919]).

Charleville. Ein trübes Kapitel aus der Etappen-Geschichte des Weltkrieges 1914/18 (Dortmund: Gerisch, 1927).

Bathe, Rolf, *Der Zusammenbruch: So war der Krieg! So war sein Ende!* (Wuppertal: Freie Presse, 1931).

Becker, Wilhelm, *Der unbekannte Soldat: Erlebnisse aus dem Weltkriege* (Paderborn: Schöningh, 1934).

Benjamin, Walter, 'The Storyteller: Observations on the Works of Nikolai Leskow' (1936), in *Selected Writings*, 4 vols., Vol. III, ed. Howard Eiland and Michael W. Jennings (Cambridge, MA; London: Belknap Press, 2002), pp. 143–66.

Beyer, Paul, *Düsseldorfer Passion: Ein deutsches National-Festspiel in zehn Bildern* (Munich: Eher, 1933).

Boveri, Margret, *Wir lügen alle: Eine Hauptstadtzeitung unter Hitler* (Olten; Freiburg: Walter, 1965).

Braun, Otto, *Von Weimar zu Hitler* (Hildesheim: Gerstenberg, 1979 [1940]).

Bröger, Karl, *Der unbekannte Soldat: Kriegstaten und Schicksale des kleinen Mannes* (Leipzig: Reclam, n.d. [1917]).

Cron, Hermann (ed.), *Das Archiv des Deutschen Studentendienstes von 1914*, Inventare des Reichsarchivs, Series 1: Kriegsbrief-Sammlungen 1 (Potsdam: Reichsarchiv, 1926).

Dietz, Otto, *Der Todesgang der deutschen Armee: Militärische Ursachen* (Berlin: Karl Curtius, 1919).

Distelbarth, Paul H., *Das andere Frankreich: Aufsätze zur Gesellschaft, Kultur und Politik Frankreichs und zu den deutsch–französischen Beziehungen 1932–1953*, ed. Hans Manfred Bock (Berne: Peter Lang, 1997).

Der 'Dolchstoß': Warum das deutsche Heer zusammenbrach (Berlin: Zentralverlag, 1920).

Der Dolchstoß-Prozeß in München Oktober–November 1925: Eine Ehrenrettung des deutschen Volkes (Munich: G. Birk, 1925).

Duderstadt, Henning, *Vom Reichsbanner zum Hakenkreuz. Wie es kommen musste: Ein Bekenntnis* (Stuttgart: Union, 1933).

Duesterberg, Theodor, *Das Reichsehrenmal im Walde südlich Bad Berka: Gedanken und Anregungen für die Ausgestaltung* (Halle: Vaterländischer Verlag, 1931).

Endres, Franz Carl, *Die Tragödie Deutschlands: Im Banne des Machtgedankens bis zum Zusammenbruch des Reiches. Von einem Deutschen*, 3rd edn (Stuttgart: Moritz, 1924 [1921]).

Der Etappensumpf: Dokumente des Zusammenbruchs des deutschen Heeres aus den Jahren 1916/1918. Aus dem Kriegstagebuch eines Gemeinen (Jena: Volksbuchhandlung, 1920).

Glaeser, Ernst, *Class of 1902* (London: Martin Secker, 1929).

Hammer, Walter, *Das Buch der 236. I. D.* (Elberfeld: Baedecker, 1919).

Hilpert, Fritz, *Das Reichsehrenmal und die Frontkämpfer* (Berlin: Deutsche Verlagsgesellschaft für Politik und Geschichte, 1927).

Himmelfahrt 1927: Reichsbanner Schwarz–Rot–Gold, Kameradschaft Eberswalde (Eberswalde: n.p., 1927).

Hirche, Kurt, *Immer in Bewegung: Lebensweg eines deutschen Sozialisten*, 3 vols., Vol. I: *Unruhe und Aufbruch* (Marburg: Schüren, 1994).

Hirschberg, Max, *Jude und Demokrat: Erinnerungen eines Münchener Rechtsanwalts 1883 bis 1939* (Munich: Oldenbourg, 1998).

Hitler, Adolf, *Mein Kampf* (London: Hutchinson, 1969).

Hobohm, Martin, *Untersuchungsausschuß und Dolchstoßlegende* (Charlottenburg: Weltbühne, 1926).

Hurwitz-Stranz, Helene (ed.), *Kriegerwitwen gestalten ihr Schicksal: Lebenskämpfe deutscher Kriegerwitwen nach eigenen Darstellungen* (Berlin: Heymann, 1931).

Jünger, Ernst, *Copse 125: A Chronicle from the Trench Warfare of 1918*, trans. Basil Creighton (London: Chatto & Windus, 1930).

Das Wäldchen 125: Eine Chronik aus den Grabenkämpfen des Jahres 1918 (1925), in *Sämtliche Werke*, 23 vols., Vol. I.1 (Stuttgart: Klett–Cotta, 1978), pp. 301–438.

Kehr, Eckart, 'Zur Genesis des Königlich Preußischen Reserveoffiziers' (1928), in *Der Primat der Innenpolitik: Gesammelte Aufsätze zur preußisch-deutschen Sozialgeschichte im 19. und 20. Jahrhundert*, ed. Hans-Ulrich Wehler (Frankfurt am Main; Berlin; Vienna: Ullstein, 1976), pp. 53–63.

Kuttner, Erich, *Der Sieg war zum Greifen nahe! Authentische Zeugnisse vom Frontzusammenbruch* (Berlin: Verlag für Sozialwissenschaft, 1921).

Lambach, Walther, *Ursachen des Zusammenbruchs* (Hamburg: Deutschnationale Verlagsanstalt, n.d. [1919]).

Löwenstein, Prince Hubertus, *The Tragedy of a People: Germany, 1918–1934* (London: Faber & Faber, 1934).

Lutz, Günther, *Die Frontgemeinschaft: Das Gemeinschaftserlebnis in der Kriegsliteratur*, Ph.D. dissertation (University of Greifswald, 1936).

Mahraun, Artur, 'Das Fronterlebnis', *Der Meister: Jungdeutsche Monatsschrift für Führer und denkende Brüder* 3 (1927), 3–7.

'Das Martyrium der Frontsoldaten', *Der Meister: Jungdeutsche Monatsschrift für Führer und denkende Brüder* 1.2 (1925/6), 6–11.

Mann, Heinrich, *Der Untertan: Roman* (Frankfurt am Main: Fischer Taschenbuch Verlag, 1991 [1919]).

Mayr, Karl, 'Der deutsche Einmarsch in Belgien', *Sozialistische Monatshefte* 34 (1928), 210–14.

'Die deutsche Kriegs-Theorie und der Weltkrieg', *Die deutsche Nation: Eine Zeitschrift für Politik* 5 (1923), 193–210, 274–84.

'Kriegsplan und staatsmännische Voraussicht', *Zeitschrift für Politik* 14 (1925), 385–411.

'"Nie wieder Krieg"?', in *Republikanischer Volkskalender 1927* (Dillingen: Lange, 1927), pp. 63–6.

Muralt, Ferdinand, 'Der "Stahlhelm" und die Große Politik', *Hochland: Monatsschrift für alle Gebiete des Wissens, der Literatur und der Kunst* 30 (1932/3), 193–204.

Norton Cru, Jean, *Wo ist die Wahrheit über den Krieg? Eine kritische Studie mit Berichten von Augenzeugen* (Potsdam: Müller & Kiepenheuer, 1932).

Ortsgruppe Potsdam des Reichsbanners Schwarz–Rot–Gold (ed.), *Das Reichsbanner und Potsdam* (Berlin: Dr Hiehold, 1924).

Ossietzky, Carl von, *Sämtliche Schriften*, 8 vols. (Reinbek: Rowohlt, 1994).

Persius, Lothar, *Die Tirpitz-Legende* (Berlin: Engelmann, 1918).

Wie es kam daß der Anstoß zur Revolution von der Flotte ausging (Berlin: Arbeitsgemeinschaft für staatsbürgerliche und wirtschaftliche Bildung, 1919).

Philipp, Albrecht and Walther Schücking, *Entschließung und Verhandlungsbericht: Die allgemeinen Ursachen und Hergänge des deutschen Zusammenbruches, 1. Teil*, *WUA* 4 (Berlin: Deutsche Verlagsgesellschaft für Politik und Geschichte, 1928).

Gutachten des Sachverständigen Dr. Hobohm, Soziale Heeresmißstände als Teilursache des deutschen Zusammenbruchs von 1918, *WUA* 11.1 (Berlin: Deutsche Verlagsgesellschaft für Politik und Geschichte, 1929).

Gutachten des Sachverständigen Reichsarchivrat Volkmann, Soziale Heeresmißstände als Mitursache des deutschen Zusammenbruches von 1918, *WUA* 11.2 (Berlin: Deutsche Verlagsgesellschaft für Politik und Geschichte, 1929).

Verhandlungsbericht: Die allgemeinen Ursachen und Hergänge des inneren Zusammenbruches, 2. Teil, *WUA* 5 (Berlin: Deutsche Verlagsgesellschaft für Politik und Geschichte, 1928).

Piper, Otto, 'Die Krise der Kriegsteilnehmergeneration', *Neue Blätter für den Sozialismus* 1 (1930), 441–51.

Remarque, Erich Maria, *All Quiet on the Western Front* (London: Putnam, 1929).

Scher, Peter, 'Immer mal wieder', *Simplicissimus* 36.5 (1931), 58.

Schmitt, Carl, *Verfassungslehre* (Berlin: Duncker & Humblot, 1954 [1928])

Schoenaich, Paul Freiherr von, *Zehn Jahre Kampf für Frieden und Recht* (Hamburg: Fackelreiter, 1929).

Schützinger, Hermann, 'Das Friedenswerk der Frontsoldaten', *Die Glocke* 10 (1924), 1100–2.

Der Kampf um die Republik: Ein Kampfbrevier für republikanische Frontsoldaten (Leipzig: Ernst Oldenburg, 1924).

Das Lied vom jungen Sterben: Kriegsroman aus dem Ban-de-Sapt (Dresden; Leipzig: Pierson, 1918).

Zusammenbruch: Die Tragödie des deutschen Feldheeres (Leipzig: Ernst Oldenburg, 1924).

Schwarz, Hans, *Die Wiedergeburt des heroischen Menschen: Eine Langemarck-Rede vor der Greifswalder Studentenschaft am 11. November 1928* (Berlin: Der Nahe Osten, 1930).

Seeberg, D[avid], *Dem unbekannt gefallenen Krieger* (Dortmund: Ruhfus, 1921).

Sozialdemokratischer Parteitag in Leipzig 1931 vom 31. Mai bis 5. Juni im Volkshaus: Protokoll (Berlin: Dietz, 1931).

Taut, Bruno, 'Das Reichsehrenmal für die Kriegsopfer', *Die Baugilde* 6 (1924), 590.

Toller, Ernst, 'Der deutsche Hinkemann' (1923), in *Gesammelte Werke*, 5 vols., Vol. II (Munich: Carl Hanser, 1978), pp. 191–248.

Tucholsky, Kurt, *Gesammelte Werke*, 10 vols., ed. Mary Gerold-Tucholsky and Fritz J. Raddatz (Reinbek: Rowohlt, 1975).

*Der unbekannte Soldat erzählt: Von **** (Berlin: Mosse Stiftung, n.d. [1934]).

Unruh, Friedrich Franz von, 'Nationalistische Jugend', *Die neue Rundschau* 43.5 (1932), 577–92.

Unruh, Fritz von, 'Heinrich aus Andernach' (1925), in *Sämtliche Werke*, 13 vols., Vol. V (Berlin: Haude & Spener, 1991), pp. 7–64.

Verzeichnis der im Bundesverlage erschienenen Männer-, Frauen-, gemischten und Kinderchöre (Berlin: Deutscher Arbeiter-Sängerbund, n.d. [1930]).

Vetter, Karl, *Der Zusammenbruch der Westfront: Ludendorff ist schuld! Die Anklage der Feldgrauen* (Berlin: Koch & Jürgens, n.d. [1919]).

Walther, Karl August, Cornelius Gurlitt and Johannes Keßler, *Vom Reichsehrenmal* (Munich: Callwey, 1926).

Wandt, Heinrich, *Erotik und Spionage in der Etappe Gent* (Vienna; Berlin: Agis-Verlag, 1929 [1928]).

Etappe Gent, 2nd edn (Vienna; Berlin: Agis-Verlag, 1926 [1920]).

Das Justizverbrechen des Reichsgerichts an dem Verfasser der 'Etappe Gent' (Berlin: Der Syndikalist, 1926).

Wegweiser für Funktionäre, Führer und alle Bundeskameraden des Reichsbanners Schwarz–Rot–Gold, 3rd edn (Magdeburg: Verlag des Bundesvorstandes, 1929).

Weniger, Erich, 'Das Bild des Krieges: Erlebnis, Erinnerung, Überlieferung', *Die Erziehung* 5 (1929), 1–21.

Wilke, G. (ed.), *Reden für republikanische Gelegenheiten und für Reichsbanner-Veranstaltungen* (Berlin: Hoffmann, 1926).

Zickler, Artur, *Im Tollhause* (Berlin: Verlag Vorwärts, n.d. [1919]).

Der Zusammenbruch der Kriegspolitik und die Novemberrevolution: Beobachtungen und Betrachtungen eines ehemaligen Frontsoldaten (Berlin: Verlagsgenossenschaft Freiheit, 1919).

SECONDARY LITERATURE

Achilles, Manuela, 'Performing the Reich: Democratic Symbols and Rituals in the Weimar Republic', in Canning, Barndt and McGuire, *Weimar Publics*, pp. 175–91.

'With a Passion for Reason: Celebrating the Constitution in Weimar Germany', *CEH* 43 (2010), 666–89.

Ackermann, Volker, '"Ceux qui sont pieusement morts pour la France ...": Die Identität des Unbekannten Soldaten', in Koselleck and Jeismann, *Der politische Totenkult*, pp. 281–314.

Alter, Reinhard, 'Heinrich Manns *Untertan*: Prüfstein für die "Kaiserreich-Debatte"?', *GG* 17 (1991), 370–89.

Appelius, Stefan, 'Der Friedensgeneral Paul Freiherr von Schoenaich: Demokrat und Pazifist in der Weimarer Republik', *Demokratische Geschichte* 7 (1992), 165–80.

Applegate, Celia, *A Nation of Provincials: The German Idea of Heimat* (Berkeley: University of California Press, 1990).

Ashworth, Tony, *Trench Warfare 1914–1918: The Live and Let Live System* (London: Macmillan, 1980).

Assmann, Jan, 'Collective Memory and Cultural Identity', *New German Critique* 65 (1995), 125–33.

Audoin-Rouzeau, Stéphane and Annette Becker, *14–18, Understanding the Great War* (New York: Hill and Wang, 2003).

Baron, Ulrich and Hans Harald Müller, 'Die Weltkriege im Roman der Nachkriegszeiten', in Niedhart and Riesenberger, *Lernen aus dem Krieg?*, pp. 300–18.

Barth, Boris, *Dolchstoßlegenden und politische Desintegration: Das Trauma der deutschen Niederlage im Ersten Weltkrieg 1914–1933* (Düsseldorf: Droste, 2003).

Beaupré, Nicolas, *Ecrire en guerre, écrire la guerre: France, Allemagne 1914–1920* (Paris: CNRS, 2006).

Das Trauma des großen Krieges 1918–1932/33 (Darmstadt: Wissenschaftliche Buchgesellschaft, 2009).

Becker, Annette, 'Der Kult der Erinnerung nach dem Grossen Krieg: Kriegerdenkmäler in Frankreich', in Koselleck and Jeismann, *Der politische Totenkult*, pp. 315–24.

Behrenbeck, Sabine, 'Heldenkult oder Friedensmahnung? Kriegerdenkmale nach beiden Weltkriegen', in Niedhart and Riesenberger, *Lernen aus dem Krieg?*, pp. 344–64.

Der Kult um die toten Helden: Nationalsozialistische Mythen, Riten und Symbole 1923 bis 1945 (Vierow: SH-Verlag, 1996).

Berghahn, Volker R., *Der Stahlhelm: Bund der Frontsoldaten 1918–1935* (Düsseldorf: Droste, 1966).

Bessel, Richard, 'The "Front Generation" and the Politics of Weimar Germany', in Mark Roseman (ed.), *Generations in Conflict: Youth Revolt and Generation Formation in Germany 1770–1968* (Cambridge University Press, 1995), pp. 121–36.

Germany after the First World War (Oxford: Clarendon Press, 1993).

Beutler, Kurt, 'Der Militärpädagoge Erich Weniger', in Martina Tschirner and Heinz-Werner Göbel (eds.), *Wissenschaft im Krieg – Krieg in der Wissenschaft* (Marburg: Eigenverlag AMW, 1990), pp. 293–304.

Blume, Dorlis, Ursula Breymayer and Bernd Ulrich (eds.), *Im Namen der Freiheit! Verfassung und Verfassungswirklichkeit in Deutschland* (Dresden: Sandstein, 2009).

Bock, Sigrid, 'Wirkungsbedingungen und Wirkungsweisen der Antikriegsliteratur in der Weimarer Republik', *Zeitschrift für Germanistik* 5 (1984), 19–32.

Breymayer, Ursula and Bernd Ulrich (eds.), *Unter Bäumen: Die Deutschen und der Wald* (Dresden: Sandstein, 2011).

Brocke, Bernhard vom, '"An die Europäer": Der Fall Nicolai und die Biologie des Krieges. Zur Entstehung und Wirkungsgeschichte eines unzeitgemäßen Buches', *HZ* 240 (1985), 363–75.

Brühl, Reinhard, *Militärgeschichte und Kriegspolitik: Zur Militärgeschichtsschreibung des preußisch–deutschen Generalstabes 1816–1945* (Berlin: Militärverlag der DDR, 1973).

Bryden, Eric, 'Heroes and Martyrs of the Republic: Reichsbanner *Geschichtspolitik* in Weimar Germany', *CEH* 43 (2010), 639–65.

Bucher, Peter, 'Die Errichtung des Reichsehrenmals nach dem Ersten Weltkrieg', *Jahrbuch für westdeutsche Landesgeschichte* 7 (1981), 359–86.

Buchner, Bernd, *Um nationale und republikanische Identität: Die deutsche Sozialdemokratie und der Kampf um die politischen Symbole in der Weimarer Republik* (Bonn: J. H. W. Dietz, 2001).

Busch, Rolf, 'Imperialismus und Arbeiterliteratur im Ersten Weltkrieg', *AfS* 14 (1974), 293–350.

Büttner, Ursula, *Weimar: Die überforderte Republik 1918–1933. Leistung und Versagen in Staat, Gesellschaft, Wirtschaft und Kultur* (Stuttgart: Klett–Cotta, 2008).

Canetti, Elias, *Masse und Macht* (Frankfurt am Main: Fischer, 1980).

Canning, Kathleen, Kerstin Barndt and Kristin McGuire (eds.), *Weimar Publics/Weimar Subjects: Rethinking the Political Culture of Germany in the 1920s* (New York: Berghahn, 2010).

Caplan, Greg, *Wicked Sons, German Heroes: Jewish Soldiers, Veterans and Memories of World War I in Germany* (Saarbrücken: VDM Verlag, 2008).

Cohen, Deborah, *The War Come Home: Disabled Veterans in Britain and Germany, 1914–1939* (Berkeley: University of California Press, 2001).

Confino, Alon, 'Collective Memory and Cultural History: Problems of Method', *American Historical Review* 102 (1997), 1386–1403.

Davy, Jennifer A., '"Manly" and "Feminine" Antimilitarism: Perceptions of Gender in the Antimilitarist Wing of the Weimar Peace Movement', in Jennifer A. Davy, Karen Hagemann and Ute Kätzel (eds.), *Frieden, Gewalt, Geschlecht: Friedens- und Konfliktforschung als Geschlechterforschung* (Essen: Klartext, 2005), pp. 144–65.

Deist, Wilhelm, 'The Military Collapse of the German Empire', *War in History* 3 (1996), 186–207.

Diehl, James M., 'Germany: Veterans' Politics under Three Flags', in Stephen R. Ward (ed.), *The War Generation: Veterans of the First World War* (Port Washington: Kennikat Press, 1975), pp. 135–86.

'The Organization of German Veterans, 1917–1919', *AfS* 11 (1971), 141–84.

Paramilitary Politics in Weimar Germany (Bloomington; London: Indiana University Press, 1977).

Diers, Michael (ed.), *Mo(nu)mente: Formen und Funktionen ephemerer Denkmäler* (Berlin: Akademie, 1993).

Dimitrova, Snezhana, '"Taming the Death": The Culture of Death (1915–1918) and Its Remembering and Commemorating through First World War Soldier Monuments in Bulgaria (1917–1944)', *Social History* 30 (2005), 175–94.

Donat, Helmut, 'Kapitänleutnant a.D. Heinz Kraschutzki (1891–1982): Ein Offizier im Kampf für ein "anderes" Deutschland', in Wette and Donat, *Pazifistische Offiziere*, pp. 339–62.

Donson, Andrew, *Youth in the Fatherless Land: War Pedagogy, Nationalism, and Authority, 1914–1918* (Cambridge, MA; London: Harvard University Press, 2010).

Dörner, Andreas, *Politischer Mythos und symbolische Politik. Der Hermannmythos: Zur Entstehung des Nationalbewußtseins der Deutschen* (Reinbek: Rowohlt, 1996).

Dülffer, Jost and Gerd Krumeich (eds.), *Der verlorene Frieden: Politik und Kriegskultur nach 1918* (Essen: Klartext, 2002).

Ebert, Jens, 'Der Roman *Im Westen nichts Neues* im Spiegel der deutschsprachigen kommunistischen Literaturkritik der 20er und 30er Jahre', in Schneider, *Erich Maria Remarque*, pp. 99–108.

Ehrke-Rothermund, Heidrun, '"Durch die Erkenntnis des Schreckens zu seiner Überwindung"? Werner Beumelburg: *Gruppe Bosemüller*', in Schneider and Wagener, *Von Richthofen*, pp. 299–318.

Eksteins, Modris, *The Limits of Reason: The German Democratic Press and the Collapse of Weimar Democracy* (Oxford University Press, 1975).

Rites of Spring: The Great War and the Birth of the Modern Age (Boston, MA: Houghton Mifflin, 1989).

'War, Memory and Politics: The Fate of the Film *All Quiet on the Western Front*', *CEH* 13 (1980), 60–82.

Elliott, Christopher James, 'The Kriegervereine in the Weimar Republic', *JCH* 10 (1975), 109–29.

Faatz, Martin, *Vom Staatsschutz zum Gestapo-Terror: Politische Polizei in Bayern in der Endphase der Weimarer Republik und der Anfangsphase der nationalsozialistischen Diktatur* (Würzburg: Echter, 1995).

Fagerberg, Elliot Pennell, 'The "Anciens combattants" and French Foreign Policy', Ph.D. dissertation (University of Geneva, 1966).

Forner, Sean A., 'War Commemoration and the Republic in Crisis: Weimar Germany and the Neue Wache', *CEH* 25 (2002), 513–49.

Fricke, Dieter (ed.), *Lexikon zur Parteiengeschichte: Die bürgerlichen und kleinbürgerlichen Parteien und Verbände in Deutschland (1789–1945)*, 4 vols. (Cologne: Pahl-Rugenstein, 1983–6).

Friedeburg, Robert von, 'Klassen-, Geschlechter- oder Nationalidentität? Handwerker und Tagelöhner in den Kriegervereinen der neupreußischen Provinz Hessen-Nassau 1890–1914', in Ute Frevert (ed.), *Militär und Gesellschaft im 19. und 20. Jahrhundert* (Stuttgart: Klett–Cotta, 1997), pp. 229–44.

Friedrich, Walter, 'Die Ideenwelt der mehrheitssozialistischen Bergarbeiter des Ruhrgebiets', Ph.D. dissertation (University of Bonn, 1923).

Fritzsche, Peter, 'The Case of Modern Memory', *Journal of Modern History* 73 (2001), 87–117.

'Did Weimar Fail?', *Journal of Modern History* 68 (1996), 629–56.

'The Economy of Experience in Weimar Germany', in Canning, Barndt and McGuire, *Weimar Publics*, pp. 360–83.

'Presidential Victory and Popular Festivity in Weimar Germany: Hindenburg's 1925 Election', *CEH* 23 (1990), 205–24.

The Turbulent World of Franz Göll: An Ordinary Berliner Writes the Twentieth Century (Cambridge, MA; London: Harvard University Press, 2011).

Fröschle, Ulrich, '"Radikal im Denken aber schlapp im Handeln?" Franz Schauwecker: *Aufbruch der Nation* (1929)', in Schneider and Wagener, *Von Richthofen*, pp. 261–98.

Fuge, Janina, '"Ohne Tod und Sterben kein Sieg": Die gefallenen Soldaten des Ersten Weltkrieges in der Hamburger Erinnerungskultur der Weimarer Republik', *Historical Social Research* 34 (2009), 356–73.

Fulda, Bernhard, *Press and Politics in the Weimar Republic* (Oxford University Press, 2009).

Gerstenberg, Günther, *Freiheit! Sozialdemokratischer Selbstschutz im München der zwanziger und frühen dreißiger Jahre*, 2 vols. (Andechs: Edition Ulenspiegel, 1997).

Gerwarth, Robert, 'The Past in Weimar History', *CEH* 15 (2006), 1–22.

Geyer, Martin H., 'Contested Narratives of the Weimar Republic: The Case of the "Kutisker–Barmat Scandal"', in Canning, Barndt and McGuire, *Weimar Publics*, pp. 215–35.

Verkehrte Welt. Revolution, Inflation und Moderne: München 1914–1924 (Göttingen: Vandenhoeck & Ruprecht, 1998).

Geyer, Michael, 'Eine Kriegsgeschichte, die vom Tod spricht', in Thomas Lindenberger and Alf Lüdtke (eds.), *Physische Gewalt: Studien zur Geschichte der Neuzeit* (Frankfurt am Main: Suhrkamp, 1995), pp. 136–61.

'Das Stigma der Gewalt und das Problem der nationalen Identität in Deutschland', in Christian Jansen, Lutz Niethammer and Bernd Weisbrod (eds.), *Von der Aufgabe der Freiheit: Politische Verantwortung und bürgerliche Gesellschaft im 19. und 20. Jahrhundert* (Berlin: Akademie, 1995), pp. 673–98.

'The Stigma of Violence: Nationalism and War in Twentieth-Century Germany', *German Studies Review* 15 (1992), 75–110.

'Ein Vorbote des Wohlfahrtsstaates: Die Kriegsopferversorgung in Frankreich, Deutschland und Großbritannien nach dem Ersten Weltkrieg', *GG* 9 (1983), 230–77.

Goebel, Stefan, *The Great War and Medieval Memory: War, Remembrance and Medievalism in Britain and Germany, 1914–1940* (Cambridge University Press, 2007).

Gollbach, Michael, *Die Wiederkehr des Weltkrieges in der Literatur: Zu den Frontromanen der späten Zwanziger Jahre* (Kronberg: Scriptor, 1978).

Goltz, Anna von der, *Hindenburg: Power, Myth, and the Rise of the Nazis* (Oxford University Press, 2009).

Gotschlich, Helga, *Zwischen Kampf und Kapitulation: Zur Geschichte des Reichsbanners Schwarz–Rot–Gold* (Berlin: Dietz Verlag, 1987).

Graf, Rüdiger, *Die Zukunft der Weimarer Republik: Krisen und Zukunftsaneignungen in Deutschland 1918–1933* (Munich: Oldenbourg, 2008).

Grammel, Wolfgang, 'Das Reichsbanner Schwarz–Rot–Gold in Freising', *Amperland* 30 (1994), 325–31.

Gräper, Friederike, 'Die Deutsche Friedensgesellschaft und ihr General: Generalmajor a.D. Paul Freiherr von Schoenaich (1866–1954)', in Wette and Donat, *Pazifistische Offiziere*, pp. 201–17.

Gregory, Adrian, *The Silence of Memory: Armistice Day, 1919–1946* (Oxford: Berg, 1994).

Groh, Dieter and Peter Brandt, *'Vaterlandslose Gesellen': Sozialdemokratie und Nation 1860–1990* (Munich: C. H. Beck, 1992).

Großmann, Anton, 'Milieubedingungen von Verfolgung und Widerstand am Beispiel ausgewählter Ortsvereine der SPD', in Martin Broszat and Hartmut Mehringer (eds.), *Bayern in der NS-Zeit*, 6 vols., Vol. V: *Die Parteien KPD, SPD, BVP in Verfolgung und Widerstand* (Munich; Vienna: Oldenbourg, 1983), pp. 433–540.

Grossmann, Kurt R., *Ossietzky: Ein deutscher Patriot* (Munich: Kindler, 1963).

Gruner, Wolfgang, *Ein Schicksal, das ich mit sehr vielen geteilt habe. Alfred Kantorowicz: Sein Leben und seine Zeit von 1899 bis 1935* (Kassel University Press, 2007).

Gündisch, Dieter, *Arbeiterbewegung und Bürgertum in Wetzlar 1918–1933* (Wetzlar: Geschichtsverein, 1992).

Halbwachs, Maurice, *On Collective Memory*, trans. and ed. Lewis A. Coser (Chicago; London: University of Chicago Press, 1992).

La Mémoire collective, ed. Gérard Namer (Paris: Albin Michel, 1997).
Hall, Alex, *Scandal, Sensation and Social Democracy: The SPD Press and Wilhelmine Germany 1890–1914* (Cambridge University Press, 1977).
Harsch, Donna, *German Social Democracy and the Rise of Nazism* (Chapel Hill: University of North California Press, 1993).
Harter, Hans, '"Das Bürgertum fehlt und überläßt dem Arbeiter den Schutz der Republik": Die Ortsgruppe Schiltach des Reichsbanners Schwarz–Rot–Gold', *Die Ortenau* 72 (1992), 271–302.
Hartung, Günter, 'Gegenschriften zu *Im Westen nichts Neues* und *Der Weg zurück*', in Schneider, *Erich Maria Remarque*, pp. 109–50.
Hausen, Karin, 'The German Nation's Obligations to the Heroes' Widows of World War I', in Margaret Higonnet, Jane Jenson, Sonya Michel and Margaret Collins Weitz (eds.), *Behind the Lines: Gender and the Two World Wars* (New Haven; London: Yale University Press, 1987), pp. 126–40.
Heffen, Annegret, *Der Reichskunstwart: Kunstpolitik in den Jahren 1920–1933. Zu den Bemühungen um eine offizielle Reichskunstpolitik in der Weimarer Republik* (Essen: Die Blaue Eule, 1986).
Heidenreich, Frank, *Arbeiterbildung und Politik: Kontroversen in der sozialdemokratischen Zeitschrift 'Kulturwille' 1924–1933* (Berlin: Argument, 1983).
Heinemann, Ulrich, 'Die Last der Vergangenheit: Zur politischen Bedeutung der Kriegsschuld- und Dolchstoßdiskussion', in Karl-Dietrich Bracher, Manfred Funke and Hans-Adolf Jacobsen (eds.), *Die Weimarer Republik 1918–1933: Politik, Wirtschaft, Gesellschaft* (Düsseldorf: Droste, 1987), pp. 371–86.
Die verdrängte Niederlage: Politische Öffentlichkeit und Kriegsschuldfrage in der Weimarer Republik (Göttingen: Vandenhoeck & Ruprecht, 1983).
Hettling, Manfred, *Totenkult statt Revolution: 1848 und seine Opfer* (Frankfurt am Main: S. Fischer, 1998).
Hilbig, Henrik, *Das Reichsehrenmal bei Bad Berka: Entstehung und Entwicklung eines Denkmalprojekts der Weimarer Republik* (Aachen: Shaker, 2006).
Horne, John, 'Kulturelle Demobilmachung 1919–1939: Ein sinnvoller Begriff?', in Wolfgang Hardtwig (ed.), *Politische Kulturgeschichte der Zwischenkriegszeit 1918–1939* (Göttingen: Vandenhoeck & Ruprecht, 2005), pp. 129–50.
'Der Schatten des Krieges: Französische Politik in den zwanziger Jahren', in Hans Mommsen (ed.), *Der Erste Weltkrieg und die europäische Nachkriegsordnung: Sozialer Wandel und Formveränderung der Politik* (Cologne: Böhlau, 2000), pp. 145–64.
Horne, John and Alan Kramer, *German Atrocities, 1914: A History of Denial* (New Haven; London: Yale University Press, 2001).
Houlihan, Patrick J., 'Was There an Austrian Stab-in-the-Back Myth? Interwar Military Interpretations of Defeat', in Günter Bischof, Fritz Plasser and Peter Berger (eds.), *Postwar: Legacies of World War I in Interwar Austria* (University of New Orleans Press, 2010), pp. 67–89.
Ingenthron, Maximilian, *"Falls nur die Sache siegt". Erich Kuttner (1887–1942): Publizist und Politiker* (Mannheim: Palatium, 2000).
Inglis, Ken, 'Entombing Unknown Soldiers: From London and Paris to Baghdad', *History & Memory* 5 (1993), 7–31.

Jäger, Wolfgang, *Bergarbeitermilieus und Parteien im Ruhrgebiet: Zum Wahlverhalten des katholischen Bergarbeitermilieus bis 1933* (Munich: C. H. Beck, 1996).

Janz, Oliver, 'Trauer und Gefallenenkult nach 1918: Italien und Deutschland im Vergleich', in Ute Daniel, Inge Marszolek, Wolfram Pyta and Thomas Welskopp (eds.), *Politische Kultur und Medienwirklichkeiten in den 1920er Jahren* (Munich: Oldenbourg, 2010), pp. 257–78.

Jax, Stefan, *Der Hofgeismarkreis der Jungsozialisten und seine Nachwirkungen in der Weimarer Zeit* (Oer-Erkenschwick: Archiv der Arbeiterjugendbewegung, 1999).

Jeismann, Michael and Rolf Westheider, 'Wofür stirbt der Bürger? Nationaler Totenkult und Staatsbürgertum in Deutschland und Frankreich seit der Französischen Revolution', in Koselleck and Jeismann, *Der politische Totenkult*, pp. 23–50.

Jindra, Zdeněk, 'Zur Entwicklung und Stellung der Kanonenausfuhr der Firma Friedrich Krupp/Essen 1854–1912', in Wilfried Feldenkirchen (ed.), *Wirtschaft, Gesellschaft, Unternehmen: Festschrift für Hans Pohl zum 60. Geburtstag* (Stuttgart: Steiner, 1995), pp. 956–76.

Jürgens-Kirchhoff, Annegret, 'Kunst gegen den Krieg im Antikriegsjahr 1924', in Dülffer and Krumeich, *Der verlorene Frieden*, pp. 287–310.

Kaes, Anton, *Shell Shock Cinema: Weimar Culture and the Wounds of War* (Princeton University Press, 2009).

Kaiser, Alexandra, *Von Helden und Opfern: Eine Geschichte des Volkstrauertags* (Frankfurt am Main: Campus, 2010).

Kalthoff, Horst, 'Felden, Emil', in *Biographisch-Bibliographisches Kirchenlexikon*, ed. Friedrich Wilhelm Bautz, 33 vols., Vol. XXII (Nordhausen: Bautz, 2003), pp. 316–19.

Kelly, Andrew, '*All Quiet on the Western Front*: "Brutal Cutting, Stupid Censors and Bigoted Politicos" (1930–84)', *Historical Journal of Film, Radio and Television* 9 (1989), 135–50.

Kienitz, Sabine, *Beschädigte Helden: Kriegsinvalidität und Körperbilder 1914–1923* (Paderborn: Schöningh, 2008).

Kiesel, Helmuth, *Ernst Jünger: Eine Biographie* (Munich: Pantheon, 2009).

Kittsteiner, Heinz-Dieter, 'Waldgänger ohne Wald: Bemerkungen zur politischen Metaphorik des deutschen Waldes', in Bernd Weyergraf (ed.), *Waldungen: Die Deutschen und ihr Wald. Ausstellungskatalog der Akademie der Künste* (Berlin: Nicolai, 1987), pp. 113–20.

Klenke, Dietmar and Franz Walter, 'Der Deutsche Arbeiter-Sängerbund', in Dietmar Klenke, Peter Lilje and Franz Walter, *Arbeitersänger und Volksbühnen in der Weimarer Republik* (Bonn: J. H. W. Dietz, 1992), pp. 15–248.

Klotzbach, Kurt, *Gegen den Nationalsozialismus: Widerstand und Verfolgung in Dortmund 1930–1945* (Hanover: Verlag für Literatur und Zeitgeschehen, 1969).

Klotzbücher, Alois, *Der politische Weg des Stahlhelm, Bund der Frontsoldaten, in der Weimarer Republik*, Ph.D. dissertation (University of Erlangen-Nuremberg, 1964).

Kolb, Eberhard, 'Rettung der Republik: Die Politik der SPD in den Jahren 1930 bis 1933', in Heinrich August Winkler (ed.), *Weimar im Widerstreit: Deutungen der ersten deutschen Republik im geteilten Deutschland* (Munich: Oldenbourg, 2002), pp. 85–104.

Koselleck, Reinhart, 'Einleitung', in Koselleck and Jeismann, *Der politische Totenkult*, pp. 9–20.

'"Space of Experience" and "Horizon of Expectation": Two Historical Categories', in *Futures Past: On the Semantics of Historical Time* (New York: Columbia University Press, 2004), pp. 255–75.

'War Memorials: Identity Formations of the Survivors', in *The Practice of Conceptual History: Timing History, Spacing Concepts* (Stanford: Stanford University Press, 2002), pp. 285–326.

Zur politischen Ikonologie des gewaltsamen Todes: Ein deutsch–französischer Vergleich (Basel: Schwabe, 1998).

Koselleck, Reinhart and Michael Jeismann (eds.), *Der politische Totenkult: Kriegerdenkmäler in der Moderne* (Munich: Fink, 1994).

Kramer, Alan, 'The First World War and German Memory', in Heather Jones, Jennifer O'Brien and Christoph Schmidt-Supprian (eds.), *Untold War: New Perspectives in First World War Studies* (Leiden; Boston, MA: Brill, 2008), pp. 385–415.

Krassnitzer, Patrick, 'Die Geburt des Nationalsozialismus im Schützengraben: Formen der Brutalisierung in den Autobiographien von nationalsozialistischen Frontsoldaten', in Dülffer and Krumeich, *Der verlorene Frieden*, pp. 119–48.

Krumeich, Gerd, 'Die Dolchstoß-Legende', in Hagen Schulze and Etienne François (eds.), *Deutsche Erinnerungsorte*, 3 vols., Vol. I (Munich: C. H. Beck, 2001), pp. 585–99.

Krumeich, Gerd (ed.), *Nationalsozialismus und Erster Weltkrieg* (Essen: Klartext, 2010).

Kruse, Kai and Wolfgang Kruse, 'Kriegerdenkmäler in Bielefeld: Ein lokalhistorischer Beitrag zur Entwicklungsanalyse des deutschen Gefallenenkultes im 19. und 20. Jahrhundert', in Koselleck and Jeismann, *Der politische Totenkult*, pp. 91–128.

Kruse, Wolfgang, *Krieg und nationale Integration: Eine Neuinterpretation des sozialdemokratischen Burgfriedensschlusses 1914/15* (Essen: Klartext, 1993).

Kühne, Thomas, *Belonging and Genocide: Hitler's Community, 1918–1945* (New Haven; London: Yale University Press, 2010).

Laclau, Ernesto, 'Why Do Empty Signifiers Matter to Politics?', in Jeffrey Weeks (ed.), *The Lesser Evil and the Greater Good* (London: Rivers Oram Press, 1994), pp. 167–78.

Langewiesche, Dieter, *Republik und Republikaner: Von der historischen Entwertung eines Begriffs* (Essen: Klartext, 1993).

Lehmann, Albrecht, 'Der deutsche Wald', in Hagen Schulze and Etienne François (eds.), *Deutsche Erinnerungsorte*, 3 vols., Vol. III (Munich: C. H. Beck, 2001), pp. 187–200.

'Militär und Militanz zwischen den Weltkriegen', in Dieter Langewiesche and Heinz-Elmar Tenorth (eds.), *Handbuch der deutschen Bildungsgeschichte*,

6 vols., Vol. V: *Die Weimarer Republik und die nationalsozialistische Diktatur* (Munich: C. H. Beck, 1989), pp. 407–29.

Lehnert, Detlef and Klaus Megerle (eds.), *Politische Teilkulturen zwischen Integration und Polarisierung: Zur politischen Kultur in der Weimarer Republik* (Opladen: Westdeutscher Verlag, 1990).

Lidtke, Vernon L., *The Alternative Culture: Socialist Labor in Imperial Germany* (Oxford; New York: Oxford University Press, 1985).

Linder, Ann P., *Princes of the Trenches: Narrating the German Experience of the First World War* (Columbia: Camden House, 1996).

Linsmayer, Ludwig, *Politische Kultur im Saargebiet 1920–1932: Symbolische Politik, verhinderte Demokratisierung, nationalisiertes Kulturleben in einer abgetrennten Region* (St Ingbert: Röhrig, 1992).

Lipp, Wilfried, *Natur–Geschichte–Denkmal: Zur Entstehung des Denkmalbewußtseins der bürgerlichen Gesellschaft* (Frankfurt am Main; New York: Campus, 1987).

Lösche, Peter and Franz Walter, 'Zur Organisationskultur der sozialdemokratischen Arbeiterbewegung in der Weimarer Republik: Niedergang der Klassenkultur oder solidargemeinschaftlicher Höherpunkt?', *GG* 15 (1989), 511–36.

Lowry, Thomas, 'Symbolische Gesten: Paul Freiherr von Schoenaich und die französischen Friedensgeneräle Martial-Justin Verraux (1855–1939) und Alexandre Percin (1846–1928)', in Wette and Donat, *Pazifistische Offiziere*, pp. 218–29.

Lucas, Erhard, *Vom Scheitern der deutschen Arbeiterbewegung* (Frankfurt am Main: Roter Stern, 1983).

Lütgemeier-Davin, Reinhold, 'Basismobilisierung gegen den Krieg: Die Nie-wieder-Krieg-Bewegung in der Weimarer Republik', in Karl Holl and Wolfram Wette (eds.), *Pazifismus in der Weimarer Republik* (Paderborn: Schöningh, 1981), pp. 47–76.

Macht, Rudolf, *Niederlage: Geschichte der Hofer Arbeiterbewegung*, Vol. III.2: *1924–1945* (Hof: Selbstverlag, 1996).

Marnau, Björn, '"Wir, die wir am Feuer von Chevreuse die Hand erhoben haben ...": Itzehoer Pazifisten in der Weimarer Republik', *Demokratische Geschichte* 10 (1996), 141–66.

Mergel, Thomas, 'High Expectations – Deep Disappointment: Structures of the Public Perception of Politics in the Weimar Republic', in Canning, Barndt and McGuire, *Weimar Publics*, pp. 192–210.

Parlamentarische Kultur in der Weimarer Republik: Politische Kommunikation, symbolische Politik und Öffentlichkeit im Reichstag (Düsseldorf: Droste, 2002).

'Überlegungen zu einer Kulturgeschichte der Politik', *GG* 28 (2002), 574–606.

Meteling, Wencke, 'Der deutsche Zusammenbruch 1918 in den Selbstzeugnissen adeliger preußischer Offiziere', in Eckart Conze and Monika Wienfort (eds.), *Adel und Moderne: Deutschland im europäischen Vergleich im 19. und 20. Jahrhundert* (Cologne: Böhlau, 2004), pp. 289–321.

Ehre, Einheit und Ordnung: Preußische und französische Städte und Regimenter im Krieg, 1870/71 und 1914/19 (Baden-Baden: Nomos, 2010).

Mews, Karl, 'Dr. Theodor Reismann-Grone', *Beiträge zur Geschichte von Stadt und Stift Essen* 79 (1963), 5–32.

Mick, Christof, 'Der Kult um den "Unbekannten Soldaten" im Polen der Zwischenkriegszeit', in Martin Schulze-Wessel (ed.), *Nationalisierung der Nation und Sakralisierung der Religion im östlichen Europa* (Stuttgart: Steiner, 2006), pp. 181–200.

Millington, Chris, *From Victory to Vichy: Veterans in Inter-War France* (Manchester University Press, 2012).

Mintert, David Magnus, *'Sturmtrupp der deutschen Republik': Das Reichsbanner Schwarz–Rot–Gold in Wuppertal* (Wuppertal: Edition Wahler, 2002).

Mommsen, Hans, *The Rise and Fall of Weimar Democracy* (Chapel Hill; London: University of North Carolina Press, 1996).

'Social Democracy on the Defensive: The Immobility of the SPD and the Rise of National Socialism', in *From Weimar to Auschwitz: Essays in German History* (Cambridge: Polity, 1991), pp. 39–61.

Mommsen, Wolfgang A. (ed.), *Die Nachlässe in den deutschen Archiven*, 2 vols., Vol. I (Boppard: Boldt, 1971).

Montgomery, Garth, '"Realistic" War Films in Weimar Germany: Entertainment as Education', *Historical Journal of Film, Radio and Television* 9 (1989), 115–33.

Morat, Daniel, 'Kalte Männlichkeit? Weimarer Verhaltenslehren im Spannungsfeld von Emotionen- und Geschlechtergeschichte', in Manuel Borutta and Nina Verheyen (eds.), *Die Präsenz der Gefühle: Männlichkeit und Emotion in der Moderne* (Bielefeld: Transkript, 2010), pp. 153–77.

Mosse, George L., *Fallen Soldiers: Reshaping the Memory of the World Wars* (New York; Oxford: Oxford University Press, 1990).

The Nationalization of the Masses: Political Symbolism and Mass Movements in Germany from the Napoleonic Wars through the Third Reich (Ithaca, NY; London: Cornell University Press, 1991).

'La sinistra Europea e l'esperienza della guerra (Germania e Francia)', in *Rivoluzione e reazione in Europa, 1917–1924: Convegno storico internazionale, Perugia, 1978* (Rome: Avanti, 1978), pp. 151–67.

Müller, Gerhard, *Für Vaterland und Republik: Monographie des Nürnberger Schriftstellers Karl Bröger* (Pfaffenweiler: Centaurus, 1985).

Müller, Hans Harald, *Der Krieg und die Schriftsteller: Der Kriegsroman in der Weimarer Republik* (Stuttgart: Metzler, 1986).

Niedhart, Gottfried and Dieter Riesenberger (eds.), *Lernen aus dem Krieg? Deutsche Nachkriegszeiten 1918 und 1945* (Munich: C. H. Beck, 1992).

Nipperdey, Thomas, 'Nationalidee und Nationaldenkmal in Deutschland im 19. Jahrhundert', *HZ* 206 (1968), 529–85.

Nora, Pierre, 'General Introduction: Between Memory and History', in Pierre Nora (ed.), *Realms of Memory: Rethinking the French Past*, 3 vols., Vol. I (New York: Columbia University Press, 1996), pp. 1–20.

Offenstadt, Nicolas, *Les Fusillés de la Grande Guerre et la mémoire collective (1914–1999)* (Paris: Editions Odile Jacob, 1999).

Ossietzky, Carl von, 'Nie wieder Krieg: Der Rundlauf einer Parole', in *Sämtliche Schriften*, 8 vols., Vol. II: *1922–1924* (Reinbek: Rowohlt, 1994), pp. 267–70.

'Schutz der Republik: Die große Mode', in *Sämtliche Schriften*, 8 vols., Vol. II: *1922–1924* (Reinbek: Rowohlt, 1994), pp. 364–6.

Petersen, Klaus, *Zensur in der Weimarer Republik* (Stuttgart: J. B. Metzler, 1995).

Peukert, Detlev J. K., *Jugend zwischen Krieg und Krise: Lebenswelten von Arbeiterjungen in der Weimarer Republik* (Cologne: Bund, 1987).

The Weimar Republic: The Crisis of Classical Modernity (New York: Hill & Wang, 1993).

Pöhlmann, Markus, '"Daß sich ein Sargdeckel über mir schlösse": Typen und Funktionen von Weltkriegserinnerungen militärischer Entscheidungsträger', in Dülffer and Krumeich, *Der verlorene Frieden*, pp. 149–70.

Kriegsgeschichte und Geschichtspolitik: Der Erste Weltkrieg. Die amtliche deutsche Militärgeschichtsschreibung 1914–1956 (Paderborn: Schöningh, 2002).

Pöppinghege, Rainer, '"Kriegsteilnehmer zweiter Klasse?": Die Reichsvereinigung ehemaliger Kriegsgefangener 1919–1933', *MGZ* 64 (2005), 391–423.

Prangel, Matthias, 'Das Geschäft mit der Wahrheit: Zu einer zentralen Kategorie der Rezeption von Kriegsromanen in der Weimarer Republik', in Jos Hoogeveen and Hans Würzner (eds.), *Ideologie und Literaturwissenschaft* (Amsterdam: Rodopi, 1986), pp. 47–78.

Prost, Antoine, *Les Anciens Combattants et la société francaise, 1914–1939*, 3 vols. (Paris: Presse de la Fondation Nationale des Sciences Politiques, 1977).

'The Impact of War on French and German Political Cultures', *Historical Journal* 37 (1994), 209–17.

In the Wake of War: 'Les Anciens Combattants' and French Society 1914–1939 (Providence, RI; Oxford: Berg, 1992).

Prost, Antoine and Jay Winter, *René Cassin et les droits de l'Homme: Le projet d'une génération* (Paris: Fayard, 2011).

Rauh-Kühne, Cornelia, *Katholisches Milieu und Kleinstadtgesellschaft: Ettlingen 1918–1939* (Sigmaringen: Thorbecke, 1991).

Reichardt, Sven, 'Die SA im "Nachkriegs-Krieg"', in Gerd Krumeich (ed.), *Nationalsozialismus und Erster Weltkrieg* (Essen: Klartext, 2010), pp. 243–59.

'Totalitäre Gewaltpolitik? Überlegungen zum Verhältnis von nationalsozialistischer und kommunistischer Gewalt in der Weimarer Republik', in Wolfgang Hardtwig (ed.), *Ordnungen in der Krise: Zur politischen Kulturgeschichte Deutschlands 1900–1933* (Munich: Oldenbourg, 2007), pp. 377–402.

Reuveni, Gideon, *Reading Germany: Literature and Consumer Culture in Germany before 1933* (New York: Berghahn, 2006).

Richards, Donald Day, *The German Bestseller in the 20th Century: A Complete Bibliography and Analysis 1915–1940* (Berne: Herbert Lang, 1968).

Riesenberger, Dieter, '"Soldat der Republik": Polizeioberst Hermann Schützinger (1888–*ca.* 1960)', in Wette and Donat, *Pazifistische Offiziere*, pp. 287–301.

Robb, George, *Culture and the First World War* (Basingstoke: Palgrave, 2002).

Robert, Jean-Louis, 'The Image of the Profiteer', in Jay Winter and Jean-Louis Robert (eds.), *Capital Cities at War: Paris, London, Berlin 1914–1919* (Cambridge University Press, 1997), pp. 104–32.

Rohe, Karl, *Das Reichsbanner Schwarz Rot Gold: Ein Beitrag zur Geschichte und Struktur der politischen Kampfverbände zur Zeit der Weimarer Republik* (Düsseldorf: Droste, 1966).

Wahlen und Wählertraditionen in Deutschland: Kulturelle Grundlagen deutscher Parteien und Parteiensysteme im 19. und 20. Jahrhundert (Frankfurt am Main: Suhrkamp, 1992).

Rosenhaft, Eve, 'Working-Class Life and Working-Class Politics: Communists, Nazis and the State in the Battle for the Streets. Berlin, 1928–1932', in Richard Bessel and E. J. Feuchtwanger (eds.), *Social Change and Political Development in Weimar Germany* (London: Croom Helm, 1981), pp. 207–40.

Rossol, Nadine, 'Flaggenkrieg am Badestrand: Lokale Möglichkeiten repräsentativer Mitgestaltung in der Weimarer Republik', *Zeitschrift für Geschichtswissenschaft* 56 (2008), 617–37.

Performing the Nation in Interwar Germany: Sport, Spectacle and Political Symbolism 1926–1936 (Basingstoke: Palgrave, 2010).

Rother, Rainer, 'Der unbekannte Soldat', in Gerhard P. Groß (ed.), *Die vergessene Front: Der Osten 1914/15. Ereignis, Wirkung, Nachwirkung* (Paderborn: Schöningh, 2006), pp. 353–71.

Rumold, Rainer, 'Rereading Heinrich Mann's *Der Untertan*: The Seeds of Fascism, or Satire as Anticipation', in Volker Dürr, Kathy Harms and Peter Hayes (eds.), *Imperial Germany* (Madison: University of Wisconsin Press, 1985), pp. 168–81.

Rumschöttel, Hermann, 'Kriegsgeschichtsschreibung als militärische Geschichtspolitik? Zur publizistischen Arbeit des Bayerischen Kriegsarchivs nach 1918', *Zeitschrift für Bayerische Landesgeschichte* 61 (1998), 233–54.

Rusinek, Bernd-A., 'Der Kult der Jugend und des Krieges: Militärischer Stil als Phänomen der Jugendkultur in der Weimarer Zeit', in Dülffer and Krumeich, *Der verlorene Frieden*, pp. 171–97.

Saehrendt, Christian, *Der Stellungskrieg der Denkmäler: Kriegerdenkmäler im Berlin der Zwischenkriegszeit (1919–1939)* (Bonn: J. H. W. Dietz, 2004).

Sammet, Rainer, *'Dolchstoss': Deutschland und die Auseinandersetzung mit der Niederlage im Ersten Weltkrieg (1918–1933)* (Berlin: Trafo, 2003).

Sarasin, Philipp, *Geschichtswissenschaft und Diskursanalyse* (Frankfurt am Main: Suhrkamp, 2003).

Schaerer, Simon, 'Franz Carl Endres (1878–1954): Kaiserlich-osmanischer Major, Pazifist, Journalist, Schriftsteller', in Wette and Donat, *Pazifistische Offiziere*, pp. 231–45.

Scheer, Friedrich-Karl, *Die Deutsche Friedensgesellschaft (1892–1933): Organisation, Ideologie, politische Ziele. Ein Beitrag zur Geschichte des Pazifismus in Deutschland* (Frankfurt am Main: Haag und Herchen, 1981).

Schellack, Fritz, *Nationalfeiertage in Deutschland von 1871 bis 1945* (Frankfurt am Main: Lang, 1990).

Scherb, Ute, 'Kriegerdenkmäler in Freiburg: Von der Gründerzeit bis nach dem Zweiten Weltkrieg', in Christian Geinitz, Volker Ilgen and Holger Skor, *Kriegsgedenken in Freiburg: Trauer–Kult–Verdrängung* (Freiburg: Haug, 1995), pp. 12–60.

Schieder, Theodor, *Das Deutsche Kaiserreich von 1871 als Nationalstaat*, 2nd edn (Göttingen: Vandenhoeck & Ruprecht, 1992).

Schivelbusch, Wolfgang, *The Culture of Defeat: On National Trauma, Mourning, and Recovery* (London: Granta, 2004).

Schleier, Hans, *Die bürgerliche deutsche Geschichtsschreibung der Weimarer Republik* (Berlin: Akademie Verlag, 1975).

Schmidt, Jürgen and Bernd Ulrich, 'Pragmatischer Pazifist und Demokrat: Hauptmann a.D. Willy Meyer (1885–1945)', in Wette and Donat, *Pazifistische Offiziere*, pp. 303–17.

Schmiechen-Ackermann, Detlef, *Nationalsozialismus und Arbeitermilieus: Der nationalsozialistische Angriff auf die proletarischen Wohnquartiere und die Reaktion in den sozialistischen Vereinen* (Bonn: J. H. W. Dietz, 1998).

Schmölders, Ralf, 'Anna Siemsen (1882–1951). Zwischen den Stühlen: Eine sozialdemokratische Pädagogin', in Peter Lösche, Michael Scholing and Franz Walter (eds.), *Vor dem Vergessen bewahren: Lebenswege Weimarer Sozialdemokraten* (Berlin: Colloquium, 1988), pp. 332–61.

Schneider, Gerhard, *'Nicht umsonst gefallen'? Kriegerdenkmäler und Kriegstotenkult in Hannover* (Hanover: Hahn, 1991).

Schneider, Thomas F., *Erich Maria Remarques Roman* Im Westen nichts Neues: *Test, Edition, Entstehung, Distribution und Rezeption* (Tübingen: Max Niemeyer, 2004).

Schneider, Thomas F., '"Es ist ein Buch ohne Tendenz": *Im Westen nichts Neues* – Autor- und Textsysteme im Rahmen eines Konstitutions- und Wirkungsmodells für Literatur', *Krieg und Literatur/War and Literature* 1 (1989), 23–40.

'Die Revolution in der Provinz. Erich Maria Remarque: *Der Weg zurück* (1930/31)', in Ulrich Kittstein and Regine Zeller (eds.), *'Friede, Freiheit, Brot!' Romane zur deutschen Novemberrevolution* (New York; Amsterdam: Rodopi, 2009), pp. 255–67.

'Das virtuelle Denkmal des Unbekannten Soldaten: Erich Maria Remarques *Im Westen nichts Neues* und die Popularisierung des Ersten Weltkriegs', in Barbara Korte, Sylvia Paletschek and Wolfgang Hochbruck (eds.), *Der Erste Weltkrieg in der populären Erinnerungskultur* (Essen: Klartext, 2008), pp. 89–98.

Schneider, Thomas [F.] (ed.), *Erich Maria Remarque: Leben, Werk und weltweite Wirkung* (Osnabrück: Rasch, 1998).

Schneider, Thomas F. and Hans Wagener, 'Einleitung', in *Von Richthofen*, pp. 11–16.

Schneider, Thomas F. and Hans Wagener (eds.), *Von Richthofen bis Remarque: Deutschsprachige Prosa zum I. Weltkrieg* (Amsterdam; New York: Rodopi, 2003).

Schott, Dieter, *Die Konstanzer Gesellschaft 1918–1924: Der Kampf um Hegemonie zwischen Novemberrevolution und Inflation* (Constance: Stadler, 1989).

Schröder, Hans-Joachim, 'Fritz von Unruh (1885–1970): Kavallerieoffizier, Dichter und Pazifist', in Wette and Donat, *Pazifistische Offiziere*, pp. 319–37.

Schüddekopf, Otto Ernst, *Linke Leute von rechts: Die nationalrevolutionären Minderheiten und der Kommunismus in der Weimarer Republik* (Stuttgart: W. Kohlhammer, 1960).

Schulze, Hagen, *Otto Braun oder Preußens demokratische Sendung* (Frankfurt am Main: Propyläen, 1977).

Schumann, Dirk, *Political Violence in the Weimar Republic 1918–1933: Battles for the Streets and Fears of Civil War* (New York: Berghahn, 2009).

Schuster, Kurt G. P., *Der Rote Frontkämpferbund 1924–1929* (Düsseldorf: Droste, 1975).

Schwede, Olaf, *Karl Mayr: Frontsoldat, Förderer Hitlers, Kämpfer gegen den Nationalsozialismus*, M.A. dissertation (University of Hamburg, 2006).

Sherman, Daniel J., 'Bodies and Names: The Emergence of Commemoration in Interwar France', *American Historical Review* 103 (1998), 443–66.

Smith, Leonard V., *The Embattled Self: French Soldiers' Testimony of the Great War* (Ithaca, NY: Cornell University Press, 2007).

Sontheimer, Kurt, *Antidemokratisches Denken in der Weimarer Republik* (Munich: Deutscher Taschenbuch-Verlag, 1978 [1962]).

Speitkamp, Winfried, '"Erziehung zur Nation": Reichskunstwart, Kulturpolitik und Identitätsstiftung im Staat von Weimar', in Helmut Berding (ed.), *Nationales Bewußtsein und kollektive Identität*, Studien zur Entwicklung des kollektiven Bewußtseins in der Neuzeit 2 (Frankfurt am Main: Suhrkamp, 1994), pp. 541–80.

Sprenger, Matthias, *Landsknechte auf dem Weg ins Dritte Reich? Zu Genese und Wandel des Freikorpsmythos* (Paderborn: Schöningh, 2008).

Stargardt, Nicholas, *The German Idea of Militarism: Radical and Socialist Critics, 1866–1914* (Cambridge University Press, 1994).

Steinkamp, Peter, 'Kapitän zur See a.D. Lothar Persius (1864–1944): Ein Seeoffizier als Kritiker der deutschen Flottenpolitik', in Wette and Donat, *Pazifistische Offiziere*, pp. 99–109.

Stiasny, Philipp, *Das Kino und der Krieg: Deutschland 1914–1929* (Munich: edition text + kritik, 2009).

Stokes, Lawrence D., 'Die Anfänge des Eutiner Reichsbanners (1924–1929/30)', *Demokratische Geschichte* 3 (1988), 335–43.

Streubel, Christiane, *Radikale Nationalistinnen: Agitation und Programmatik rechter Frauen in der Weimarer Republik* (Frankfurt am Main; New York: Campus, 2006).

Tallgren, Vappu, *Hitler und die Helden: Heroismus und Weltanschauung* (Helsinki: Suomaleinen Tiedeakatemia, 1981).

Teichler, Hans Joachim and Gerhard Hauk (eds.), *Illustrierte Geschichte des Arbeitersports* (Bonn: J. H. W. Dietz, 1987).

Tenfelde, Klaus, 'Historische Milieus: Erblichkeit und Konkurrenz', in Manfred Hettling and Paul Nolte (eds.), *Nation und Gesellschaft in Deutschland: Historische Essays* (Munich: C. H. Beck, 1996), pp. 247–68.

Ther, Vanessa, '"Humans are cheap and the bread is dear": Republican Portrayals of the War Experience in Weimar Germany', in Heather Jones, Jennifer O'Brien and Christoph Schmidt-Supprian (eds.), *Untold War: New Perspectives in First World War Studies* (Leiden; Boston, MA: Brill, 2008), pp. 357–84.

Thier, Erich, *Gestaltwandel des Arbeiters im Wandel seiner Lektüre: Ein Beitrag zu Volkskunde und Leserführung* (Leipzig: Harassowitz, 1939).

Tilmans, Karin, Frank van Vree and Jay Winter (eds.), *Performing the Past: Memory, History and Identity in Modern Europe* (Manchester University Press, 2010).

Toury, Jacob, 'Die Judenfrage in der Entstehungsphase des Reichsbanners Schwarz–Rot–Gold', in Ludger Heid and Arnold Paucker (eds.), *Juden und deutsche Arbeiterbewegung bis 1933* (Tübingen: Mohr, 1992), pp. 215–35.

Tracey, Donald R., 'Der Aufstieg der NSDAP bis 1930', in Detlev Heiden and Gunther Mai (eds.), *Thüringen auf dem Weg ins 'Dritte Reich'* (Erfurt: Landeszentrale für Politische Bildung, 1996), pp. 65–93.

Trommler, Frank, *Sozialistische Literatur in Deutschland* (Stuttgart: Kröner, 1976).

Überegger, Oswald, *Erinnerungskriege: Der Erste Weltkrieg, Österreich und die Tiroler Kriegserinnerung in der Zwischenkriegszeit (1918–1939)* (Innsbruck: Wagner, 2011).

Ulrich, Axel, *Freiheit! Das Reichsbanner Schwarz–Rot–Gold und der Kampf von Sozialdemokraten in Hessen gegen den Nationalsozialismus 1924–1938* (Frankfurt am Main: SPD–Bezirk Hessen Süd, 1988).

Ulrich, Bernd, *Die Augenzeugen: Deutsche Feldpostbriefe in Kriegs- und Nachkriegszeit 1914–1933* (Essen: Klartext, 1997).

'Die Perspektive "von unten" und ihre Instrumentalisierung am Beispiel des Ersten Weltkrieges', *Krieg und Literatur/War and Literature* 1 (1989), 47–64.

'Die umkämpfte Erinnerung: Überlegungen zur Wahrnehmung des Ersten Weltkrieges in der Weimarer Republik', in Jörg Duppler and Gerhard P. Groß (eds.), *Kriegsende 1918: Ereignis–Wirkung–Nachwirkung* (Munich: Oldenbourg, 1999), pp. 367–75.

Ulrich, Bernd and Benjamin Zieman (eds.), *German Soldiers in the Great War: Letters and Eyewitness Accounts* (Barnsley: Pen & Sword, 2010).

Verhey, Jeffrey, *The Spirit of 1914: Militarism, Myth and Mobilization in Germany* (Cambridge University Press, 2000).

Voelker, Judith, '"Unerträglich, unerfüllbar und deshalb unannehmbar": Kollektiver Protest gegen Versailles im Rheinland in den Monaten Mai und Juni 1919', in Dülffer and Krumeich, *Der verlorene Frieden*, pp. 229–41.

Vogel, Jakob, 'Der Undank der Nation: Die Veteranen der Einigungskriege und die Debatte um ihren "Ehrensold" im Kaiserreich', *MGZ* 60 (2001), 343–66.

Vogt, Stefan, *Nationaler Sozialismus und Soziale Demokratie: Die sozialdemokratische Junge Rechte, 1918–1945* (Bonn: J. H. W. Dietz, 2006).

Voigt, Carsten, *Kampfbünde der Arbeiterbewegung: Das Reichsbanner Schwarz-Rot-Gold und der Rote Frontkämpferbund in Sachsen 1924–1933* (Cologne: Böhlau, 2009).

Vollmer, Jörg, 'Imaginäre Schlachtfelder: Kriegsliteratur in der Weimarer Republik. Eine literatursoziologische Untersuchung', Ph.D. dissertation (Freie Universität Berlin, 2003).

Walter, Franz, *'Republik das ist nicht viel': Partei und Jugend in der Krise des Weimarer Sozialismus* (Bielefeld: Transkript, 2011).

Watson, Alexander, *Enduring the Great War: Combat, Morale and Collapse in the German and British Armies, 1914–1918* (Cambridge University Press, 2008).

Weber, Jürgen, 'Das Reichsbanner im Norden: Ein Bollwerk der Demokratie?', *Demokratische Geschichte* 20 (2009), 127–46.

Weber, Thomas, *Hitler's First War: Adolf Hitler, the Men of the List Regiment, and the First World War* (Oxford University Press, 2010).

Weiß, Christian, '"Soldaten des Friedens": Die pazifistischen Veteranen und Kriegsopfer des "Reichsbundes" und ihre Kontakte zu den französischen *anciens combattants* 1919–1933', in Wolfgang Hardtwig (ed.), *Politische Kulturgeschichte der Zwischenkriegszeit 1918–1939* (Göttingen: Vandenhoeck & Ruprecht, 2005), pp. 183–204.

Weitz, Eric D., *Creating German Communism, 1890–1990: From Popular Protests to Socialist State* (Princeton University Press, 1997).

'Weimar Germany and Its Histories', *CEH* 43 (2010), 581–91.

Weimar Germany: Promise and Tragedy (Princeton University Press, 2007).

Welzbacher, Christian, *Edwin Redslob: Biografie eines unverbesserlichen Idealisten* (Berlin: Matthes & Seitz, 2009).

Werth, German, *Verdun: Die Schlacht und der Mythos* (Bergisch Gladbach: Bastei Lübbe, 1982).

Wette, Wolfram, 'Befreiung vom Schwertglauben: Pazifistische Offiziere in Deutschland 1871–1933', in Wette and Donat, *Pazifistische Offiziere*, pp. 9–39.

'Ideologien, Propaganda und Innenpolitik als Voraussetzungen der Kriegspolitik des Dritten Reiches', in Wilhelm Deist, Manfred Messerschmidt and Hans-Erich Volkmann, *Ursachen und Voraussetzungen des Zweiten Weltkrieges* (Frankfurt am Main: Fischer, 1989 [1979]), pp. 23–208.

Wette, Wolfram and Helmut Donat (eds.), *Pazifistische Offiziere in Deutschland 1871–1933* (Bremen: Donat, 1999).

Whalen, Robert W., *Bitter Wounds: German Victims of the Great War, 1914–1939* (Ithaca, NY; London: Cornell University Press, 1984).

Wiedner, Hartmut, 'Soldatenmißhandlungen im Wilhelminischen Kaiserreich (1890–1914)', *AfS* 22 (1982), 159–99.

Winkler, Heinrich August, *Der Schein der Normalität: Arbeiter und Arbeiterbewegung in der Weimarer Republik 1924 bis 1930*, 2nd edn (Berlin; Bonn: J. H. W. Dietz, 1988).

Von der Revolution zur Stabilisierung: Arbeiter und Arbeiterbewegung in der Weimarer Republik 1918 bis 1924 (Berlin; Bonn: J. H. W. Dietz, 1984).

Winter, Jay, 'Forms of Kinship and Remembrance in the Aftermath of the Great War', in Jay Winter and Emmanuel Sivan (eds.), *War and Remembrance in the Twentieth Century* (Cambridge University Press, 1999), pp. 40–60.

Remembering War: The Great War between Memory and History in the Twentieth Century (New Haven; London: Yale University Press, 2006).

Sites of Memory, Sites of Mourning: The Great War in European Cultural History (Cambridge University Press, 1996).

Wohl, Robert, *The Generation of 1914* (Cambridge, MA: Harvard University Press, 1979).

Wohlfeil, Rainer, 'Reichswehr und Republik', in Militärgeschichtliches Forschungsamt (ed.), *Handbuch zur deutschen Militärgeschichte*, 9 vols., Vol. VI (Frankfurt am Main: Bernard & Graefe, 1969), pp. 1–306.

Woods, Roger, 'Die neuen Nationalisten und ihre Einstellung zum 1. Weltkrieg', *Krieg und Literatur/War and Literature* 1 (1989), 59–79.

Woyke, Meik, *Albert Schulz (1895–1974): Ein sozialdemokratischer Regionalpolitiker* (Bonn: J. H. W. Dietz, 2006).

Ypersele, Laurence Van, 'Mourning and Memory, 1919–45', in John Horne (ed.), *A Companion to World War I* (Chichester: Wiley, 2010), pp. 576–90.

Zibell, Stephanie, *Politische Bildung und demokratische Verfassung: Ludwig Bergsträsser (1883–1960)* (Bonn: J. H. W. Dietz, 2006).

Ziemann, Benjamin, '"Charleville" und "Etappe Gent": Zwei kriegskritische Bestseller der Weimarer Republik', *Krieg und Literatur/War and Literature* 23 (2012), 59–82.

'"Gedanken eines Reichsbannermannes auf Grund von Erlebnissen und Erfahrungen": Politische Kultur, Flaggensymbolik und Kriegserinnerung in Schmalkalden 1926. Dokumentation', *Zeitschrift des Vereins für Thüringische Geschichte* 53 (1999), 214–32.

'Germany 1914–1918: Total War as a Catalyst of Change', in Helmut Walser Smith (ed.), *The Oxford Handbook of Modern German History* (Oxford University Press, 2011), pp. 378–99.

'Germany after the First World War: A Violent Society? Results and Implications of Recent Research on Weimar Germany', *Journal of Modern European History* 1 (2003), 80–95.

'Republikanische Kriegserinnerung in einer polarisierten Öffentlichkeit: Das Reichsbanner Schwarz-Rot-Gold als Veteranenverband der sozialistischen Arbeiterschaft', *HZ* 267 (1998), 357–98.

'Wanderer zwischen den Welten: Der Militärkritiker und Gegner des entschiedenen Pazifismus Major a.D. Karl Mayr (1883–1945)', in Wette and Donat, *Pazifistische Offiziere*, pp. 273–85.

War Experiences in Rural Germany, 1914–1923 (Oxford: Berg, 2007).

'Weimar was Weimar: Politics, Culture and the Emplotment of the German Republic', *German History* 28 (2010), 542–71.

Ziemann, Benjamin and Miriam Dobson, 'Introduction', in Miriam Dobson and Benjamin Ziemann (eds.), *Reading Primary Sources: The Interpretation of Texts from Nineteenth- and Twentieth-Century History* (London: Routledge, 2008), pp. 1–18.

Zirkel, Kirsten, *General Berthold von Deimling: Eine politische Biographie* (Essen: Klartext, 2008).

Index